Fodor's 2015

NEW ORLEANS

OLIMPIA

May 2015

WELCOME TO NEW ORLEANS

New Orleans is a vibrant, bursting at the seams melting pot of a city that famously inspires indulgence. This is the place to eat, drink, listen to jazz or R&B, take part in a parade, and immerse yourself in the atmosphere. Whether you come for Mardi Gras or the New Orleans Jazz & Heritage Festival or any other reason, a visit to this unique destination is never the same trip twice, but always memorable. Sugar-dusted beignets are a must, cocktail hour is anytime you want it, and the street musicians will have you dancing on the sidewalk.

TOP REASONS TO GO

★ **Food:** Seafood, cutting-edge cuisine, and Creole and Cajun specialties.

★ **Music:** You'll hear brass bands and funk rhythms in the street and in the clubs.

★ **History:** Frenchmen, Spaniards, Africans, and others forged the city's culture.

★ **French Quarter:** Elegant streets have everything from antiques to Bourbon Street raunch.

★ **Garden District:** A stroll here takes in centuries-old oaks and historic mansions.

★ **The Vibe:** More northern Caribbean than Southern U.S., NOLA lives like no other city.

Fodor's NEW ORLEANS 2015

Publisher: Amanda D'Acierno, *Senior Vice President*

Editorial: Arabella Bowen, *Editor in Chief*; Linda Cabasin, *Editorial Director*

Design: Fabrizio La Rocca, *Vice President, Creative Director*; Tina Malaney, *Associate Art Director*; Chie Ushio, *Senior Designer*; Ann McBride, *Production Designer*

Photography: Melanie Marin, *Associate Director of Photography*; Jessica Parkhill and Jennifer Romains, *Researchers*

Maps: Rebecca Baer, *Senior Map Editor*; David Lindroth and Mark Stroud, Moon Street Cartography *Cartographers*

Production: Linda Schmidt, *Managing Editor*; Evangelos Vasilakis, *Associate Managing Editor*; Angela L. McLean, *Senior Production Manager*

Sales: Jacqueline Lebow, *Sales Director*

Marketing & Publicity: Heather Dalton, *Marketing Director*; Katherine Punia, *Senior Publicist*

Business & Operations: Susan Livingston, *Vice President, Strategic Business Planning*; Sue Daulton, *Vice President, Operations*

Fodors.com: Megan Bell, *Executive Director, Revenue & Business Development*; Yasmin Marinaro, *Senior Director, Marketing & Partnerships*

Copyright © 2015 by Fodor's Travel, a division of Random House LLC

Writers: Nathalie Jordi, Alexis Korman, Susan Granger, Cameron Todd

Lead Editor: Caroline Trefler

Editor: Stephen Brewer

Production Editor: Carrie Parker

ISBN 978-0-8041-4270-0

ISSN 0743-9385

SPECIAL SALES

This book is available at special discounts for bulk purchases for sales promotions or premiums. For more information, e-mail specialmarkets@randomhouse.com

PRINTED IN THE UNITED STATES OF AMERICA

10 9 8 7 6 5 4 3 2 1

CONTENTS

Fodor's Features

MAPS

ABOUT
THIS GUIDE

Fodor's Recommendations

Everything in this guide is worth doing—we don't cover what isn't—but exceptional sights, hotels, and restaurants are recognized with additional accolades. Fodor's Choice ★ indicates our top recommendations; and **Best Bets** call attention to notable hotels and restaurants in various categories. Care to nominate a new place? Visit Fodors.com/contact-us.

Trip Costs

We list prices wherever possible to help you budget well. Hotel and restaurant price categories from **$** to **$$$$** are noted alongside each recommendation. For hotels, we include the lowest cost of a standard double room in high season. For restaurants, we cite the average price of a main course at dinner or, if dinner isn't served, at lunch. For attractions, we always list adult admission fees; discounts are usually available for children, students, and senior citizens.

Hotels

Our local writers vet every hotel to recommend the best overnights in each price category, from budget to expensive. Unless otherwise specified, you can expect private bath, phone, and TV in your room. For expanded hotel reviews, facilities, and deals visit Fodors.com.

Top Picks	Hotels & Restaurants
★ Fodor's Choice	🏨 Hotel
Listings	↳ Number of rooms
✉ Address	ⵙ Meal plans
✉ Branch address	✗ Restaurant
☎ Telephone	⌂ Reservations
🖷 Fax	👔 Dress code
⊕ Website	▭ No credit cards
✉ E-mail	$ Price
▦ Admission fee	**Other**
⊗ Open/closed times	⇨ See also
Ⓜ Subway	☞ Take note
✛ Directions or Map coordinates	⅄ Golf facilities

Restaurants

Unless we state otherwise, restaurants are open for lunch and dinner daily. We mention dress code only when there's a specific requirement and reservations only when they're essential or not accepted. To make restaurant reservations, visit Fodors.com.

Credit Cards

The hotels and restaurants in this guide typically accept credit cards. If not, we'll say so.

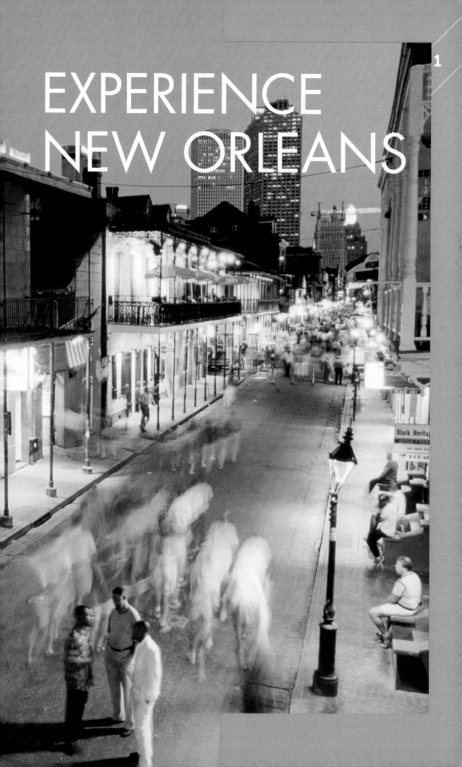

EXPERIENCE
NEW ORLEANS

NEW ORLEANS TODAY

New Orleans is the ultimate urban illustration of the Japanese concept *wabi-sabi*, which translates literally to "perfect-imperfect," but which suggests that, like a sidewalk buckled with cracks where an oak tree root grew up beneath the concrete, or an old plaster wall with bricks showing through, sometimes things are even more special when they are just a little bit broken. New Orleans is perfect in its sheer persistence: this comeback city's age, incredible heritage and history, and unwavering determination to live on and let the good times roll are what makes it so endearing, and so easy to return to again and again.

Like no other place in America. It sounds like a tourist brochure cliché, but it's true: New Orleans feels like a place out of step with the rest of the country. Some of that is due to geography: this port city has seen an influx of many, many cultures over the course of its history. It welcomes diversity and tolerates lifestyles that deviate from the norm—a big reason artists and other creative types have long put down roots here. And the fact that the city lies mostly below sea level lends it a certain degree of fatalism and probably, if unconsciously, informs the New Orleans live-for-today attitude.

Proud of tradition. Red beans and rice on Monday, St. Joseph's altars, jazz funerals, a Christmas visit to Mr. Bingle in City Park—this is a destination steeped in tradition, one that guards its unique customs. Take Mardi Gras, for example: some of the parading organizations, known as krewes, have been around for more than 150 years, building elaborate floats annually and parading through the streets in masks. The Mardi Gras Indian tradition, likewise, is shrouded in secrecy and ritual: "tribes" of mostly African American revelers spend months constructing fanciful, Native American–influenced costumes in tribute to actual tribes that once helped escaped slaves find freedom.

A giant movie set. Or that's how it seems these days, with multiple film projects going on at any given moment. The scenic backdrop is one reason for all the activity; generous tax credits and a growing local film industry are the other drivers behind what civic boosters have dubbed "Hollywood South." Movies and shows filmed here recently include HBO's *Tremé*, Quentin Tarantino's *Django Unchained*, FX's *American Horror Story,* and Bravo's *Top Chef: New Orleans.*

WHAT WE'RE TALKING ABOUT

After many delays, a massive $30 million "Reinventing the Crescent" riverfront development project is underway. The plan is to create a series of parks, jogging and biking paths, art spaces, and retail areas along the riverfront. The first fruits of the project are visible in Crescent Park, which runs along the riverfront of the Faubourg Marigny and Bywater neighborhoods. Look for the large, rust-colored arch at Piety Street, which leads over the flood wall and into Piety Gardens, scheduled to open in mid-2014.

It may not be named Desire, but the newest part of the famed New Orleans streetcar line is now in operation. The project connects Amtrak's Union Station with Canal Street and the Canal Street streetcar route, giving train passengers access to

Still recovering. Eight years after Katrina hit the city, the areas where tourists tend to wander—downtown, the riverfront, the French Quarter, Faubourg Marigny, the Warehouse District, and the Garden District/Uptown—all show little outward sign of the storm's devastating floods. But predominantly residential areas like parts of Lakeview and the Lower Ninth Ward are still struggling to recover. As of July 2012, Census Bureau estimates indicated that the city's population was still 81% of what it had been before the storm.

Popular mayor Mitch Landrieu, who won an easy re-election in 2014, has taken great strides toward getting the city back on track, but he has also seen controversy and some turmoil within reform efforts. The success of grassroots recovery programs is a bright contrast to any lingering skepticism locals feel about projects started by previous administrations and elected officials. Locally led projects continue to gain ground, including the Ninth Ward's George Washington Carver High School sports program, Brad Pitt's Make it Right housing-renewal program, the New Orleans Hope and Heritage Project, and Tipitina's Foundation for musicians.

On the verge of ____. Fill in the blank; your guess is as good as anybody's. New Orleans has survived an insane number of fires, floods, epidemics, and scandals since its founding in 1718, and there are many encouraging signs—new buildings, streetcar lines, restorations, festivals—that even Hurricane Katrina couldn't keep this amazing city down. But questions remain: the repaired levees held fast against 2012's Hurricane Isaac, but will they withstand an even larger storm? Will New Orleans manage to move past its propensity for political scandals, crime, and all the ills of urban poverty? Despite the many fortune-tellers plying their trade on Jackson Square, no one knows for sure what the future holds for the Crescent City.

the French Quarter and the Central Business District (CBD) and passing just steps away from the Mercedes-Benz Superdome and the New Orleans Arena.

Forget hair of the dog, Nola is increasingly the spot for Downward Facing Dog as the city's yoga scene continues to grow. New Orleans yoga studios have grown from a paltry six pre-Katrina to currently more than 25, in neighborhoods from the Garden District to Uptown and the CBD. Visitors can even find their chi within view of the St. Louis Cathedral at Yoga at the Cabildo on Jackson Square, Tuesday and Thursday mornings at 7:30 and Saturdays at 8:30, for just $12.

WHAT'S WHERE

Numbers refer to chapters.

2 The French Quarter.
The geographic and cultural heart of the city since the early 1700s, the Quarter is a vibrant commercial and residential hodgepodge of wrought-iron balconies, beckoning courtyards, antiques shops—and, of course, tawdry Bourbon Street bars. Elsewhere in the Quarter, you'll find fine dining and fabulous local music.

3 Faubourg Marigny, Bywater, and Tremé.
The Faubourg Marigny is home to restored Creole cottages and famous Frenchman Street, lined with music clubs, restaurants, and bars. Bywater has gentrified but retains its working-class credentials, with a burgeoning arts scene and an influx of hipster professionals. Tremé, the cradle of jazz and second-line parades, fell into decline but is back on the map.

4 CBD and Warehouse District. The city's trendy urban area is undergoing a building boom; it's also where most of the newer hotels are clustered, near Canal Street or the sprawling Morial Convention Center. There also are museums, art galleries, fine restaurants, and a casino.

5 The Garden District.
Stunning early-19th-century mansions make this a great neighborhood for walking, followed by an afternoon browsing the shops and cafés along ever-evolving Magazine Street. Take the streetcar for a gander at the massive and stately St. Charles Avenue homes.

6 Uptown and Carrollton-Riverbend. Audubon Park and the campuses of Tulane and Loyola universities anchor oak-shaded Uptown; hop on the St. Charles streetcar to survey it in period style. You'll find boutiques, eateries, and pubs at the uptown end of Magazine Street, on Maple Street between Broadway and Carrollton, and in the Riverbend.

7 Mid-City and Bayou St. John. City Park is Mid-City's playground and encompasses the New Orleans Museum of Art and the adjacent Besthoff Sculpture Garden. A stroll along Bayou St. John and a visit to Pitot House on its banks are good ways to see this residential neighborhood.

12 Side Trips. If you have time, head to Plantation Country to visit the gorgeous antebellum homes, or explore Cajun County.

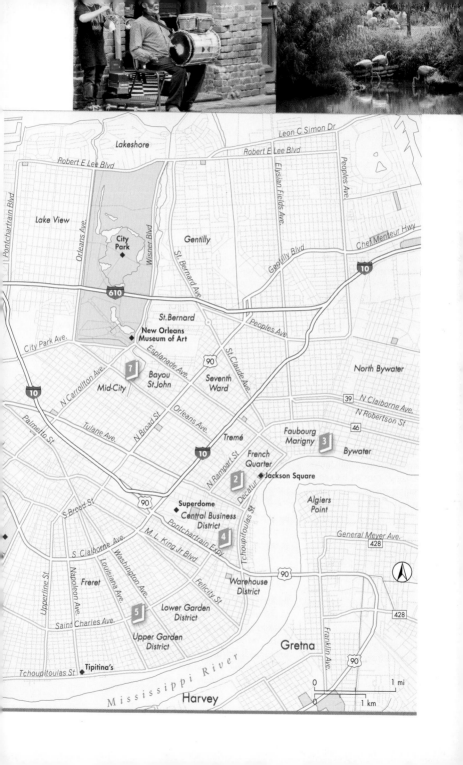

NEW ORLEANS PLANNER

Getting Here

By air: Most major and a few regional airlines serve **Louis Armstrong International Airport** (☎ 504/464–0831), 15 miles east of downtown New Orleans. A taxi from the airport to the French Quarter costs a flat rate of $33 for two people; for more than two passengers the fixed rate is $14 per person. Shared-ride shuttles to hotels are available for about $20 per person. If you're traveling light and have a lot of extra time, you can take Jefferson Transit's airport bus, which runs between the main terminal entrance and the Central Business District (CBD). Fare is $2.

By car: Interstate 10 is the major thoroughfare into and out of New Orleans and can be used to reach downtown from the airport. Lanes can get backed up during morning and evening rush hours; plan accordingly.

By train: Three Amtrak lines serve New Orleans: the *City of New Orleans* from Chicago; the *Sunset Limited* service between New Orleans and Los Angeles; and the *Crescent*, which connects New Orleans and New York by way of Atlanta. For tickets and schedules, call ☎ 800/872–7245 or visit ⊕ www.amtrak.com.

Getting Around

By streetcar: The St. Charles line runs from Canal Street to the intersection of Claiborne and Carrollton avenues; along the way it passes the Garden District, Audubon Park, and Tulane and Loyola universities. The Riverfront line skirts the French Quarter along the Mississippi, from Esplanade Avenue to the Ernest N. Morial Convention Center. Some Canal line streetcars make a straight shot from the Quarter to the cemeteries at City Park Avenue; others take a spur at Carrollton Avenue that goes to City Park and the New Orleans Museum of Art. The Loyola line runs from Union Passenger Terminal (rail and bus station) down to Canal Street, where it meets the other lines.

By Bus: Once an unpredictable affair, bus travel in New Orleans is now reasonably reliable and comfortable; you can even get the status of your bus via text message. The Magazine bus runs the length of Magazine Street, from Canal and Camp streets to the Audubon Zoo entrance at the far edge of Audubon Park. The Esplanade bus serves City Park, and drops Jazz Fest passengers off a few blocks from the Fair Grounds.

Fares for streetcars and buses are $1.25 ($1.50 for express lines); unlimited-ride Jazzy Pass cards are available for one day ($3; available on bus and streetcar); unlimited 3-day and 31-day passes ($9 and $55) are available at some hotels and grocery stores and at Walgreens. For info, visit ⊕ www.norta.com.

By car: If you don't plan to drive outside the city limits, you probably won't need a car—you'll save money traveling by streetcar, cab, and on foot. If you do decide to drive, keep in mind that some streets are in ragged condition, traffic lights routinely malfunction, and parking in the Quarter is tight (and parking regulations vigorously enforced).

By taxi: Taxis are often convenient, and drivers are used to short trips, so grab a cab if you're leery about walking back to your hotel at night. Most locals recommend United Cabs, Yellow Checker, and Veterans. Don't get into an unlicensed, unmarked "gypsy" cab. Rates are $2 per mile or 20¢ for every 40 seconds of waiting, plus a base of $3.50; each additional passenger is $1.

Safety

Much of the post-Katrina media coverage has focused on New Orleans's escalating crime rate. Sadly, this isn't just sensationalism—gangs operate in the city's underpopulated neighborhoods, there's a significant homelessness problem, the murder rate is among the highest in the nation, and armed robberies occur all too frequently. These grim statistics should not dissuade you from visiting, but you need to exercise caution if you venture outside the well-touristed areas—especially at night.

The French Quarter is generally safe, but pay attention to your surroundings and your possessions (especially expensive cameras and dangling shoulder bags). Use special caution in the areas near Rampart Street and below St. Philip Street at night, and be alert on all quiet Quarter side streets.

The CBD and Warehouse District are safe, but take a cab at night if there aren't many other pedestrians around.

Be alert and exercise caution walking around in the Bywater or the lower part of Faubourg Marigny at night, and take a cab when traveling between spread-out destinations. Avoid Garden District side streets after dark.

All that said, the New Orleans Police Department does take pains to keep violent crime out of the tourist zones, with many uniformed and plainclothes police stationed throughout the Quarter and at special events.

Helpful Websites

⊕ *www.fodors.com:* Log on to the Travel Talk Forums to get advice from New Orleanians and travelers who have recently visited the Crescent City.

⊕ *www.neworleanscvb.com:* Head here for up-to-date information from the New Orleans Convention and Visitors Bureau.

⊕ *www.nola.com:* Find out what's happening from the city's newspaper, the *New Orleans Times-Picayune*.

⊕ *www.neworleans.com:* This site has often-updated special events and entertainment info.

⊕ *www.offbeat.com:* The website for the monthly magazine *Offbeat* has extensive club and live-music listings, along with features covering the local music scene.

When to Go

May through September is hot and humid—double-100 days (100°F and nearly 100% humidity) aren't uncommon. Just mustering the energy to raise a mint julep to your lips can cause exhaustion. These long, hot summers may explain why things are less hurried down here. But if you visit during sticky July and August, you'll find lower hotel prices and plenty of tables at the top restaurants.

June through November brings heavy rains and occasional hurricanes. Although winters are mild compared with those in northern climes, the high humidity can put a chill in the air December through February. Nevertheless, the holiday season is a great time to visit, with few conventions in town, a beautifully bedecked French Quarter, and "Papa Noel" discounted rates at many hotels.

Perhaps the best time to visit the city is early spring. Days are pleasant, except for seasonal cloudbursts, and nights are cool. The azaleas are in full bloom, the apricot scent of sweet olive trees wafts through the evening air, and the city bustles from one outdoor festival to the next.

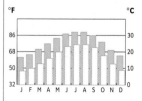

NEW ORLEANS TOP ATTRACTIONS

Bourbon Street

(A) Crude and crass, New Orleans's most famous entertainment strip isn't to everyone's taste, but you have to see it at least once—preferably under the nighttime neon lights. Tawdry strip clubs and souvenir shops scream for attention, but take a closer look: you'll find local jazz musicians showing off their chops, elegant restaurants, and faded bars where luminaries like Mark Twain and Tennessee Williams imbibed.

Jackson Square

(B) Flanked by St. Louis Cathedral, the antebellum Pontalba apartment buildings, and the Mississippi River, postcard-pretty Jackson Square has been the hub of New Orleans life since the city's colonial start. Artists, musicians, and fortune-tellers congregate on the plaza surrounding the square, but the manicured park itself is a peaceful oasis in the midst of the French Quarter bustle.

Garden District

(C) A field day for architecture buffs and gardeners, the leafy Garden District is a remarkably intact collection of 19th-century Greek Revival mansions and raised cottages, many built by wealthy merchants during the city's cotton heyday. Cap a visit here with lunch at Commander's Palace and browsing the shops and cafés on Magazine Street.

St. Charles Avenue Streetcar

(D) Three streetcar lines converge on Canal Street, but this one packs the most bang for the buck-and-a-quarter. Following a route in use since a steam train first plied the avenue in 1835, the old-school streetcars clatter through the CBD, then roll along the oak-shaded median (or "neutral ground," in local parlance) past some of the city's most exclusive addresses. Stops include Audubon Park, the Garden District, and the Riverbend shopping district.

Audubon Park

(E) Picturesque Audubon Park, across from the campuses of Tulane and Loyola universities and on the St. Charles Avenue streetcar line, is an Uptown oasis featuring waterfowl-filled lagoons, oak trees draped in Spanish moss, and wide-open green spaces. The park also includes the world-class Audubon Zoo, the Audubon Park Golf Course, Audubon Stables, and Audubon Tennis Courts, and it has great views of the Mississippi River.

French Market

(F) French trappers, seafood vendors, and more than a few rowdy sailors traipsed through these open-air stalls once upon a time. Today the place more resembles a bazaar, and alongside vegetable stalls and charcuteries selling alligator-on-a-stick, crawfish, and Cajun sausages, you'll find stands packed with jewelry, bags, cheap sunglasses, and antiques. The quality of the merchandise varies (it's a great place to pick up Mardi Gras beads and hot sauces), but the scene is a lot of fun—especially on weekends and whenever live music takes over the market.

City Park

(G) Accessible by the Canal Street streetcar line, City Park offers 1,300 acres of recreational and cultural opportunities in the heart of New Orleans's Mid-City. The park is home to the New Orleans Museum of Art and the adjacent, first-rate Besthoff Sculpture Garden. The New Orleans Botanical Gardens, the Carousel Gardens Amusement Park, Storyland, and the miniature train that tours the park are other big draws. There's a walking track around the lake near the museum, where you'll find a genuine Venetian gondola for hire. The Spanish mission–style Old Casino Building houses the Parkview Café for a light bite, a cool drink, or an ice-cream treat on a hot day.

NEW ORLEANS
TOP ATTRACTIONS

Food

The city of New Orleans has long been a cultural melting pot, and that goes for her cooking pots as well. There's a stunning variety of homegrown cuisines and styles here—everything from traditional Creole to fresh-caught seafood, from slow-cooked soul food to upscale urban fusions, from gorgeous French-style five-course meals to corner-store po'boys. For the upscale connoisseurs, this is a city where chefs come to make a name for themselves. Internationally recognized stars like John Besh, Paul Prudhomme, and Emeril Lagasse are joined by inventive culinary masterminds such as Susan Spicer (Bayona), Donald Link (Herbsaint), and Scott Boswell (Stella!). This is also a place that puts a high premium on simple pleasures, and it's the unsung cooks and chefs of the corner shops, pubs, late-night grills, and even taco stands that deliver some of the best eats.

Cocktails

New Orleans is home to several of the world's oldest and most popular cocktails, dating back to the turn of the 19th century, so it's no surprise that an old guard of traditional New Orleans bartenders has kept the sacred flame alight, honing their skills on homegrown classics like the Sazerac, the Ramos gin fizz, and the ever-popular Hurricane. A new generation of innovative mixologists is, however, combining their prowess with some of the most venerable cocktail traditions and settings, bringing new recipes, fresh ingredients, hand-squeezed juices, and homemade syrups, mixers, and reductions. Hot spots like Cure, Bar Tonique, and Twelve Mile Limit lead the cocktail renaissance. The popular Tales of the Cocktail festival in July celebrates all things shaken and stirred.

Music

Music is so organic to New Orleans that it's almost like humidity—hanging in the air, drifting down the street, working its way in between the clapboards on the sides of houses and clubs. When you follow those strains a little more closely, you'll realize that every style of music, every band, and every musician has a unique energy that pours into the city, from the stride piano blues of Jon Cleary to the high-energy brass jams of the world-renowned Rebirth Brass Band. Old-school kings of rhythm and blues like Walter Wolfman Washington or Little Freddie King still keep people half their age (and less) dancing into the wee hours of the night. Meanwhile, the young hipsters of the New Orleans Cottonmouth Kings play swing jazz standards that are old enough to be their grandparents' age (and then some).

Festivals

To many people a festival is an event that arrives once a year, spans a few days, and then fades to nice memories. In New Orleans, however, the term "festival" has transcended any single event and has become a lifestyle, a state of mind, and possibly even an obsession. Regardless of the time of year you might be visiting, there's likely something happening—from the large-scale, musical mega-events like Jazz Fest (where jazz is only the beginning of the offerings), Essence Fest (hip-hop and R&B), and the Voodoo Experience (rock and electronic) to the funky neighborhood celebrations like the Bayou Boogaloo or Festivus. Legendary figures like Louis Armstrong and Tennessee Williams have events thrown in their honor. So pack your sunscreen and a hat, slip on some dancing shoes, and get ready to plunge into the festival state of mind.

NEW ORLEANS SPORTS: SAINTS AND STINGERS

For a city that loves to play, New Orleans was never considered much of a professional sports town. Season after season of disappointing scores had even earned the New Orleans NFL team the pitiful nickname "The Aints." But things changed in the last few years, when two of the city's pro teams saw unprecedented success. The victories represented comeback—not just for the teams, but for the entire city.

New Orleans Saints

The Saints went marching in to victory in Miami in 2010 when they became Super Bowl champions for the first time, and the win meant more than just a football championship. Throughout the winning season—which opened with 13 wins in a row—New Orleans was abuzz and united with Saints spirit like never before. The New Orleans Saints Super Bowl XLIV victory parade, which fell just a week before Mardi Gras, drew 800,000 people. It was the largest parade crowd some locals claim they've ever seen, which is truly impressive for America's party city.

Today, despite an ethics scandal that has rocked the NFL, Saints fever continues unabated. Fans are as enthusiastic as ever, and celebrate in Champions Square, just outside the rechristened Mercedes-Benz Superdome, a hot spot for pre- and postgame partying. Whether you're at the Dome or watching the Saints on TV, keep an eye out for some of the Saints' most famous fans: Halo Saint, who wears a gold Transformer-esque getup; Da Pope, dressed as the pontiff himself; Whistle Monsta, in black-and-gold face paint, Saints uniform, and a giant gold whistle atop his helmet; and Voodoo Man, sporting a tux jacket, top hat, and ghostly face paint.

Where they play: Mercedes-Benz Superdome (⌧ *Sugar Bowl Dr., CBD*)

Season: August–January

How to buy tickets: With a wish and a prayer, or at least your fingers crossed. Individual tickets are technically not for sale—the Saints have been sold out on season tickets alone since 2006. Your best bet is the **NFL Ticket Exchange** (⊕ *www.nfl.com*).

Famous players, past and present: Drew Brees, Rickey Jackson, Archie Manning

Past highlights: Won Super Bowl XLIV in 2010; made playoffs in 2011, 2012, and 2013

New Orleans Pelicans

The Pelicans, who from 2002 through 2012 kept the "Hornets" moniker they arrived with from Charlotte, have seen mixed results over the years. Hurricane Katrina sent the team to Oklahoma City in 2005–2007, but they returned to New Orleans for the 2007–2008 season and the team made the NBA playoffs that season and the next. After a less successful 2009–2010 season, the team made it back to the playoffs in spring 2011. A disappointing 2012 season followed, but with a new owner (Tom Benson, the colorful owner of the Saints) and the new team name, there is renewed enthusiasm for this young team, which plays in the newly renamed Smoothie King Arena.

Where they play: New Orleans Arena (⌧ *1501 Girod St., CBD*)

Season: October–April

How to buy tickets: Ticket office (☎ *504/525-HOOP* ⊕ *www.nba.com/hornets*)

Past highlights: Made the NBA playoffs in 2008, 2009, and 2011

INSPIRATION: BOOKS AND MOVIES

New Orleans is a strange, wonderful, and evocative place, and it has inspired some incredible books, movies, and television shows.

Movies

To prepare for your trip to New Orleans, rent *A Streetcar Named Desire*, starring Marlon Brando and Vivien Leigh. Seedy, steamy, and emotionally charged, this is the quintessential New Orleans film. Also check out Elvis in *King Creole*, a music-filled noir tale set in the French Quarter. Other New Orleans classics are *Jezebel, The Buccaneer*, and *Easy Rider*. More contemporary movies include the movie adaptation of Anne Rice's *Interview with the Vampire*, John Grisham's *The Pelican Brief* starring Julia Roberts and Denzel Washington, *Double Jeopardy* with Ashley Judd, *Runaway Jury* starring John Cusack, *Déja Vu* with Denzel Washington, and *The Curious Case of Benjamin Button*, set in the Garden District.

Television Shows

The HBO series *Treme* highlights New Orleans music and culture post-Katrina. The third season of the anthology series *American Horror Story* is set in New Orleans, as was the 11th season of *Top Chef*.

Books: fiction

A necessary read for any New Orleans visitor is John Kennedy Toole's *A Confederacy of Dunces*. Ignatius J. Reilly, the book's bumbling protagonist, is as quirky as the city itself. Tim Gautreaux's *The Missing* is a literary mystery set in 1920s. For a look into life in New Orleans in the late 1800s, pick up anything by George Washington Cable.

For a more contemporary take on the city, Tom Piazza's *City of Refuge* takes a look at two fictional families—one black and one white—in the aftermath of Hurricane Katrina. (Piazza's nonfiction *Why New Orleans Matters*, written right after the hurricane, is a short but moving book about what makes the city so unique and why it was so important that it be rebuilt.) James Lee Burke's well-known series starring detective Dave Robicheaux is set in and around New Orleans (several of the books have been made into movies as well).

Books: nonfiction

For a somewhat lighter look at the city, try NPR commentator Andrei Codrescu's *New Orleans, Mon Amour*, a touching and humorous collection of short essays about living in his adopted city of New Orleans.

Several excellent nonfiction books have been written about New Orleans and Hurricane Katrina, including Dan Baum's excellent *Nine Lives*, which traces the story of 40 years of New Orleans through the lives of nine very different people.

There is much dark and interesting history to this city. Walter Johnson's *Soul by Soul: Life Inside the Antebellum Slave Market* is an insightful account of how slavery shaped New Orleans. *Lords of Misrule: Mardi Gras and the Politics or Race in New Orleans,* by James Gill, delves into the history of Carnival, one of the quintessential parts of the city.

While you're in New Orleans, visit any of the locally owned bookstores to talk to the booksellers and get a local's perspective on the city's literary scene.

LOCAL FOR A DAY

Tired of time-share hawkers and tap dancers? Want to spend some time enjoying New Orleans the way locals do? Step one: get out of the Quarter.

Get Some Exercise

Go for a jog along the **St. Charles Avenue streetcar tracks.** You'll have plenty of company anywhere between Jackson Avenue and the university area—just follow the well-worn trails along the median (locals refer to it as the "neutral ground"). Keep an eye out for streetcars as well as vehicles crossing the tracks. If that sounds too risky, hit the paths in **City Park**, or rent a bicycle and head for **Audubon Park**, where you can get on a paved jogging and bike trail that runs along the Mississippi River levee well into Jefferson Parish.

Find a Market

The **Crescent City Farmers Market** sets up at the corner of Girod and Magazine streets in the CBD on Saturday mornings; on Tuesday from 9 am to 1 pm, it's held Uptown at Tulane Square, on Leake Avenue at Broadway. Although you may not want to lug a bag of broccoli back to your hotel, there's always some good prepared food for sale, local chefs foraging for ingredients, and an entertaining bunch of vendors. If you're in town the first Saturday of the month (except July and August), head to the **Freret Market Uptown**, a food, art, and flea fest where the merchandise is high quality and the crowd never less than colorful. The **Frenchmen Art Market**, at 619 Frenchmen Street, takes place Thursday through Saturday, from 7 pm to 1 am, and on Sunday from 6 pm to midnight.

Queue Up for Breakfast

After a long Saturday of cavorting, locals need a Sunday morning recovery meal as much as visitors. Every New Orleanian has a favorite brunch spot, where you'll find lines of hungry customers. Hit **Dante's Kitchen** (✉ *736 Dante St. Uptown* ☎ *504/861–3121*; brunch Sun.) for buttermilk biscuits, shrimp and grits, and bread-pudding French toast. A more elegant option is **Patois** (✉ *6078 Laurel St., Uptown* ☎ *504/895–9441*; brunch Sun.), for bacon or hash browns paired with fried rabbit or almond-crusted Gulf fish. **Elizabeth's** (✉ *601 Gallier St., Bywater* ☎ *504/944–9272*; breakfast daily) gets its share of tourists, but the brunch crowd still mostly consists of neighborhood denizens.

Hang Out by the River

Locals love Riverview Drive—better known as **The Fly**—the riverside stretch of Audubon Park behind the zoo, even if they have no idea how it got its nickname (probably from a butterfly-shaped building that used to stand here). There is a Little League baseball complex (where spectators can sip Abita beer sold at the snack bar) and a football-soccer field, but most people are content to spread out on a blanket, have a picnic or barbecue, and watch the ships go by on the Mississippi.

Shop Local

Whether it's at the incredibly diverse array of boutiques on the "six miles of style" that make up **Magazine Street** or at the stately antiques dealerships in the **French Quarter,** locals prefer to spend their money at businesses owned and staffed by New Orleanians. Look for the lime-green-and-blue "Stay Local!" logo stickers on store windows.

NEW ORLEANS WITH KIDS

New Orleans is a grown-up town in a lot of ways, but there are lots of activities to keep the kids interested, too. See the full listings in the neighborhood exploring chapters for contact info.

Get Out and Play

Audubon Park. This beautiful Uptown park is the perfect place to let the kids run free for a couple of hours. They can explore the lagoon complex, where they'll find ducks and an impressive (sometimes squawky) assortment of migratory birds nesting on Bird Island. Several play structures throughout the park—the biggest is at the downtown, lakeside corner of the park near St. Charles Avenue—provide a place for kids to swing, slide, and climb. And a walk around the 1.8-mile paved jogging path is an ever-popular family pastime. (*Uptown*)

City Park. There's plenty to do here for the younger set, including two free playgrounds: one with swings near the Peristyle, and a playground for older kids, just off Marconi Drive, that has more challenging things to clamber on. Storyland, a fairy-tale theme park, is open on weekends year-round, and features a number of sculptures created by Blaine Kern Studios, the maker of Mardi Gras floats. Adjacent Carousel Gardens Amusement Park has low-impact rides, a miniature train that tours the park, and a beautiful 100-year-old carousel as a centerpiece. (*Mid-City*)

Animals Everywhere!

Audubon Aquarium of the Americas. Loads of exotic sea creatures, a penguin exhibit, and an interactive area where kids can get their hands wet make the aquarium a favorite family destination. There's a fun museum shop and an IMAX theater next door. (*The French Quarter*)

Audubon Butterfly Garden and Insectarium. This amazing attraction features insects for everyone—from a beautiful exhibit on butterflies to gross-out fun with the bug chef. (*The French Quarter: Riverfront*)

Audubon Zoo. A well-designed showcase with animals from all over the world, the zoo also has a hands-on area for kids—where young volunteers show off real live zoo residents—and a petting zoo with docile goats, among other beasties. (*Uptown*)

Kiddie Culture

Louisiana Children's Museum. The Warehouse District museum tries to sneak in a little education while giving kids a place to romp, role-play, and dabble in the arts. (*Warehouse District*)

For Kids of All Ages

Blaine Kern's Mardi Gras World at Kern Studios. The city's most famous float-building family offers tours of their company's vast studio, where kids can try on costumes and watch the artists at work. (*Warehouse District*)

Streetcars. You can't leave New Orleans without taking the kids for a ride in a streetcar, which you can also use to get to several of the sites listed here, including City Park (on the Canal Street line) and Audubon Park (St. Charles Avenue). (*See the "Riding the Streetcar" feature in the Uptown and Carrollton-Riverbend chapter.*)

FREE AND ALMOST FREE

Free Museums and Galleries

Buy a **Power Pass** (three days, $129.99 per adult ⊕ *www.visiticket.com*) to save a significant amount on the admission fees to the city's leading museums and attractions. It costs nothing, however, to browse the **Warehouse District galleries** on and around Julia Street, where you'll find works by established and up-and-coming artists.

The Sydney and Walda Besthoff Sculpture Garden in City Park, next to the New Orleans Museum of Art, is free and has major work by important 20th-century artists, including Henry Moore, Jacques Lipchitz, Barbara Hepworth, and Seymour Lipton, dramatically set among lagoons and moss-laden oak trees.

Uptown, on the Tulane University campus, the **Newcomb Art Gallery** hosts shows featuring work by internationally known artists—photographer Diane Arbus and master silversmith William Spratling are two examples—as well as themed exhibitions and work by Newcomb's art school alumni.

Free Music

Outdoor festivals like the **Satchmo Summer Fest** and **French Quarter Festival** are great places to hear live music for free. Street bands also serenade visitors daily in the French Quarter—although if you linger, you'll be asked to toss a few bucks into the hat.

Drop by the **Jean Lafitte National Historic Park's French Quarter visitor center** (✉ *419 Decatur St.* ☎ *504/589–3882*) to get a schedule of upcoming shows; the park hosts concerts by Louisiana musicians in the courtyard.

The **New Orleans Jazz National Historical Park** (✉ *916 N. Peters St.* ☎ *504/589–4806*) sponsors free live performances and lectures Tuesday to Saturday at its French Market office and at its smart new performance space in the Old U.S. Mint. The performers—almost invariably good—cover the jazz spectrum, from traditional brass band music to modern jazz.

If you're in town on a Wednesday from early April to late June or from mid-September to October, check out the free **Wednesday at the Square** and **Harvest the Music** concert series at Lafayette Square in the CBD, across from Gallier Hall. At both festivals around 5 pm, a horde of downtown workers and fest-loving residents converge on the square to hear good local bands, dance, and socialize. There's plenty of food and drink available for purchase.

Free Ride

The **Canal–Algiers Ferry** offers some of the best views of the city. It's a fun thing to do with kids, and a great way to get a sense of the Mississippi River's magnitude. The pedestrian entrance is on the plaza at the foot of Canal Street, across from Harrah's Casino; it docks on the West Bank at Algiers Point, a quaint historic neighborhood that makes for a good daytime stroll. At night, though, stay onboard for the return trip.

OFFBEAT
NEW ORLEANS

Cemeteries

The old cemeteries in and around New Orleans, where tombs have to be built above the boggy ground to keep the remains of loved ones from drifting away, are fascinating places to visit. Those near the French Quarter (**St. Louis No. 2** and **St. Roch**, for example) are best visited on a tour or with a group. **Lake Lawn Metairie Cemetery** (✉ *5100 Pontchartrain Blvd.* ☎ *504/486–6331*), on the other hand, is safe to visit on your own: the office even has audio guides to help motorists find their way around the stately cemetery, the final resting place of luminaries like Al Hirt, Louis Prima, and Civil War general P.G.T. Beauregard. Guided tours are available by appointment. Because it's a busy cemetery, officials prefer that people visit between 8:30 and 10:30 am or after 3:30 pm, when there's less chance of disrupting a funeral in progress.

Weird Museums

Home to a small but interesting collection of art and artifacts related to voodoo history and practice in the city, the **New Orleans Historic Voodoo Museum** (✉ *724 Dumaine St.* ☎ *504/680–0128*) offers insight into a spiritual tradition that persists to this day. If you're not squeamish about toying with the black arts, there are handcrafted voodoo dolls and gris-gris (magic talisman) bags sold in the small shop. *(See the French Quarter listings.)*

Louis Dufilho, America's first licensed pharmacist, operated an apothecary, La Pharmacie Francaise, in an 1823 town home. Today it holds the **New Orleans Pharmacy Museum** (✉ *514 Chartres St.* ☎ *504/565–8027*), a collection of ancient medicine bottles, a huge leech jar, eyeglasses, and some truly unsettling surgical instruments. *(See the French Quarter listings.)*

In a former funeral home, the small, quirky **Backstreet Cultural Museum** (✉ *1116 St. Claude St.* ☎ *504/522–4806*) has everything you want to know about second line and Mardi Gras Indian traditions, with fascinating displays of Mardi Gras Indian suits, the fans and umbrellas of the Social Aid and Pleasure Clubs, and the vestments of lesser-known traditions, such as the Baby Dolls and Skull and Bone Gangs. *(See the Tremé listings.)*

Tiny Abita Springs, north of Lake Pontchartrain, is notable for three things: artesian spring water, Abita beer, and an oddball institution known as the **Abita Mystery House** (✉ *22275 Hwy. 36, at Grover St., Abita Springs* ☎ *985/892–2624* ⊕ *www.abitamysteryhouse.com*). Artist John Preble's obsessive collection of found objects includes combs, old musical instruments, paint-by-number art, and taxidermy experiments gone awry. *(See the Side Trips from New Orleans listings.)*

Sno-balls

In the days before air-conditioning, New Orleanians developed the sno-ball as a way to cope with stifling summers: it's a ball of shaved ice served in a cup or Chinese take-out container, topped with anything from simple syrup to condensed milk. A New Orleans inventor designed the patented SnoWizard machine to produce the finest shaved ice imaginable, so a sno-ball in New Orleans is different from those elsewhere. **Hansen's Sno-Blitz Sweet Shop** (✉ *4801 Tchoupitoulas St., Uptown* ☎ *504/891–9788* ⊗ *May–Aug.*) has been dishing them out since 1939; another stalwart is **Plum Street Snoball** (✉ *1300 Burdette St., Carrollton-Riverbend* ☎ *504/866–7996* ⊗ *Mar.–Oct.*).

GREAT ITINERARIES

NEW ORLEANS HIGHLIGHTS

Including a trip to Plantation Country.

Day 1: The French Quarter

Start by getting to know the city's most famous neighborhood. The café au lait and beignets at **Café du Monde** are a good place to begin, followed by a stroll around **Jackson Square** and **St. Louis Cathedral.** Cross the seawall and take in the views of the Mississippi River from **Woldenberg Riverfront Park.** Wander along North Peters Street to the shops and market stalls in the **French Market,** followed by a walk in the mostly residential **Lower Quarter** and **Faubourg Marigny.** After lunch, explore the antiques stores and art galleries on **Royal and Chartres streets,** winding it all up with a cocktail in a shady courtyard; try **Napoleon House,** an atmospheric bar and café that makes a mean Pimm's Cup, or the French Quarter mainstay **Pat O'Brien's.** Save **Bourbon Street** for after dinner at one of the Quarter's esteemed restaurants; like anything that's lived hard and been around as long, it's much more attractive in low light.

Day 2: The Garden District and Uptown

The **St. Charles Avenue streetcar** rumbles past some of the South's most prized real estate; take a seat in one of the antique wooden seats and admire the scenery on the way to leafy **Audubon Park.** In the park you can follow the paved footpath to the **Audubon Zoo,** keeping an eye out for the zoo's white tiger and rare white alligators. Board an inbound **Magazine Street** bus near the zoo entrance and take it a couple of blocks past Louisiana Avenue, where a number of restaurants, some with sidewalk tables, are clustered.

Continue on Magazine to Washington Avenue and head left through the **Garden District.** Prytania Street, just past **Lafayette Cemetery No. 1** (Anne Rice fans, take note), is a good axis from which to explore the neighborhood's elegant side streets. Catch a downtown-bound streetcar on St. Charles, or wrap up the afternoon shopping and dining on Magazine Street.

Day 3: Art, History, and Culture

Dedicate one day to a deeper exploration of the city's cultural attractions. Art lovers shouldn't miss the **Warehouse District,** where a pair of fine museums—the **Ogden Museum of Southern Art** and the **Contemporary Arts Center**—anchor a vibrant strip of contemporary art galleries, most of which feature local artists. History buffs will want to check out the **National World War II Museum,** also in the Warehouse District, and the **Historical New Orleans Collection** in the French Quarter, which hosts changing exhibits in a beautifully restored town home.

Day 4: Remembering Katrina

It may strike some as macabre, but touring neighborhoods that were devastated by Hurricane Katrina and its subsequent floods has become a ritual for many visitors, much as Lower Manhattan's Ground Zero has become a pilgrimage site. You can opt for a guided bus tour, which takes you to **Lakeview** and the infamous **17th Street Canal levee breach;** some companies also travel to the **Lower Ninth Ward** and **Chalmette.** ⇨ *If you have your own transportation, follow a drive through Hurricane Katrina's aftermath in our Remembering Katrina feature at the end of this chapter.* After a somber tour of Katrina's devastation, a good antidote is to look to the many signs of renewal and rebirth. **City Park,** which sustained extensive wind and flood damage, reopened its stately botanical gardens; nearby stands the venerable **New Orleans Museum of Art** and the adjacent **Sydney and Walda Besthoff Sculpture Garden.** Wrap the day up with dinner and live music downtown at one of the clubs on **Frenchmen Street,** in the Faubourg Marigny neighborhood, where the city's inexhaustible party spirit is in evidence.

Day 5: Head Out of Town

Consider a day trip out of town to visit one of the region's elegant **plantation homes,** explore **Cajun Country,** or take a guided **swamp tour.** Some tour companies offer a combination of these destinations, with lunch included. Many of the antebellum mansions between New Orleans and Baton Rouge have been painstakingly restored and filled with period furniture; nature lovers will want to set aside time to explore the grounds and lush flower gardens. Swamp tours may sound hokey, but they're actually a good way to see south Louisiana's cypress-studded wetlands (and get up close and personal with the alligators and other critters that live there). Continue the nautical theme in the evening with a ride to **Algiers Point** aboard the Canal Street Ferry for lovely sunset views of the New Orleans skyline.

TIPS

If you're venturing out in your own vehicle, be aware that street conditions aren't great. Some roads are undergoing massive repaving, so prepare to be patient with construction-zone traffic patterns.

Summers in New Orleans arrive early and stick around longer than most people would like. If visiting in the hot months, stay hydrated, limit your midday outdoor activities, and be prepared for sudden, sometimes torrential downpours.

Bring a sweater or light jacket with you: air-conditioning in restaurants and other destinations can be excessive.

New Orleanians are friendly, but odd offers from people on the street to tell you where you got your shoes ("You got them on your feet," followed by a demand that you pay for this information) and other overtures from chatty, rather dubious-looking types should be ignored (feel free to pretend you don't speak English). Trust your intuition; if something doesn't feel right, don't worry about coming across as mean; just continue along your way.

Before you book your trip, visit ⊕ *www.neworleansonline.com*, click travel tools, and download coupons for lodging, dining, attractions, tours, and shopping discounts. This site is owned by the New Orleans Tourism Marketing Corporation and is a great source for event information. The site ⊕ *www.neworleanscvb.com* also has a selection of downloadable coupons.

A GOOD GARDEN DISTRICT WALK

As New Orleans expanded upriver from Canal Street in the 19th century, wealthy newcomers built their majestic homes in the Garden District. Today the area is home to politicians, fifth-generation New Orleanians, and celebrities. A walk through the Garden District, just a 20-minute street-car ride from the French Quarter, provides a unique look at life in New Orleans, past and present.

Start at **the Rink,** a small shopping complex at the Washington Avenue and Prytania Street intersection, a block from the streetcar stop. Walk east on Prytania (the main artery of the district) to the corner of Fourth Street to see **Colonel Short's Villa** (1448 Fourth St.), known for its ornate cornstalk fence, supposedly built for his wife, who was homesick for Kentucky. Toward Third Street, the **Briggs-Staub House** (2605 Prytania St.) is one of the few Gothic Revival houses in the city. No expense was spared in building the **Lonsdale House** (2521 Prytania St.) across the street, which was a Catholic chapel for more than 70 years. The **Maddox House** (2507 Prytania St.) next door is an example of the five-bay Greek Revival expansion. Across Prytania at the corner of Second is the **Women's Guild of the New Orleans Opera Association House** (2504 Prytania St.), with its distinctive octagonal turret; it's now a catering hall for weddings and social events. At First and Prytania streets are the regal **Bradish-Johnson House** (2343 Prytania St.), now a private girls' school, and the relatively modest raised **Toby-Westfeldt House** (2340 Prytania St.), an example of a Creole colonial home.

Turn right and walk down First Street. Built in 1869, **Morris House** (1331 First St.), on the corner of Coliseum, and **Carroll House** (1315 First St.) next door, where *Toys in the Attic* was filmed, are decorated with "iron lace," exemplifying the era's romantic Italianate style. Across Chestnut Street, **Brevard House** (1239 First St.), also known as Rosegate for the ornate cast-iron gate that extends the length of the block, used to be the home of author Anne Rice. A block farther on the right is the **Payne House** (1134 First St.), where Confederate president Jefferson Davis died.

Walk back up First Street toward Coliseum, which takes you past some of the most beautiful and historic homes in the South. The **Italianate Mansion** at 2425 Coliseum Street, at First Street, is the home of actor John Goodman. Across the street from each other at Coliseum and Third streets are the white-columned **Robinson House** (1413 Third St.), thought to be the first house in New Orleans with indoor plumbing, and the intricate iron-balconied **Musson House** (1415 Third St.) built by Edgar Degas's uncle. The white-columned **Nolan House,** at 2707 Coliseum, is where Benjamin Button was raised in the film *The Curious Case of Benjamin Button.* Next door, one of New Orleans's most famous restaurants, **Commander's Palace** (1403 Washington Ave.), is a great stop for lunch. Across Washington Avenue is the white-walled **Lafayette Cemetery No. 1,** arguably the most beautiful cemetery in the city.

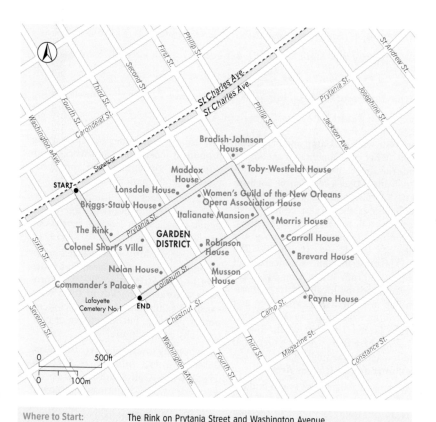

Where to Start:	The Rink on Prytania Street and Washington Avenue
Distance:	1 mile
Timing:	45 minutes (without stops inside)
Where to Stop:	Women's Guild of the New Orleans Opera Association House for interior tours on Monday; Lafayette Cemetery No. 1, open to visitors from Monday through Saturday
Best Time to Go:	Mornings, especially in spring and fall; Monday for the Women's Guild tours
Worst Time to Go:	Midday, especially in summer; Sunday when the cemetery is closed
Good in the Hood:	Stein's Deli, Tracey's Irish Channel Bar, Coquette bistro and wine bar, Commander's Palace

A GOOD GALLERY WALK IN THE WAREHOUSE DISTRICT

Julia Street in the Warehouse District is the epicenter of New Orleans's contemporary art scene, and for art enthusiasts a day on (and just off) Julia is a requirement. The street is lined with galleries, specialty shops, and modern apartment buildings, with the greatest concentration stretching from South Peters Street to Carrollton Avenue.

Start your walk on Camp and St. Joseph streets. Whet your appetite for art buying inside the airy, contemporary, stone-and-glass-walled **Ogden Museum of Southern Art** (⊠ *925 Camp St.* ☎ *504/539–9600*), which houses the largest collection of Southern art anywhere. Across the street, the multidisciplinary **Contemporary Arts Center** (⊠ *900 Camp St.* ☎ *504/528–3805*) hosts performances, concerts, and lectures, and runs stimulating and eclectic exhibitions by local and foreign artists. Pop in if there's an exhibition, and then continue on your way down Camp to Julia Street. Turn left when you get to Julia, where there are five gallery and studio spaces in the single block between this corner and St. Charles Avenue.

At Camp and Julia streets you'll find the **Jean Bragg Gallery of Southern Art** (⊠ *600 Julia St.* ☎ *504/895–7375*), in the first of the Thirteen Sisters addresses that make up the historic Julia Street Row. Jean Bragg shows a mix of contemporary and historical paintings depicting Louisiana scenery and life, works by the famed Mississippi artist Walter Anderson, and pottery and crafts from the renowned Newcomb College.

Longtime champion of the visual arts scene in New Orleans, **Arthur Roger** maintains a world-class gallery (⊠ *432-434 Julia St.* ☎ *504/522–1999*) that occupies two adjacent Julia Street addresses behind gleaming glass-walled facades.

The gallery is a leader in representing prominent local artists and works from around the globe, and is an influential presence in the national art scene.

In the next block you'll find contemporary work with a political edge and a public conscience at **Jonathan Ferrara Gallery** (⊠ *400a Julia St.* ☎ *504/522–5471*).

Next door, the lofty whitewashed brick-and-glass space inside **Søren Christensen** (⊠ *400 Julia St.* ☎ *504/569–9501*) provides a gorgeous backdrop for always excellent exhibitions, largely of contemporary painting, but sometimes of photography and sculpture.

Keep heading toward the river to **Le Mieux Galleries** (⊠ *332 Julia St.* ☎ *504/522–5988*), where Gulf South artists are the stars; drawings, paintings, photography, and sculpture from throughout the region are showcased here.

1

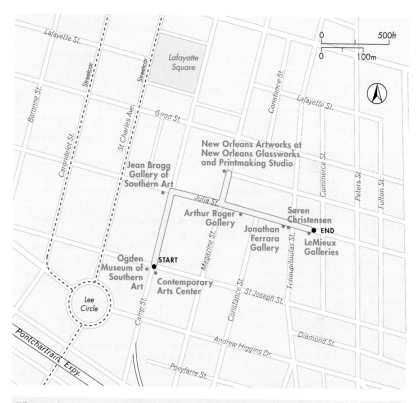

Where to Start:	Camp Street at the Ogden Museum of Southern Art
Distance:	About a half mile
Timing:	Several hours to all day, depending on how much time you have and how much you want to see
Where to Stop:	Julia and Commerce streets
Best Time to Go:	First Saturday of every month, when Art Walks are hosted by Warehouse District galleries from 6 to 9 pm. Two Saturdays not to be missed if you happen to be in town are Jammin' on Julia in April and Whitney White Linen Night in August, wildly popular, all-out art block parties enjoyed by enthusiastic crowds.
Worst Time to Go:	Sunday, when nearly all galleries are closed
Good in the Hood:	Charcuterie and Southern cuisine are showcased at Cochon (✉ 930 Tchoupitoulas St. ☎ 504/588–2123). Next door, Cochon Butcher (✉ 930 Tchoupitoulas St. ☎ 504/588–7675) is more casual, with sandwiches and small plates. Root (✉ 220 Julia St. ☎ 504/252–9480) serves modern American cuisine and crafted cocktails.

BEST FESTS AND PARADES

New Year's Eve

Join the crowd on the Mississippi River near Jax Brewery for fireworks, live music, and the annual countdown to midnight (marked by "Baby Bacchus" dropping from the top of the brewery).

Mardi Gras, February or March

The biggest event in the city's busy festival calendar has been around for well over a century, and for a celebration of frivolity, people here take Carnival very seriously. There are almost daily parades—even one for dogs (the Krewe of Barkus)—in the two weeks leading up to Fat Tuesday, when pretty much the entire city takes the day off, gets in costume, and hits the streets (⇨ *See our Mardi Gras feature in Chapter 2*). ⊕ *www.mardigrasneworleans.com.*

St. Patrick's Day, March

A couple of big parades roll on the weekend closest to March 17: one starts at Molly's in the Market and winds through the French Quarter; the other, in Uptown, goes down Magazine Street. On St. Paddy's Day the streets around Parasol's Restaurant & Bar, in the Irish Channel neighborhood, turn into one big, green block party. Two days later (March 19) the town celebrates St. Joseph's Day with home-cooked food and goodie bags filled with cookies and lucky fava beans. Check the *Times-Picayune* classified ads for announcements of altars that you can visit, and be prepared to make a small contribution to cover costs—$5 a person or so.

Tennessee Williams/New Orleans Literary Festival, March

This annual tribute to the *A Streetcar Named Desire* playwright, who spent much of his career in New Orleans, draws well-known and aspiring writers, lecturers, and a handful of Williams's acquaintances. It closes with contestants reenacting Stanley Kowalski's big "Stella-a-a!" moment. ☎ *504/581–1144* ⊕ *www. tennesseewilliams.net.*

Easter, March or April

Three fun parades hit the streets of the French Quarter on Easter Sunday: one led by local entertainer Chris Owens, another dedicated to the late socialite Germaine Wells, and a gay parade that takes the festive bonnet tradition to a whole new level.

French Quarter Festival, April

A lot of locals consider this the best festival. With stages set up throughout the Quarter and on the river at Woldenberg Park, the focus is on local entertainment—and, of course, food. ☎ *504/522–5730* ⊕ *www.fqfi.org.*

New Orleans Jazz & Heritage Festival, April–May

Top-notch local and international talent takes to several stages the last weekend of April and first weekend of May. The repertoire covers much more than jazz, with big-name rock and pop stars in the mix, and there are dozens of lectures, quality arts and crafts, and awesome food to boot. Next to Mardi Gras, Jazz Fest is the city's biggest draw; book your hotel as far in advance as possible (⇨ *See the Jazz Fest feature listing*). ☎ *504/410–4100* ⊕ *www. nojazzfest.com.*

New Orleans Wine & Food Experience, May

Winemakers and oenophiles from all over the world converge for five days of seminars, tastings, and fine food. The Royal Street Stroll, when shops and galleries host pourings and chefs set up tables on the street, is especially lively. ☎ *504/529–9463* ⊕ *www.nowfe.com.*

Essence Music Festival, July

Held around Independence Day, this three-day festival draws top names in R&B, pop, and hip-hop to the Mercedes-Benz Superdome. The event also includes talks by prominent African American figures and empowerment seminars. ⊕ *www.essence.com/festival.*

Tales of the Cocktail, late July

Every summer, heralded mixologists, distillers, writers, chefs, and cocktail connoisseurs converge in the city that gave birth to the Sazerac and the Ramos gin fizz—among other libations—for several days of cocktail competitions, seminars, tastings, pairing dinners, and many more spirited events. ⊕ *www.talesofthecocktail.com.*

Satchmo SummerFest, August

This weekend-long tribute to the late, great Louis Armstrong honors Satchmo in the French Quarter, with jazz performances staged throughout the streets, seminars and discussions with Louis Armstrong scholars, a Satchmo Club Strut down Frenchman Street, and the Louis Armstrong Birthday Party. ⊕ *www.fqfi. org/satchmosummerfest.*

Southern Decadence, early September

On Labor Day weekend hundreds of drag-queens-for-a-day parade through the Quarter. What began as a small party among friends has evolved into one of the South's biggest gay celebrations. The parade rolls (and as the day wears on, staggers) on Sunday, but Decadence parties and events start Thursday evening.

Art for Art's Sake, early October

Art lovers and people-watchers pack the Warehouse District and Magazine Street galleries for this annual Saturday-evening kickoff to the arts season. What's on the walls usually plays second fiddle to the party scene, which spills out into the streets.

Voodoo Experience, October

Part music festival, part giant interactive art exhibition, Voodoo Experience is an evolving festival held every Halloween weekend; it attracts eclectic young masses with its mix of edgy national acts, local bands, and art installations in various mediums. ⊕ *www.worshipthemusic.com.*

Celebration in the Oaks, late November–early January

City Park's majestic oaks, Botanical Gardens, Carousel Garden, and Storyland amusement park are awash in holiday lights and decorations during this popular weeks-long event. There are food and rides, a miniature train decked out for Christmas, and entertainment by local school groups. ☎ *504/482–4888* ⊕ *www. neworleanscitypark.com.*

A New Orleans Christmas, December

The lighting of Canal Street kicks off this monthlong celebration. Royal Street shops and historic homes don holiday decorations, restaurants feature special *reveillon* menus, and thousands of carolers gather in Jackson Square for a candlelit sing-along. Around Christmas, bonfires are lit on the levee at various points along the Mississippi, from below New Orleans up into Cajun Country. Legend says the bonfires were lighted by the early settlers to help Papa Noel (the Cajun Santa Claus) find his way up the river. Steamboat tour companies offer special cruises for the occasion.

GETTING OUT OF TOWN

Cajun Country

The land that gave the world one of its great cuisines—and a refuge for French-Canadian exiles in the 18th century—is worth at least one overnight. **Lafayette**, with its attractive downtown and plentiful accommodations, makes a good hub for exploring the region. The Cajun kitsch can be a bit much at times, but there are some outstanding restaurants and museums, including the **Paul and Lulu Hilliard University Art Museum** and **Acadian Village**, a re-creation of an early-19th-century Acadian settlement. Venture south to picturesque **Abbeville**, where restaurants serve up some mean oysters on the half shell, or to **New Iberia** and nearby **Avery Island**, home of the famous Tabasco hot sauce and a gorgeous 250-acre botanical garden. **Breaux Bridge**, site of the annual Crawfish Festival, has antiques shops and some excellent Cajun restaurants, including **Café des Amis** and **Mulate's**, both known for their dance parties. **St. Martinville**, south of Breaux Bridge, is an attractive small town and home of the **Evangeline Oak**, immortalized in Longfellow's classic poem "Evangeline."

To the north lie **Grand Coteau**, a quaint, historic village set on a natural bluff, and **Opelousas**, a hotbed of zydeco music; nearby **Plaisance** hosts the annual **Southwest Louisiana Zydeco Music festival** each Labor Day weekend. A bit farther afield, the normally quiet town of **Mamou** goes bonkers on Fat Tuesday, when the traditional **Courir de Mardi Gras** takes to the streets; Saturday mornings little **Fred's Lounge** gets packed to the gills with locals and more than a few tourists two-stepping and waltzing to live Cajun music.

Plantation Country

For *Gone with the Wind* fans, the stretch of the Mississippi north of New Orleans is the ultimate Southern experience. Tour buses ply the highway on both sides of the river, but with a car and a map, it's easy to explore on your own. Fortunes were made here in the 18th and 19th centuries—on the backs of the slaves that worked these plantations—and vestiges of the Old South's wealthy heyday remain in the region's lavish homes, many lovingly restored and open to the public. Highlights include **Oak Alley**, with its procession of ancient oak trees that flank the entrance; **Houmas House**, notable for its architecture, gardens, and fine Latil's Landing restaurant; and **Nottoway**, the largest extant plantation house. Several homes offer accommodations and dining for those who want to linger.

Many of the small towns that dot Plantation Country are fun to explore, but **St. Francisville**, about 25 miles north of Baton Rouge, deserves special mention. The historic town center is a well-preserved collection of antebellum homes and buildings, and the river landing there is one of the few places in south Louisiana where the Mississippi isn't hemmed in by levees. A cluster of fine plantation homes are nearby, including **Rosedown Plantation and Gardens** and the attractive **Oakley House at Audubon State Historic Site**, where John James Audubon taught drawing to the plantation owner's daughter while executing some of the works in his Birds of America series. **Baton Rouge** itself is worth a visit to see the **Old State Capitol** (and the new one, where Governor Huey P. Long met his untimely end) and its lively downtown.

REMEMBERING KATRINA

For nearly 300 years, New Orleans captured the imaginations of people around the world with its unique heritage and lifestyle—a rich tapestry of food, music, pageantry, and irreverent, laissez-faire culture. On August 29, 2005, however, New Orleans captured the attention of the world in a different way: as the site of one of the country's worst natural and manmade disasters and, for a few terrifying days, as a pit of human suffering.

New Orleans is the first major American city to be nearly drained of its population, and even today, nearly a decade later, the city has recovered only about three-quarters of its former population. Some neighborhoods are still recovering, and while businesses and residents have trickled back into the heavily damaged areas, many are still waiting for a number of factors to kick in—insurance settlements, rebuilding of infrastructure, and direction from city officials.

That being said, much of New Orleans has been restored and rejuvenated, and visitors are finding that the city retains its sense of joy and hospitality. It is, again, one of the most exciting cities in the United States.

Nevertheless, Hurricane Katrina is still an essential part of city's landscape, mentally and physically, and it will not soon be forgotten.

The following pages include a recap of the disaster and its immediate aftermath, and information on organizations that have made, and continue to make, a profound impact on the rebuilding of the city.

Above, post-Katrina devastation

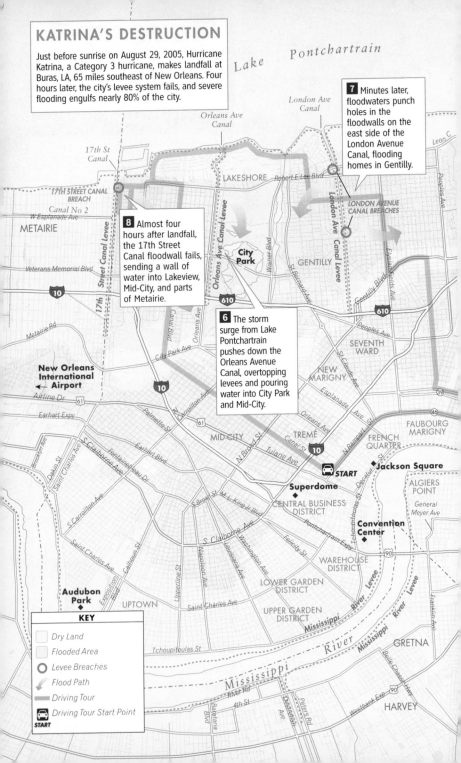

KATRINA'S DESTRUCTION

Just before sunrise on August 29, 2005, Hurricane Katrina, a Category 3 hurricane, makes landfall at Buras, LA, 65 miles southeast of New Orleans. Four hours later, the city's levee system fails, and severe flooding engulfs nearly 80% of the city.

7 Minutes later, floodwaters punch holes in the floodwalls on the east side of the London Avenue Canal, flooding homes in Gentilly.

8 Almost four hours after landfall, the 17th Street Canal floodwall fails, sending a wall of water into Lakeview, Mid-City, and parts of Metairie.

6 The storm surge from Lake Pontchartrain pushes down the Orleans Avenue Canal, overtopping levees and pouring water into City Park and Mid-City.

KEY

- Dry Land
- Flooded Area
- ○ Levee Breaches
- ↙ Flood Path
- ▬ Driving Tour
- 🚗 Driving Tour Start Point

1

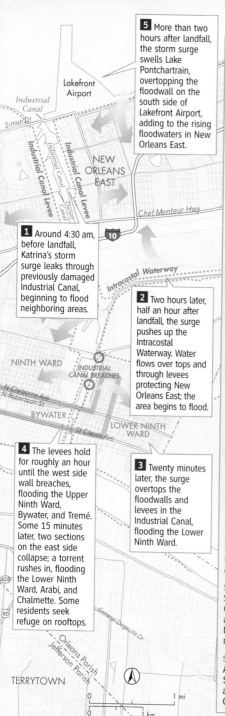

5 More than two hours after landfall, the storm surge swells Lake Pontchartrain, overtopping the floodwall on the south side of Lakefront Airport, adding to the rising floodwaters in New Orleans East.

Lakefront Airport

Industrial Canal

Simon Dr

Industrial Canal

Industrial Canal

Industrial Canal Levee

NEW ORLEANS EAST

Chef Menteur Hwy

10

Intracoastal Waterway

1 Around 4:30 am, before landfall, Katrina's storm surge leaks through previously damaged Industrial Canal, beginning to flood neighboring areas.

2 Two hours later, half an hour after landfall, the surge pushes up the Intracostal Waterway. Water flows over tops and through levees protecting New Orleans East; the area begins to flood.

NINTH WARD

INDUSTRIAL CANAL BREACHES

N Claiborne Ave
N Robertson St

BYWATER

St Claude Ave

LOWER NINTH WARD

4 The levees hold for roughly an hour until the west side wall breaches, flooding the Upper Ninth Ward, Bywater, and Tremé. Some 15 minutes later, two sections on the east side collapse; a torrent rushes in, flooding the Lower Ninth Ward, Arabi, and Chalmette. Some residents seek refuge on rooftops.

3 Twenty minutes later, the surge overtops the floodwalls and levees in the Industrial Canal, flooding the Lower Ninth Ward.

428

General Degaulle Dr

90

Orleans Parish
Jefferson Parish

TERRYTOWN

0   1 mi

0   1 km

THE DAYS THAT FOLLOWED

August 30
The breach at the 17th Street Canal gets larger; Lakeview floodwaters rise to nine feet. Many people climb onto roofs to escape. Crowds build at the Superdome, seeking refuge. Rescuers in helicopters and boats pick up hundreds of stranded people, and reports of looting begin to emerge.

August 31
The first buses arrive at the Superdome to take refugees to the Astrodome in Houston.

September 1
National Guard arrives. Looting, carjacking, and other violence spreads. Crowds at the Superdome swell to 25,000, with another 20,000 at the New Orleans Convention Center.

September 2
Congress approves $10.5 billion for immediate rescue and relief efforts.

September 4
Superdome and Convention Center are fully evacuated. Nearly 45,000 refugees.

September 8
An additional $52 billion in aid approved by Congress.

September 17
Business owners are allowed back into Algiers, French Quarter, the CBD, and Uptown.

September 23
A storm surge from Hurricane Rita overtops an Industrial Canal levee, reflooding the Lower Ninth Ward; surge also tops the London Avenue Canal, reflooding Gentilly.

September 26
After suspending re-entry due to Hurricane Rita, the city allows residents to return.

February 18, 2006
The first official Mardi Gras parade (in Orleans Parish), Pontchartrain, rolls.

February 28
Amid controversy, thousands turn out to celebrate Mardi Gras.

April 28
First day of New Orleans Jazz and Heritage Festival.

May 20
C. Ray Nagin is re-elected Mayor of New Orleans.

June 24
Approximately 20,000 attend American Library Association meeting, the largest conference in the city post-Katrina.

REBUILDING NEW ORLEANS

Habitat for Humanity

The immediate aftermath of Hurricane Katrina is over, but the hard work of rebuilding a city continues. Some remarkable organizations stepped up to that challenge, and many others were formed in direct response. These are a few of the players that continue to inspire hope around the city and the region. For a list of voluntourism opportunities, go to www.neworleanscvb.com/travel-professionals/toolkit/voluntourism/.

BUILD NOW

Helping hard-hit New Orleanians navigate the maze of claims, licenses, permits, and zoning laws, the Build Now Foundation has put dozens of families and individuals back into homes on their original lots. The organization constructs elevated site-built homes in flood-damaged neighborhoods; find the homes in neighborhoods including the Lower Ninth Ward, Lakeview, Gentilly, and Chalmette. ⊕ *www.buildnownola.com*

COMMON GROUND RELIEF

Combining recovery efforts with environmental awareness and grassroots activism, Common Ground Relief has organized some 25,000 volunteers. They have gutted more than 3,000 homes, founded an independent health clinic and women's shelter, created a free legal clinic, and cofounded the Lower Ninth Ward Urban Farming Coalition. They also run a wetlands restoration program and a job training program. ⊕ *www.commongroundrelief.org*

HABITAT FOR HUMANITY

Utilizing an incredible array of volunteer forces and partnerships with Ameri-Corps, Habitat for Humanity has rebuilt hundreds of homes in New Orleans, including one of the most prominent and beloved post-Katrina projects, the Musician's Village. Located on Roman Street in the Upper Ninth Ward, the site has provided home and shelter for dozens of returning musicians and is now home to the new Ellis Marsalis Center for Music, dedicated to the education, development, and preservation of New Orleans unique musical heritage. ⊕ *www.habitatnola.org*

MAKE IT RIGHT

With Brad Pitt as one of its founders, the Make it Right Foundation altered the landscape of post-Katrina Lower Ninth Ward, from one of despair to one of hope—not to mention wonder. The futuristic designs of the affordable, environmentally friendly houses makes each home more than a living unit—they're works of art. ⊕ *www.makeitrightnola.org*

REBUILDING TOGETHER NEW ORLEANS (RTNO)

Along with parent organization the Preservation Resource Center of New Orleans, RTNO has been a champion of efforts to rebuild New Orleans in a way that is sensitive to its past and heritage. One of the great New Orleans landmarks they helped restore was the historic Doullut Steamboat Houses, a pair of architectural and aesthetic wonders, built next to the river in the Holy Cross neighborhood. ⊕ *www.rtno.org*

Rebuilding Together

THE FRENCH QUARTER

GETTING ORIENTED

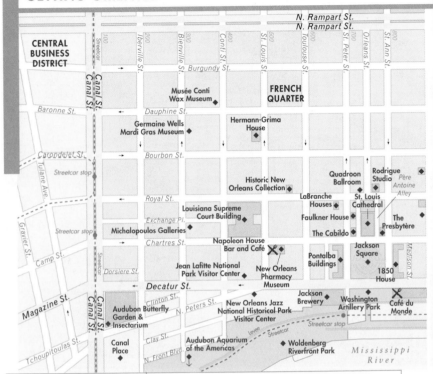

GETTING AROUND

French Quarter streets are laid out in a **grid pattern**. Locals describe locations based on the proximity to the river or the lake and to uptown or downtown. Thus, "it's on the downtown, lakeside corner" indicates that a destination in the Quarter is on the northeast corner. Locals also refer to the **number block** that a site is on (as in "the 500 block of Royal Street"). Numbers across the top of the map are applicable to all streets parallel to North Rampart Street. Streets perpendicular to North Rampart start at 500 at Decatur Street and progress north in increments of 100.

MAKING THE MOST OF YOUR TIME

Many visitors never leave the French Quarter, which is the center of New Orleans. Daytime offers history buffs, antiques lovers, shoppers, and foodies a feast of delights; street performers around **Jackson Square** are always entertaining; and the Quarter lights up with fine and casual dining, live music, and the infamous **Bourbon Street** debauchery at night. This is a destination you can enjoy 24 hours a day.

SAFETY

Exercise the same caution here that you would in any major city. Close to the river, the French Quarter is busy day and night, and there is safety in numbers. Farther from the river and closer to Rampart Street or the more residential area, crowds thin, and opportunities for theft grow slightly higher. It's advisable to use extra caution at these outer edges of the French Quarter.

2

The French Quarter

TOP REASONS TO GO

Queue up for beignets. Anytime is the right time for powdered-sugar-topped beignets and cafe au lait from Café du Monde.

Take in Jackson Square. Mule-drawn carriage tours, artists selling their wares, and quirky street performers and musicians converge around the square, with the historic St. Louis Cathedral as a backdrop.

Go treasure hunting. The French Market and the random stores and warehouses that surround it are great for finding inexpensive souvenirs.

Drink up. From rowdy Bourbon Street to fancy hotel bars, you'll never go thirsty. Savor your cocktail in a beautiful courtyard, or ask for a "go cup."

Gallery hop on Royal Street. Fine antiques, upscale boutiques, and artwork abound on this classy thoroughfare.

Groove to live music. The French Quarter has some great music venues, including Preservation Hall, the Palm Court Jazz Cafe, Fritzel's European Jazz Pub, and One-Eyed Jack's.

QUICK BITES

Café du Monde. Open around the clock for late-night treats or a sweet breakfast, Café du Monde has been serving café au lait and beignets (and not much else) for more than a century. If the open-air café is crowded, go around back to the take-out window and enjoy your treats on the Mississippi riverfront. ⊠ *800 Decatur St., French Quarter* ☎ *504/525–4544* ⊕ *www.cafedumonde.com.*

Napoleon House Bar and Café. The house specialty, Pimm's Cup (a refreshing mixture of lemonade and Pimm's, a light gin-based liquor), can be enjoyed in the lush courtyard or the cool, darkened interior. ⊠ *500 Chartres St., French Quarter* ☎ *504/524–9752* ⊕ *www.napoleonhouse.com.*

Verti Marte Deli. Pick up a sandwich or hot lunch to go from this distinctly New Orleans take on a deli, open 24 hours and a prime refueling point for the late-night bar crawl. ⊠ *1201 Royal St., French Quarter* ☎ *504/525–4767* ⊕ *www.vertimarte.com.*

Sightseeing
★★★★★
Dining
★★★★★
Lodging
★★★★☆
Shopping
★★★★★
Nightlife
★★★★★

Even locals love to get lost in the history and romance of the French Quarter, the city's oldest neighborhood. From the narrow side streets flanked with historic architecture you'll marvel at the city's power to endure. Keep walking, slowly, and take the time to look up at the fabled wrought-iron balcony railings or to peer down cobblestone corridors for a glimpse of secret courtyard gardens.

Updated
by Susan
Granger

The neighborhood will not run out of ways to entertain you. The Vieux Carre, French for "Old Square," is technically the entire French Quarter, but you'll notice a divide at Decatur Street to the river, as things start to feel more modern, and chain stores and restaurants pop up. The historic part of the French Quarter is where you can slip down a quiet street, gaze up at a row of balconies, and forget for a moment that you are living in the 21st century. During the day the French Quarter offers several different faces to its visitors. The streets running parallel to the river all bear distinct personas: Decatur Street is a strip of tourist shops, hotels, restaurants, and bars uptown from Jackson Square; downtown from the square it becomes a hangout for hipsters and leather-clad regulars drawn to shadowy bars, vintage clothing resellers, funky antiques emporiums, and novelty shops. Modern development along the river side of Decatur Street can make this strip feel like a suburban corridor, but some of the best of old New Orleans is still here: the massive Mississippi River, Café du Monde, and the French Market.

Chartres Street remains a relatively calm stretch of inviting shops and eateries. Royal Street is, perhaps aptly, the address of sophisticated antiques shops and many of the Quarter's finest residences. Bourbon Street claims the strip bars, sex shops, extravagant cocktails, and flashy music clubs filmmakers love to feature. Dauphine and Burgundy streets are more residential, with just a few restaurants and bars serving as retreats for locals.

After dark you'll find fine dining and easygoing eateries aplenty, and music pouring from the doorways of bars as freely as the drinks flowing within them (and out of their doors—plastic "go cups" for your cocktails are standard at the exit of every bar and club, and consuming alcohol on public streets is legal in New Orleans). On any ordinary evening a stroll through the French Quarter is a moving concert.

GET A GO CUP

Open containers of alcohol are allowed on the streets of New Orleans, as long as they're not in glass containers. So when you're ready to leave, ask your bartender for a "go cup," pour your drink into the plastic cup, and head out, drink in hand.

Strains of traditional jazz, blues, classic rock and roll, and electronic dance beats all flow from the various bars and nightclubs while street musicians add their unique sound to the mix.

For all its evening-time adult entertainment, the French Quarter by day is quite kid-friendly. Children adore eating beignets; watching ships ply the Mississippi; walking through the Caribbean tunnel fish tank at the Aquarium of the Americas; munching crunchy treats made out of bugs at the Audubon Insectarium; and savoring the same delicious po'boy sandwiches and fried seafood that their parents enjoy.

TOP ATTRACTIONS

FAMILY

Fodor'sChoice ★

Audubon Aquarium of the Americas. The giant aquatic showplace perched on the Mississippi Riverfront has four major exhibit areas: the Amazon Rain Forest, the Mississippi River, the Gulf of Mexico, and the new Great Maya Reef gallery, all of which have fish and animals native to those environments. The aquarium's spectacular design allows you to feel like you're part of the watery worlds by providing close-up encounters with the inhabitants. A special treat is Parakeet Pointe, where you can get up close to hundreds of parakeets and feed them by hand. A gift shop and café are on the premises. Woldenberg Riverfront Park, which surrounds the aquarium, is a tranquil spot with a view of the Mississippi. ■TIP→ You can combine tickets for the aquarium and the Entergy IMAX Theater ($27.50), but the best deal is the "Audubon Experience": aquarium, IMAX, Audubon Insectarium, and Audubon Zoo for $39.50 (tickets are good for 30 days). ⊠ 1 Canal St., French Quarter ☎ 504/581–4629, 800/774–7394 ⊕ www.auduboninstitute. org ⊴ $22.50 ⊙ Mar. 1–Labor Day, daily 10–5; Sept.–Feb., Tues.–Sun. 10–5.

FAMILY

Audubon Butterfly Garden and Insectarium. Shrink down to ant size and experience "Life Underground," explore the world's insect myth and lore, venture into a Louisiana swamp, and marvel at the hundreds of delicate denizens in the Japanese butterfly garden. Then tour the termite galleries and other sections devoted to the havoc insects wreak so you can sample Cajun-fried crickets and other insect cuisine without a twinge of guilt. ⊠ 423 Canal St., French Quarter ☎ 800/774–7394 ⊕ auduboninstitute.org ⊴ $16.50 ⊙ Mar. 1–Labor Day, daily 10–5; Sept.–Feb., Tues.–Sun. 10–5.

Bourbon Street. Ignore your better judgment and take a stroll down Bourbon Street, past the bars, restaurants, music clubs, and novelty shops that have given this strip its reputation as the playground of the South. The bars of Bourbon Street were among the first businesses of the city to reopen after Katrina; catering to the off-duty relief workers, they provided a different form of relief. Today, the spirit of unbridled revelry here is as big as ever. The noise, raucous crowds, and bawdy sights are not family fare; if you go with children, do so before sundown. St. Ann Street marks the beginning of a short strip of gay bars, some of which retain links to the long history of gay culture in New Orleans. Although Bourbon is usually well patrolled, it is wise to stay alert to your surroundings. The street is blocked to make a pedestrian mall at night; often the area is shoulder to shoulder, especially during major sports events, on New Year's Eve, and during Mardi Gras. ✉ *French Quarter.*

The Cabildo. Dating from 1799, this Spanish colonial building is named for the Spanish council—or *cabildo*—that met there. The transfer of Louisiana to the United States was made in 1803 in the front room on the second floor overlooking the square. This historic transaction was reenacted in the same room for the 200th anniversary of the purchase in 2003. The Cabildo later served as the city hall and then the Supreme Court.

Three floors of multicultural exhibits recount Louisiana history—from the colonial period through Reconstruction—with countless artifacts, including the death mask of Napoléon Bonaparte. In 1988 the building suffered terrible damage from a four-alarm fire. Most of the historic pieces inside were saved, but the top floor (which had been added in the 1840s), the roof, and the cupola had to be replaced. The Cabildo is almost a twin to the **Presbytère** on the other side of the cathedral. ■TIP→ **Both sites—as well as the Old U.S. Mint and the 1850 House— are part of the Louisiana State Museum system. Buy tickets to two or more state museums and receive a 20% discount.** ✉ *Jackson Sq., 701 Chartres St., French Quarter* ☎ *504/568–8975* ⊕ *lsm.crt.state.la.us* 🖂 *$6* ☼ *Tues.–Sun. 10–4:30 (last entrance at 4).*

French Market. The sounds, colors, and smells here are alluring: street performers, ships' horns on the river, pralines, muffulettas, sugarcane, and Creole tomatoes. Originally a Native American trading post, later a bustling open-air market under the French and Spanish, the French Market historically began at Café du Monde and stretched along Decatur and North Peters streets all the way to the downtown edge of the Quarter. Today the market's graceful arcades have been mostly enclosed and filled with shops and eateries, and the fresh market has been pushed several blocks downriver, under sheds built in the 1930s as part of a Works Progress Administration project. **Latrobe Park,** a small recreational area at the uptown end of the French Market, honors Benjamin Latrobe, designer of the city's first waterworks. A modern fountain evoking a waterworks marks the spot where Latrobe's steam-powered pumps once stood. Sunken seating, fountains, and greenery make this a lovely place to relax with a drink from one of the nearby kiosks. ✉ *Decatur St., French Quarter* ⊕ *www.frenchmarket.org* ☼ *Shops daily 9–6; flea market daily 9–6 (may vary depending on season and weather).*

WHEN TO GO

Save Bourbon Street for after dinner at one of the Quarter's esteemed restaurants; like anything that has lived hard and been around a long time, Bourbon Street is much more attractive in low light.

Hermann-Grima House. Noted architect William Brand built this Georgian-style house in 1831, and it's one of the largest and best-preserved examples of American architecture in the Vieux Carré. Cooking demonstrations on the open hearth of the Creole kitchen are held most Thursdays from October through May. You'll want to check the gift shop, which has many local crafts and books. ⊠ *820 St. Louis St., French Quarter* ☎ *504/525–5661* ⊕ *www.hgghh.org* ☜ *$12, $15 with open-hearth cooking demonstration* ⊙ *Mon., Tues., Thurs., and Fri. 10–3, Sat. noon–4; tours on the hr.*

BORDERLAND

In New Orleans street medians are known as "neutral grounds." Why? The term evolved in the days following the Louisiana Purchase, when the Europeans and Creoles who inhabited the French Quarter did little to welcome American immigrants into their neighborhood. Americans instead settled outside the city center and established what are now the CBD, Warehouse, and Garden districts. Canal Street became the first "neutral ground" in the clash of cultures.

Historic New Orleans Collection. This private archive and exhibit complex, with thousands of historic photos, documents, and books, is one of the finest research centers in the South. It occupies the 19th-century town house of General Kemper Williams and the 1792 Merieult House. Changing exhibits focus on aspects of local history. Architecture, history, and house tours are offered several times daily, and a museum shop sells books, prints, and gifts. The Williams Research Center addition, at 410 Chartres Street, hosts additional free exhibits. ⊠ *533 Royal St., French Quarter* ☎ *504/523–4662* ⊕ *www.hnoc.org* ☜ *Free, tours $5* ⊙ *Tues.–Sat. 9:30–4:30 (museum and research library), Sun. 10:30–4:30 (museum only). Tours daily at 10, 11, 2, and 3 (no 10 am tour Sun.).*

FAMILY
Fodor'sChoice
★

Jackson Square. Surrounded by historic buildings and atmospheric street life, this beautifully landscaped park is the heart of the French Quarter. **St. Louis Cathedral** sits at the top of the square, while the **Cabildo** and **Presbytère,** two Spanish colonial buildings, flank the church. The handsome brick apartments on each side of the square are the **Pontalba Buildings.** The park is landscaped in a sun pattern, with walkways set like rays streaming from the center, a popular garden design in the royal court of King Louis XIV, the Sun King. In the daytime, dozens of artists hang their paintings on the park fence and set up outdoor studios where they work on canvases or offer to draw portraits of passersby. These artists are easy to engage in conversation and are knowledgeable about many aspects of the Quarter and New Orleans. Musicians, mimes, tarot-card readers, and magicians perform on the flagstone pedestrian mall, many of them day and night.

Originally called the Place d'Armes, the square was founded in 1718 as a military parade ground. It was also the site of public executions carried out in various manners, including burning at the stake, beheading, breaking on the wheel, and hanging. A **statue of Andrew Jackson,** victorious leader of the Battle of New Orleans in the War of 1812, commands the center of the square; the park was renamed for him

A statue of General Andrew Jackson presides over his namesake park, Jackson Square.

in the 1850s. The words carved in the base on the cathedral side of the statue—"The Union must and shall be preserved"—are a lasting reminder of the Federal troops who occupied New Orleans during the Civil War and who inscribed them. ⊠ *French Quarter* ⊙ *Park daily 8 am–dusk; paths on park's periphery open 24 hrs.*

LaBranche Houses. This complex of lovely town houses, built in the 1830s by sugar planter Jean Baptiste LaBranche, fills the half block between Pirate's Alley and Royal and St. Peter streets behind the Cabildo. The house on the corner of Royal and St. Peter streets, with its elaborate, rounded cast-iron balconies, is among the most frequently photographed residences in the French Quarter. ⊠ *700 Royal St., French Quarter.*

Mississippi River. When facing the river with the French Quarter at your back, you will see, to your right, the **Crescent City Connection,** a twin-span bridge between downtown New Orleans and the Westbank, and a ferry that crosses the river every 30 minutes. The river flows to the left downstream for another 100 miles until it merges with the Gulf of Mexico. **Woldenberg Riverfront Park** and **Spanish Plaza** are prime territory for watching everyday life along the Mississippi: steamboats carrying tour groups, tugboats pushing enormous barges, and ocean-going ships. Directly across the river from the Quarter are the ferry landing and a ship-repair dry dock. ⊠ *French Quarter.*

Fodor'sChoice
★

The Presbytère. One of the twin Spanish colonial buildings flanking St. Louis Cathedral, this one, on the right, was built on the site of the priests' residence, or presbytere. It served as a courthouse under the Spanish and later under the Americans. It is now a museum showcasing

DID YOU KNOW?

In the French Quarter you're never too far from a Lucky Dog, one of New Orleans's most prized before-, during-, or after-drinking snacks. The hot-dog-shape vending carts were immortalized by John Kennedy Toole in *A Confederacy of Dunces*, his Pulitzer Prize–winning novel set in the Crescent City.

a spectacular collection of Mardi Gras memorabilia. Displays highlight both the little-known and popular traditions associated with New Orleans's most famous festival. "Living with Hurricanes: Katrina and Beyond" is a $7.5 million exhibition exploring the history, science, and powerful human drama of one of nature's most destructive forces. The building's cupola, destroyed by a hurricane in 1915, was restored to match the one atop its twin, the Cabildo. Allow at least an hour to see the exhibits. ⊠ *751 Chartres St., on Jackson Sq., French Quarter* ☎ *504/568–6964* ⊕ *lsm.crt.state.la.us* ✆ *$6* ☉ *Tues.–Sun. 10–4:30 (last entrance at 4).*

St. Louis Cathedral. The oldest active Catholic cathedral in the United States, this beautiful church and basilica at the heart of the Old City is named for the 13th-century French king who led two crusades. The current building, which replaced two structures destroyed by fire, dates from 1794 (although it was remodeled and enlarged in 1851). The austere interior is brightened by murals covering the ceiling and stained-glass windows along the first floor. Pope John Paul II held a prayer service for clergy here during his New Orleans visit in 1987; to honor the occasion, the pedestrian mall in front of the cathedral was renamed Place Jean Paul Deux. Of special interest is his portrait in a Jackson Square setting, which hangs on the cathedral inner side wall. Pick up a brochure ($1) for a self-guided tour; books about the cathedral are available in the gift shop. Docents often give free tours.

■TIP→ **Nearly every evening in December brings a free concert at the cathedral, in addition to the free concert series throughout the year.**

The statue of the Sacred Heart of Jesus dominates St. Anthony's Garden, which extends behind the cathedral-basilica to Royal Street. The garden is also the site of a monument to 30 members of a French ship who died in a yellow-fever epidemic in 1857. The garden has been redesigned by famed French landscape architect Louis Benech, who also redesigned the Tuileries gardens in Paris. ⊠ *615 Père Antoine Alley, French Quarter* ☎ *504/525–9585* ⊕ *www.stlouiscathedral.org* ✆ *Free* ☉ *Daily 8–4.*

Woldenberg Riverfront Park. This stretch of green from Canal Street to Esplanade Avenue overlooks the Mississippi River as it curves around New Orleans, which inspired the Crescent City moniker. The wooden promenade section in front of Jackson Square is called the **Moon Walk**, named for Mayor Moon Landrieu (father of current mayor Mitch Landrieu), under whose administration in the 1970s the riverfront beyond the flood wall was reopened to public view. Today, the French Quarter Festival's main stages are located here every April. It's a great place for a rest (or a muffuletta sandwich or café au lait and beignet picnic) after touring the Quarter, and you'll often be serenaded by musicians and amused by street performers. The park also is home to art pieces including the modest **Holocaust Memorial,** with its spiral walkway clad in Jerusalem stone. At the center of the spiral are nine sculptural panels by Jewish artist Yaacov Agam. A statue of local businessman Malcolm Woldenberg, the park's benefactor, is located near *Ocean Song,* local artist John T. Scott's large kinetic sculpture whose wind-powered movements are intended to evoke the patterns of New Orleans music. ⊠ *French Quarter.*

WORTH NOTING

1850 House. This well-preserved town house and courtyard provide rare public access beyond the storefronts and into the interior of the exclusive **Pontalba Buildings.** The rooms are furnished in the style of the mid-19th century, when the buildings were built as upscale residences and retail spaces. Notice the ornate ironwork on the balconies of the apartments: the original owner, Baroness Micaela Pontalba, popularized cast (or molded) iron with these buildings, and it eventually replaced much of the old handwrought ironwork in the French Quarter. The initials for her families, *A* and *P*—Almonester and Pontalba—are worked into the design. A gift shop and bookstore run by the Friends of the Cabildo is downstairs. The Friends of the Cabildo offer an informative two-hour walking tour of the French Quarter ($15; 10 and 1:30) from this location every day but Monday that includes admission to the house tour. ⊠ *523 St. Ann St., on Jackson Sq., French Quarter* ☎ *504/523–3939* ⊕ *crt.state.la.us, friendsofthecabildo.org* ⊠ *$3* ☾ *Tues.–Sun. 10–4:30.*

Beauregard-Keyes House. The Confederate general and Louisiana native P.G.T. Beauregard briefly made his home at this stately 19th-century mansion. A more long-term resident, however, was the novelist Frances Parkinson Keyes, who found the place in a sad state when she arrived in the 1940s. Keyes restored the home, today filled with period furnishings. Her studio at the back of the large courtyard remains intact, complete with family photos, original manuscripts, and her doll, fan, and teapot collections. Keyes wrote 40 novels there, all in longhand, among them the local favorite, *Dinner at Antoine's.* Even if you don't have time to tour the house, take a peek through the gates at the beautiful walled garden at the corner of Chartres and Ursulines streets. Landscaped in the same sun pattern as Jackson Square, it blooms throughout the year. ⊠ *1113 Chartres St., French Quarter* ☎ *504/523–7257* ⊕ *www. bkhouse.org* ⊠ *$10* ☾ *Mon.–Sat. 10–3, tours on the hr.*

Canal Place. At the foot of Canal Street, this mall offers high-end shopping and the **Theatres at Canal Place,** a upscale moviegoing experience, with reserved seating and waiters to deliver snacks, drinks, or even a full meal in the middle of a showing. The **Westin New Orleans at Canal Place** tops the complex; its dining rooms and lobby have fantastic river views. ⊠ *333 Canal St., French Quarter* ☎ *504/522–9200* ☾ *Mon.–Sat. 10–7, Sun. noon–6.*

CLOSE UP

Micaela Pontalba

Every life has its little dramas, but how many of us can claim a life dramatic enough to inspire an opera? The Baroness Micaela Almonester de Pontalba is in that rarefied number, albeit posthumously. In 2003, on the 200th anniversary of the Louisiana Purchase, the New Orleans Opera Association commissioned an opera based on Pontalba and the mark she left on New Orleans—a legacy you can easily see even now in the Pontalba Buildings, the elegant brick apartments lining Jackson Square.

Micaela Almonester was of Spanish stock, the daughter of the wealthy entrepreneur and developer Don Andres Almonester, who was instrumental in the creation of the Cabildo and Presbytère on Jackson Square. Don Almonester died while Micaela was still young, but not before passing on to his daughter a passion for building and urban design. The rest of her life became a tale of the impact a single will can have upon an urban environment, as well as a tragedy-torn drama of international scope.

At the time of the Louisiana Purchase, in 1803, New Orleans was in cultural upheaval. Following a period under Spanish rule during the late 18th century, the French had reacquired the colony—and merrily sold it to the Americans. The often-complex blending of French and Spanish society was further complicated by the anticipated imposition of American laws and mores, so foreign to the population of New Orleans. Micaela Almonester was right in the middle of the confusion: daughter of Spanish gentry, she fell in love and married a Frenchman, who took her to Paris with his family to avoid coming under American rule in New Orleans.

The Pontalbas' marriage was particularly unhappy, and Micaela's relationship to her in-laws was poisoned by mistrust over family property. Control of her New Orleans inheritance became part of an increasingly bitter feud that included separation from her husband and, at its dramatic pinnacle, her attempted murder by her father-in-law. After the old baron inflicted four gunshot wounds on his daughter-in-law, he committed suicide, believing he had protected his son and his property. But Micaela, now Baroness de Pontalba following the old baron's death, survived her wounds. Within two years, she had recovered enough to conceive the plan for the buildings that bear her name, but a long series of delays, including a bitter divorce, halted the project. Micaela finally returned to New Orleans in the 1840s in order to direct construction of the elegant apartment buildings that would complete the square her father had been so instrumental in developing during the previous century. The Pontalba Buildings, designed by James Gallier in the French style favored by Micaela, were dedicated in 1851 to great fanfare. Each building (one along each side of Jackson Square) contained 16 grand and lavishly detailed apartments.

Following the dedication of the buildings, Pontalba returned to France. She had been living in Paris for nearly 50 years by then, her children had grown up there, and it had become her home. Yet the pilgrimage she had made to New Orleans in order to complete a dream in the name of her father's memory, hints that her heart never really left her childhood home.

Canal Street. At 170 feet wide, Canal Street is the widest street (as opposed to avenue or boulevard) in the United States and one of the liveliest—particularly during Carnival parades. It was once scheduled to be made into a canal linking the Mississippi River to Lake Pontchartrain; plans changed, but the name remains. In the early 1800s, after the Louisiana Purchase, the French Creoles residing in the French Quarter segregated themselves from the Americans who settled upriver from Canal Street. What is now Canal Street—and, most specifically, the central median running down Canal Street—was neutral ground between them. Today, animosities between these two groups are history, but the term "neutral ground" has survived as the name for all medians throughout the city.

> ## PIRATE'S ALLEY
>
> Pirate's Alley takes its name, in part, from the popular myth that Jean Lafitte met here with General Andrew Jackson before the Battle of New Orleans. During this meeting, Lafitte supposedly made his offer to double-cross the British. The legend apparently has no historical foundation, but its romance was so appealing that the name of the alley (originally Orleans Alley) was officially changed. It's a picturesque way to get from Jackson Square to the shops and galleries of Royal Street.

Some of the grand buildings that once lined Canal Street remain, many of them former department stores, now serve as hotels, restaurants, or souvenir shops. The Werlein Building (605 Canal St.), once a multilevel music store, is now the **Palace Café** restaurant. The former home of Maison Blanche (921 Canal St.), once the most elegant of the downtown department stores, is now a **Ritz-Carlton hotel**. One building still serving its original purpose is **Adler's** (722 Canal St.), the city's most elite jewelry and gift store. For the most part, these buildings are faithfully restored, so you can still appreciate the grandeur that once reigned on this fabled strip. ✉ *French Quarter.*

Faulkner House. The young novelist William Faulkner lived and wrote his first book, *Soldiers' Pay,* here in the 1920s. He later returned to his native Oxford, Mississippi, where his explorations of Southern consciousness earned him the Nobel Prize for literature. The house is not open for tours, but the ground-floor apartment Faulkner inhabited is now a bookstore, **Faulkner House Books** (⇨ *Shopping, French Quarter*), which specializes in local and Southern writers. The house is also home to the **Pirate's Alley Faulkner Society** literary group, which sponsors the annual Words & Music literary festival. ✉ *624 Pirate's Alley, French Quarter* ☎ *504/524-2940* ⊕ *www.faulknerhouse.net* ☉ *Daily 10–5:30.*

Gallier House. Irish-born James Gallier Jr. was one of the city's most famous 19th-century architects; he died in 1866, when a hurricane sank the paddle-steamer on which he was a passenger. This home, where he lived with his family, was built in 1857 and contains an excellent collection of early Victorian furnishings. During the holiday season, the entire house is filled with Christmas decorations. ✉ *1132 Royal St., French Quarter* ☎ *504/525-5661* ⊕ *www.hgghh.org* ✐ *$12, combination ticket with Hermann-Grima House $20* ☉ *Tours Mon., Thurs., and Fri. 10, 11, noon, and 2; Sat. noon, 1, 2, and 3.*

Continued on page 63

IT'S MARDI GRAS TIME IN NEW ORLEANS!

by Todd Price

Odds are, most of what you know about Mardi Gras is wrong. The bare breasts of Bourbon Street have nothing to do with the real experience—a party steeped in tradition that New Orleanians throw (and pay for) themselves. They generously invite the rest of the world to join in the fun, so hold on to your fairy wings, your tutus, and your beads; things are about to get crazy!

Mardi Gras (French for "Fat Tuesday") is actually the final day of Carnival, a Christian holiday season that begins on the Twelfth Night of Christmas (January 6) and comes crashing to a halt on Ash Wednesday, the first day of Lent. The elite celebrate with private balls, while the rest of the city takes to the streets for weeks of parades and mischief. Don't be shy—after a few moments of astonished gaping, and maybe some Hurricane cocktails, you too will be bebopping to the marching bands, yelling for throws, and draped in garlands of beads.

On Mardi Gras day, New Orleanians don costumes and masks, drink Bloody Marys for breakfast and roam the streets until dark. It's an official city holiday, with just about everyone but the police and bartenders taking the day off. Two of Carnival's most important parades, Zulu and Rex, roll that day before noon, smaller walking crews meander through the side streets, tribes of Mardi Gras Indians emerge in Tremé, and silent bands of skeletons mysteriously appear. For one day, an entire city becomes a surreal, flamboyant party.

(top) Masked revelers get in the Mardi Gras spirit

MARDI GRAS HISTORY

"The Carnival at New Orleans," a wood engraving drawn by John Durkin and published in *Harper's Weekly*, March 1885.

On February 24, 1857, a group of men dressed like demons paraded through the streets of New Orleans in a torch-lighted cavalcade. They called themselves the **Mistick Krewe of Comus,** after the Greek god of revelry. It was the start of modern Mardi Gras.

Based on European traditions, these men formed a secret society and sent 3,000 invitations to a ball held at New Orleans's Gaiety Theater. Many years later, when a 1991 City Council ordinance—later ruled unconstitutional—required all krewes to reveal their members to obtain a parade permit, Comus stopped parading. Its annual ball, however, remains one of the city's most exclusive.

Through the years, other groups of men organized Carnival krewes, each with its own character. In 1872, 40 businessmen founded the School of Design, whose ruler would be dubbed **Rex.** The krewe still parades on Mardi Gras morning and holds its lavish ball Mardi Gras night. Rex and his queen are considered the monarchs of the entire Carnival celebration, and their identities are kept secret until Lundi Gras morning.

For many decades, these "old-line" crews were strictly segregated, so other parts of society started their own clubs. The **Zulu Social Aid and Pleasure Club** was organized in 1909 by working-class black men, and they started parading in 1915. Zulu was one of the first krewes to integrate, and today members spanning the racial and economic spectrums parade down St. Charles Avenue on Mardi Gras day, preceding Rex.

Parade standards changed in 1969, when a group of businessmen founded the **Krewe of Bacchus,** named after the god of wine. The sassy group stunned the city with a stupendous show featuring lavish floats that dwarfed the old-line parades. The king was Danny Kaye, not a homegrown humanitarian, as was custom, but a famous entertainer. And you didn't have to be socially prominent—or white—to join the after-party, which they called a rendezvous, not a ball.

The arrival of Bacchus ushered in an era of new krewes with open memberships, including satiric krewes such as **Tucks** and **Muses,** that put on many of today's most popular parades.

PEOPLE STILL TALK ABOUT...

1972: Major parades rolled one last time through the French Quarter's narrow streets.

2000: The 19th century Krewe of Proteus returned after a seven-year hiatus.

2006: Despite the 2005 devastation of Katrina, New Orleanians insisted on holding a smaller (but no less enthusiastic) Mardi Gras.

2010: Saints quarterback Drew Brees reigned as king of Bacchus, tossing Nerf footballs to the crowds a week after winning the Super Bowl.

EXPERIENCE MARDI GRAS

Don't forget your costume! Mardi Gras spectators are often the wackiest.

Carnival parades begin in earnest two weekends before Mardi Gras day, with krewes rolling day and night on the final weekend. Almost all krewes each year select a different theme, ranging from the whimsical to hard-edged satire. Off-color jokes and political incorrectness are part and parcel of the subversiveness that characterizes Carnival. Throws will sometimes reflect a parade's theme, which is one reason why locals dive for the cups, doubloons, and other plastic trinkets. The floats and high school marching bands make up the bulk of the parades, with the odd walking club, dance troupe, or convertible car tossed into the mix.

Night parades also have the flambeaux, torch-bearing dancers who historically lighted the way for the parades. These days they provide little more than nostalgia and some fancy stepping to the bands, but they still earn tips for their efforts.

There are no day parades Monday, but Lundi Gras, literally "Fat Monday," has become a major event downtown by the riverfront. Rex and the Zulu King each arrive by boat to greet their subjects and each other. Zulu also hosts free concerts throughout the day. On Mardi Gras day, nearly every corner of New Orleans sees something marvelous, including walking clubs that follow unannounced routes and Mardi Gras Indians who wage mock battles to prove who's the prettiest. Mardi Gras and the Carnival season end with the arrival of Ash Wednesday.

FOR EARLY BIRDS

While most revelers arrive in New Orleans the Friday before Mardi Gras, many major parades actually start earlier in the week. They follow the traditional route down St. Charles Avenue to Canal Street. Note: times might change

Wednesday: Krew of Druids, 6:30 pm; Krewe of Nyx, 7 pm

Thursday: Knights of Babylon, 5:45 pm; Knights of Chaos, 6:30 pm; Krew of Muses, 6:30 pm

MARDI GRAS PARADE SCHEDULE: NOTEABLE KREWES

KREWES (EST.)	Rolls	Participants	Claim to fame	Watch for	Prize throws
Hermes (1937)	Friday 6 pm	Local businessmen	Oldest continuous night parade	Large line-up of marching bands	Lighted medallion beads
Le Krewe d'Etat (1996)	Friday 6:30 pm	Sardonic lawyers and well-heeled elites	Led by a dictator instead of a king	The Dictator's "Banana Wagon" pulled by mules	"D'Etat Gazette" with drawings of every float
Morpheus (2000)	Friday 7 pm	Lovers of traditional parades	Youngest parading krewe in New Orleans	Old-school floats and generous throws	Plush moons
Iris (1917)	Saturday 11 am	Upper crust ladies	Oldest all-female krewe	Flirtatious ladies throwing silk flowers	Ceramic beads
Tucks (1969)	Saturday 12 pm	Exuberant and irreverent young men and women	Took name from defunct Friar Tucks bar	Tongue-in-cheek themes	Plastic plungers and stuffed Friar Tucks dolls
Endymion (1966)	Saturday 4:15 pm	Partiers from around the country	Largest Mardi Gras parade; follows a unique route through Mid-City	Massive, spectacular floats and celebrity riders	Plush Endymion mascots
Okeanos (1949)	Sunday 11 am	Civic-minded business leaders	Queen selected by lottery	Trailer carrying a traditional jazz band	Frisbees
Mid-City (1934)	Sunday 11:45 am	Men from Mid-City	First krewe to have "animated" floats	Floats decorated in colored tinfoil	Bags of potato chips
Thoth (1947)	Sunday 12 pm	Guys with a charitable bent	Unique route passes retirement homes and Children's Hospital	Lavishing throws on children	Thoth baseballs
Bacchus (1968)	Sunday 5:15 pm	Devotees of the god of wine	First "superkrewe"	The Bacchagator and King Kong floats	Wine colored "king" doubloons
Proteus (1882)	Monday 5:15 pm	Members of the city's oldest families	Second-oldest krewe	Beautiful floats built on 19th century wagons	Plush seahorses
Orpheus (1993)	Monday 6 pm	Musicians and music lovers of any gender	Founded by singer Harry Connick Jr.	Latest parade technology, including confetti blowers	Stuffed Leviathan with flashing eyes
Zulu (1916)	Tuesday 8 am	Predominantly African American	Oldest African American Mardi Gras parade	Riders in blackface	Hand-painted coconuts
Rex (1872)	Tuesday 10 am	The most elite men in New Orleans society	King of Carnival	Crossing St. Charles to toast Rex mansion	Traditional Rex beads

WHERE TO WATCH THE PARADES

French Quarter side streets offer some degree of refuge while still sustaining a high party pitch.

Canal Street on the edge of the French Quarter is party animal central; mostly tourists.

The corner of **Napoleon and St. Charles** avenues is a crowded but exciting place to watch.

Great acoustics under the 610 overpass before **Lee Circle** make this a favorite spot for brass bands.

The **Columns Hotel** front porch provides a good vantage point for those who don't need to catch more beads. It charges a fee for access to its bar and bathrooms.

Energetic (sometimes rowdy) revelers camp out in front of bars between **Jackson Avenue and Lee Circle.**

FRENCH QUARTER

CENTRAL BUSINESS DISTRICT

Lee Circle

WAREHOUSE DISTRICT

LOWER GARDEN DISTRICT

UPTOWN

Columns Hotel

UPPER GARDEN DISTRICT

Most big parades begin Uptown, either at Jefferson Avenue and Magazine Street or Napoleon Avenue and Magazine, turn down St. Charles Avenue toward Canal Street, then follow

Canal to their finish. Although it's chaotic all along the route, Uptown is more family friendly; as you head downtown you'll encounter fewer locals and families and more lewd acts. By Mardi Gras weekend it is difficult to walk down Bourbon Street, where drinking, exchanging

beads, and exhibitionism are popular activities. Unlike in Uptown, where parades are the focal point, downtown the parades seem merely a blip on the screen of general frenzy.

KREWES START HERE

- Thoth
- Le Krewe d'Etat
  Mid-City
  Morpheus
  Okeanos
- Bacchus
  Hermes
  Iris
  Orpheus
  Proteus
  Tucks
- Rex
- Zulu

MARDI GRAS TRADITIONS

Royalty

Indian

Dancer

New Orleans's many Carnival traditions often collide on Mardi Gras. Here are some of the characters you're bound to meet.

Mardi Gras Royalty. Each krewe selects monarchs to preside over its parade and ball. In old-line krewes, members choose the king, who is often a prominent local philanthropist and businessman. Super krewes like Bacchus and Endymion pick celebrity kings or grand marshals. Some krewes elect a queen; others have a more elaborate process. To become the reigning woman of the Twelfth Night Revelers, a debutante must find a golden bean in a faux king cake.

Mardi Gras Indians. The African American Mardi Gras Indians began their rituals in the late 19th century in response to being excluded from white Mardi Gras festivities. On Fat Tuesday morning—dressed in intricately beaded and feathered "suits" that often take all year to create—the tribes chant songs and square off in mock battles to decide whose Big Chief is the prettiest. You'll find the Uptown tribes across St. Charles Avenue from the Garden District between Jackson and Washington avenues. Downtown tribes generally meander through Tremé on Ursulines Street.

Dancers. First it was troupes of suburban middle-school girls—dressed a tad too provocatively for their age—that entertained between parade floats. Later, grown women thought this looked fun and created groups like the Pussyfooters and Camel Toe Lady Steppers. Despite the risqué names, many members are lawyers, professors, and other professionals; all members practice choreographed routines for months. In 2010, the 610 Stompers, the first all-male troupe, took to the streets in tight blue gym shorts and red satin jackets. Their motto was "Ordinary Men, Extraordinary Moves."

MARDI GRAS SAFETY

■ Use common sense; don't bring excess cash, valuables, or tempting jewelry.

■ Establish a meeting spot where your family or group will convene at preset times throughout the day.

■ Do not throw anything at the floats or bands, a ticketable and truly hazardous act.

■ You will probably get away with flashing in the French Quarter, but elsewhere you might get ticketed.

■ Be aware that cell phone photos and videos shot on Bourbon Street can wind up on the Internet; think twice before you flash for beads.

■ Each year accidents occur when children (or adults) venture too near the wheels of floats. If you have kids with you, pick a spot some way back from the parade.

MARDI GRAS YEAR-ROUND

A sculptor working on a float at Blaine Kern's Mardi Gras World.

BACKSTREET CULTURAL MUSEUM
This small museum in Tremé chronicles New Orleans's street culture, including the Mardi Gras Indians. Elaborate costumes are on display.

BLAINE KERN'S MARDI GRAS WORLD
Tour the workshop of one of the most prominent Carnival float builders. Floats from previous parades are on display in the warehouse.

GERMAINE WELLS MARDI GRAS MUSEUM
This free Mardi Gras museum is full of photos, masks, and more than two dozen mid-20th-century ball gowns, most worn by Germaine Wells, daughter of the restaurant's founder and queen of more than twenty-two Mardi Gras balls.

THE PRESBYTERE
Part of the Louisiana State Museum, this historic building on Jackson Square hosts a permanent Mardi Gras exhibit on the second floor.

MARDI GRAS LINGO

King cake: An oval cake decorated with purple, green, and gold sugar and glaze, eaten from January 6—"Twelfth Night"—until Mardi Gras. A plastic baby is hidden inside, and by tradition whoever gets it must buy the next cake.

Krewe: A term used by Carnival organizations to describe themselves, as in Krewe of Iris.

Lundi Gras: French for "Fat Monday," the day before Mardi Gras.

Mardi Gras: "Fat Tuesday" in French; the day before Ash Wednesday and the culmination of the festivities surrounding Carnival season.

Purple, green, and gold: The traditional colors of Mardi Gras (purple represents justice, green faith, and gold power), chosen by the first Rex in 1872.

Throw: Anything tossed off a float, such as beads, plastic cups, doubloons (fake metal coins), or stuffed animals.

"Throw me somethin', mister": Phrase shouted at float riders to get their attention so they will throw you beads.

MARDI GRAS RESOURCES

■ **Arthur Hardy's Mardi Gras Guide** (⊕ www.mardigrasguide.com).

■ **MardiGras.com** (⊕ www.mardigras.com).

■ **New Orleans Convention and Visitors Bureau** (⊕ www.neworleanscvb.com).

MARDI GRAS DATES

2015 February 17

2016 February 9

2017 February 28

Gauche House. The cherub design of the effusive ironwork on this distinctive house stops people in the street. Built in 1856, this mansion and its service buildings were once the estate of businessman John Gauche, who lived there until 1882. Although the privately owned house is not open to the public, its exterior still merits a visit to snap a few photos. ⊠ *704 Esplanade Ave., French Quarter.*

Germaine Wells Mardi Gras Museum. During a 31-year period (1937–68), Germaine Cazenave Wells, daughter of Arnaud's restaurant founder Arnaud Cazenave, was queen of Carnival balls a record 22 times for 17 different krewes, or organizations. Many of her ball gowns, in addition to costumes worn by other family members, are on display in this dim, quirky, one-room museum above Arnaud's restaurant. ⊠ *Arnaud's restaurant, 813 Bienville St., 2nd fl. (enter through restaurant), French Quarter* ☎ *504/523–5433* ⊕ *www.arnaudsrestaurant. com/mardi-gras-museum* ⌨ *Free* ☉ *Daily during restaurant hrs.*

Jackson Brewery. A brewery from the days when New Orleans was the beer capital of the South, was remodeled in the 1980s. Jax Brewery, as it's commonly known, is home to a three-section shopping-and-entertainment complex and caters mainly to tourists with national clothing chains and souvenir shops. The local retailer Perlis, however, brings Uptown New Orleans style, and its crawfish-logo Polo-style shirts, to the masses with its Cajun Clothing Co. store here. The outside features multilevel terraces with sweeping views of the Mississippi River. Inside, there's a small museum that preserves the history of the brewery along with several casual restaurants, although better dining options are found elsewhere. ⊠ *600 Decatur St., French Quarter* ☎ *504/566–7245* ⊕ *www.jacksonbrewery.com* ☉ *Daily 10–7.*

Jean Lafitte National Park Visitor Center. Visitors who want to explore the areas around New Orleans should stop here first. The office supervises and provides information on Jean Lafitte National Park Barataria Unit, a beautiful swamp nature preserve across the river from New Orleans, along with the Chalmette Battlefield, where the Battle of New Orleans was fought in the War of 1812. Each year in January, near the anniversary of the battle, a reenactment is staged at the Chalmette site. This visitor center has free visual and sound exhibits on the customs of various communities throughout the state, as well as information-rich riverfront tours called "history strolls," offered Tuesdays through Saturdays. The one-hour daily tour leaves at 9:30 am; tickets are handed out one per person (you must be present to get a ticket), beginning at 9 am, for that day's tour only. Arrive at least 15 minutes before tour time to be sure of a spot. You'll need a car to visit the preserve or the battlefield. ⊠ *419 Decatur St., French Quarter* ☎ *504/589–2636* ⊕ *www.nps.gov/ jela* ☉ *Tues.–Sat 9–4:30.*

LaLaurie Mansion. Locals, or at least local tour guides, say this is the most haunted house in a generally haunted neighborhood. Most blame the spooks on Madame LaLaurie, a wealthy but ill-fated 19th-century socialite who fell out with society when, during a fire, neighbors who rushed into the house found mutilated slaves in one of the apartments. Madame LaLaurie fled town that night, but there have been stories of hauntings ever since. The home is a private residence, not open to the public. Actor Nicolas Cage bought the property in 2007. Two years later, the house sold at a foreclosure auction. ✉ *1140 Royal St., French Quarter.*

Latrobe House. Architect Benjamin Henry Latrobe, who designed the U.S. Capitol, built this modest house with Arsene Latour in 1814. Its smooth lines and porticoes started a passion for Greek Revival architecture in Louisiana, evidenced later in many plantation houses upriver as well as in a significant number of buildings in New Orleans. Latrobe would die in New Orleans six years later

TALK OF THE TOWN

Although it's just two blocks away from Bourbon Street in the French Quarter, Burgundy Street is not pronounced like the wine (New Orleanians say "bur-GUN-dee" instead). And if you trot out your high school French to ask for directions to Chartres Street, a bemused local will probably ask if you mean "CHAW-tuhs." Farther uptown, the streets named for the muses offer more challenges: Calliope ("CAL-ee-ope") and Melpomene ("MELL-pa-meen").

from yellow fever. This house, believed to be the earliest example of Greek Revival in the city, is not open to the public. ✉ *721 Governor Nicholls St., French Quarter.*

Louisiana Supreme Court Building. The imposing building that takes up the whole block of Royal Street between St. Louis and Conti streets is the Old New Orleans Court, erected in 1908. Later it became the office of the Wildlife and Fisheries agency. After years of vacancy and neglect, this magnificent edifice was restored and reopened in 2004 and is now the elegant home of the Louisiana Supreme Court. The public can visit the courthouse but must pass through security and cannot take photos inside. ✉ *400 Royal St., French Quarter* ⊙ *Weekdays 9–5.*

Madame John's Legacy. Now a state museum, this is the only example in the French Quarter of West Indies architecture and early Creole-colonial home design. The large, dark rooms of the main living space occupy the second story, and a porch (called a gallery) runs along the front and back of the house, providing ventilation during the steamy summers and protection from both sun and rain. The current building was constructed in 1789, following the 1788 fire that destroyed much of the Quarter. The house has a colorful past. The first owner, Jean Pascal, a French sea captain, was killed by Natchez Indians. The name "Madame John's Legacy" was adopted in the late 1800s from a short story by New Orleans writer George Washington Cable. The popular tale was about Madame John, a "free woman of color" who, like many mulatto women at that time, became the mistress of a Frenchman. Having never married, the Frenchman, John (Jean), bequeathed his house and estate to her on his deathbed. ✉ *632 Dumaine St., French Quarter* ☎ *504/568–6968* ⊕ *www.crt.state.la.us* 🎫 *Free* ⊙ *Tues.–Sun. 10–4:30.*

Michalopoulos Galleries. One of New Orleans's most beloved artists, James Michalopoulos exhibits his expressionistic visions of New Orleans architecture in this small gallery. Michalopoulos's palette-knife technique of applying thick waves of paint invariably brings van Gogh to mind—but his vision of New Orleans, where no line is truly straight and every building appears to have a soul, is uniquely his own. His work has become a prized adornment of many a New Orleanian's walls. Michalopoulos was commissioned to create the official poster of the New Orleans Jazz and Heritage Festival in 1998, 2001, 2003, 2006, 2009, and 2013, bringing a new perspective to some of New Orleans's greatest musicians: Mahalia Jackson, Louis Armstrong, Dr. John, Fats Domino, and Aaron Neville. ⊠ *617 Bienville St., French Quarter* ☎ *504/558–0505* ⊕ *www.michalopoulos.com* ⊘ *Mon.–Sat. 10–6, Sun. 11–6.*

FAMILY **Musée Conti Wax Museum.** The history of New Orleans and Louisiana unfolds in colorful vignettes in this kitschy but fun museum. Local legends are captured life-size at seminal moments: Madame LaLaurie discovered torturing her slaves; Napoléon in his bathtub, arguing with his brothers over the Louisiana Purchase; Marie Laveau selling gris-gris to downtown customers; the Duke and Duchess of Windsor attending a Mardi Gras ball. Written and audio explanations supplement the visual scenes. A miniature Mardi Gras parade fills one corridor. The museum provides an enjoyable way to get acquainted with New Orleans history, although the history depicted here tends toward the sensational and, occasionally, the unsubstantiated. ⊠ *917 Conti St., French Quarter* ☎ *504/525–2605* ⊕ *www.neworleanswaxmuseum. com* ⊡ *$8* ⊘ *Mon., Fri., Sat. 10–4.*

New Orleans Historic Voodoo Museum. This homegrown museum will turn skeptics into believers. Voodoo isn't just something marketed to visitors; it lingers on in the lives of many New Orleanians, who still light candles for good luck or rely on a potion to find love. The large collection of artifacts and displays here include portraits by and of voodoo legends, African artifacts believed to have influenced the development of the religion, and lots of gris-gris (bundles with magical ingredients). The gift shop sells customized gris-gris, potions, and handcrafted voodoo dolls. A psychic reader is on duty to divine your future. ⊠ *724 Dumaine St., French Quarter* ☎ *504/680–0128* ⊕ *www. voodoomuseum.com* ⊡ *$7* ⊘ *Daily 10–6.*

FAMILY **New Orleans Jazz National Historical Park.** In 1987, the U.S. Congress declared jazz a "national American Treasure," and in the following years, the New Orleans Jazz National Historical Park was created to preserve and display that treasure. The park offers free performances and educational events in two locations around the French Quarter: the Visitor Center and the **Old U.S. Mint,** which also houses the state's jazz collection. Some of the park's rangers are also working musicians; don't miss the chance to catch their lively and informative demonstrations exploring the full range of Louisiana's musical heritage. ⊠ *Visitor Center, 916 N. Peters St., French Quarter* ☎ *504/589–4841* ⊕ *www. nps.gov/jazz* ⊡ *Free* ⊘ *Visitor Center Tues.–Sat. 9–5; Old U.S. Mint Tues.–Thurs. noon–4, Sat. 10–4.*

New Orleans Pharmacy Museum. To tour this musty shop is to step back into 19th-century medicine: even the window display, with its enormous leech jar and other antiquated paraphernalia, is fascinating. This building was the apothecary shop and residence of Louis J. Dufilho Jr., America's first licensed pharmacist with his own shop, in the 1820s. His botanical and herbal gardens are still cultivated in the courtyard. Watch for free 19th-century seasonal health tips posted in the front window. ⊠ *514 Chartres St., French Quarter* ☎ *504/565–8027* ⊕ *www.pharmacymuseum.org* ⊠ *$5* ⊙ *Tues.–Fri. 10–2, Sat. 10–5.*

DON'T BET ON IT!

At some point during your visit to the French Quarter, you are bound to come across someone on the street who will offer you the following wager: "I bet you [insert dollar amount] I know where you got them shoes." It's a con, of course, and an old one at that. The answer is, "You got them on your feet in New Orleans, Louisiana."

Old Ursuline Convent. The Ursulines were the first of many orders of religious women who came to New Orleans and founded schools, orphanages, and asylums and ministered to the needs of the poor. The current structure, a replacement for the original convent, was completed in 1752 and is now the oldest French-colonial building in the Mississippi Valley, having survived the disastrous 18th-century fires that destroyed the rest of the Quarter. **St. Mary's Church,** adjoining the convent, was added in 1845. The original tract of land for a convent, school, and gardens covered several French Quarter blocks. Now an archive for the archdiocese, the convent was used by the Ursulines for 90 years. The Ursuline Academy, the convent's girls' school founded in 1727, is now Uptown on State Street, where the newer convent and chapel were built. The academy is the oldest girls' school in the country. The Old Ursuline Convent is open to the public for self-guided tours Monday through Saturday. ⊠ *1110 Chartres St., French Quarter* ☎ *504/525–9585* ⊕ *www.stlouiscathedral.org/convent.html* ⊠ *$5* ⊙ *Mon.–Sat. 10–4.*

Old U.S. Mint. Minting began in 1838 in this ambitious Ionic structure, a project of President Andrew Jackson. The New Orleans mint was to provide currency for the South and the West, which it did until Louisiana seceded from the Union in 1861. Both the short-lived Republic of Louisiana and the Confederacy minted coins here. When Confederate supplies ran out, the building served as a barracks, then a prison, for Confederate soldiers. The production of U.S. coins recommenced only in 1879; it stopped again, for good, in 1909. After years of neglect, the federal government handed the Old Mint over to Louisiana in 1966. The state now uses the building to exhibit collections of the Louisiana State Museum, although the feds have returned with New Orleans Jazz National Historical Park, which also has exhibits and collections here. At the main Barracks Street entrance, which is set back from the surrounding gates and not well marked, notice the one remaining sample of the mint's old walls—it'll give you an idea of the building's deterioration before its restoration. Hurricane Katrina ripped away a large section of the copper roof, and for months the twisted metal remained on the ground here, one of the most dramatic reminders in the French Quarter of the storm. After repairs, the museum reopened to the public in 2007.

The first floor explores the history of the mint. The principal draw, however, is the second floor dedicated to items from the **New Orleans Jazz Collection**. At the end of the exhibit, displayed in its own room like the Crown Jewels, you'll find Louis Armstrong's first cornet. The third floor of the building is now a performance space for the Jazz National Historical Park, which has a packed calendar of free performances throughout the week. Check in with the helpful Park Ranger office for performance details.

The **Louisiana Historical Center,** which holds the French and Spanish Louisiana archives, is open free to researchers by appointment. At the foot of Esplanade Avenue, notice the memorial to the French rebels against early Spanish rule. The rebel leaders were executed on this spot and give nearby Frenchmen Street its name. ✉ *400 Esplanade Ave., French Quarter* ☎ *504/568–6993* ⊕ *www.crt.state.la.us, www.nps.gov/ jazz* 🖥 *$6* ⊙ *Tues.–Sun. 10–4:30.*

Pontalba Buildings. Baroness Micaela Pontalba built this twin set of town houses, one on each side of Jackson Square, around 1850; they are known for their ornate cast-iron balcony railings. Baroness Pontalba's father was Don Almonester, who sponsored the rebuilding of St. Louis Cathedral in 1788. The strong-willed Miss Almonester also helped fund the landscaping of the square and the erection of the Andrew Jackson statue in its center. The Pontalba Buildings are publicly owned; the side to the right of the cathedral, on St. Ann Street, is owned by the state, and the other side, on St. Peter Street, by the city. On the state-owned side is the **1850 House,** and at 540-B St. Peter Street on the city-owned side is a plaque marking this apartment as that of Sherwood Anderson, writer and mentor to William Faulkner. ✉ *French Quarter.*

Quadroon Ballroom. In the early 1800s, the wooden-rail balcony extending over Orleans Street was linked to a ballroom where free women of color met their French suitors, as Madame John of Madame John's Legacy is said to have done. The quadroons (technically, people whose racial makeup was one-quarter African) who met here were young, unmarried women of legendary beauty. A gentleman would select a favorite beauty and, with her mother's approval, buy her a house and support her as his mistress. The sons of these unions, which were generally maintained in addition to legal marriages with French women, were often sent to France to be educated. This practice, known as *plaçage*, was unique to New Orleans at the time. The Quadroon Ballroom later became part of a convent and school for the Sisters of the Holy Family, a religious order founded in New Orleans in 1842 by the daughter of a quadroon to educate and care for African American women. The ballroom itself is not open to visitors, but a view of the balcony from across the street is enough to set the historical stage. ✉ *Bourbon Orleans Hotel, 717 Orleans St., 2nd fl., French Quarter.*

Rodrigue Studio. Cajun artist George Rodrigue began his career as a painter with moody yet stirring portraits of rural Cajun life, but he gained popular renown in 1984 when he started painting blue dogs, inspired by the spirit of his deceased pet, Tiffany. Since then, the blue dog has found thousands of manifestations in various settings in the cult artist's paintings. Though Rodrigue died in late 2013 of cancer, his principal gallery, a space rather eerily lined almost entirely with paintings of the blue dog, remains open. ⊠ *730 Royal St., French Quarter* ☎ *504/581–4244* ⊕ *www.georgerodrigue.com* ⊙ *Mon.–Sat. 10–6, Sun. noon–5.*

> ## WHISTLING "DIXIE"
>
> One popular theory for the origin of the term "Dixie" points back to Citizens Bank of New Orleans, which issued bilingual $10 bank notes bearing the French word "dix" (meaning "ten") on the reverse. The notes thus became known as "dixies," and the term eventually became synonymous with Louisiana, and then with the entire South. Historians are still debating this etymology—but it's a good story nonetheless.

Washington Artillery Park. This raised concrete area on the river side of Decatur Street, directly across from Jackson Square, is a great spot to photograph the square and the barges and paddle wheelers on the Mississippi. The cannon mounted in the center and pointing toward the river is a model 1861 Parrot Rifle used in the Civil War. This monument honors the local 141st Field Artillery of the Louisiana National Guard that saw action from the Civil War through World War II. Marble tablets at the base give the history of the group, represented today by the Washington Artillery Association. ⊠ *Decatur St., between St. Peter and St. Ann Sts., French Quarter.*

3

FAUBOURG MARIGNY, BYWATER, AND TREMÉ

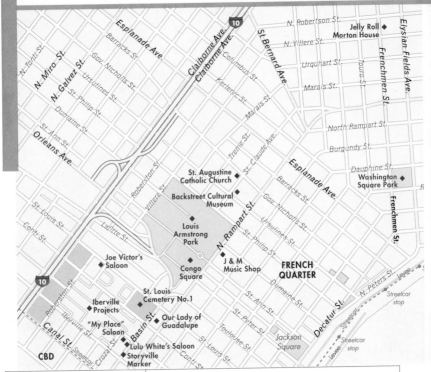

SAFETY

Use common sense when exploring these neighborhoods, especially at night. The Marigny is the safest of the three to explore during daylight hours, and Frenchmen Street is a safe, crowded, nightlife hotspot. Outside of Frenchmen Street, it's best to drive or cab at night. Bywater is mostly safe, but it's next to some rough neighborhoods; it's advisable to travel by car, especially if you're going into the Lower Ninth Ward. The part of Tremé closest to Canal Street is home to the Iberville Projects, an area you'll generally want to steer clear of. Use caution throughout Tremé.

GETTING HERE AND AROUND

The Marigny and Tremé border the French Quarter to the east and north, and are within easy walking distance. The **bus** and **streetcar** will also land you in or around these neighborhoods. Biking is a great way to get around the French Quarter and the Marigny (See Travel Smart for bike rental companies).

Bywater is a little farther out, past the Marigny to the east. It makes the most sense to drive or take the bus or a cab. The **No. 5 Marigny/Bywater bus** runs along the south edge (river side) of the French Quarter, out to the far edge of Bywater. The **No. 88 St. Claude/Jackson Barracks bus** runs along the north edge (lake side) of the French Quarter all the way into the Lower Ninth Ward. The ride from the French Quarter takes about 15 minutes.

Faubourg Marigny, Bywater, and Tremé

Marigny St. Manderville St. Spain St. St. Roch Ave. Music St.

New Orleans Healing Center

St Claude St.

St Ferdinand St. Press St. Montegut St. Clouet St. Louisa St.

St Claude St.

FAUBOURG MARIGNY

Franklin Ave Port St.

North Rampart St.

House of Dance and Feathers →

Burgundy St.

Christopher Porché-West Galerie

Dauphine St.

Royal St.

Cake Café

Venusian Gardens and Art Gallery

Mercury Injection Studio Arts

Satsuma Café

Chartres St.

Studio Inferno Glassworks

Decatur St.

N. Peters St.

New Orleans Center for Creative Arts (NOCCA)

Dr. Bob

Mickey Markey Playground

Pauline St. **BYWATER**

• Streetcar stop

Mississippi River

0 — 1,000ft
0 — 200m

MAKING THE MOST OF YOUR TIME

The Marigny and Tremé are easy to visit from the French Quarter. At night Frenchmen Street is *the* place for live music. In Bywater, spend some time exploring galleries, parks, cafés, and vintage stores. At night off-the-beaten-path bars, restaurants, and music clubs light up.

QUICK BITES

Cake Café. A beloved local favorite, this corner bakery and café serves breakfast, lunch, pastries, and baked goods indoors and on the sidewalk patio daily until 3 pm. ⊠ *2440 Chartres St., Faubourg Marigny* ☎ *504/943–0010* ⊕ *www.nolacakes.com.*

Satsuma Café. Drop into this lively bohemian hangout for a healthy breakfast, a filling lunch, or a restorative glass of juiced fruits and vegetables. ⊠ *3218 Dauphine St., Bywater* ☎ *504/304–5962* ⊕ *satsumacafe.com.*

TOP REASONS TO GO

Explore Frenchmen Street. This bustling strip of bars, clubs, restaurants, cafés, and shops is the heart of the Marigny. At night this is *the* place to hear live music and watch eccentric street artists.

Experience the birthplace of jazz. Tremé is fertile ground for New Orleans musical traditions. Visit the site of Congo Square, where jazz was born (now in Louis Armstrong Park), or drop by the Backstreet Cultural Museum.

Discover the Bywater arts scene. This rapidly gentrifying neighborhood is an enclave of artists, musicians, and creative outliers, and you'll see it in everything from the decorated cars and funky boutiques to the intricate street art on warehouses and buildings.

Enjoy the Marigny architecture. In 1974 the entire Marigny neighborhood was added to the National Register of Historic Places; 35 years later it was awarded the distinguished "Great Places in America" designation by the American Planning Association.

Sightseeing
★★
Dining
★★
Lodging
★
Shopping
★★
Nightlife
★★★★

From Tremé's musical history to the alternative-arts scene in Bywater, to the bohemian comingling of the two in the Marigny, these three neighborhoods only look like sleepy rows of houses. In fact, they're engines for much of New Orleans's most innovative and energetic activity, where newly arrived artists and entrepreneurs add to the area's historic legacy.

FAUBOURG MARIGNY

Updated by
Cameron Todd

The Faubourg Marigny (pronounced "FOE-berg MAR-ah-nee," and mostly just referred to as "The Marigny") is made up of two distinct sections. The Marigny Triangle is the trendy area, with the Frenchmen Street commercial district on the border of the French Quarter. Mazelike streets here are lined with beautiful cottages, Creole plantation homes, and charming guesthouses. You'll have no problem finding great restaurants, bars, music clubs, and hip shops. On the other side of Elysian Fields Avenue the Marigny Rectangle begins.

The Marigny is one of the earliest neighborhoods in the city, formed in 1805 when the young Bernard Xavier Philippe de Marigny de Mandeville embarked on what is now practically an American pastime—creating subdivisions. With architectural styles ranging from classic Creole cottages to Victorian mansions, the streets are mainly peaceful and the residents often bohemian—what the French Quarter used to be like 30 years ago.

TOP ATTRACTIONS

Fodor'sChoice
★

Frenchmen Street. The three-block stretch closest to the French Quarter is where it's at, complete with cafés, bars, and music clubs. While the true magic happens come nightfall—when live music spills from the doorways of clubs and crowds gather for street performers—it is still a great daytime destination, too. ✉ *Frenchmen St. between Decatur and Dauphine Sts., Faubourg Marigny.*

An artist works on a Mardi Gras mural that's right at home in the colorful Marigny neighborhood.

New Orleans Healing Center. This is a great place to explore and touch base with the spiritual side of New Orleans. An innovative collaboration includes more than a dozen of New Orleans's most progressive (and intriguing) organizations. Visitors can check out everything from the Wild Lotus Yoga Studio to the New Orleans Food Co-Op, from the Café Istanbul Performance Hall to the Island of Salvation Botanica, the famous voodoo shop run by the internationally renowned priestess Sallie Ann Glassman. Fatoush, an excellent Mediterranean restaurant and juice bar, is also located here. ✉ *2372 St. Claude Ave., Faubourg Marigny* ☎ *504/940–1130* ⊕ *www.neworleanshealingcenter.org.*

WORTH NOTING

New Orleans Center for Creative Arts (*NOCCA*). Many of New Orleans's most talented musicians, artists, actors, and writers have passed through this high school arts program on their way to fame, including Harry Connick Jr., the Marsalis brothers, Donald Harrison, Terence Blanchard, Anthony Mackie, and Wendell Pierce. More than just a beautiful campus built along the Marigny's industrial riverfront area, NOCCA hosts a year-round schedule of celebrated performances, showings, and events open to the public. ✉ *2800 Chartres St., Faubourg Marigny* ☎ *504/940–2787* ⊕ *www.nocca.com.*

House of Dance and Feathers. One of the most fascinating and heartwarming locations in the Lower Ninth Ward has to be the House of Dance and Feathers, a tiny backyard museum that is a labor of love for community character Ronald Lewis, a retired streetcar conductor. Formed almost by accident (after his wife threw his extensive collection of Mardi Gras Indian and second-line paraphernalia out of the house

CLOSE UP

The Lower Ninth Ward

The Lower Ninth Ward has long been a cultural touchstone for New Orleans, generating some of the most venerable artists and colorful traditions in the city. In the wake of post-Katrina flooding, the neighborhood became a touchstone for the whole nation, and indeed the world, as a symbol of tragedy. No neighborhood endured as much destruction or suffering as this low-lying residential stretch that fell victim to the failed levees.

Nowadays the neighborhood is a very changed place. Signs of the deluge persist—empty lots where houses were literally swept off their foundations, boarded-up buildings with overgrown weeds and an eerie quiet—but signs of life and renewed vigor show, too. A slow but steady rebuilding effort by hard-hit locals joined by aid organizations and volunteers is reclaiming the landscape one lot at a time. Traditional New Orleans shotgun-style homes are now joined by sleek, raised, modern houses, compliments of the Brad Pitt–led efforts of the

Make It Right foundation. In addition, groups like Habitat for Humanity and Global Green have embarked on innovative and environmentally sustainable rebuilding projects in and around this neighborhood, such as the New Orleans Musicians Village and the Holy Cross Project.

The Lower Ninth Ward is not the safest area of New Orleans, and we advise you to visit during the day in a car or with a tour. One safe and informative way to learn about Hurricane Katrina's effect on the city, including the Lower Ninth Ward, is to sign up for a bus tour offered by a number of companies (*see the Travel Smart chapter*).

and into the yard), this small glass-paneled building is a trove of Mardi Gras Indian lore and local legend. Intricately beaded panels from Indian costumes, huge fans and plumes of feathers dangling from the rafters, and photographs cover almost every available inch of wall space.

Lewis, who, among many other things, can list "president of the Big Nine Social and Pleasure Club" and "former Council Chief of the Choctaw Hunters" on his résumé, is a qualified and dedicated historian whose vision and work have become a rallying point for a hardscrabble neighborhood. ⊠ *1317 Tupelo St., Faubourg Marigny* ☎ *504/957–2678* ⊕ *houseofdanceandfeathers.org* 🖃 *Free* ⊙ *Mon.–Sat. 10–6.*

Venusian Gardens and Art Gallery. This 19th-century former church building now serves as Eric Ehlenberger's otherworldly art studio, gallery, and event space, displaying his luminous sculptures and dioramas. Take a stroll beneath a sea of glowing jellyfish or bask in a neon-lit landscape. ⊠ *2601 Chartres St., Faubourg Marigny* ☎ *504/943–7446* ⊕ *www.venusiangardens.com* ⊙ *By appointment only.*

BYWATER

Bywater, a once crumbling but now rapidly gentrifying beautiful old neighborhood east of the train tracks at Press Street, has become a magnet for wealthy newcomers seeking an "authentic" New Orleans. The Mississippi River runs the length of its boundary, and the bars and coffee shops scattered around the often still gritty neighborhood combine elements of its working-class roots with the more recent hipster influx for a lively and distinctly local experience. It doesn't have the head-swiveling density of sights that you'll find in the French Quarter, but a visit to Bywater gives you a feel for New Orleans as it lives day to day, in a colorful, overgrown, slightly sleepy cityscape reminiscent of island communities and tinged with a sense of perpetual decay.

TOP ATTRACTIONS

Alternative Art Spaces. The Bywater neighborhood is home to dozens of alternative art spaces, many of which have banded together under the loose umbrella of the St. Claude Arts District (SCAD). From old candle factories to people's living rooms, this burgeoning scene—centered around St. Claude Avenue and nearby streets—is producing some of the most intriguing and innovative work in the city, with several major artists and arts organizations involved. In addition to gallery space, several independent theater spaces have sprung up as well, offering venues for live performances, magic and burlesque shows, fringe theater, and more. The second Saturday of each month is opening night when galleries and venues host new shows and parties. ⊠ *Bywater* ⊕ *www.scadnola.com.*

WORTH NOTING

Christopher Porché-West Galerie. Legendary independent photographer Christopher Porché-West operates out of this working studio and exhibit space. The atmosphere depends on the current focus and vigor of Porché-West's activities; sometimes it is more work-oriented, sometimes more formally set up for exhibits of his work or of other artists. The gallery occupies an old pharmacy storefront, which has become the hub of a hip block boasting restaurants, boutiques, and a yoga studio. Whenever the artist happens to be in, the gallery is open. You can also make an appointment (he's almost always nearby). ⊠ *3201 Burgundy St., Bywater* ☎ *504/947–3880* ⊕ *porche-west.com.*

Dr. Bob. A small compound of artists' and furniture-makers' studios includes the headquarters of this beloved local folk artist whose easily recognizable work can be found hanging all across New Orleans. "Be Nice or Leave," "Be Gay and Stay," "Shalom, Ya'll," and "Shut Up and Fish" are just a few of his popular themes. Dr. Bob's shop is chock-full of original furniture, colorful signs, and unidentifiable objects of artistic fancy. Prices start as low as $30 for a small "Be Nice" and most pieces are in the $200–$500 range. The sign outside advertises the open hours: "9 am–'til." Best to call ahead. ⊠ *3027 Chartres St., Bywater* ☎ *504/945–2225* ⊕ *drbobart.net.*

Mercury Injection Studio Arts. Glassworks, mirrors, sculptures, and paintings fill this tiny studio of artist Michael Cain. Michael is usually around, so don't be discouraged if the doors are closed. Knock, and if he's in, you're in for a show as he blows his fanciful pieces into existence. ✉ 727 Louisa St., Bywater ☎ 504/723–6397 ⊙ By appointment only.

Studio Inferno Glassworks. Famous for their New Orleans–themed glasswork, flaming hearts, and innovative designs, artists at this working studio give demonstrations of glass casting in a spacious red warehouse in the heart of Bywater. You can also see the artists at local festivals and events, including Jazz Fest, where they have been a popular feature for years. The gallery and gift shop is a wonderland of vivid color and design. ✉ 3000 Royal St., Bywater ☎ 504/945–1878 ⊙ Mon.–Sat. 10–4.

JAZZ FUNERALS AND SECOND LINES

If you're lucky, you'll get swept up in a jazz street parade while you're in New Orleans. The parades themselves are often referred to as "second lines," a term that originated in the city's jazz funerals. Traditionally, a brass band accompanies a New Orleans funeral procession to the grave site, playing dirges along the way. On the return from the grave, however, the music becomes upbeat, celebrating the departed's passage to heaven. Behind the family, friends, and recognized mourners, a second group often gathers, taking part in the free entertainment and dancing—hence, the "second line."

TREMÉ

Just across Rampart Street from the French Quarter, is Tremé (pronounced truh-MAY), one of the oldest neighborhoods in the city, perhaps in the country. The rows of cottages, churches, and corner stores belie the raucous historical and musical legacy of this area, originally built and populated largely by free people of color. This is the birthplace of jazz after all, not to mention the site of the old Congo Square gathering place for African and Caribbean slaves, and the location of the fabled Storyville red-light district. Through its many incarnations it has remained true to its heritage as one of the oldest African American neighborhoods in the nation. Tremé continues to be one of the great driving forces in the musical culture of New Orleans.

TOP ATTRACTIONS

Backstreet Cultural Museum. Local photographer and self-made historian Sylvester Francis is an enthusiastic guide through this rich collection of Mardi Gras Indian costumes and other musical artifacts tied to the street traditions of New Orleans, and the museum hosts traveling and featured exhibits in addition to its permanent collection. Sylvester is also an excellent source for current musical goings-on in Tremé and throughout town. ✉ 1116 Henriette Delille St., Tremé ☎ 504/522–4806 ⊕ www.backstreetmuseum.org ☛ $8 ⊙ Tues.–Sat. 10–5.

A unique Creole cottage in Tremé, across the street from the Backstreet Cultural Museum

St. Louis Cemetery No. 1. The oldest and most famous of New Orleans's cities of the dead, founded in the late 1700s, is just one block from the French Quarter. Stately rows of crypts are home to many of the city's most legendary figures, including Homer Plessy of the *Plessy vs. Ferguson* 1896 U.S. Supreme Court decision establishing the separate but equal "Jim Crow" laws, and voodoo queen Marie Laveau, whose grave is still a choice destination among the spiritual, the superstitious, and the curious. The cemetery is near a downtown housing project, so visitors are advised to exercise great caution when exploring this site. The safest way to visit is to join one of the many group tours that come through each day; the nonprofit group **Save Our Cemeteries** (☎ *504/525–3377*) gives guided tours every day at 10 pm (with an additional tour at 1 pm on Fridays and Saturdays) leaving from the Basin Street Station Visitors Center at 501 Basin Street. ⊠ *499 Basin St., bounded by Basin, Conti, Tremé, and St. Louis Sts., Tremé* ☉ *Mon.–Sat. 9–3, Sun. 9–noon.*

WORTH NOTING

J&M Music Shop. Although the patrons of the laundromat that now occupies this space probably don't pay the historical provenance much heed, this is one of the most significant musical landmarks in New Orleans. A plaque on this 1835 building marks it as the former site of the recording studio that launched the rock-and-roll careers of such greats as Fats Domino, Jerry Lee Lewis, Little Richard, and Ray Charles. Owned by Cosimo Matassa, the studio operated from 1945 to 1955. ⊠ *840 N. Rampart St., Tremé.*

HBO's Treme

The Tremé neighborhood has always held a special place in the hearts of musicians and musical historians for its role in the development of jazz and other African American musical traditions, but it wasn't until more recently that the neighborhood captured the imagination of a much wider audience, thanks to the HBO series *Treme*. In the wake of Hurricane Katrina, the award-winning team of David Simon and Eric Overmyer (*The Wire*) decided to turn their lens on the Crescent City. They found the ornate and deeply rooted traditions of working-class Tremé to be the perfect focal point for the larger story of recovery and perseverance in New Orleans. *Treme*, the fourth and final season of which was completed in 2013, is widely regarded as one of the best and most accurate representations of New Orleans ever captured on film—which is no small feat for anyone trying to render the intricacies of the social, cultural, musical, political, and socioeconomic dynamics of this city.

"The aesthetic has an anthropological quality," says Henry Griffin, a New Orleans writer, filmmaker, and professor who plays a character in the series based loosely on himself. "They're trying to re-create an exact period of history: the years right after the storm."

To that end, the producers employed a small army of local writers, fact-checkers, and historians to help ensure that the script and scene work were as accurate and realistic as possible. The casting team used locals whenever possible, and the location scouts and set producers went to remarkable lengths to ensure the authenticity of sets,

props, and costumes. "What really sets it apart," Griffin says, "is that other shows or films about New Orleans are always made for a bigger audience first, and then later the directors might consider what locals think of it. *Treme*, on the other hand, is made for New Orleans first, and then developed for the wider audience."

The show cast a spotlight on many of New Orleans's underground spots. Suddenly, crowds of music lovers swelled on Tuesday nights to catch Kermit Ruffins performing at **Bullets Sports Bar** (✉ *2441 AP Tureaud* ☎ *504/948–4003*)—a bar that has long been a staple of Tremé nightlife. Local institutions like Bywater nightclub **Vaughan's** (✉ *4229 Dauphine St.* ☎ *504/947–5562*), the Mid-City café **Angelo Brocato's** (✉ *214 N. Carrollton Ave.* ☎ *504/486–1465*), and the French Quarter restaurant **Bayona** (✉ *430 Dauphine St.* ☎ *504/525–4455*) were also featured.

Treme proved to be a galvanizing creative force in the city of New Orleans, bringing people together to celebrate their own world and traditions. More than that, it's a recognition, a rendering, and a celebration of the perseverance and unique temperament of this city and its denizens in the face of an unprecedented national tragedy—and that has a healing quality all its own.

The Tremé Brass Band marches in the Day of the Dead second-line parade, on Claiborne Avenue.

Louis Armstrong Park. There's a certain sad irony to this park. On the one hand, it's a joy to behold, with its huge, lighted gateway entrance and its meandering pathways through 32 acres of grassy knolls, lagoons, and historic landmarks. Elizabeth Catlett's famous statue of Louis Armstrong is joined by other artistic landmarks, such as the bust of Sidney Bechet, and it now houses the New Orleans Jazz National Historical Park. On the other hand, it's often nearly deserted, and bordered by some rough stretches of neighborhood, not a place to visit after dark.

To the left inside the park is **Congo Square,** marked by an inlaid-stone space, where slaves in the 18th and early 19th centuries gathered on Sunday, the only time they were permitted to play their music openly. The weekly meetings held here have been immortalized in the travelogues of visitors, leaving invaluable insight into the earliest stages of free musical practices by Africans in America and African Americans. Neighborhood musicians still congregate here at times for percussion jams, and it is difficult not to think of the musical spirit of ancestors hovering over them. Marie Laveau, the greatly feared and respected voodoo queen of antebellum New Orleans, had her home a block away on St. Ann Street and is reported to have held voodoo rituals here regularly.

Behind Congo Square is a large gray building, the **Morris F.X. Jeff Municipal Auditorium;** to the right, behind the auditorium, is the newly renovated **Mahalia Jackson Center for the Performing Arts,** which is home to the New Orleans Opera and the New Orleans Ballet and hosts an excellent year-round calendar of events—everything from readings to rock concerts. The St. Philip Street side of the park houses the **Jazz National Historical Park,** anchored by **Perseverance Hall,** the oldest Masonic temple in the state. △ Armstrong Park is patrolled by a security detail, but be very careful when wandering, and do not visit after dark. ⊠ *N. Rampart St. between St. Philip and St. Peter Sts., Tremé* ◷ *Auditorium and performing arts center open by event; check local newspapers for listings.*

St. Augustine Catholic Church. Ursuline nuns donated the land for this church in 1841. Upon its completion in 1842, St. Augustine's became an integrated place of worship; slaves were relegated to the side pews, but free blacks claimed just as much right to center pews as whites did. The architect, J.N.B. de Pouilly, attended the École des Beaux-Arts in Paris and was known for his idiosyncratic style, which borrowed freely from a variety of traditions and resisted classification. Some of the ornamentation in his original drawings was eliminated when money ran out, but effusive pink-and-gold paint inside brightens the austere structure. The church grounds now also house the Tomb of the Unknown Slave, a monument dedicated in 2004 to the slaves buried in unmarked graves in the church grounds and surrounding areas. Following Hurricane Katrina, the Archdiocese of New Orleans planned to close seven churches in the city, including St. Augustine. Public outcry, the church's historical significance, and parishioners' dedication saved the parish, and its 10 am Sunday gospel-jazz services continue. ⊠ *1210 Governor Nicholls St., Tremé* ☎ *504/525–5934* ⊕ *staugustinecatholicchurch-neworleans.org.*

CBD AND WAREHOUSE DISTRICT

GETTING ORIENTED

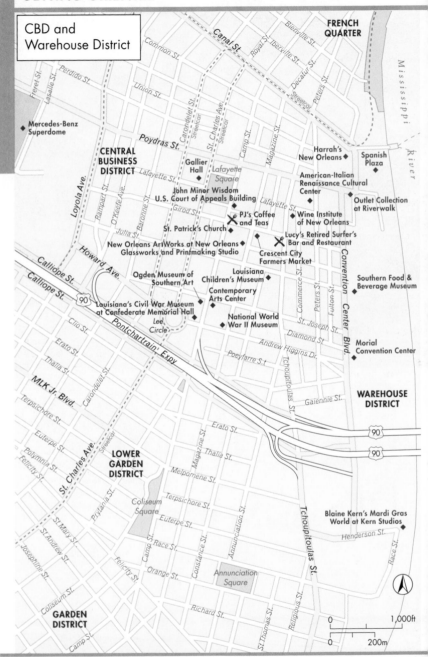

CBD and
Warehouse District

GETTING HERE AND AROUND

The CBD and Warehouse District together comprise a fairly small area and can easily be traveled on foot; the close proximity of the Warehouse District's museums and galleries makes for some especially easy sightseeing. The CBD is adjacent to the French Quarter, just across Canal Street. To travel to or from Uptown or the Garden District, you can take a cab, drive, or take the **streetcar**—use any stop from Canal Street to Lee Circle. If you have an extra 20 minutes, walking is also feasible.

MAKING THE MOST OF YOUR TIME

Arts- and culture-loving travelers can easily spend a few days visiting the **museums, auction houses, and galleries** here (check gallery listings for days of operation). The area also is a great **nightlife destination,** with some of the city's most acclaimed restaurants, music clubs, and Harrah's New Orleans.

QUICK BITES

Lucy's Retired Surfers Restaurant and Bar. This brightly decorated bar, courtyard, and dining room provide a nice spot for a margarita, fresh seafood, or a Southwestern-style snack. The restaurant serves brunch, lunch and dinner, and the bar is open to the wee hours for late-night thirst quenching. ⊠ *701 Tchoupitoulas St., Warehouse District* ☎ *504/523–8995* ⊕ *www.lucysretiredsurfers.com.*

PJ's Coffee and Teas. Founded in 1978, this local chain serves snacks, traditional hot or frozen beverages, and their signature cold-drip coffee (brewed with cold water and refrigerated). Seasonal flavors with New Orleans flair (like king cake–flavored blend, available during Carnival) are favorites. ⊠ *644 Camp St., CBD* ☎ *504/529–3658* ⊕ *www.pjscoffee.com.*

TOP REASONS TO GO

Gallery crawl through the Warehouse District. Browse the many art galleries that line Julia Street and its surroundings.

Feast on cutting-edge dining. Sample some of the finest in Louisiana contemporary cuisine from chefs who are quickly becoming household names.

Get cultured. Revisit a defining chapter of our nation's history at the National World War II Museum, or discover a new favorite artist in the airy, urban oasis of the Ogden Museum of Southern Art.

Experience Carnival season year-round. At Blaine Kern's Mardi Gras World at Kern Studios, see floats from years past, watch video footage, observe artists working on next year's creations, and stock up on souvenirs.

SAFETY

Parts of the CBD can be more deserted at night than other highly trafficked tourist areas. Staying close to the river while downtown and near the pulse of Warehouse District nightlife is the safest bet after the sun sets. By day, these areas are bustling with workers, shoppers, and tourists.

4

Sightseeing
★★★★
Dining
★★★★
Lodging
★★★★
Shopping
★★
Nightlife
★★

With a particularly welcoming atmosphere for art, design, and entertainment, the CBD (Central Business District) and Warehouse District (also, appropriately, known as the Arts District) comprise a vibrant, vital sector of downtown New Orleans that's becoming increasingly residential, with high-end apartments, condos, and shops taking root in once dilapidated historic buildings.

CENTRAL BUSINESS DISTRICT

Updated by Susan Granger

The CBD covers the ground between Canal and Poydras streets, with some spillover into the Warehouse District's official territory. By day the CBD hums with commerce and productivity. You'll find the National World War II Museum, the Ogden Museum of Southern Art, the Contemporary Arts Center, the Louisiana Children's Museum, and Louisiana's Civil War Museum at Confederate Memorial Hall—all within a three-square-block radius. The neighborhood includes the Mercedes-Benz Superdome, the convention center, and Harrah's Casino. Around central Lafayette Square you'll also find historic architecture, government buildings, and office complexes. Canal Street is the CBD's main artery and the official dividing line between the business district and the French Quarter; street names change from American to French as they cross Canal into the Quarter. Served by the streetcar, the palm tree–lined Canal Street is regaining its former elegance, particularly as it nears the river.

TOP ATTRACTIONS

Harrah's New Orleans. Some 115,000 square feet of gaming space is divided into five areas, each with a New Orleans theme: Jazz Court, Court of Good Fortune, Smugglers Court, Mardi Gras Court, and Court of the Mansion. There are also table games, 2,100-plus slots, and live entertainment at Masquerade, which includes a lounge, video tower, and dancing show. Check the website for seasonal productions, including music, theater, and comedy. Dining and libation choices include the extensive Harrah's buffet, Cafés on Canal food court, Besh Steak House, Gordon Biersch, Grand Isle, Manning's, and Ruth's Chris Steak House. The last four are part of Harrah's Fulton Street Mall, a pedestrian promenade that attracts casual strollers, club goers, and diners. ⊠ *8 Canal St., CBD* ☎ *504/533–6000, 800/427–7247* ⊕ *www. harrahs.com* ⊙ *Daily 24 hrs.*

Mercedes-Benz Superdome. Home to the NFL's New Orleans Saints, the Mercedes-Benz Superdome has been the site of many Sugar Bowls, several NCAA Final Four basketball tournaments, the BCS championship game, a record seven Super Bowls (including 2013), and the 1998 Republican National Convention.

The Superdome was badly damaged during Hurricane Katrina and in its aftermath, when it served as a shelter of last resort for evacuees. The stadium underwent extensive renovations in the years that followed and reopened for football in September 2006, when the Saints beat the Atlanta Falcons, at the time setting a record for the largest TV audience in ESPN history.

Built in 1975, the Superdome seats approximately 71,000 people, has a 166,000-square-foot main arena and a roof that covers almost 10 acres at a height of 27 stories. Since the Saints' Super Bowl victory in 2010, the Superdome has been covered in gold-hued anodized aluminum siding and given a brand-new outdoor festival space appropriately named Champions Square. Exterior LED lighting added in 2011 gives the stadium an eye-catching, ever-changing facade. The bronze statue on the Poydras Street side of the Superdome is the Vietnam Veterans Memorial. Across from it is a large abstract sculpture called the *Krewe of Poydras*. The sculptor, Ida Kohlmeyer, meant to evoke the frivolity and zany spirit of Mardi Gras. A couple of blocks down Poydras Street from the Superdome is the Bloch Cancer Survivors Monument, a block-long walkway of whimsical columns, figures, and a triumphal arch in the median of Loyola Avenue. The Smoothie King Center (formerly called the New Orleans Arena) behind the Superdome is home to the NBA's New Orleans Pelicans. The streets around the Superdome and arena are usually busy during business hours, but at night and on weekends, except during a game, the area should not be explored alone.

■ **TIP→ The Superdome does not offer public tours, but visitors can walk along the exterior Plaza and Champions Square to get a better view. The Plaza by Champions Square offers the best photo opportunity.** ⊠ *1 Sugar Bowl Dr., CBD* ☎ *504/587–3663* ⊕ *www.superdome.com.*

WORTH NOTING

Gallier Hall. This Greek Revival building, modeled on the Erectheum of Athens, was built in 1845 by architect James Gallier Sr. It served as City Hall in the mid-20th century and today hosts special events. It's the mayor's official perch during Carnival parades, where kings and queens of many krewes stop to be toasted by city officials and dignitaries. The grand rooms inside the hall are adorned with portraits and decorative details ordered by Gallier from Paris. ⊠ *545 St. Charles Ave., CBD* ☎ *504/658–4000* ⊕ *nola.gov/gallier-hall.*

John Minor Wisdom United States Court of Appeals Building. New York architect James Gamble Rogers was commissioned to design this three-story granite structure as a post office and court building in 1909, and it opened in 1915. By the 1960s the post office had moved to larger digs, and McDonough No. 35 High School found refuge here after Hurricane Betsy in 1965. Today the Italian Renaissance building houses the Fifth Circuit Court of Appeals in an elaborately paneled and ornamented series of three courtrooms, one of which, the En Banc courtroom, boasts a bronze glaze ceiling. The Great Hall's plaster ceiling has been restored to its original appearance and color, a light gray. As you enter the building and pass security, turn left and continue around the corner to find the library, where you can pick up information on the courthouse. Outside, a repeating sculpture of four women stands atop each corner of the building's penthouse level: the four ladies represent History, Agriculture, Industry, and the Arts. The building is named for Judge John Minor Wisdom, the New Orleans native who was instrumental in dismantling the segregation laws of the South. Judge Wisdom received the Presidential Medal of Freedom in 1993. ⊠ *600 Camp St., CBD* ☏ *504/310–7777* ⊘ *Weekdays 8–5.*

> **FREE FUN**
>
> From mid-March to June the Young Leadership Council, the Downtown Development District, and several corporate sponsors present Wednesday at the Square, a weekly event that features food, beer and soft drinks, local arts and crafts vendors, and a free evening concert in Lafayette Square. Bring a blanket and enjoy the music from 5 to 8.

Lafayette Square. Planned in 1788 as a public place for Faubourg St. Marie, Lafayette Square occupies one city block in the midst of the Federal Complex and Gallier Hall. The leafy square shaded by oak, magnolia, and maple trees, and landscaped with hydrangeas and azaleas, offers a shady spot to sit. Statues include Benjamin Franklin, Henry Clay, and New Orleans philanthropist John McDonogh. Recently, the Square has been experiencing a renaissance brought about in large part by the Young Leadership Council's Wednesday at the Square concert series, held in the spring and early summer. ⊠ *Between Camp St., St. Charles Ave., N. Maestri and S. Maestri Sts., CBD.*

The Outlet Collection at Riverwalk. This riverfront shopping center went through major renovations and is scheduled to reopen in 2014 as an outlet mall with retail chains, including Coach, Neiman Marcus Last Call, Forever 21, and many others. Various cruise ships leave from the Julia Street Wharf slightly upriver; you can often see them from the front of the Riverwalk. ⊠ *1 Poydras St., CBD* ☏ *504/522–1555* ⊕ *www.riverwalkmarketplace.com.*

Spanish Plaza. For a terrific view of the river and a place to relax, go behind the **World Trade Center** at 365 Canal Street to Spanish Plaza, a large, sunken space with beautiful inlaid tiles and a fountain. The plaza was a gift from Spain in 1976; here you can hear occasional live music and purchase tickets for riverboat cruises in the offices that face the river. ■ TIP→ If you happen to be in town on the Monday before Mardi Gras (Lundi Gras), you can watch Rex, the King of Carnival, arrive here from across the river to greet King Zulu and take symbolic control of the city for a day. ⊠ *365 Canal St., CBD.*

A ride on the streetcar is a great way to tour New Orleans in period style.

WAREHOUSE DISTRICT

Bordered by the river, St. Charles Avenue, Poydras Street, and the Pontchartrain Expressway, and filled with former factories and cotton warehouses, the Warehouse District began its renaissance when the city hosted the World's Fair here in 1984. Structures that housed the international pavilions during the fair now make up the New Orleans Morial Convention Center and a number of hotels, restaurants, bars, and music venues.

Today the Warehouse District is one of the trendiest residential and arts-and-nightlife areas of the city, dotted with modern renovations of historic buildings and upscale loft residences. A concentration of upscale galleries, auction houses, and artist studios lines Julia Street, a main thoroughfare, and you can try your hand at glassmaking and printmaking in some of the studios. By night you'll find excellent eateries, bustling live-music venues old and new, and numerous neighborhood and hotel bars ranging from casual to the very chic. All are patronized by scores of young professionals, mixing with tourists and longtime residents.

TOP ATTRACTIONS

FAMILY
Fodor'sChoice
★

Blaine Kern's Mardi Gras World at Kern Studios. If you're not in town for the real thing, here's a fun (and family-friendly) backstage look at the history and artistry of Carnival. The massive 400,000-square-foot complex, just upriver from the New Orleans Convention Center, has an enhanced guided tour through a maze of video presentations, decorative sculptures, and favorite megafloats from Mardi Gras parades such as Bacchus, Rex, and Endymion. A gift shop offers souvenirs

The Mercedes-Benz Superdome is home to the NFL New Orleans Saints.

like masks, beads, and Mardi Gras posters, as well as tickets for the tour, during which participants can sample king cake and coffee and see artists at work on papier-mâché and fiberglass floats. For special events, visitors enter through a plantation alley that is part Cajun swamp-shack village, part antebellum Disneyworld (Kern was a friend of, and inspired by, Walt Disney). Hour-long tours begin on the half hour. ⊠ *1380 Port of New Orleans Pl., Warehouse District* ☏ *504/361–7821* ⊕ *www.mardigrasworld.com* ✉ *$19.95* ⊙ *Daily 9:30–5:30, tours run every half hour. Last tour at 4:30.*

Contemporary Arts Center. Take in cutting-edge exhibits, featuring both local artists and the work of national and international talent, at this cornerstone of the now vibrant Warehouse District arts scene. Two theaters present jazz productions, films, dance, plays, lectures, and experimental and conventional concerts, including a New Orleans music series. Hours vary during concerts, performances, lectures, and special events; call or check the website for details. ⊠ *900 Camp St., Warehouse District* ☏ *504/528–3805, 504/528–3800 theater box office* ⊕ *www.cacno.org* ✉ *$8* ⊙ *Wed.–Mon. 11–5.*

Julia Street. Contemporary art dealers have adopted this strip in the Warehouse District as their own. The street is lined with galleries and specialty shops, with the greatest concentration stretching from South Peters Street to St. Charles Avenue. The first Saturday evening of each month gallery owners throw open their doors to show off new exhibits, to the accompaniment of wine, music, and general merriment. ⊠ *Warehouse District.*

FAMILY **Louisiana Children's Museum.** An invaluable resource for anyone traveling with kids, this top-notch museum is 30,000 square feet of hands-on educational fun. Favorites include a mini grocery store (with both carts and registers manned by visitors), a role-play café, a bayou-themed literacy center, an exhibit on New Orleans architecture featuring a miniature French Quarter courtyard, and a giant bubble station. If they still have steam, they can burn it off at the mini fitness center with a kid-size stationary bicycle and rock-climbing wall. A welcoming environment is provided for children with disabilities: most exhibits are accessible. Art teachers lead classes daily; there's also daily theatrical storytelling, and weekly special educational programs on topics like dinosaurs, Earth Week, and cultural heritage. An indoor playground is reserved for toddlers ages three and under, and Toddler Time activities are held at 10 am on Tuesday and Thursday. ⊠ *420 Julia St., Warehouse District* ☎ *504/523–1357* ⊕ *www.lcm.org* ⊠ *$8.50* ☾ *Summer: Mon.–Sat. 9:30–5, Sun. noon–5; winter: Tues.– Sat. 9:30–4:30, Sun. noon–4:30.*

Fodor's Choice ★ **National World War II Museum.** This vast and still expanding museum is a moving and well-executed examination of World War II events and its aftermath. Seminal moments are re-created through vintage propaganda posters, radio and film clips from the period; more than 7,500 oral histories of the military personnel involved; a number of short documentary films; and collections of weapons, personal items, and other artifacts from the war. Highlights of the museum include "Final Mission: The USS *Tang* Experience," which re-creates the experience of being in an immersive submarine, and the 4-D theater experience (across the street from the main exhibits) called "Beyond All Boundaries" produced and narrated by Tom Hanks. (Buy timed tickets in advance for the "Final Mission" and "Beyond All Boundaries," as there is limited availability.) Other popular exhibits are the replicas of the Higgins boat troop landing craft, which was invented and manufactured in New Orleans by Andrew Jackson Higgins during WWII, and the U.S. Freedom Pavilion: The Boeing Center, which honors all service branches and includes a restored Boeing B-17. This latter is the third of five new pavilions proposed for the expanded campus, due to be completed in 2016. The Stage Door Canteen features WWII-era entertainment and an adjoining restaurant serving the food of celebrity-chef John Besh. Check the website for updates on the expansion and a list of current movies, lectures, events, and programs. ⊠ *945 Magazine St., main entrance on Andrew Higgins Dr., Warehouse District* ☎ *504/528–1944* ⊕ *www.nationalww2museum. org* ⊠ *$22; combination ticket with 4-D presentation $27; with 4-D presentation and submarine experience $32* ☾ *Daily 9–5.*

FAMILY Fodor's Choice ★ **Ogden Museum of Southern Art.** Art by Southern artists, made in the South, about the South, and exploring Southern themes fills this elegant building. The basis of the museum's permanent collection are 1,200 works collected by local developer Roger Ogden since the 1960s. It has now grown to more than 4,000 pieces, including paintings, ceramic, drawings, sculpture, photographs, and design. These pieces, along with special exhibitions, showcase artists from Washington, D.C., and 15

Southern states spanning the 18th–21st centuries. A central stair hall filters natural light through the series of galleries, and a rooftop patio affords lovely views of the surrounding area. The gift shop sells crafts and jewelry by Southern artists, and books and movies celebrating the South. Thursday nights (6–8) come alive with Ogden After Hours, featuring live music, artist interviews, refreshments, children's activities, and special gallery exhibitions. ⊠ *925 Camp St., Warehouse District* ☎ *504/539–9650* ⊕ *www.ogdenmuseum.org* ◻ *$10* ۞ *Wed.–Mon. 10–5, additional hours Thurs. 6–8 pm.*

WORTH NOTING

Crescent City Farmers Market. This year-round market offers an array of locally grown produce, baked goods, cut flowers, wild-caught Louisiana seafood, fresh dairy, and handcrafted meals from regional vendors; special events and holidays bring appearances by local musicians and cooking demonstrations. Meet and greet the local farmers, chefs, and fishers who make this city's amazing food culture possible. ⊠ *700 Magazine St., Warehouse District* ☎ *504/861–4488* ⊕ *www. crescentcityfarmersmarket.org* ۞ *Sat. 8–noon.*

Louisiana's Civil War Museum at Confederate Memorial Hall. Established in 1891, this ponderous stone building is the oldest museum in Louisiana and features heavy trusses, gleaming cypress paneling, and elaborate Richardsonian Romanesque architecture. It houses a collection of artifacts from the Civil War, including uniforms, flags, soldiers' personal effects, and a rudimentary hand grenade. ⊠ *929 Camp St., Warehouse District* ☎ *504/523–4522* ⊕ *www.confederatemuseum. com* ◻ *$8* ۞ *Tues.–Sat. 10–4.*

FAMILY **New Orleans ArtWorks at New Orleans Glassworks and Printmaking Studio.** See free demonstrations of glassmaking and design, printmaking, and silver alchemy in this 25,000-square-foot warehouse space. The studio offers group and individual classes. Call in advance to make reservations for hands-on instruction. A shop and gallery display and sell the finished products. ⊠ *727 Magazine St., Warehouse District* ☎ *504/529–7279* ⊕ *www.neworleansglassworks.com* ۞ *Mon.–Sat. 10–5.*

Wine Institute of New Orleans. This hybrid institute known by the acronym w.i.n.o. is part wine school, part wine store, and part high-tech wine-tasting experience. A state-of-the-art Italian wine-serving system dispenses wine by the ounce so patrons can design their own flights and taste many more wines than at traditional tastings. Educate your palate with their selection of 120 wines, or sip a beer or cocktail— both pair just as well with charcuterie, artisanal cheese, and other small plates. w.i.n.o. also offers a weekly wine-tasting class on Tuesday evenings. Classes fill up quickly, so plan ahead. ⊠ *610 Tchoupitoulas St., Warehouse District* ☎ *504/324–8000* ⊕ *www.winoschool. com* ۞ *Mon., Tues. 1–10, Wed., Thurs. 1–midnight, Fri., Sat. 1 pm– 2 am, Sun. 2–10.*

5

THE GARDEN
DISTRICT

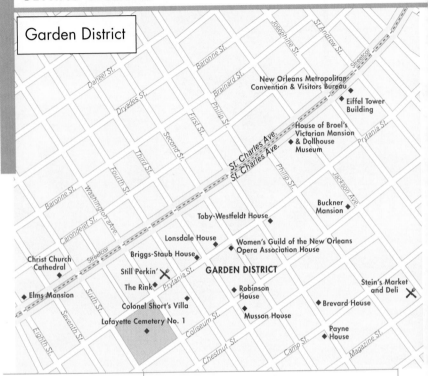

Garden District

QUICK BITES

Stein's Market and Deli. It's a traditional Jewish-Italian deli, but the "Muphuletta" is a take on the New Orleans muffuletta. ✉ *2207 Magazine St., Garden District* ☎ *504/527–0771* ⊕ *www.steinsdeli.net* ⊗ *Tues.–Fri. 7–7, weekends 9–5.*

Still Perkin'. This popular café offers coffees, teas, muffins, scones, and tarts made by local bakeries. ✉ *2727 Prytania St., Garden District* ☎ *504/899–0335* ⊕ *www.neworleanscoffeeshop.com* ⊗ *Weekdays 7–6, Sat. 8–6, Sun. 8–5.*

GETTING HERE AND AROUND

The Garden District is easily accessible by car, streetcar, and city bus, or on foot from the CBD or Uptown. It's easy and free to park your car on any side street, but you have to pay to park along busier stretches of Magazine Street and Prytania Street.

The **streetcar** runs every 20 or 30 minutes (more frequently during rush hour), 24 hours a day, and makes several stops along St. Charles Avenue. Because the tracks are undergoing maintenance, segments of the line are periodically out of commission, and in those instances a shuttle service is available. You may have to wait longer than 30 minutes for the streetcar to arrive at night, but it's generally a safe, if leisurely, mode of transportation. It takes about 20 minutes on the streetcar to get to Jackson Avenue in the lower Garden District from Canal Street. The **No. 11 bus** runs up Magazine Street, making stops at all major intersections every 20 minutes. The ride from Canal Street to Jackson Avenue takes about 10 minutes depending on traffic.

GARDEN DISTRICT

Annunciation Square

Coliseum Square Park

Goodrich-Stanley House

```
0          500ft
0     100m
```

TOP REASONS TO GO

Architecture. View antebellum homes built during New Orleans's most prosperous era by renowned architects, including Henry Howard, Lewis E. Reynolds, William Freret, and Samuel Jamison.

Feast on Magazine Street. Rubbing shoulders with vintage boutiques and dive bars, the eateries along this stretch serve a mélange of cuisines—you'll find everything from po'boys to French crepes to crawfish-stuffed sushi rolls.

Check out local art. Peruse fine and funky jewelry, paintings, pottery, and other locally made artwork at the galleries on Magazine Street. Or visit Garden District Gallery, featuring gorgeous work by local artists.

Take in some history. View the aboveground tombs at Lafayette Cemetery No. 1, in continual use since 1833 and one of the most beautiful burial grounds in the city.

MAKING THE MOST OF YOUR TIME

Plan at least a day to see the Garden District's gorgeous mansions, shop Magazine Street, and visit the historic **Lafayette Cemetery No. 1.** Historic New Orleans Tours runs quality tours of the Garden District that includes the former house of Anne Rice and Lafayette Cemetery No. 1 *(see the Travel Smart chapter for more information).*

SAFETY

Safety isn't a major concern in the Garden District, as the neighborhood hires its own security service in addition to what the New Orleans police offer. At night the neighborhood is quiet and the streets are not well lit, so it's always wise to walk with someone, especially in the lower Garden District. Visitors should avoid the rougher area bordered by Tchoupitoulas and Magazine streets around Jackson Avenue, as well as Central City on the opposite side of St. Charles Avenue, particularly at night.

Sightseeing
★★★
Dining
★★
Lodging
★★
Shopping
★★★★
Nightlife
★

Boasting some of the most stunning homes in the city, the Garden District has acquired fame for its antebellum mansions and manicured gardens. Residents take great pride in their gorgeous properties, and the neighborhood is in bloom 12 months a year. Although most homes are closed to the public, with the exception of special-event tours, the views from the other side of the intricate cast-iron fences are still impressive. A stroll through the neighborhood is a peaceful break from more touristy areas of New Orleans.

Updated by Susan Granger

Originally the Livaudais Plantation, the Garden District was laid out in the late 1820s and remained part of the city of Lafayette until incorporated into New Orleans in 1852. The neighborhood attracted "new-moneyed" Americans who, snubbed by the Creole residents of the French Quarter, constructed grand houses with large English-style gardens featuring lush azaleas, magnolias, and camellias. Three architectural styles were favored: the three-bay Greek Revival, center-hall Greek Revival, and raised cottage. Renovations and expansions to these designs through the years allowed owners to host bigger and more ostentatious parties, particularly during the social season between Christmas and Carnival. Today many of the proud residents represent fourth- or fifth-generation New Orleanians.

The lower Garden District, along Magazine Street east of Jackson Avenue, boasts offbeat boutiques selling original art, antiques, vintage clothing, and jewelry, catering in particular to a young professional and student crowd. A "green light district" of eco-friendly shops has taken root in its 2000–2100 blocks. Coliseum Square, in the center of the neighborhood, features a fountain and walking trails that wind around looming oak trees, and the mansions flanking the park display a distinctly faded beauty. The neighborhood quiets down a lot in the evening; however, there are a few nighttime hangouts and restaurants, especially near the triangular intersection of roads at St. Mary Street and Sophie Wright Place.

A morning walk in the upper Garden District, west of Jackson Avenue, provides a peaceful break from more touristy areas of New Orleans. Besides beautiful mansions with wrought-iron fences that wrap around vibrant manicured gardens, the neighborhood has Lafayette Cemetery No. 1, one of the city's oldest and most beautiful cemeteries. Return to the present day by visiting the stretch of Magazine Street that runs alongside the upper Garden District, which boasts an eclectic mix of restaurants and chichi boutiques.

TOP ATTRACTIONS

Brevard House. Though Anne Rice moved out of her elegant Garden District home in 2004, the famous novelist's fans still flock to see the house that inspired the Mayfair Manor in her series *Lives of the Mayfair Witches*. The house is a three-bay Greek Revival, extended over a luxurious, lemon tree–lined side yard and surrounded by a fence of cast-iron rosettes that earned the estate's historical name, Rosegate. ✉ *1239 1st St., Garden District.*

Coliseum Square Park. Established in the mid-19th century, this lush green space is the centerpiece of the lower Garden District. With bike and walking trails as well as a beautiful fountain, the wedge-shaped park is a great spot to stop and relax after a walk through the neighborhood. Though the area bordered by Race Street and Melpomene Street can be bustling with activity during the day, it's best not to wander around alone at night. ✉ *1700 Coliseum St., Garden District.*

Van Benthuysen-Elms Mansion. Built in 1869, this home saw the Confederate president Jefferson Davis as a frequent guest. In the early 20th century, it served as the German consulate until the start of World War II. The house has been meticulously maintained and furnished with period pieces and is the site of many private receptions and special events. Highlights include a carved oak staircase and mantelpiece and 24-karat gilt moldings and sconces. ✉ *3029 St. Charles Ave., Garden District* ☎ *504/895–9200* ⊕ *elmsmansion.com.*

Goodrich-Stanley House. This restored Creole cottage is an excellent example of the modest prototype for much of the far more elaborate architecture of the surrounding Garden District. The scale, derived from the climate-conscious design prevalent in the West Indies, made the style easily adaptable to the higher pretensions of the Greek Revival look, as well as the slightly more reserved Colonial Revival. Built in 1837, the house has had one famous occupant: Henry Morton Stanley, renowned explorer of Africa and founder of the Congo Free States who most famously uttered the phrase "Dr. Livingstone, I presume" upon encountering the long-lost Scottish missionary. ✉ *1729 Coliseum St., Garden District.*

House of Broel's Victorian Mansion and Dollhouse Museum. This restored antebellum home was built in two periods. The upstairs was constructed in 1850, and a new first floor was added when the house was elevated in 1884. The extensive dollhouse collection includes 60 historically accurate, scale-model miniatures of Victorian, Tudor, and plantation-style houses and covers more than 3,000 square feet on the mansion's second floor. All were created by owner Bonnie Broel over a 15-year period. Walk-in and groups tours are available, and the mansion offers a setting for weddings, receptions, and parties. Visitors can only view the property on the tours, so be sure to call ahead. ⊠ *2220 St. Charles Ave., Garden District* ☎ *504/494–2220, 504/522–2220* ⊕ *www.houseofbroel. com* ⊠ *Mansion tour $10* ⊗ *Weekdays 11–3 by appointment.*

Fodor's Choice
★

Lafayette Cemetery No. 1. New Orleans was seeing a large influx of Italian, German, Irish, and American immigrants from the North when this magnolia-shaded cemetery opened in 1833. Many who fought or played a role in the Civil War have plots here, indicated by plaques and headstones that detail the site of their death. Several tombs also reflect the toll taken by the yellow fever epidemic, which affected mostly children and newcomers to New Orleans; 2,000 yellow fever victims were buried here in 1852. Movies such as *Interview with the Vampire* and *Double Jeopardy* have used this walled cemetery for its eerie beauty. Save Our Cemeteries, a nonprofit, offers hour-long, volunteer-led tours daily at 10:30 am. All proceeds benefit the organization's cemetery restoration and advocacy efforts. ⊠ *1400 block of Washington Ave., Garden District* ⊗ *Weekdays 7:30–3, weekends 9–6.*

Lonsdale House. As a 16-year-old immigrant working in the New Orleans shipyards, Henry Lonsdale noticed how many damaged goods were arriving from upriver. Spotting a need for more-protective shipping materials, he developed the burlap bag (clued in by his parents, who had picked up a sample in India). He made a fortune in burlap, only to lose it all in the 1837 depression. Lonsdale next turned to coffee importing, an industry that ran into problems during the Civil War: the Union blocked imports from Brazil, the major supplier of coffee to New Orleans. Lonsdale hit upon the momentous idea of cutting the limited coffee grinds with chicory, a bitter root, and New Orleanians have been drinking the blend ever since. The house, built with his entrepreneurial dollars, displays many fine details, including intricate cast-iron work on the galleries and a marble entrance hall. The statue of Our Mother of Perpetual Help in the ornate gazebo in the front yard is a remnant of the house's more than 70 years as an active Catholic chapel, which ended with its controversial sale to novelist Anne Rice in 1996. Actor Nicholas Cage purchased the home in 2005 and put it up for sale in 2009 after facing foreclosure on the property, as well as on the LaLaurie mansion he owned in the French Quarter. ⊠ *2523 Prytania St., Garden District.*

Women's Guild of the New Orleans Opera Association House. This fundamentally Greek Revival house, built in 1865, has a distinctive Italianate octagonal turret, added in the late 19th century. The last private owner, Nettie Seebold, willed the estate to the guild in 1955. Furnished with 18th- and 19th-century European and American pieces, the house underwent extensive renovations in 2008 and is once again being used for receptions, weddings, and private parties. ⊠ *2504 Prytania St., Garden District* ☎ *504/267–9539* ⊕ *neworleansopera. org/guild-home.*

WORTH NOTING

Briggs-Staub House. The only Gothic Revival house in the district was built in 1849. Garden District Americans shunned the Gothic Revival style as linked to Creole-Catholic tradition, but Londoner Charles Briggs ignored decorum and had James Gallier Sr. design this anomaly, touted as a "Gothic cottage." The interior departs from a strict Gothic breakup of rooms to make it better suited for entertaining. ⊠ *2605 Prytania St., Garden District.*

Buckner Mansion. This 1856 home was built by cotton king Henry S. Buckner in overt competition with the famous Stanton Hall in Natchez, built by Buckner's former partner. Among the luxurious details are 48 fluted cypress columns and a rare honeysuckle-design cast-iron fence. Now privately owned, the house served as the campus of Soulé College from 1923 to 1975. ⊠ *1410 Jackson Ave., Garden District.*

Christ Church Cathedral. This English Gothic church completed in 1887 has steeply pitched gables, an architectural detail that was a precursor to the New Orleans Victorian style. The cathedral is the oldest non–Roman Catholic church in the Louisiana Purchase: the congregation was established in 1805. Jefferson Davis was among its parishioners, and the altar from his home is at the church, as is the grave of Confederate general Leonidas Polk. Visitors are welcome to walk into the main building when daily services are not in session. ⊠ *2919 St. Charles Ave., Garden District* ⊕ *www.cccnola.org* ⊗ *Services weekdays at 12:15, Sat. at 9:30, Sun. at 7:30, 10, and 6.*

Colonel Short's Villa. This house, built in 1859, was stylistically influential in the district because the two-story galleries of its dining room wing had railings made of cast iron rather than wood. Its architect, Henry Howard, is known for designing Nottaway—the largest plantation home in America—and other monumental homes. The fence, with a pattern of morning glories intertwining with cornstalks, is the most famous example of cast iron in the Garden District. Legend has it that Colonel Short purchased the fence for his wife, who was homesick for her native Iowa. A similar cornstalk fence appears in the French Quarter at 915 Royal Street. After the Shorts, the house was occupied for a brief time by the Union governor Michael Hahn and subsequently by occupational governor Nathaniel Banks during the Civil War. ⊠ *1448 Fourth St., Garden District.*

Eiffel Tower Building. Thirty years ago, engineers in Paris discovered hairline fractures in the Eiffel Tower supports. To lighten the load, they removed the restaurant on the second platform. New Orleans auto dealer McDonald Stephens bought the restaurant, which was disassembled into 11,000 pieces for shipping. Ever the romantic, Stephens hired New Orleans architect Steven Bingler to build a "jewel box" out of the pieces for his four beloved daughters. Bingler's vision, assembled on St. Charles Avenue in 1986, incorporated scattered pieces from the

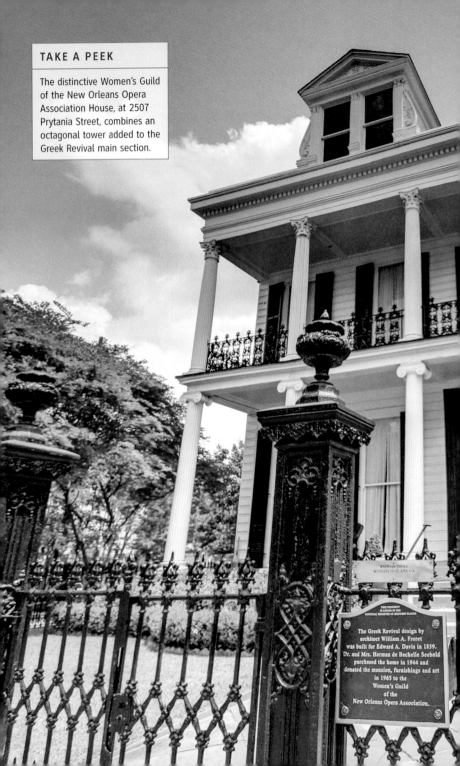

TAKE A PEEK

The distinctive Women's Guild of the New Orleans Opera Association House, at 2507 Prytania Street, combines an octagonal tower added to the Greek Revival main section.

The Greek Revival design by architect William A. Freret was built for Edward A. Davis in 1859. Dr. and Mrs. Herman de Bachelle Seebold purchased the home in 1944 and donated the mansion, furnishings and art in 1965 to the Women's Guild of the New Orleans Opera Association.

original restaurant into a contemporary outer structure meant to resemble the Eiffel Tower. The building went through many reincarnations, most unsuccessful. Today it is a lounge and events venue catering to a younger crowd. ⊠ *2040 St. Charles Ave., Garden District* ☎ *504/525–2951* ⊕ *eiffelsociety.com.*

Musson House. This Italianate house was built by impressionist Edgar Degas's maternal uncle, Michel Musson—a rare Creole inhabitant of the predominantly American Garden District. Musson had moved to his Esplanade Street residence before Degas made his visit to New Orleans, so it's unlikely the artist ever stayed at this address. A later owner added the famous "lace" iron galleries. ⊠ *1331 Third St., Garden District.*

Payne House. Confederate president Jefferson Davis died here on December 6, 1889; a monument out front outlines his political and military careers. Cast iron ornaments the capitals of the Ionic columns, each embossed with the date (1848) and place (New York) of manufacture. ⊠ *1134 1st St., Garden District.*

The Rink. This small collection of specialty shops was once the location of the South's first roller-skating rink. Locals can be found here browsing the **Garden District Book Shop,** which stocks regional, rare, and old books, along with a wide assortment of autographed first editions by local and regional writers, **Judy's at the Rink,** an upscale gift and housewares boutique, and **Loomed NOLA,** which imports hand-woven, organic textiles from Turkey. ⊠ *2727 Prytania St., Garden District.*

Robinson House. Styled after an Italian villa, this home built in the late 1850s is one of the largest in the district. Doric and Corinthian columns support the rounded galleries. It is believed to be the first house in New Orleans with "waterworks," as indoor plumbing was called then. Years of extensive renovation based on the original plans culminated with a re-landscaping in 2005. ⊠ *1415 Third St., Garden District.*

Toby-Westfeldt House. Dating from the 1830s, this unpretentious Greek Revival raised cottage sits amid a large, plantation-like garden, surrounded by a copy of the original white-picket fence. Thomas Toby, a Philadelphia businessman, moved to New Orleans and had this house built well above the ground to protect it from flooding and promote air circulation. The house is thought to be the oldest in this part of the Garden District. ⊠ *2340 Prytania St., Garden District.*

UPTOWN AND CARROLLTON-RIVERBEND

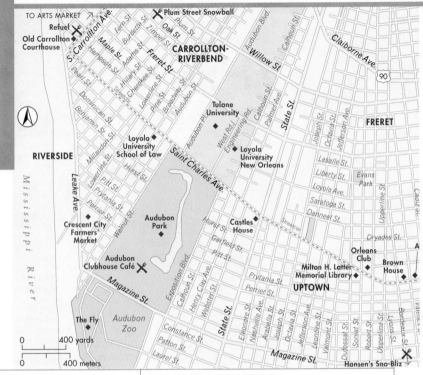

Audubon Clubhouse Café. Have breakfast, brunch, or lunch in the dining room overlooking the Audubon Park, or relax with a drink on the shady veranda. ✉ *Golf Club Dr., off Magazine St., Uptown* ☎ *504/212–5285, 800/774–7394* ⊕ *www.auduboninstitute.org.*

Refuel. Stop for breakfast and lunch at this modern café. At weekend brunch, try the hand-whisked grits, said to be the best in the city. ✉ *8124 Hampson St., Carrollton-Riverbend* ☎ *504/872–0187* ⊕ *www.refuelcafe.com* ☽ *No lunch Mon.*

Uptown and Carrollton-Riverbend are easily walkable neighborhoods. The **St. Charles Avenue streetcar** is a reliable and picturesque mode of transportation, running approximately every 20 minutes 24 hours a day (less frequently at night), from Canal Street at the edge of the French Quarter to South Claiborne Avenue. It stops at all main intersections across St. Charles Avenue, leaving you within walking distance of Audubon Park and Zoo. Expect the entire ride, from Canal Street to Carrollton-Riverbend, to take about an hour (more during rush hour or on holidays). Because the tracks are undergoing maintenance, segments on the line are occasionally out of commission; visit the RTA's website (⊕ *www.norta.com*) for updates. The **No. 11 bus** runs the length of Magazine Street up to Audubon Park from Canal Street. A bit quicker, it runs every 20 minutes, making stops at five major intersections. The fare is $1.25 for both the streetcar and the bus.

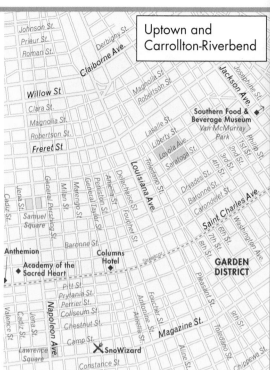

Uptown and Carrollton-Riverbend

6

TOP REASONS TO GO

Ride the streetcar. Take the scenic and leisurely trolley ride from Canal Street to Audubon Park, ogling the stately mansions that stretch along St. Charles Avenue.

Monkey around in Audubon Park and Zoo. Considered one of the best in the nation, Audubon Zoo offers a wide range of interesting exhibits for visitors of all ages. The adjoining park has beautiful walking trails lined with 100-year-old oaks.

Hang with locals at The Fly. This quieter stretch of Audubon Park is known locally as "The Fly." The levee, a riverside walkway along one side of the park, provides spectacular views of the Mississippi

Explore Carrollton-Riverbend. This bustling neighborhood along Oak Street, Maple Street, and South Carrollton Avenue has restaurants, shops, and popular hangouts for college students and locals.

Shop 'til you drop. Magazine Street is the city's premier shopping destination.

MAKING THE MOST OF YOUR TIME

You could easily spend two days in this neighborhood: a day visiting the **Audubon Zoo** and enjoying the park that surrounds it, and a day exploring the boutiques, galleries, and restaurants along **Magazine Street**. If you have extra time, head to **The Fly,** the riverside park on the back side of the zoo, where locals like to picnic and play ball on weekends.

SAFETY

Most of Uptown and Carrollton-Riverbend is safe to walk around during the day and evening. However, travelers should always exercise caution, especially when walking at night in the area between Magazine Street and the river up to Jefferson. Also avoid the area close to the river west of Audubon Park and dark side streets when out late at night.

RIDING THE STREETCAR

Take in the beautiful mansions and fun local vibe of Uptown via the St. Charles Avenue streetcar, which runs the length of the avenue, from Canal Street right outside of the French Quarter to Carrollton-Riverbend. The relaxing ride takes about an hour and costs $1.25 one way.

The St. Charles streetcar line runs through Uptown (above) and the CBD (right page, bottom).

If you're coming from the French Quarter, board at Canal and Carondelet. Jump off at Jackson Avenue (the ride will take 20 minutes) and follow our Garden District Walking Tour (⇨ *See Chapter 1*). Reboard at Louisiana Avenue, which forms the boundary between the Garden District and Uptown. As you approach Louisiana Avenue, the huge white mansion on your left at the intersection was formerly the **Bultman Funeral Home,** where Tennessee Williams staged his play *Suddenly Last Summer.* It's now a Fresh Market grocery store. Note that unless you have an unlimited day pass ($3) for the streetcar, you'll need to ask for a 25¢ transfer when you pay—otherwise you'll have to repay the fare (in exact change) each time you board.

STREETCAR HISTORY

In the 1900s, streetcars were the most prominent mode of public transit in New Orleans, and by the early 20th century the city had almost 200 miles of streetcar lines; a ride cost just 5¢. In the 1920s, however, buses started to overtake the old-fashioned system. Today just three lines operate, with plans for additional ones underway.

The **Columns Hotel,** formerly a private home, is on the right after Peniston Street. It's a great place for a cocktail on the grand veranda. Next you'll pass the Gothic-style **Rayne Memorial Methodist Church,** built in 1875, a block past the hotel on the left. The 1887 Queen Anne–style **Grant House** up the block was designed by local architect Thomas Sully with a decorative porch and balcony balustrades.

As you continue, the large avenue at the next stop is Napoleon. The spectacular **Academy of the Sacred Heart,** a private girls' school, is on the right in the next block, past Jena Street. Across the street, the Mediterranean **Smith House** claims one of the most picturesque settings on the avenue. It was built in 1906 for William Smith, president of the New Orleans Cotton Exchange. The oldest house on St. Charles Avenue (circa 1850s) is the **4621 St. Charles House** on the right, before Valence Street. Next door, **Anthemion** is an early example of the Colonial Revival movement. The **Brown House,** on the right before Bordeaux Street, is one of the largest mansions on St. Charles Avenue.

Several houses in the next block past the Brown House are turn-of-the-20th-century buildings that re-create an antebellum style. On the left, the neighboring **Rosenberg House** and **Stirling House** contrast Colonial and Classical

Revival. The Tudor style of the Stirling House, with its steep gables, Gothic arches, and half timbering, was popular when banana magnate Joseph Vaccaro built it in 1910. The **Milton H. Latter Memorial Library,** a Beaux-Arts mansion that is now a public library, is on the left at Soniat Street. It's one of the few mansions along St. Charles open to the public.

Several blocks ahead, the **Benjamin House,** between Octavia and Joseph streets, is a stunning mansion (circa 1912) made of limestone, an expensive and unusual building material for New Orleans. In the next block, past Joseph Street on the right, is the **McCarthy House,** a 1903 Colonial Revival home with ornate columns and flattop doors and windows. The plantation home used in the film *Gone With the Wind* was a set, but it inspired the columned New Orleans **Tara,** built in 1941, at the corner of Arabella.

As you cross Nashville Avenue, the **Wedding Cake House,** an elaborate Victorian built circa 1896, is on the right. Its most notable feature is the beveled leaded glass in its front door, one of the most beautiful entryways in the city. As you enter the university district, dominating the next block on the left is the neo-Gothic **St. Charles Avenue Presbyterian Church.**

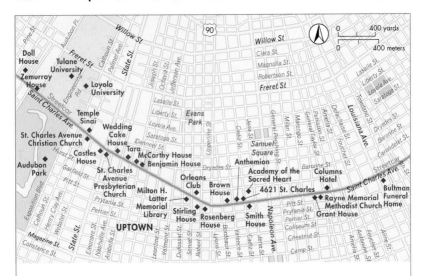

Castles House, on the left after State Street, is a similar Colonial Revival, as is the **St. Charles Avenue Christian Church,** two blocks up on the left. On the right, across from the church, is **Temple Sinai,** the first Reform Jewish congregation in New Orleans. This building dates from 1928; the annex on the corner was built in 1970.

Just beyond Calhoun Street, **Loyola University,** on the right, takes up the block past Temple Sinai. **Tulane University,** founded in 1884, is directly beside Loyola. Campuses for both universities extend back several blocks off the avenue. On the left, across the avenue from the two universities is **Audubon Park and Zoo.**

Back on the streetcar, the heavy stone archway on the right just after Tulane University is the guarded entrance to **Audubon Place.** The private drive has some of the most elegant mansions in the city. **Zemurray House,** the columned white home facing the archway, was built in 1907 by the president of the United Fruit Company. It is now the official residence of Tulane's president. The **Doll House,** a miniature house in the corner yard on the right at Broadway, is said to be the smallest house in New Orleans to have its own postal address.

At Broadway, to the left, is the **Loyola University School of Law,** an Italianate building that housed the Dominican Sisters and the college they operated until the 1980s. The street continues several more stops past Broadway along St. Charles until it turns at the Riverbend onto Carrollton Avenue, once the entrance to a former resort town.

You'll travel through the Carrollton-Riverbend neighborhood before reaching the end of the line at **Palmer Park,** where an arts market is held the last Saturday of every month. Reboard the streetcar headed downtown at South Carrollton Avenue and Claiborne Avenue, where the St. Charles Avenue line both begins and ends.

Sightseeing
★★

Dining
★★★

Lodging
★

Shopping
★★★★

Nightlife
★★★

Discover the more residential face of New Orleans in the sprawling Uptown and Carrollton-Riverbend neighborhoods. Just a 30-minute streetcar ride from Canal Street, you'll find blocks of shops on bustling Magazine Street, stunning homes along oak-lined streets, and the first-class Audubon Park and Zoo. Head farther into Uptown and spend a couple of hours walking the length of the levee in Riverbend for stunning views of the Mississippi.

UPTOWN

Updated
by Susan
Granger

Uptown encompasses the area upriver from Louisiana Avenue between Tchoupitoulas Street and South Claiborne Avenue, on the west side of the Garden District. Stately mansions line the length of St. Charles Avenue, where you'll find colorful Mardi Gras beads hanging from tree limbs throughout the year. Traveling along the avenue from downtown to uptown provides something of a historical narrative: the city's development unfolded upriver, and the houses grow more modern the farther uptown you go. Smaller shotgun and Victorian-style homes on the side streets display old-world charm, and the family-oriented neighborhood is home to Loyola and Tulane universities. Magazine Street bustles with six miles of shops, bars, and restaurants all the way from the CBD up to Audubon Park.

TOP ATTRACTIONS

FAMILY

Fodor's Choice
★

Audubon Park. Formerly the plantation of Etienne de Boré, the father of the granulated sugar industry in Louisiana, this large, lush stretch of greenery is between St. Charles Avenue and Magazine Street, continuing across Magazine Street to the river. Designed by John Charles Olmsted, nephew of Frederick Law Olmsted (who laid out New York City's Central Park), it contains the world-class **Audubon Zoo**; a 1.7-mile track for running, walking, or biking; picnic and play areas; Audubon Park Golf Course; tennis courts; a swimming pool; horse stables; and a river view. Calm lagoons wind through the park, harboring egrets and other indigenous species. The park and zoo were named for the famous ornithologist and painter John James Audubon, who spent many years working in and around New Orleans. ✉ *6500 Magazine St., Uptown* ☎ *504/581–4629* ⊕ *www. auduboninstitute.org* ✉ *Free.*

Audubon Zoo. Consistently ranked as one of the top zoos in the nation, the Audubon Zoo presents a wide array of animals in exhibits that mimic their natural habitats. The Louisiana Swamp exhibit re-creates the natural habitat of alligators, including rare white alligators (technically leucistic gators), nutrias (large swamp rodents), and catfish; alligator-feeding time is always well attended. Among other highlights are the Reptile Encounter, Komodo Dragon exhibit, and a white Bengal tiger. Several attractions are available for additional ticket fees, including a zoo train tour that departs every 30 minutes from the swamp exhibit, a Dinosaur Adventure exhibit with moving dinosaur replicas, and the Safari Simulator Ride. "Cool Zoo," a splash park featuring a 28-foot white alligator slide, bubbling fountains, and splash zones is set aside for toddlers and young children. (Cool Zoo is open daily April–Labor Day, then weekends only through September; separate admission is $8 for non-members and $6 for members.) ✉ *6500 Magazine St., Uptown* ⊕ *www.auduboninstitute.org* ✉ *$17.50 adults, $12 children 2–12, $13 seniors; combination ticket for zoo and Audubon Aquarium of the Americas, $36 adults, $25 children, $22.50 seniors.* ☉ *Mar. 1–Labor Day, Tues.–Sun. 10–5, Sat.–Sun. 10–6; Sept.–Feb., Tues.–Sun. 10–4.*

Loyola University New Orleans. Chartered by the Jesuits in 1912, Loyola University is a landmark in New Orleans. Its communications, music, and law degree programs are world-renowned. The Gothic- and Tudor-styled Marquette Hall, facing St. Charles Avenue and Audubon Park, provides the backdrop for a quintessential New Orleans photo opportunity. The fourth floor of the neo-Gothic J. Edgar and Louise S. Monroe Library houses the university's Collins C. Diboll Art Gallery, open to the public seven days a week (Mon.–Sat. 10–6, Sun. noon–6). ✉ *6363 St. Charles Ave., Uptown* ⊕ *www.loyno.edu.*

Tulane University. Next to Loyola University on St. Charles Avenue, the university's three original buildings face the avenue: **Tilton Hall** (1902) on the right, **Gibson Hall** (1894) in the middle, and **Dinwiddie Hall** (1924) on the left. The Romanesque style, with its massive stone look and arches, is repeated in several buildings around a quad. Modern campus buildings extend another three blocks to the north. These include Newcomb Art Gallery, a 3,600-square-foot exhibition

---

PERFECT PICNIC

Spicy seafood to go makes for the perfect New Orleans picnic. For seasonal boiled specialties—crawfish, crabs, shrimp, corn, potatoes, and garlic—stop by the **Big Fisherman** (⊕ *3301 Magazine St.*) on your way to Audubon Park. Ask if there are fresh crawfish pies available. And don't forget to pick up paper towels at the supermarket next door.

Kids love feeding the giraffes at the Audubon Zoo.

facility offering contemporary and historical exhibits (free, Tues.–Fri. 10–5, Sat.–Sun. 11–4). Tulane offers undergraduate, graduate, and professional degrees in the liberal arts, science and engineering, architecture, business, law, social work, medicine, public health, and tropical medicine.

The **Middle American Research Institute and Gallery** *(☎ 504/865–5110 ⊕ mari.tulane.edu)*, located on the third floor of Tulane's Dinwiddie Hall, includes the world's oldest documented Guatemalan textile collection and replicas of classic Maya sculpture. Established in 1924, the institute's collection also includes rare artifacts like poison-dart arrows from Venezuela and shrunken heads from the Brazilian rain forest. The pre-Columbian artifacts are complemented by an associated collection of books on Latin American culture housed in Tulane's main library (free, Mon.–Fri., 9–4, appointments are recommended). ✉ *6823 St. Charles Ave., Uptown ⊕ www.tulane.edu*

WORTH NOTING

Academy of the Sacred Heart. This Colonial Revival building, housing a Catholic girls' school, was built in 1900 and features wide, wraparound balconies (or galleries) and colonnades facing a large garden. The academy is exceptionally beautiful during the December holidays, when the galleries are decked with wreaths and garlands. ✉ *4521 St. Charles Ave., Uptown.*

Anthemion. The emergence of Colonial Revival architecture in the late 19th century indicated local weariness with the excesses of the Greek Revival craze that had dominated the mid-century. Anthemion is an excellent example of this return to simplicity. Built in 1896 for the druggist Christian Keppler, it served as the headquarters of the Japanese consulate from 1938 to 1941. ⊠ *4631 St. Charles Ave., Uptown.*

Brown House. This mansion, completed in 1904 for cotton magnate William Perry Brown, is one of the largest houses on St. Charles Avenue. Its solid monumental look, Syrian arches, and steep gables make it a choice example of Romanesque Revival style. ⊠ *4717 St. Charles Ave., Uptown.*

Castles House. Local architect Thomas Sully designed this 1895 Colonial Revival house after the Longfellow House in Cambridge, Massachusetts. The interior has often appeared in the pages of design magazines. ⊠ *6000 St. Charles Ave., Uptown.*

Milton H. Latter Memorial Library. A former private home now serves as the most elegant public library in New Orleans. Built in 1907 and taking up an entire city block, this Italianate–beaux arts mansion was once the home of silent-screen star Marguerite Clark. It was then purchased by the Latter family and given to the city as a library in 1948 in memory of their son, who was killed in World War II. Sit and leaf through a copy of Walker Percy's *The Moviegoer* or John Kennedy Toole's *Confederacy of Dunces* (two popular novels set in New Orleans), or just relax in a wicker chair in the solarium. This is one of the few mansions on St. Charles Avenue open to the public, and the gardens are lovely. ⊠ *5120 St. Charles Ave., Uptown* ☎ *504/596–2626* ⊕ *www.neworleanspubliclibrary.org* ☾ *Mon., Wed. 9–8, Tues., Thurs. 9–6, Sat. 10–5, Sun. noon–5.*

Orleans Club. This sumptuous mansion was built in 1868 as a wedding gift from Colonel William Lewis Wynn to his daughter. The side building, on the uptown side of the main building, is an auditorium added in the 1950s. The house is closed to the public but serves as headquarters to a ladies' social club and hosts many debutante teas and wedding receptions. ⊠ *5005 St. Charles Ave., Uptown.*

CARROLLTON-RIVERBEND

Before becoming part of New Orleans in 1874, the area was a resort town, providing a relaxing getaway with riverfront views. Now the neighborhood is mostly composed of smaller one- and two-story family homes, shady oak-lined streets, and plenty of small restaurants and cafés. With the success of local events, such as the annual Oak Street Po'Boy Festival in November (⊕ *www.poboyfest.com*), the retail strip on Oak Street has blossomed with shops, clothing boutiques, restaurants, and popular bars such as the Maple Leaf, where the Rebirth Brass Band plays every Tuesday night. Nearby Maple Street is a great shopping destination in its own right, attracting the college crowd with an array of bars and cafés. Walk the stretch of the levee from Riverbend back downtown along the river and relax at "The Fly," a popular hangout on the back side of Audubon Zoo, where locals enjoy views of the river while setting up picnics or team sports.

EXPLORING

Arts Market of New Orleans. Spend a morning perusing the craftsmanship of more than 100 artists from all over the region in this open-air market held the last Saturday of each month in beautiful Palmer Park. Vendors include jewelry artists, painters, textile designers, soap makers, and potters. Musicians, a kids' tent, and food stands round out the event. ⊠ *Palmer Park, corner of S. Carrolton and S. Claiborne Aves., Carrollton-Riverbend* ⊕ *www. artscouncilofneworleans.com* 🖾 *Free* ⊗ *Last Sat. of month, 10–4.*

Crescent City Farmers Market. Rub shoulders with New Orleans chefs as they rush to pick up fresh veggies, fish, and meat before their restaurants open. The market caters to both home cooks and professionals who embrace the concept of showcasing local and seasonal ingredients. A new chef is featured each month to prepare delicious lunches. Visitors can indulge in tasty treats like homemade popsicles, fresh-squeezed juice, and hot-from-the-oven bread, as well as sampling the local produce. ⊠ *200 Broadway St., between Leake Ave. and Broadway, Carrollton-Riverbend* ⊕ *www.crescentcityfarmersmarket. org* 🖾 *Free* ⊗ *Tues. 9–1.*

The Fly. Spend an afternoon picnicking at this lush green park with spectacular views of the Mississippi, just on the other side of Audubon Zoo. Officially called The Riverview, locals call it "The Fly" after a butterfly-shaped building that used to be on-site. It is a popular place for picnics and pickup sports. The park is particularly beautiful in the early evening, when you can watch the sunset just beyond the river. ⊠ *Exposition Blvd., Carrollton-Riverbend.*

MID-CITY AND
BAYOU ST. JOHN

GETTING ORIENTED

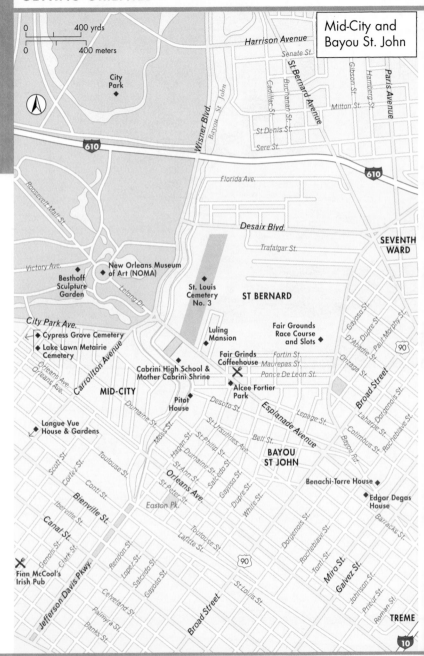

Mid-City and
Bayou St. John

Harrison Avenue
Senate St.
St Bernard Avenue
Gibson St.
Hamberg St.
Paris Avenue
City
Park
Cadillac St.
Buchanan St.
Milton St.
St Denis St.
Wisner Blvd.
Bayou St. John
Sere St.
610
610
Roosevelt Mall St.
Florida Ave.
Desaix Blvd.
Trafalgar St.
SEVENTH WARD
Victory Ave.
New Orleans Museum
of Art (NOMA)
Besthoff
Sculpture
Garden
Lelong Dr.
St. Louis
Cemetery
No. 3
ST BERNARD
Gayoso St.
Dupre St.
Paul Murphy St.
City Park Ave.
Cypress Grove Cemetery
Lake Lawn Metairie
Cemetery
Carrollton Avenue
Luling
Mansion
Fair Grounds
Race Course
and Slots
D'Abadie St.
Onzaga St.
90
Orleans Ave.
Orleans Ave.
Cabrini High School &
Mother Cabrini Shrine
Fair Grinds
Coffeehouse
Fortin St.
Maurepas St.
Ponce De Leon St.
Broad Street
Dorgenois St.
LaHarpe St.
Rocheblave St.
MID-CITY
Dumaine St.
Pitot
House
Alcee Fortier
Park
Desoto St.
Esplanade Avenue
Lepage St.
Columbus St.
Bayou Rd.
Longue Vue
House & Gardens
Moss St.
Hagan St.
St. Ursulines Ave.
St Philip St.
Salcedo St.
Bell St.
BAYOU
ST JOHN
Benachi-Torre House
Scott St.
Cortez St.
Toulouse St.
Conti St.
St Ann St.
Dumaine St.
Gayoso St.
Dupre St.
White St.
Dorgenois St.
Rocheblave St.
Edgar Degas
House
Barracks St.
Bienville St.
Iberville St.
Orleans Ave.
St Peter St.
Easton Pk.
Toni St.
Miro St.
Galvez St.
Canal St.
Genois St.
Clark St.
Rendon St.
Lopez St.
Salcedo St.
Toutouse St.
Lafitte St.
90
Dorgenois St.
Johnson St.
Prieur St.
Finn McCool's
Irish Pub
Jefferson Davis Pkwy.
Cleveland St.
Palmyra St.
Gayoso St.
St Louis St.
Broad Street
Roman St.
TREME
Banks St.
10

0 400 yrds
0 400 meters

GETTING HERE AND AROUND

From downtown there are two easy ways to get into Mid-City: Canal Street or Esplanade Avenue, both of which border the French Quarter. There are two **streetcar** lines that run down Canal Street: one will take you straight down Canal to Metairie Cemetery, and the other will turn down Carrollton Avenue and deposit you in an ideal location right in front of City Park. The **No. 91 Jackson-Esplanade bus,** which you can catch anywhere along Rampart Street in the French Quarter, turns onto Esplanade Avenue, has a stop right by the Degas House, and takes you right in front of City Park. The streetcar ride from downtown takes approximately 30 minutes. Allow about 15 minutes for the bus ride down Esplanade.

MAKING THE MOST OF YOUR TIME

City Park and the Mid-City **cemeteries** are generally open during daylight hours, but the **outdoor patios** of Esplanade Avenue restaurants and cafés stay open well into the night. Allow yourself at least half a day, starting in the afternoon, so you can enjoy both activities. **City Park** is one of the largest urban parks in the nation, and you could easily spend an entire vacation exploring its art collections, hiking trails, vintage carousel, botanical gardens, and gondola rides.

SAFETY

Things can change from cute to creepy in the span of a block or so, so exercise good judgment if you go walking off the main thoroughfares. The areas around Bayou St. John and City Park tend to be safe, especially during daylight hours, but areas closer to Broad Street (which runs roughly parallel to the bayou about half a mile south toward the French Quarter) are rougher, and should definitely be avoided on foot at night. Carrollton Avenue is the main thoroughfare through Mid-City (and connects to the Uptown and Carrollton-Riverbend neighborhoods) and is usually well trafficked, but elsewhere in the neighborhood it's advisable to drive at night.

TOP REASONS TO GO

Explore City Park. This gorgeous and sprawling park is home to dozens of attractions, including a museum, sculpture garden, and amusement park.

Take a cemetery tour. Mid-City has some of the largest, safest, and best-kept cemeteries in New Orleans.

Stroll along Bayou St. John. The grassy banks offer biking and walking trails and splendid views of some of the most historic and lovely homes and landmarks in the city.

QUICK BITES

Fair Grinds Coffeehouse. Just off Esplanade Avenue, Fair Grinds Coffeehouse is the neighborhood spot for fair trade coffee, tea, and small snacks—including vegan treats. Recent renovations opened the upstairs balcony for alfresco dining, and there's live music at least twice a week. ✉ *3133 Ponce de Leon St., Bayou St. John* ☏ *504/913– 9072* ⊕ *www.fairgrinds.com.*

Finn McCool's Irish Pub. This convivial spot is more than just your average corner bar: it streams European football games (opening as early as 7am to do so) and hosts a popular trivia quiz on Monday nights. The kitchen serves delicious BBQ and burgers. ✉ *3701 Banks St., Mid-City* ☏ *504/486– 9080* ⊕ *finnmccools.com.*

7

Sightseeing
★★
Dining
★
Lodging
★
Shopping
★
Nightlife
★

With their tree-lined streets and avenues, neighborhood gathering places and historic landmarks, the Mid-City and Bayou St. John neighborhoods are decidedly more tranquil than their downtown counterparts. Instead of music blaring out of every doorway, you will find a quieter form of charm in the gardens, galleries, and lagoons of City Park, in the elaborately constructed tombs of the cemeteries, and on the tree-shaded patios and decks of the restaurants and cafés where you can listen to the church bells keep time as you relax with a cold drink.

MID-CITY

Updated by
Cameron Todd

Above the French Quarter and below the lakefront, neither Uptown nor quite downtown, Mid-City is primarily a working-class neighborhood, embracing everything from massive, lush City Park to storefronts along gritty Broad Street. Much of this area was low-lying swamp until the late 1800s, and you can still see where the high ground was, such as along the Esplanade Ridge (now Esplanade Avenue). These are the stretches with many of the largest historic homes, churches, and landmarks. Along Carrollton Avenue you can find everything from an old-school Italian ice-cream parlor to strips of inexpensive Central American restaurants. The neighborhood hosts more than a dozen festivals and celebrations a year, from block parties like Bayou Boogaloo to grand-scale mega-events like the Voodoo Experience. It's easy to discern which festival is approaching by the bright flags that spring up on people's porches.

TOP ATTRACTIONS

FAMILY
Fodor'sChoice
★

City Park. This 150-year-old, 1,300-acre expanse of moss-draped oaks and 11 miles of gentle lagoons is just 2 miles from the French Quarter, but feels like it could be another world. With the largest collection of live oaks in the world, including old grove trees that are more than 600 years old, the park offers a certain natural majesty that's difficult to find in urban areas. The art deco benches, fountains, bridges, and ironwork are remnants of a 1930s Works Progress Administration refurbishment and add to the dreamy scenery that visitors enjoy boating and biking through. Within the park are the **New Orleans Museum of Art,** the **Sydney and Walda Besthoff Sculpture Garden,** the **New Orleans Botanical Garden,** the kid-friendly **Carousel Gardens Amusement Park and Storyland,** a golf course, equestrian stable, sports facilities, and picnic areas. Check the park's website for seasonal activities and special events, such as music festivals, the annual Easter egg hunt, and the eye-popping wonderland that is Celebration in the Oaks between Thanksgiving and New Year's Day. Morning Call, an eatery behind the Sculpture Garden, serves up hot beignets and café au lait 24-7. Most of the park's offerings are free, but several of the venues inside City Park charge their own separate admission fees.

Open seasonally, the 17-ride **Carousel Gardens Amusement Park** (*⊕ 504/483–9402 ✉ $3 admission; rides $3 each*) has a New Orleans treasure as its centerpiece—a 1906 carousel, one of only 100 antique wooden carousels left in the nation, that is on the National Register of Historic Places. In addition to the cherished "flying horses," the park has rides like the new Musik Express, Rockin' Tug, Coney Tower, Ferris Wheel, Bumper Cars, Monkey Jump, Red Baron miniplane, Scrambler, and Tilt-A-Whirl. The rides here are mostly geared to children, not hard-core thrill seekers, but adults and kids both like the miniature train that takes passengers on a gentle sightseeing tour through City Park. In 2013, two 18-hole miniature golf courses opened, one with a New Orleans theme and one with a Louisiana theme. The park's minigolf tradition, which started in the 1940s, returns after more than two decades of absence.

New Orleans Botanical Garden (*☎ 504/483–9386 ✉ $6 ⊘ Closed Mon.*), opened in 1936 as a Depression-era project of the Works Progress Administration (WPA), is one of the few remaining examples of public garden design from the WPA and art-deco period. The garden's collections contain over 2,000 varieties of plants from all over the world, which are complemented by sites such as The Conservatory, Pavilion of the Two Sisters, and the Yakumo Nihon Teien Japanese Garden, and theme gardens containing aquatics, roses, native plants, ornamental trees, and shrubs and perennials. The garden serves as a showcase of three notable talents: New Orleans architect Richard Koch, landscape architect William Wiedorn, and artist Enrique Alférez. Adding a touch of fun, the Historic Train Garden, open on weekends, offers visitors the chance to enjoy baguette-sized cars rolling through a miniature New Orleans village.

Featuring figures and settings culled from children's literature, whimsical **Storyland** (*☎ 504/483–9402 ✉ $3 ⊘ Closed Mon.*), adjacent to the amusement park, has been a favorite romping ground for generations of New Orleans kids. With more than 25 larger-than-life storybook exhibits, kids can climb aboard Captain Hook's pirate ship, visit the old lady who lived in a shoe, and journey with Pinocchio into the mouth of a whale. ✉ *Bordered by City Park Ave., Robert E. Lee Blvd., Marconi Dr., and Bayou St. John, Mid-City ☎ 504/482–4888 ⊕ www.neworleanscitypark.com.*

Fodor's Choice ★ **New Orleans Museum of Art (NOMA).** Gracing the main entrance to City Park since 1911, this traditional fine-arts museum draws from classic Greek architecture, with several modern wings that bring additional light and space to the grand old building. NOMA now has 46 galleries housing an outstanding permanent collection. With nearly 40,000 objects, the installations and exhibitions represent historical periods from the Italian Renaissance to the best of the contemporary world. A wealth of American and European art—particularly French—makes up much of the collection, with works by Monet, Renoir, Picasso, and Pollock. Louisiana artists also have a marked presence, and the museum boasts photography, ceramics, and glassworks from cultures around the globe, plus outstanding holdings in African, Pre-Columbian, and Asian art. In addition, the museum offers a year-round schedule of traveling and special exhibitions, events, tours, and public programs.

Henry Moore's handsome *Reclining Mother and Child* greets visitors at the entrance of the Sydney and Walda Besthoff Sculpture Garden. Most of the garden's 60-some sculptures, representing some of the biggest names in modern art, were donated by avid local collector Sydney Besthoff. Meandering trails and bridges over bayou lagoons carry visitors past a fascinating combination of famed traditional sculpture and contemporary works, including major pieces by Jacques Lipchitz, Barbara Hepworth, and Joel Shapiro. The garden is open daily from 10 until 4:45; admission is free. ⊠ *City Park, 1 Collins Diboll Circle, Mid-City* 🖅 *504/658–4100* ⊕ *www. noma.org* 🖾 *$10* ☉ *Tues.–Thurs. 10–6, Fri. 10–9, weekends 11–5.*

WORTH NOTING

Cypress Grove Cemetery. This expansive and still-used cemetery was founded by the Fireman's Charitable and Benevolent Association in 1840. Over time, as the cemetery expanded, other societies and individuals joined the volunteer firemen in building impressive monuments. Leading architects and craftsmen were called upon to design and build tombs commemorating the lives of many of New Orleans's most prominent citizens. Crafted in marble, granite, and cast iron, tombs at Cypress Grove are among the nation's leading examples of memorial architecture. Of note is the Chinese Soon On Tong Association's tomb that holds a grate in front so that visitors can burn prayers in it. ⊠ *120 City Park Ave., Mid-City* ☉ *Daily 8–5.*

Lake Lawn Metairie Cemetery. The largest cemetery in the metropolitan area, known to locals simply as Metairie Cemetery, is the final resting place of nine Louisiana governors, seven New Orleans mayors, three Confederate generals, and musician Louis Prima. Many of New Orleans's noted families are also interred here in elaborate monuments ranging from Gothic crypts to Romanesque mausoleums to Egyptian pyramids. The arrangement of tombs reflects the cemetery's former life as a horse-racing track, with the tombs arranged around the perimeter and interior. ⊠ *5100 Pontchartrain Blvd., Mid-City* ⊕ *www. lakelawnmetairie.com* ☉ *Daily 8–5.*

Longue Vue House and Gardens. While technically in the Lakewood neighborhood, this beautiful destination is in easy walking distance of the Mid-City streetcar. Fourteen separate gardens are arranged throughout 8 acres of beautifully maintained property, embellished with fountains,

City Park is one of the most serene places in all of New Orleans.

architectural flourishes, and gorgeous pathways of hand-laid Mexican pebbles and rough-cut marble. This city estate, now a National Historic Landmark, was fashioned in the 1940s after the great country houses of England, and the villa-style mansion is decorated with its original furnishings of English and American antiques, priceless tapestries, modern art, and porcelain. Longue Vue is open Tuesday through Sunday, and guests can visit the house by guided tour or explore the gardens at their own leisure. Themed gardens include the formal Spanish court, modeled after a 14th-century Spanish garden, as well as a Discovery Garden, which introduces kids to the intricacies and wonders of horticulture.

■ TIP→ **While the verdant gardens are open year round, March and April see the amarillos, daffodils, azaleas, spring snowdrops, tulips, and poppies in full bloom.** ⊠ *7 Bamboo Rd., Lakewood* ☎ *504/488–5488* ⊕ *www.longuevue.com* ⌑ *full tour $10; garden-only tour $7* ⊙ *House and garden Tues.–Sat. 10–5, Sun. 1–5; shop Tues.–Sat. 10–4, Sun. 1–4.*

BAYOU ST. JOHN

Just up Esplanade Avenue from the French Quarter, the Bayou St. John neighborhood is known for its beautiful shady lanes, gorgeous homes, and laid-back vibe. Great restaurants, cafés, and bars dot the landscape, with sidewalk seating and relaxed patios. It's also home to the New Orleans Fairgrounds Race Course and Slots, one of the nation's premier horse-racing venues, and the world-famous New Orleans Jazz and Heritage Festival. St. Louis Cemetery No. 3 opens its gates onto Esplanade Avenue, inviting visitors to explore the rows of aboveground tombs and mausoleums. At the end of the avenue you'll discover Bayou St. John, the scenic waterway that begins in Mid-City, meanders through Faubourg St. John, and ends at the lakefront. You'll find all sorts of people out enjoying the wide grassy banks—biking, fishing, or just strolling along and admiring the reflection of a sunset in the smooth water.

TOP ATTRACTIONS

Bayou St. John. A bayou is a natural inlet, usually a slow moving, narrow waterway that emerges from the swamp at one end and joins a larger body of water at the other. This bayou—the only one remaining in New Orleans—borders City Park on the east and extends about 7 miles from Lake Pontchartrain to just past Orleans Avenue. It is named for John the Baptist, whose nativity (St. John's Eve, June 23), the most important day in the year for voodoo practitioners, was notoriously celebrated on the bayou's banks in the 1800s. The first European settlers in the area, believed to have been trappers, coexisted with Native Americans here beginning in 1704. Today, the Bayou is still a popular destination among New Orleanians, whether for tradition's sake, such as the famed Mardi Gras Indians who gather for their annual celebrations, a festival such as the Bayou Boogaloo in May, or simply for a relaxing afternoon of fishing, canoeing, or picnicking along the grassy banks. Scenic biking and walking trails run alongside the waterway all the way to the lakefront, where you can watch the graceful old homes of picturesque Moss Street morph into the dazzling waterfront mansions of Bancroft Drive. ⊠ *From the foot of Jefferson Davis Parkway to Lakeshore Dr., Bayou St. John.*

Pitot House. One of the few surviving houses that lined the bayou in the late 1700s, and the only Creole-colonial style country house in the city open to the public, is named for James Pitot, who bought the property in 1810 as a country home for his family. In addition to being one of the city's finest merchants, Pitot served as New Orleans mayor from 1804 to 1805, the city's first mayor after the Louisiana Purchase, and later as parish court judge. The Pitot House was restored and moved 200 feet to its current location in the 1960s to make way for the expansion of Cabrini High School. It is noteworthy for its stucco-covered brick-between-post construction, an example of which is exposed on the second floor. The house is typical of the West Indies style brought to Louisiana by early colonists, with galleries around the house that protect the interior from both rain and sunshine. There aren't any interior halls to stifle ventilation, and opposing doors encourage a cross breeze. The house is furnished with period antiques from the United States, including special pieces from Louisiana. ⊠ *1440 Moss St., Bayou St. John* ☎ *504/482–0312* ⊕ *www. louisianalandmarks.org* ⊡ *$7* ☉ *Wed.–Sat. 10–3 or by appointment.*

St. Louis Cemetery No. 3. One block from the entrance to City Park, at the end of Esplanade Avenue, this cemetery was opened in 1854 on an old leper colony. Governor Galvez exiled the lepers to this area of high ground along Bayou St. John, but during the yellow fever outbreak of 1853 they were removed yet again to make room for the dead. Storyville photographer E. J. Bellocq lies here, and the cemetery is notable now for its neat rows of elaborate aboveground crypts, mausoleums, and carved stone angels soaring overhead. ⊠ *3428 Esplanade Ave., Bayou St. John* ☉ *Mon.–Sat. 9–3, Sun. 9–noon.*

CLOSE UP

Mid-City's Cemeteries

Of all Mid-City's charms, one of the most fascinating is its prolific number of cemeteries, and the haunting beauty of these "cities of the dead." These evocative graves hold the final resting places of famous musicians, Storyville madams, voodoo practitioners, politicians, and pirates.

The historical development of these aboveground cemeteries emerges from two main points. New Orleans, most of which lies below sea level, has a high water table, which caused (and continues to cause, in some circumstances) buried coffins to pop out of the ground when a heavy rain occurred. Raised graves and vaulted tombs were also an old tradition among the French and Spanish.

Mid-City cemeteries are some of the safest and most-trafficked in the city. Our favorite out here is **St. Louis**

Cemetery No. 3 but **Cypress Grove Cemetery** or **Lake Lawn Metairie Cemetery** are good alternatives. It all depends on what's most convenient.

Save Our Cemeteries. This is a great source for historical knowledge, safety info, and tours. ✉ Mid-City ☎ 504/525–3377 ⊕ www.saveourcemeteries.org.

CEMETERY SYMBOLISM

Most vaults or plots are infused with funerary symbolism, revealing a secret language between the living and dead. An anchor stands for hope, a broken column represents life cut short, and a broken flower symbolizes a life terminated. Sculpted ivy is a symbol of enduring friendship. Clasped hands stand for unity and love, even after death. There's more at ⊕ www.nolacemeteries.com.

7

WORTH NOTING

Alcee Fortier Park. Situated at Esplanade Avenue and Mystery Street, this tiny sliver of a park was named for philanthropist Alcee Fortier, who owned much of the surrounding area in the late 19th century and founded a public school. A neighborhood favorite, the park is almost completely maintained by the efforts of local volunteers who tend the lush landscaping, which includes palms, caladiums, and azaleas, keep up the collection of whimsical sculptures and art, and make sure the concrete tables with chess boards built into them are ready for game time (complete with baskets of chess pieces). It's a focal point of the Bayou St. John neighborhood, surrounded by a concentration of hip restaurants and neighborhood grocers. ✉ *Esplanade Ave. and Mystery St., Bayou St. John.*

Benachi-Torre House. This historic Greek Revival mansion was built in 1859 for the Greek consul in New Orleans and was a significant part of the original expansion of New Orleans into this neighborhood. Directly across from the Degas House, this intersection forms something of a historical hub. The house earned the nickname "Rendezvous des Chasseurs" (meeting place of hunters) during the 19th century when much of this area was still undeveloped swampland. The gorgeous house and gardens are now primarily a private event space and a popular setting for New Orleans weddings. ✉ *2257 Bayou Rd., at N. Tonti St., Bayou St. John* ☎ *800/308–7040* ⊕ *www.benachihouse.com.*

Cabrini High School and Mother Cabrini Shrine. Mother Frances Cabrini, the first American-citizen saint (she was canonized in 1946), purchased the land between Esplanade Avenue and Bayou St. John near City Park in 1905 and built the Sacred Heart Orphan Asylum here. She stayed in the Pitot House, which was on her property until she gave it to the city during construction of the orphanage. In 1959 the institution was converted to a girls' high school in St. Cabrini's name. Her bedroom has been preserved as it was when she lived here, filled with personal effects and maintained as a shrine. Tours of her room and Sacred Heart Chapel are available by appointment. ⊠ *1400 Moss St., Bayou St. John* ☎ *504/483–8690* ⊕ *www. cabrinihigh.com/saint-frances-cabrini-shrine.*

Edgar Degas House Museum, Courtyard and Inn. Impressionist Edgar Degas, whose Creole mother and grandmother were born in New Orleans, stayed with his Musson cousins in this house during an 1872 visit to New Orleans, producing 18 paintings and 4 drawings while here. "This is a new style of painting," Degas wrote in one of the five letters he sent from New Orleans, saying the breakthrough he experienced here led to "better art." Today, this museum house and bed-and-breakfast offers public tours given by Degas's great-grandnieces, which include a viewing of an award-winning film on Degas's family and their sojourn in New Orleans and a walk through the historic neighborhood centered on the details in the artist's letters. Feel free to drop by for a look if you're in the vicinity, but check the website or call ahead for event dates or to make an appointment for a full tour. ⊠ *2306 Esplanade Ave., Bayou St. John* ☎ *504/821–5009* ⊕ *www.degashouse.com* ✉ *$29; discounts for children, seniors, and military* ☉ *Tours at 10:30 and 1:30 by reservation.*

Fair Grounds Race Course and Slots. The third-oldest racetrack in the country sits just off Esplanade Avenue, among the houses of Bayou St. John. The newly renovated facility is modern and comfortable throughout, complete with clubhouse restaurant, grandstand café, and concession-snack bars. A slots facility was added in 2008, and the popular Starlight Racing series, held Friday nights, features live music, DJs, food trucks, a beer garden, and jockey-costumed go-go dancers. The grounds are also home to the annual ⇨ *New Orleans Jazz and Heritage Festival.* For the clubhouse, be sure to make reservations and be aware that proper attire is required (collared shirts, closed shoes, no shorts). ⊠ *1751 Gentilly Blvd., Bayou St. John* ☎ *504/943–2200 for box and restaurant reservations, 504/944–5515 for general information* ⊕ *www.fairgroundsracecourse.com* ✉ *Grandstand free, clubhouse $10* ☉ *Thanksgiving–Mar., check website for days and times.*

Luling Mansion. Also called the "Jockey's Mansion," this massive, three-story Italianate mansion is a neighborhood landmark (and now a popular setting for Hollywood film crews). Designed by prominent New Orleans architect James Gallier Jr., it was built in 1865 for Florence A. Luling, whose family had made a fortune selling turpentine to Union soldiers when they occupied New Orleans during the Civil War. When the Louisiana Jockey Club took over the Creole Race Course (now the Fair Grounds) in 1871, it purchased the mansion and for the next 20-odd years used it as a clubhouse. It is not open to the public. ⊠ *1436–1438 Leda St., Bayou St. John.*

8

WHERE TO EAT

Updated by
Alexis Korman

New Orleanians are obsessed with food. Over lunch they're likely talking about dinner. Ask where to get the best gumbo, and you'll spark a heated debate among city natives.

Everyone, no matter what neighborhood they're from or what they do for a living, wants a plate of red beans and rice on Monday, has a favorite spot for a roast beef po'boy, and holds strong opinions about the proper flavor for a shaved ice "sno-ball."

The menus of New Orleans's restaurants reflect the many cultures that have contributed to this always-simmering culinary gumbo pot over the last three centuries. It's easy to find French, African, Spanish, German, Italian, and Caribbean influences—and increasingly Asian and Latin American as well. The speckled trout amandine at Antoine's could have been on the menu when the French Creole institution opened in 1840. Across the Mississippi River on the West Bank, Tan Dinh serves fragrant bowls of pho soup that remind New Orleans's large Vietnamese population of the home they left in the 1970s. And at MiLa, husband-and-wife team Slade Rushing and Allison Vines-Rushing apply the cutting-edge culinary techniques they learned in New York City to the dishes they grew up eating in Mississippi and Louisiana.

For years New Orleans paid little attention to food trends from the East and West coasts. Recently, however, the city has taken more notice of the "latest things." In Orleans Parish you'll now find gastropubs, gourmet burgers, and numerous small-plate specialists. In a town where people track the crawfish season as closely as the pennant race, no one has to preach the virtues of eating seasonally. New Orleans is still one of the most exciting places in America to eat. There's no danger that will change.

PLANNING

RESERVATIONS

Most restaurants in New Orleans accept reservations, and many popular places are booked quickly, especially on weekend nights. Reservations are always a good idea: we mention them only when they're essential or not accepted. Reserving several weeks ahead is not too far in advance for trips during Mardi Gras, French Quarter Fest, Jazz Fest, and other special events.

WHAT TO WEAR

Unless otherwise noted, restaurants listed in this book allow casual dress. Reviews mention dress only when men are required to wear a jacket or tie. In a luxury restaurant or in one of the old-line, conservative Creole places, dress appropriately.

TIPPING

The standard for tipping in New Orleans is no different from that in the rest of the country—at least 15% or 20%. Sales tax for restaurants is 9.75%, which means that calculating the tip by doubling the tax is a widespread practice.

PRICES

Meals in the city's more upscale restaurants cost about what you'd expect to pay in other U.S. cities. Bargains are found in the more casual restaurants, where a simple lunch or dinner can frequently be had for less than $25. However, even the more expensive restaurants offer fixed-price menus of three or four courses for substantially less than what an à la carte meal costs. Serving sizes are more than generous—some would say unmanageable for the average eater—so many diners order two appetizers rather than a starter and a main course, which can make ordering dessert more practical. Some restaurants offer small- or large-plate options.

Prices in the reviews are the average cost of a main course at dinner or, if dinner is not served, at lunch.

USING THE MAPS

Throughout the chapter, you'll see mapping symbols and coordinates (✛ 3:F2) at the end of each review. Maps are located within the chapter. The first number after the ✛ symbol indicates the map number. Following that is the property's coordinate on the map grid.

8

RESTAURANT REVIEWS

Listed alphabetically within neighborhood.

THE FRENCH QUARTER

In the city's oldest neighborhood grand restaurants that opened before the Civil War sit around the corner from contemporary, cutting-edge destinations. The Quarter, as locals call it, is a living neighborhood, and though it's packed with tourists, you'll certainly bump into residents grabbing a cup of coffee or tucking into a po'boy for lunch.

$
SEAFOOD
FAMILY
Fodor'sChoice
★

✕ **Acme Oyster House.** A rough-edge classic in every way, this no-nonsense eatery at the entrance to the French Quarter is a prime source for cool and salty raw Gulf oysters; legendary shrimp, oyster, and roast-beef po'boys; and tender, expertly seasoned red beans and rice. Even locals can't resist, although most opt for the less crowded, if less charming, suburban branches (there's one in Metairie). Expect lengthy lines here in the French Quarter, often a half-block long—trust us, though, it's worth it. Crowds lighten in the late afternoon, making Acme a perfect respite for a mid-afternoon snack of a dozen on the half shell washed

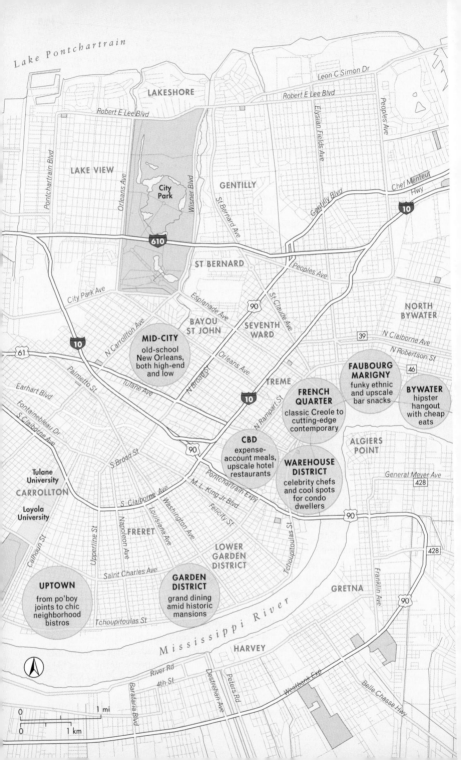

Lake Pontchartrain

LAKESHORE

Leon C Simon Dr

Robert E Lee Blvd

Robert E Lee Blvd

LAKE VIEW

City Park

GENTILLY

Chef Menteur Hwy

610

ST BERNARD

Peoples Ave

10

City Park Ave

Esplanade Ave

90

NORTH BYWATER

BAYOU ST JOHN

SEVENTH WARD

39

N Claiborne Ave

N Robertson St

MID-CITY
old-school New Orleans, both high-end and low

61

10

TREME

10

FRENCH QUARTER
classic Creole to cutting-edge contemporary

FAUBOURG MARIGNY
funky ethnic and upscale bar snacks

46

BYWATER
hipster hangout with cheap eats

CBD
expense-account meals, upscale hotel restaurants

ALGIERS POINT

90

WAREHOUSE DISTRICT
celebrity chefs and cool spots for condo dwellers

General Meyer Ave

428

Earhart Blvd

Tulane University

CARROLLTON

Loyola University

FRERET

LOWER GARDEN DISTRICT

90

428

UPTOWN
from po'boy joints to chic neighborhood bistros

GARDEN DISTRICT
grand dining amid historic mansions

GRETNA

Franklin Ave

90

Tchoupitoulas St

Mississippi River

HARVEY

River Rd

4th St

Westbank Expy

Belle Chasse Hwy

0   1 mi

0   1 km

down with an Abita beer. ⑤ *Average main: $12* ⊠ *724 Iberville St., French Quarter* ☎ *504/522–5973* ⊕ *www.acmeoyster.com* ⌖ *Reservations not accepted* ✚ *1:D3.*

$$$$ ✕ **Antoine's.** Though some people believe Antoine's heyday passed before
CREOLE the turn of the 20th century, others wouldn't leave New Orleans without at least one order of the original oysters Rockefeller—baked oysters topped with a parsley-based sauce and bread crumbs. Other notables on the bilingual menu include *pommes de terre soufflées* (fried potato puffs), pompano *en papillote* (baked in parchment paper), and baked Alaska. Tourists are generally shown to the front room, but walking through the grand labyrinth is a must. Be prepared for lackluster service. A jacket is preferred, but casually dressed diners can order most of the classic menu at the adjoining Hermes Bar. ⑤ *Average main: $36* ⊠ *713 St. Louis St., French Quarter* ☎ *504/581–4422* ⊕ *www.antoines.com* ⌖ *Reservations essential* ☾ *No dinner Sun.* ✚ *1:C3.*

$$$ ✕ **Arnaud's.** This grande dame of classic Creole restaurants still sparkles.
CREOLE In the main dining room, ornate etched glass reflects light from charming old chandeliers while the late founder, Arnaud Cazenave, gazes from an oil portrait. The adjoining jazz bistro offers the same food but is a more casual and music-filled dining experience. The ambitious menu includes classic dishes as well as more contemporary ones. Always reliable are Shrimp Arnaud (cold shrimp in a superb rémoulade), Oysters Bienville, Petit Filet Lafitte, and praline crepes. Jackets are requested in the main dining room. Check out the Mardi Gras museum upstairs. ⑤ *Average main: $35* ⊠ *813 Bienville St., French Quarter* ☎ *504/523–5433* ⊕ *www.arnaudsrestaurant.com* ⌖ *Reservations essential* ☾ *No lunch Mon.–Sat.* ✚ *1:D3.*

$$$ ✕ **Bayona.** "New World" is the label Louisiana native Susan Spicer applies
MODERN to her cooking style, and resulting delicious dishes include the goat cheese
AMERICAN crouton with mushrooms in madeira cream, a Bayona specialty, or the
Fodor's Choice Caribbean pumpkin soup with coconut. A legendary favorite at lunch is
★ the sandwich of smoked duck, cashew peanut butter, and pepper jelly. The imaginative dishes on the constantly changing menu are served in an early-19th-century Creole cottage that glows with flower arrangements, elegant photographs, and trompe-l'oeil murals suggesting Mediterranean landscapes. Don't skip the sweets, like a chocolate-bourbon panna cotta or mango cheesecake flan with pistacchio crust. ⑤ *Average main: $28* ⊠ *430 Dauphine St., French Quarter* ☎ *504/525–4455* ⊕ *www.bayona. com* ☾ *Closed Sun. No lunch Mon. and Tues.* ✚ *1:C3.*

$$ ✕ **Bourbon House.** On one of the French Quarter's busiest corners is
CREOLE Dickie Brennan's biggest and flashiest restaurant yet (he also owns Palace Café and Dickie Brennan's Steakhouse), and it's a solid hit with seafood aficionados. The raw bar is prime real estate, with its sterling oysters on the half shell, chilled seafood platters, and antique, decorative oyster plates, but the elegant main dining room is more appropriate for digging into the Creole catalog—oysters Bienville, catfish pecan, and Gulf fish on the "half shell" with lump crab meat. Take your frozen bourbon-milk punch in a to-go cup. Why? Because you can. ⑤ *Average main: $23* ⊠ *144 Bourbon St., French Quarter* ☎ *504/522–0111* ⊕ *www.bourbonhouse.com* ✚ *1:D3.*

8

BEST BETS FOR NEW ORLEANS DINING

With hundreds of restaurants to choose from, how will you decide where to eat? Fodor's writers and editors have selected their favorite restaurants by price, cuisine, and experience. In the first column, Fodor's Choice properties represent the "best of the best."

Fodor's Choice ★

Acme Oyster House, $, p. 125
August, $$$$, p. 140
Bayona, $$$, p. 127
Boucherie, $, p. 159
Café du Monde, $, p. 130
Cochon, $$, p. 149
Cochon Butcher, $, p. 149
Company Burger, $, p. 156
Coquette, $$$, p. 153
Domenica, $$, p. 147
Emeril's Delmonico, $$$, p. 153
Galatoire's, $$$$, p. 131
Herbsaint, $$$, p. 150
Patois, $$$, p. 158
Stella!, $$$$, p 137
Sucré, $, p. 153
Upperline, $$$, p. 159

BEST BY PRICE

$

Acme Oyster House, p. 125
Boucherie, p. 159
Café du Monde, p. 130
Casamento's, p. 154
Cochon Butcher, p. 149
Mahony's Po-Boy Shop, p. 157
Port of Call, p. 136

$$

Cochon, p. 149
Domenica, p. 147
Irene's Cuisine, p. 132
Rio Mar, p. 152

$$$

Bayona, p. 127
Commander's Palace, p. 152
Coquette, p. 153
Emeril's Delmonico, p. 153
Herbsaint, p. 150
Patois, p. 158
Upperline, p. 159

$$$$

Antoine's, p. 127
August, p. 140
Broussard's, p. 130
Galatoire's, p. 131
Stella!, p. 137

BEST BY CUISINE

AMERICAN

Emeril's, $$$, p. 150
Iris, $$$, p. 132

ASIAN

Chiba, $$, p. 154
Lucky Rooster, $$, p. 147
Sukho Thai, $$, p. 138

CAJUN

Bon Ton Café, $$$, p. 140
Cochon, $$, p. 149
K-Paul's Louisiana Kitchen, $$$, p. 133

CREOLE

Arnaud's, $$$, p. 127
Brigtsen's, $$$, p. 159
Commander's Palace, $$$, p. 152
Emeril's Delmonico, $$$, p. 153
Galatoire's, $$$$, p. 131
Upperline, $$$, p. 159

FRENCH

Café Degas, $, p. 160
La Crêpe Nanou, $$, p. 157

ITALIAN

A Mano, $$, p. TK
Domenica, $$, p. 147
Irene's Cuisine, $$, p. 132

SEAFOOD

Acme Oyster House, $, p. 125
Borgne, $$, p. 140
Casamento's, $, p. 154
GW Fins, $$$, p. 131
Pêche Seafood Grill, $$$, p. 150

BEST BY EXPERIENCE

BRUNCH

Atchafalaya, $$,
p. 154

Commander's Palace,
$$$, p. 152

Mr. B's Bistro, $$$,
p. 134

Palace Café, $$, p. 134

Stanley, $, p. 137

Celebrity Chefs

August (John Besh),
$$$$, p. 140

Emeril's (Emeril
Lagasse), $$$, p. 150

Herbsaint (Donald
Link), $$$, p. 150

K-Paul's (Paul
Prudhomme), $$$,
p. 133

R'Evolution (Rick
Tramonto), $$$, p. 136

CELEBRITY SPOTTING

August, $$$$, p. 140

Cochon, $$, p. 149

Lilette, $$$, p. 157

Stella!, $$$$, p. 137

CHILD-FRIENDLY

Acme Oyster House,
$, p. 125

American Sector, $$,
p. 148

Angelo Brocato's, $,
p. 160

Johnny's Po-Boys, $,
p. 133

Port of Call, $, p. 136

HISTORICAL

Antoine's, $$$$, p. 127

Arnaud's, $$$, p. 127

Galatoire's, $$$$,
p. 131

HOTEL RESTAURANTS

Borgne, $$, p. 140

Domenica, $$, p. 147

Grill Room, $$$$,
p. 147

MiLa, $$$, p. 148

LATE NIGHT

Café du Monde, $,
p. 130

Morning Call, $, p. 161

Root, $$$, p. 152

LATE-NIGHT DINING

Cleo's Mediterranean
Cuisine & Grocery, $,
p. 140

Port of Call, $, p. 136

Remoulade, $, p. 136

LIVELY SCENE

Clancy's, $$$, p. 156

Cochon, $$, p. 149

Domenica, $$, p. 147

Galatoire's, $$$$,
p. 131

Jacques-Imo's Cafe,
$$, p. 160

LOCAL FAVORITES

Bon Ton Café, $$$,
p. 140

Clancy's, $$$, p. 156

Gautreau's, $$$,
p. 156

Irene's Cuisine, $$,
p. 132

Patois, $$$, p. 158

MEATLOVERS

Cochon, $$, p. 149

Emeril's Delmonico,
$$$, p. 153

La Boca, $$$, p. 150

Toups' Meatery, $$,
p. 162

MOST ROMANTIC

Bayona, $$$, p. 127

Commander's Palace,
$$$, p. 152

Coquette, $$$, p. 153

Gautreau's, $$$,
p. 156

Iris, $$$, p. 132

Martinique Bistro, $$,
p. 158

Stella!, $$$$, p. 137

OFF THE BEATEN PATH

Elizabeth's, $, p. 139

Rue 127, $$, p. 162

OYSTER BARS

Acme Oyster House,
$, p. 125

Bourbon House, $$,
p. 127

Casamento's, $, p. 154

Grand Isle, $$, p. 147

Pascal's Manale, $$,
p. 158

PO'BOYS

Johnny's Po-Boys, $,
p. 133

Mahony's Po-Boy
Shop, $, p. 157

Parkway Bakery &
Tavern, $, p. 161

VEGGIE FRIENDLY

Carmo, $, p. 148

Green Goddess, $$,
p. 131

MiLa, $$$, p. 148

8

$$$$ ✕ **Broussard's.** If local restaurants were judged solely by the beauty
CREOLE of their courtyards, Broussard's would certainly be a standout—but
the food here is also outstanding. Expect dishes like blackened crab
cakes with Creole mustard sauce; pecan-crusted jumbo Gulf shrimp;
and slow-roasted half pheasant—you won't forget your meal anytime
soon. Fight the good fight for an outdoor table, and don't skip dessert, the lemon Napoleon is plate-licking good. ■TIP→ **A three-course**
Sunday brunch features live jazz. ⑤ *Average main: $40* ✉ *819 Conti*
St., French Quarter ☎ *504/581–3866* ⊕ *www.broussards.com* ⊙ *No*
lunch Mon.–Sat. ✚ *1:C3.*

$ ✕ **Café du Monde.** No visit to New Orleans is complete without a chic-
CAFÉ ory-laced café au lait paired with the addictive, sugar-dusted beignets
FAMILY at this venerable institution. The tables under the green-and-white-
Fodor'sChoice striped awning are jammed with locals and tourists at almost every
★ hour. ■TIP→ **If there's a wait, head around back to the takeout win-**
dow, get your coffee and beignets to go, and enjoy them overlooking
the river right next door or in Jackson Square. The most magical time
to go is just before dawn, before the bustle begins. You can hear the
birds in the crepe myrtles across the way. The metro-area satellites
(there's one in the CBD at the Port of New Orleans) lack the character
of the original. ⑤ *Average main: $3* ✉ *800 Decatur St., French Quar-*
ter ☎ *504/525–4544* ⊕ *www.cafedumonde.com* ⌂ *Reservations not*
accepted ▭ *No credit cards* ✚ *1:C4.*

$ ✕ **Central Grocery.** This old-fashioned grocery store creates authentic
DELI muffulettas, a gastronomic gift from the city's Italian immigrants. Made
FAMILY by filling nearly 10-inch round loaves of seeded bread with ham, salami,
provolone, Emmentaler cheese, and olive salad, the muffuletta is nearly
as popular locally as the po'boy. Central Grocery also sells a vegetarian version. The sandwiches are available in wholes and halves (they're
huge—unless you're starving, you'll do fine with a half). Eat at one of
the counters or get your sandwich to go and dine on a bench in Jackson
Square or the Moon Walk along the Mississippi riverfront. The Grocery
closes at 5 pm. ⑤ *Average main: $8* ✉ *923 Decatur St., French Quarter*
☎ *504/523–1620* ⊙ *Closed Sun. and Mon. No dinner* ✚ *1:C4.*

$ ✕ **Croissant d'Or Patisserie.** In a quiet corner of the French Quarter, you'll
CAFÉ have to look for the quaint Croissant d'Or Patisserie. Once you've found
it, you'll understand why locals and visitors return to the colorful pastry shop for excellent and authentic French croissants, pies, tarts, and
custards, as well as an imaginative selection of soups, salads, and sandwiches (don't miss the hot croissant sandwiches with creamy béchamel
sauce). You can get your goodies to go, but try to get a table during the
busy breakfast hours for great people-watching. During Carnival season
they bake a traditional French-style king cake filled with almond paste.
The cafe is open 6:30 am to 3 pm. ⑤ *Average main: $5* ✉ *617 Ursu-*
lines St., French Quarter ☎ *504/524–4663* ⊕ *www.croissantdornola.com*
⌂ *Reservations not accepted* ⊙ *Closed Tues. No dinner* ✚ *1:B4.*

$$$$ ✕ **Dickie Brennan's Steakhouse.** "Straightforward steaks with a New
STEAKHOUSE Orleans touch" are the words to live by at this clubby shrine to red
meat, the creation of a younger member of the Brennan family of res-
taurateurs who also runs Palace Café and the Bourbon House. Start

with stellar martinis in the dark cherrywood-paneled lounge, then head back to the cavernous dining room to dig into classic cuts of top-quality beef and seafood. The standard beefsteak treatment is light seasoning and a brush of Creole-seasoned butter, but other options include béarnaise, made-from-scratch Worcestershire sauce, and pepper-cream bourbon sauce. $ *Average main: $33* ⊠ *716 Iberville St., French Quarter* ☎ *504/522–2467* ⊕ *www.dickiebrennanssteakhouse. com* ☾ *No lunch Sat.–Thurs.* ✛ *1:D3.*

$$$$
CREOLE
Fodor'sChoice
★

✕ **Galatoire's.** With many of its recipes dating to 1905, Galatoire's epitomizes the old-style French-Creole bistro. Fried oysters and bacon en brochette are worth every calorie, and the brick-red rémoulade sauce sets a high standard. Other winners include veal chops with optional béarnaise sauce, and seafood-stuffed eggplant. Downstairs in the white-tableclothed, narrow dining room, lit with gleaming brass chandeliers, is where boisterous regulars congregate and make for excellent entertainment; you can only reserve a table in the renovated upstairs rooms. Friday lunch starts early and continues well into the evening. Shorts and T-shirts are never allowed; a jacket is required for dinner and all day Sunday. ■TIP➔ **If the lines get too long, head to Galatoire's 33 Bar & Steak, which opened next door in 2013. It offers classic cuts and cocktails in a similarly adorned space.** $ *Average main: $30* ⊠ *209 Bourbon St., French Quarter* ☎ *504/525–2021* ⊕ *www. galatoires.com* ☾ *Closed Mon.* ✛ *1:D3.*

$$
ECLECTIC

✕ **The Green Goddess.** At this cozy (read: small) restaurant in the heart of the French Quarter diners are wowed by the inventive and globally inspired cuisine, though the service is a bit eclectic, too. Menus change regularly, but may feature apple cheddar French toast, and duck confit salad for lunch, or a bacon sundae with pecan-praline ice cream for dessert. The staff weaves through the tight space with the grace of gymnasts, keeping the crowds both well fed and well lubricated with specialty cocktails. Tables are set outside when the weather's fine. $ *Average main: $15* ⊠ *307 Exchange Place, French Quarter* ☎ *504/301–3347* ⊕ *www.greengoddessrestaurant.com* ⌂ *Reservations not accepted* ☾ *Closed Mon. and Tues.* ✛ *1:D3.*

$
CREOLE
FAMILY

✕ **Gumbo Shop.** Even given a few modern touches—like the vegetarian gumbo offered daily—this place evokes a sense of old New Orleans. The menu is chock-full of regional culinary anchors: jambalaya, shrimp Creole, rémoulade sauce, red beans and rice, bread pudding, and seafood and chicken-and-sausage gumbos, all heavily flavored with tradition but easy on the wallet. The patina on the ancient painting covering one wall seems to deepen by the week, and the old tables and bentwood chairs have started to seem like museum pieces. Reservations are accepted only for groups of 10 or more. $ *Average main: $14* ⊠ *630 St. Peter St., French Quarter* ☎ *504/525–1486* ⊕ *www.gumboshop.com* ✛ *1:C4.*

$$$
SEAFOOD

✕ **GW Fins.** If you're looking for seafood, you won't be disappointed with GW Fins, which impresses with quality and variety—the bounty of fish species from around the world is among the menu's lures. Chef Tenney Flynn's menu changes daily, depending on what's fresh, but typical dishes have included luscious lobster dumplings, Hawaiian big-eye tuna, and sautéed rainbow trout with spinach, oysters, and shiitake mushrooms. For dessert, try the baked-to-order deep-dish apple pie. The spacious dining room's attractive modern decor and the enthusiastic service make this a relaxing refuge from the French Quarter's crowds. $ *Average main: $27* ⊠ *808 Bienville St., French Quarter* ☎ *504/581–3467* ⊕ *www.gwfins.com* ⊘ *No lunch* ✛ *1:D3.*

$
CREOLE
✕ **Hermes Bar.** The allure here is that you'll have your pick of the classic dishes that made Antoine's—founded in 1840—famous, without committing to a full-price meal in its austere dining room. Elegant bar snacks such as oysters Rockefeller, shrimp rémoulade, and fried eggplant sticks make just as grand a meal, with the added benefit of a front-row view of the Bourbon Street crowd. Expertly mixed old-school cocktails, such as the Sazerac and Ramos gin fizz, are a tradition here. Hermes is connected to Antoine's, but there is a separate entrance next door. It's open until midnight on weekends. ■TIP➔ **Daily happy hour deals are available from 4 to 7 pm.** $ *Average main: $11* ⊠ *713 St. Louis St., French Quarter* ☎ *504/581–4422* ⊕ *www.antoines.com* ⌨ *Reservations not accepted* ✛ *1:C3.*

$$
ITALIAN
FAMILY
✕ **Irene's Cuisine.** The walls here are festooned with enough snapshots, garlic braids, and crockery for at least two more restaurants, but it all just adds to the charm of this cozy Italian-Creole eatery. From Irene DiPietro's kitchen come succulent roasted chicken brushed with olive oil, rosemary, and garlic; delicious, velvety soups; and fresh shrimp, aggressively seasoned and grilled before they join linguine glistening with herbed olive oil. Waits here can stretch to the 60-minute mark during peak dinner hours, which is just enough time for a bottle of wine in the convivial little piano bar. The service is easily the friendliest in the French Quarter. $ *Average main: $20* ⊠ *539 St. Philip St., French Quarter* ☎ *504/529–8811* ⊘ *Closed Sun. No lunch* ✛ *1:B4.*

$$$
AMERICAN
✕ **Iris.** Chef Ian Schnoebelen's contemporary American cuisine has a West Coast attitude and a fascination with Asian flavors. The daily changing menu might include Vietnamese spicy tomato soup; duck confit and pork belly with peaches, plums, and pickled peppers; or steak frites with bone marrow butter. The restaurant has always employed some of the city's best bartenders, who are adept at creating drinks that pair with the complex cuisine. The thoughtful balance between meat and unexpected seafood entrées, the array of salads, and the generously portioned appetizers are all reasons to stop and smell the irises. $ *Average main: $26* ⊠ *Bienville House Hotel, 321 N. Peters St., French Quarter* ☎ *504/299–3944* ⊕ *www.irisneworleans.com* ⊘ *Closed Sun. and Tues. No lunch Sat.–Thurs.* ✛ *1:D3.*

$$$
ITALIAN
✕ **The Italian Barrel.** Verona-born chef Samantha Castagnetti turns out sumptuous, authentic Northern Italian pasta dishes, like fusilli with peas, shallots, and Italian prosciutto in an elegant white cream sauce along with meaty mains such as veal osso buco over decadent polenta at this tiny French Quarter eatery. This is the kind of place that turns first dates into lifelong affairs, with a space so intimate you'll feel like you're dining at nonna's house. The all-Italian wine list is surprisingly affordable, with many glasses at $10 or less. $ *Average main: $25* ⊠ *430 Barracks St., French Quarter* ☎ *504/569–0198* ⊕ *www.italianbarrel. com/* ⌨ *Reservations essential* ✛ *1:B5.*

Mardi Gras Sweet Spotlight: The King Cake

New Orleans is known for lots of local flavor, from pralines and po'boys to beignets and chicory coffee. But for a true taste of Mardi Gras, you can't beat a King Cake.

The origins of the King Cake go back to early-12th-century Europe, when a similar type of cake was baked to represent the arrival of the biblical Three Kings on the 12th day after Christmas. French settlers passed along the tradition in the late 19th century to the residents of New Orleans. Many years and iterations later, the King Cake lives on, and starting on January 6, 12 days after Christmas and the first day of Mardi Gras, through Fat Tuesday, the day before

Ash Wednesday, a party isn't complete without a King Cake at hand.

Traditional King Cakes are a ring-shaped, cinnamon-flavored brioche with purple, gold, and green icing for the colors of Mardi Gras. Nowadays King Cakes come in a variety of flavors and fillings, such as cream cheese, almond, praline, or chocolate. A small plastic toy baby, said to represent Baby Jesus, is hidden inside or on top of the cake. It's tradition that whoever gets the slice with the hidden baby must host the next Mardi Gras party or buy the King Cake for the next celebration.

You can find them all around the area in special bakeries and local grocery stores.

$ ✕ **Johnny's Po-boys.** Strangely enough, good po'boys are hard to find
DELI in the French Quarter. Established in 1950, Johnny's compensates for
FAMILY that scarcity with a cornucopia of overstuffed options, even though the quality can be inconsistent and the prices are somewhat inflated for the tourist trade. Inside the soft-crust French bread come the classic fillings, including lean boiled ham, well-done roast beef in garlicky gravy, and crisply fried oysters or shrimp. The chili may not cut it in San Antonio, but the red beans and rice are the real deal. The surroundings are rudimentary. Johnny's closes at 4:30 pm. ⑤ *Average main: $8* ✉ *511 St. Louis St., French Quarter* ☎ *504/524–8129* ⊕ *www.johnnyspoboys.com* ⋈ *Reservations not accepted* ▬ *No credit cards* ☽ *No dinner* ✛ *1:D4.*

$$$ ✕ **Kingfish.** Named after former Louisiana Governor Huey P. Long,
CREOLE who went by the nickname "Kingfish," this stylish French Quarter restaurant pays homage to the Jazz Age, with its pressed tin ceilings and suspendered bartenders (the excellent craft cocktail list is helmed by local legend Chris McMillian). Drinks do not disappoint, and as for food, expect Southern-inspired small plates with a local twist, like mirlitons (a type of squash) stuffed with corn bread dressing and smothered in an arugula and mushroom Alfredo sauce. ⑤ *Average main: $22* ✉ *337 Chartres St., French Quarter* ☎ *504/598–5005* ⊕ *www.cocktailbarneworleans.com* ✛ *1:D3.*

$$$ ✕ **K-Paul's Louisiana Kitchen.** At this comfortable French Quarter café
CAJUN with glossy wooden floors and exposed brick, chef Paul Prudhomme added "Cajun" to America's culinary vocabulary and started the craze for blackening, in which a fish fillet, coated with a thick layer of herbs

and spices, is seared until dark. More than three decades later, many still consider a visit to K-Paul's essential for his inventive gumbos, fried crawfish tails, blackened Gulf fish, and sweet potato–pecan pie. Prices are steep, but servings are generous. A casual "deli" menu of sandwiches and plate lunches is offered at midday. Although Prud-homme no longer works in the kitchen, he still often greets guests at the door. ⑤ *Average main: $30* ⊠ *416 Chartres St., French Quarter* ☎ *504/596–2530* ⊕ *www.kpauls.com* ☾ *Closed Sun. No lunch Mon.– Wed.* ✛ *1:D3.*

$$$
CREOLE
FAMILY
⤬ **Mr. B's Bistro.** Those who wonder if there really is a New Orleans res-taurant that can properly cater to both tourists and locals need look no farther than Mr. B's. Using as many Louisiana ingredients as possible, the chef offers a standout braised rabbit, an irresistible honey-ginger-glazed pork chop, and one of the best barbecued shrimp dishes in the city. First-timers must try the "Gumbo Ya-Ya," a rich chicken and sau-sage gumbo, and no meal here can end without the hot buttered pecan pie. Upscale yet accessible, Mr. B's is still on the map because of its just-right seasonings, its windows on the French Quarter world, and its dedication to service. ■ TIP➜ Don't miss Sunday brunch, featuring a live jazz trio and "eye openers" (also known as brunch cocktails). ⑤ *Average main: $26* ⊠ *201 Royal St., French Quarter* ☎ *504/523–2078* ⊕ *www. mrbsbistro.com* ✛ *1:D3.*

$$$
CREOLE
⤬ **Muriel's Jackson Square.** Among Jackson Square's many dining spots, Muriel's is easily the most ambitious, in both atmosphere and menu. In the large downstairs rooms, architectural knickknacks and artwork evoke the city's colorful past, while diners indulge in hearty updated renderings of old Creole favorites. The upstairs balcony has views of the square, with the occasional sounds of street music wafting in. The menu is diverse, ranging from a Gorgonzola-prosciutto tart appetizer to barbecue shrimp or pecan-crusted drum (a popular local fish also known as red drum) with Louisiana crawfish relish for main courses. Sunday brunch is accompanied by live jazz. ⑤ *Average main: $26* ⊠ *801 Chartres St., French Quarter* ☎ *504/568–1885* ⊕ *www. muriels.com* ✛ *1:C4.*

$$$
CREOLE
⤬ **Nola.** Fans of Emeril Lagasse will want to grab a seat at the food bar overlooking the open kitchen at this French Quarter restaurant. Freewheeling appetizers are among the big attractions, the standout being "Miss Hay's stuffed chicken wings" with hoisin dipping sauce. Entrées, such as the hickory-roasted duck with whiskey-caramel glaze and buttermilk-cornbread pudding, are heavy but delicious. Be warned: after a few bites of the buttermilk fried chicken with bourbon mashed sweet potatoes, you may start looking for prop-erty in New Orleans. Leave room in your tummy, and heart, for the banana-pudding layer cake. The space is arty and bright, but it can get pretty noisy. ⑤ *Average main: $28* ⊠ *534 St. Louis St., French Quar-ter* ☎ *504/522–6652* ⊕ *www.emerilsrestaurants.com* ⌲ *Reservations essential* ☾ *No lunch Mon.–Wed.* ✛ *1:D4.*

$$
CREOLE
FAMILY
⤬ **Palace Café.** Occupying what used to be New Orleans's oldest music store, this Dickie Brennan stalwart is a convivial spot to try some of the more imaginative contemporary Creole dishes, such as crabmeat

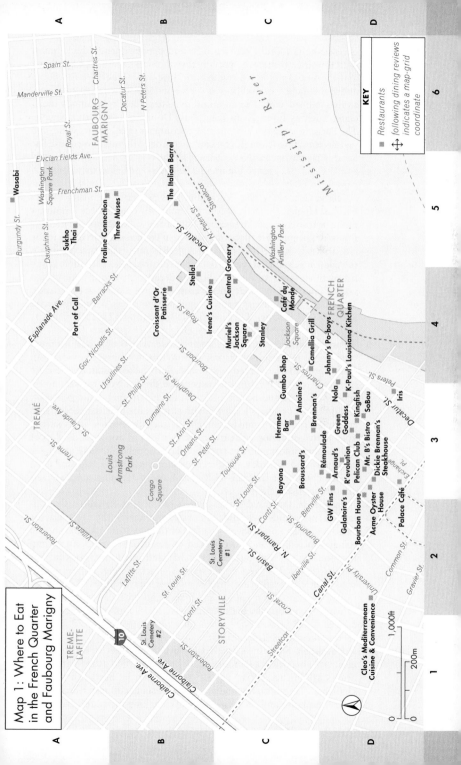

Map 1: Where to Eat in the French Quarter and Faubourg Marigny

KEY

■ Restaurants

⊕ following dining reviews indicates a map-grid coordinate

Mississippi River

FAUBOURG MARIGNY

FRENCH QUARTER

TREMÉ

TREMÉ-LAFITTE

STORYVILLE

Louis Armstrong Park

Congo Square

Washington Square Park

Washington Artillery Park

Jackson Square

St. Louis Cemetery #1

St. Louis Cemetery #2

Wasabi
Sukho Thai
Praline Connection
Three Muses
The Italian Barrel
Port of Call
Croissant d'Or Patisserie
Stella!
Irene's Cuisine
Central Grocery
Muriel's Jackson Square
Stanley
Café du Monde
Gumbo Shop
Camellia Grill
Johnny's Po-boys
K-Paul's Louisiana Kitchen
Hermes Bar
Antoine's
Brennan's
Nola
Green Goddess
Kingfish
SoBou
Iris
Bayona
Broussard's
Rémoulade
Arnaud's
R'evolution
Pelican Club
Mr. B's Bistro
Dickie Brennan's Steakhouse
GW Fins
Galatoire's
Bourbon House
Acme Oyster House
Palace Café
Cleo's Mediterranean Cuisine & Convenience

Spain St.
Manderville St.
Elysian Fields Ave.
Frenchman St.
Esplanade Ave.
Barracks St.
Gov. Nicholls St.
Ursulines St.
St. Philip St.
Dumaine St.
St. Ann St.
Orleans St.
St. Peter St.
Toulouse St.
St. Louis St.
Conti St.
Bienville St.
Iberville St.
Canal St.
Common St.
Gravier St.

Chartres St.
Decatur St.
N. Peters St.
Royal St.
Burgundy St.
Dauphine St.
Bourbon St.
Dauphine St.
Chartres St.
Decatur St.
Peters St.
Exchange Pl.
University Pl.
N. Rampart St.
Burgundy St.
Basin St.
Crozat St.
Iberville St.
Robertson St.
Villere St.
St. Claude Ave.
Treme St.
Claiborne Ave.
Robertson St.
St. Louis St.
Lafitte St.
Conti St.

Streetcar

10

1,000ft
200m

cheesecake, andouille-crusted fish, and pepper-crusted duck breast with foie gras. Desserts, especially the white-chocolate bread pudding and the house-made ice creams, are luscious. Drugstore-tile floors and stained cherrywood booths set the mood. The wraparound mezzanine is lined with a large mural depicting the city's famous musicians, such as Louis Armstrong, Fats Domino, and Aaron Neville. The Parisian-style sidewalk seating encourages small plates, wine, and people-watching (though you can also order full meals outside). The Sunday jazz brunch is New Orleans all the way. $ *Average main: $25* ⊠ *605 Canal St., French Quarter* ☎ *504/523–1661* ⊕ *www.palacecafe. com* ✛ *1:D3.*

$$$ ✕ **Pelican Club.** Sassy New York flourishes permeate the menu of chef
ECLECTIC   Richard Hughes's smartly decorated, eminently comfortable restaurant in the heart of the French Quarter, but there's still evidence of Hughes's Louisiana origins. He turns out what may be the best crab cakes in the city (infused with fresh shrimp) but with the surprise addition of pineapple-jalapeño chutney served over fried green tomatoes. The whole crispy fish with shrimp and diver scallops is decadent, while the Australian rack of lamb with rosemary-pesto crust is almost a spiritual experience. There is even a children's menu for budding gourmets. $ *Average main: $32* ⊠ *312 Exchange Pl., French Quarter* ☎ *504/523–1504* ⊕ *www. pelicanclub.com* ☽ *No lunch* ✛ *1:D3.*

$ ✕ **Port of Call.** Every night, no matter the weather, people wait for more
AMERICAN   than an hour outside Port of Call for fist-thick burgers made from
FAMILY   freshly ground beef, served with always fluffy baked potatoes (there are no fries here). For the definitive experience, drink a Neptune's Monsoon (Port of Call's mind-bending take on the Hurricane) while you wait, and order your potato "loaded" (with mushrooms, cheddar cheese, sour cream, butter, chives, and bacon bits). A juicy filet mignon is also available. In the afternoon and early evening, it's a fun stop for kids. Port of Call is open until midnight from Sunday through Thursday and 1 am on Friday and Saturday. $ *Average main: $14* ⊠ *838 Esplanade Ave., French Quarter* ☎ *504/523–0120* ⊕ *www.portofcallnola.com* ⌖ *Reservations not accepted* ✛ *1:A4.*

$ ✕ **Remoulade.** Operated by the owners of the posh Arnaud's, Remou-
CREOLE   lade is more laid-back and less pricey but serves the same Caesar
FAMILY   salad and pecan pie, as well as a few of the signature starters: shrimp Arnaud in rémoulade sauce, baked oysters, turtle soup, and shrimp bisque. The marble-counter oyster bar and mahogany cocktail bar date from the 1870s; a dozen oysters shucked here, paired with a cold beer, can easily turn into two dozen, maybe three. Tile floors, mirrors, a pressed-tin ceiling, and brass lights create an old-time New Orleans environment. It's open daily until 11 pm. $ *Average main: $13* ⊠ *309 Bourbon St., French Quarter* ☎ *504/523–0377* ⊕ *www. remoulade.com* ✛ *1:C3.*

$$$ ✕ **R'evolution.** Superstars rarely start over when they're on top—but
CREOLE   celebrity chef Rick Tramonto, best known for his avant-garde creations at Chicago's Tru, headed south when he needed a mid-life challenge. Tramonto hooked up with Louisiana culinary Renaissance man John Folse and the two set about remaking the state's creations,

combining Folse's deep knowledge of Cajun and Creole food with Tramonto's modern techniques and impeccable standards. The result is a lavish, multimillion dollar venue where the encyclopedic menu ranges from oven-roasted bone marrow and hog's head cheese to crawfish-stuffed flounder and a "triptych" of quail. $ *Average main: $33* ⊠ *Royal Sonesta Hotel, 777 Bienville St., French Quarter* ☎ *504/553–2277* ⊕ *www.revolutionnola.com* ⌂ *Reservations essential* ☾ *No lunch Sat.* ✛ *1:D3.*

$ × **SoBou.** The new venture from the Commander's Palace team puts
CREOLE   cocktails, beer, and wine front and center. The bar is nearly as big as the dining room. The cocktails are a mix of pre-Prohibition classics and crowd-pleasing originals. A row of self-service machines dispense wines by the taste or the glass, and a few coveted tables even have personal beer taps. The menu includes Southern-style snacks, such as grilled alligator sausage or cracklings with pimento cheese fondue. The chef grew up in Puerto Rico, so Latin flavors creep into many dishes, like the oyster tacos or shrimp and tasso pinchos. $ *Average main: $15* ⊠ *W Hotel French Quarter, 310 Chartres St., French Quarter* ☎ *504/552–4095* ⊕ *www.sobounola.com* ✛ *1:D3.*

$ × **Stanley.** Chefs across America are ditching the white tablecloths
CREOLE   and applying fine-dining chops to burgers, bar food, and comfort
FAMILY   fare. Here chef Scott Boswell of Stella! takes this track with the food of Louisiana. At breakfast, pancakes are covered in earthy Louisiana cane syrup and eggs Benedict are topped with Cajun boudin sausage. At lunch and dinner oyster po'boys get an extra zing from spicy rémoulade dressing and the roast beef po'boy is remade as Korean barbecue with sinus-clearing kimchi. Some grumble about prices too high for what is, at heart, New Orleans neighborhood fare, but this crisply decorated café sits on a coveted corner of Jackson Square, and that view is priceless. $ *Average main: $13* ⊠ *547 St. Ann St., French Quarter* ☎ *504/587–0093* ⊕ *www.stanleyrestaurant.com* ⌂ *Reservations not accepted* ✛ *1:C4.*

$$$$ × **Stella!.** Louisiana-born chef Scott Boswell has evolved into one of
MODERN   New Orleans's most innovative and daring culinarians, marrying
AMERICAN   wild creativity and an interest in Asian flavors with an obsession for
Fodor'sChoice precision. Dinner here now requires a full commitment to either a
★   four-course menu ($85) or a seven-course menu ($125). Dishes might include veal sweetbreads with andouille, spicy chili prawns, or butter-poached lobster. For a price, the truly decadent can add wine pairings, caviar, and truffles. A favorite of the well-heeled and famous, this is one of the city's best and most elegant fine-dining restaurants. ■TIP➜ **A vegetarian tasting menu is available on request.** $ *Average main: $85* ⊠ *Hôtel Provincial, 1032 Chartres St., French Quarter* ☎ *504/587–0091* ⊕ *www.restaurantstella.com* ⌂ *Reservations essential* ☾ *No lunch* ✛ *1:B4.*

FAUBOURG MARIGNY, BYWATER, AND TREMÉ

FAUBOURG MARIGNY

The carefully preserved and colorfully painted cottages and shotgun houses of the Faubourg Marigny are home to artists, hipsters, and gay couples. You'll find cool cafés, interesting ethnic options, and neighborhood hangouts with cheap eats. Most travelers make a beeline for Frenchmen Street, a three-block stretch of live music clubs and bars known as "Bourbon Street for locals."

$ ✕ **Praline Connection.** Down-home cooking in the southern Creole style
CREOLE   is the forte of this very Southern restaurant just a few blocks from the
FAMILY   French Quarter. The fried or stewed chicken, smothered pork chops, fried chicken livers, and collard greens are definitively done, and the soulful filé gumbo, peas with okra, and sweet-potato pie are welcome in a neighborhood otherwise in short supply of soul food. Add a congenial staff and a comfortable dining room, and the result is a fine place to enjoy a relaxing mealtime. The adjacent sweetshop holds such delights as sweet-potato cookies and Creole pralines. ■ TIP➜ **An outpost of the restaurant serves hungry travelers at Louis Armstrong International Airport.** ⑤ *Average main: $15* ⊠ *542 Frenchmen St., Faubourg Marigny* ☎ *504/943–3934* ⊕ *www.pralineconnection.com* ⊹ *1:A5.*

$$ ✕ **Sukho Thai.** Certainly the most extensive Thai restaurant in the area,
THAI   Sukho Thai fits snugly into its arty neighborhood with servers wearing all black and a hip, art-gallery approach to decorating. You can't go wrong with any of the curries, but the whole fried fish with three spicy chili sauces is a showstopper. Creative house-made desserts take the form of barely sweetened coconut custard and black-rice pudding. The most imaginative and extensive tea menu in the area compensates for the lack of a liquor license, although you can bring your own wine for a corkage fee. ■ TIP➜ **An Uptown location (4519 Magazine St.) has a larger menu, as well as Asian beer, cocktails, and sake.** ⑤ *Average main: $18* ⊠ *1913 Royal St., Faubourg Marigny* ☎ *504/948–9309* ⊕ *www. sukhothai-nola.com* ⊗ *Closed Mon.* ⊹ *1:A5.*

$ ✕ **Three Muses.** The most eclectic mix of music, food, and people can
ECLECTIC   be found on Frenchmen Street, and Three Muses captures everything that makes this vibrant stretch of the Faubourg Marigny worth seeking out. The small-plates menu by chef Daniel Esses traverses the globe, with standout delicacies including jerk duck tostones, crispy short ribs, yucca fries with Cuban mojo sauce, and Korean-style tofu bulgogi. The kitchen devotes special attention to the vegetarian offerings. There's live music most nights, too. With a no reservations policy and a tiny dining room, you'll almost always have to wait. ⑤ *Average main: $10* ⊠ *536 Frenchmen St., Faubourg Marigny* ☎ *504/252–4801* ⊕ *www.thethreemuses.com* ⌫ *Reservations not accepted* ⊗ *Closed Tues. No lunch* ⊹ *1:B5.*

BYWATER

Minutes from the French Quarter but still relatively untouched by tourists, edgy Bywater has recently seen an influx of new residents, new restaurants, and new vitality.

$
SOUTHERN
FAMILY

✕ Elizabeth's. "Real food, done real good" is the motto at Elizabeth's, where the vinyl-print tablecloths look just like grandma's and breakfast is the most important meal of the day. The menu offers everything from po'boys to a stellar seared duck. The fried-oyster po'boy is huge and irresistible. The staff is spunky, and so is the Bywater neighborhood clientele. Weekend brunch is served from 8 am to 2:30, and includes "lost bread" (also known as French toast), "red neck eggs" (fried green tomatoes with poached eggs and hollandaise), and a traditional country breakfast with a smoked pork chop. The praline bacon is a must. Breakfast is served every weekday as well, from 8 am to 2:30 pm, and has almost the same options. Reservations are accepted only for dinner. ⑤ *Average main: $15* ✉ *601 Gallier St., Bywater* ☎ *504/944–9272* ⊕ *www.elizabethsrestaurantnola.com* ⊗ *No dinner Sun.* ✛ *3:B5.*

$
SOUTHERN
FAMILY

✕ The Joint. You can't miss this bright yellow-striped building but it's the smell of the meat—pork shoulder, pork ribs, beef brisket, and chicken—cooking in the custom-made smoker that will draw you in. In a town not really known for great barbecue, the Joint is the exception, which is why it draws hungry patrons from far and wide. The meat is the thing, but don't skip the side dishes, which go above and beyond in concept and execution, particularly the sweet-and-spicy baked beans, and the crispy-on-the-outside mac and cheese. Pecan, key lime, and peanut butter pies are fitting country desserts. ⑤ *Average main: $12* ✉ *701 Mazant St., at Royal St., Bywater* ☎ *504/949–3232* ⊕ *www.alwayssmokin.com* ⌾ *Reservations not accepted* ⊗ *Closed Sun.* ✛ *3:B6.*

$$
ITALIAN

✕ Mariza. New Orleanians need no further evidence of the Bywater's gentrification: behold Mariza, the second restaurant from chef Ian Schnoebelen and general manager Laurie Casebonne (of Iris in the French Quarter). This eatery has it all: charm, comfort, and serious Italian eats at affordable prices, like the duck ragout papardelle with liver mousse, lamb meatballs with poached duck egg, and braised lamb belly atop creamy polenta. House-cured meats, homemade pastas, and excellent pizzas round out the list of menu attractions, and the exposed brick walls and high ceilings make for an airy, comfortable dining experience. ⑤ *Average main: $16* ✉ *Rice Mill Lofts, 2900 Chartres St., Bywater* ☎ *504/598–5700* ⊕ *www.marizaneworleans.com* ⌾ *Reservations not accepted* ⊗ *Closed Sun.–Mon., no lunch* ✛ *3:B5.*

$
SOUTHERN

✕ Maurepas Foods. This relative newcomer and self-proclaimed purveyor of "robust cuisine" already has the lived-in charm of a corner store with a hip edginess. The menu changes depending on what the farmers pulled up that week or the fishermen caught, and the eclectic dishes, like squash soup with hibiscus slaw, goat tacos with pickled green tomatoes, or a hot pot of shrimp, kimchi, and andouille sausage, are designed to please the Southern-born eater who has traveled the globe a few times. The Bywater neighborhood has exploded with new restaurants, but Maurepas still stands above them all. ⑤ *Average main: $13* ✉ *3200 Burgundy St., Bywater* ☎ *504/267–0072* ⊕ *maurepasfoods.com* ⊗ *Closed Wed.* ✛ *3:B5.*

8

CBD AND THE WAREHOUSE DISTRICT

The CBD, or Central Business District, is as much about pleasure as work. Amid the modern condos and high-rises, you'll discover many of New Orleans's most celebrated restaurants that keep up with national trends.

CBD

$$$$
MODERN
AMERICAN
Fodor'sChoice
★

✕ **August.** If the Gilded Age is long gone, someone forgot to tell the folks at August, where the main dining room shimmers with masses of chandelier prisms, thick brocade fabrics, and glossy woods. Service is anything but stuffy, however, and the food showcases chef John Besh's modern techniques. Nothing is mundane on the seasonally changing menu, which might include handmade gnocchi with blue crab and winter truffle or rabbit cassoulet with andouille sausage. Expect the unexpected—like pecan-smoked Two Run Farm's beef. The sommelier is happy to confer with you on the surprisingly affordable wine list. ⑤ *Average main: $35 ✉ 301 Tchoupitoulas St., CBD* ☎ *504/299–9777* ⊕ *www.restaurantaugust.com* 🍴 *Reservations essential* ⊘ *No lunch Sat.–Thurs.* ✛ *2:B4.*

$$$
CAJUN

✕ **Bon Ton Café.** The Bon Ton's opening in 1953 marked the first appearance of a significant Cajun restaurant in New Orleans, and the now-famed crawfish dishes, gumbo, jambalaya, and oyster omelet continue to draw fans. The bustle in the dining room peaks at lunchtime on weekdays, when businesspeople from nearby offices come in droves for turtle soup, eggplant with a shrimp and crab étouffée, and the warm, sugary bread pudding. If you can sacrifice the afternoon for pleasure, try a Rum Ramsey cocktail. The veteran servers are knowledgeable and fleet-footed. ⑤ *Average main: $28 ✉ 401 Magazine St., CBD* ☎ *504/524–3386* ⊕ *www.thebontoncafe.com* ⊘ *Closed weekends* ✛ *2:B4.*

$$
SEAFOOD

✕ **Borgne.** It's a mystery why New Orleans doesn't have more restaurants like Borgne. Overseen by celebrity-chef John Besh and former Galatoire's chef Brian Landry, it takes rustic Louisiana seafood dishes and adds a touch of city sophistication. A seafood-stuffed flounder comes with Meyer lemon butter, and the Gulf fish in a bag is accompanied by onions, fennel, and crab fat. Named after Lake Borgne in eastern Louisiana, the restaurant honors that area's many Spanish settlers with paella, empanadas, and goat cheese a la plancha. The one off note is the decor, which feels like a museum cafeteria furnished with stiff chairs and undersized tables. ⑤ *Average main: $24 ✉ Hyatt Regency New Orleans, 601 Loyola Ave., CBD* ☎ *504/613–3860* ⊕ *www.borgnerestaurant.com* ✛ *2:B2.*

$
MIDDLE EASTERN

✕ **Cleo's Mediterranean Cuisine & Grocery.** Good things really do come in small packages, like the outstanding falafel you can order at the back of this unpretentious, pocket-sized Middle Eastern convenience store outfitted with a handful of tables and chairs. There are plenty of mouthwatering options for carnivores, like lamb kebabs and beef gyros, but the vegetarian sampler plate, with creamy hummus, smoky baba ghanoush, and fresh tabouleh is the must-order dish. Look for international grocery items, like pistachio cotton candy from Turkey. ■ TIP➜ **The kitchen is open 24/7, making it an ideal spot to grab a pita after partying.** ⑤ *Average main: $10 ✉ 165 University Pl., CBD* ☎ *504/522–4504* ⊕ *www.facebook.com/CleosNOLA* ✛ *2:A3.*

Continued on page 147

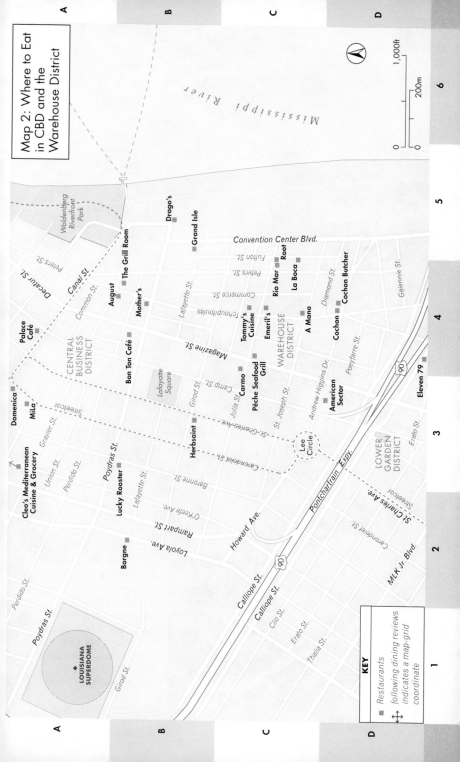

Map 2: Where to Eat in CBD and the Warehouse District

Mississippi River

Waldenberg Riverfront Park

CENTRAL BUSINESS DISTRICT

- Cleo's Mediterranean Cuisine & Grocery
- Borgne
- Lucky Rooster
- Domenica
- Mila
- Palace Café
- Herbsaint
- Bon Ton Café
- August
- Mother's
- The Grill Room
- Drago's
- Grand Isle

WAREHOUSE DISTRICT

- Carmo
- Pêche Seafood Grill
- Tommy's Cuisine
- Emeril's
- A Mano
- American Sector
- Cochon
- Cochon Butcher
- Rio Mar
- La Boca
- Root
- Eleven 79

LOWER GARDEN DISTRICT

Lafayette Square

Lee Circle

LOUISIANA SUPERDOME

Convention Center Blvd.

Fulton St.

Peters St.

Commerce St.

Magazine St.

Tchoupitoulas

Lafayette St.

Canal St.

Common St.

Decatur St.

Peters St.

Gravier St.

Union St.

Perdido St.

Poydras St.

Poydras St.

Perdido St.

Girod St.

Loyola Ave.

Rampart St.

O'Keefe Ave.

Baronne St.

Carondelet St.

St. Charles Ave. Streetcar

Camp St.

Girod St.

Julia St.

St. Joseph St.

Andrew Higgins Dr.

Diamond St.

Peeyfarre St.

Gaienne St.

Howard Ave.

Pontchartrain Expy.

Calliope St.

Clio St.

Erato St.

Thalia St.

MLK Jr. Blvd.

Carondelet St.

St. Charles Ave. Streetcar

90

Lafayette Ave.

1,000ft
200m

KEY

- ■ Restaurants
  following dining reviews indicates a map-grid coordinate

DID YOU KNOW?

Crawfish is a staple in the Louisiana diet. It is found in a number of Cajun and Creole dishes, but it is most commonly boiled and served with potatoes and corn on the cob.

THE CUISINE OF NEW ORLEANS

From humble po' boy shops to white-tablecloth temples of classic Creole cuisine, food is a major reason to visit the Crescent City. People in New Orleans love to eat, and discerning local customers support a multitude of options when it comes to dining. Innovative fine dining restaurants exist alongside more modest eateries serving red beans and rice and boiled crawfish. Whatever the cost, it's hard to find a bad meal in this culinary town.

Given New Orleans's location near the mouth of the Mississippi River and the Gulf of Mexico, it was perhaps inevitable that an outstanding food culture would develop in the area. Farmers grow an abundance of produce—locally prized Creole tomato, okra, strawberries, and chayote (locally know as mirliton)—in the fertile delta soil that surroundes the city and fishermen harvest a wealth of seafood like black drum, speckled trout, shrimp, blue crabs, oysters, and crawfish from the marshes and open waters of the Gulf of Mexico.

As a port city, New Orleans has always been something of a melting pot. The city's native Creole cuisine is a mixture of French, African, and Spanish influences; immigration from Italy and Sicily in the 19th century gave New Orleans its own version of Italian cooking. Plus, there is a lingering influence from an influx of German settlers; more recently, immigrants from Vietnam have brought their culinary traditions to New Orleans and the surrounding parishes.

Creole food is the cooking of the city, while Cajun food evolved from the rural traditions of the plains and swamps of southwest Louisiana. The Acadians, a people of French heritage, arrived in Louisiana after being expelled by the British from parts of Canada (present-day Nova Scotia and surrounding areas) in the 18th century. Like the cuisine of rural France, Cajun cooking is hearty and employs similar cooking techniques such as slow braising and the addition of a roux (a combination of flour and fat), but it features local seafood, game, and produce.

By Robert D. Peyton

(top) A café au lait and beignets served at the renowned Café du Monde.

CLASSIC CREOLE AND CAJUN FOOD

Jambalaya

Oysters Rockefeller

BEIGNETS

Beignets are fried pillows of dough, generally served with powdered sugar (and lots of it!) and steaming cups of café au lait made with New Orleans-style chicory coffee. Beignets are typically consumed for breakfast or for dessert.

ÉTOUFFÉE

Étouffée means "smothered" in French, and the dish can be made with shrimp; chicken; and, most typically, crawfish. The dish is Cajun in origin, but there are Creole versions, as well. As with many Cajun dishes, it starts with a light roux, to which chopped onion, celery, and bell pepper (called "the trinity" in South Louisiana) is added. Some versions contain tomatoes, and the sauce is finished with stock and meat, poultry, or seafood. Crawfish étouffée is best during crawfish season (March–June), but you can find it year-round.

MUFFALETTA

The Muffaletta sandwich was invented at the Central Grocery (923 Decatur St.) by Salvatore Lupo and became popular enough that it can now be found all over town. The sandwich is served on a round loaf that's stuffed with salami, ham, pro-

volone, and a local condiment called olive salad, which typically consists of olives, celery, and pickled peppers. Some restaurants heat the sandwich, but many purists consider that heresy.

OYSTERS ROCKEFELLER

Oysters Rockefeller was invented at Antoine's, the oldest continuously operated restaurant in the United States. The dish, to this day, consists of oysters baked on the half-shell with an anise-scented puree of herbs and bread crumbs. Although the recipe Antoine's uses remains a closely guarded secret, the dish typically contains parsley, chervil, tarragon, and celery leaves. This is a dish that should be ordered while oysters are at their best, between September and April.

JAMBALAYA

Jambalaya is a hearty dish that combines rice with meat, poultry, and/or seafood with a result akin to the Spanish paella. In New Orleans, the dish usually includes tomatoes, giving it a reddish hue. Ingredients can include chicken, andouille, pork, shrimp, crawfish, duck, and even alligator. The requisite "trinity" of onion, celery, and

Shrimp gumbo

Pralines

bell pepper is cooked with or without meat or seafood, and then the rice is added with stock, and the dish is covered to finish.

GUMBO

Gumbo is yet another dish that has both Cajun and Creole variations. It is a thick soup or thin stew that can include almost any meat, poultry, sausage, or seafood found in South Louisiana. Cajuns generally cook the roux for gumbo until it is very dark, giving the dish a nutty flavor, while in New Orleans a lighter roux is employed, and okra and tomatoes are often included. A common ingredient, filé powder (dried, ground sassafras leaves), used as a thickening agent and seasoning, is considered by some as a necessary ingredient for making Cajun and Creole gumbo.

BOUDIN

Boudin is a Cajun sausage that combines rice with pork or other ingredients; some of the best can be found just outside of the city at rural gas stations, where it's frequently eaten as a roadside snack. In restaurants, the stuffing is sometimes removed from its casing, formed into balls, and fried.

TASSO

Tasso is a cured and smoked pork product that is one of the treasures of Acadian charcuterie. It is a highly spiced preparation that is used as a flavor base in many local recipes such as gumbo and red beans. Though it is sometimes called tasso ham, the meat used to prepare it is from the shoulder rather than the leg.

ANDOUILLE

Andouille is a smoked sausage made with both ground and cubed pork and flavored with garlic. It is a variation of a French sausage that in the Cajun interpretation is more highly spiced and aggressively flavored. It appears as an ingredient in many South Louisiana dishes, including gumbo and jambalaya.

PRALINES

Pralines are a sweet patty-shaped Creole treats made with caramelized sugar, cream, butter, and pecans—the latter often sourced from trees that grow locally in great abundance. Modern interpretations include chocolate, peanut butter, and bourbon pralines. Be sure to pronounce it like the locals: "PRAH-line," not "PRAY-line."

TASTEMAKERS AND THEIR RESTAURANTS

DONALD LINK

Donald Link was raised in Acadia Parish, and the simple, hearty food he grew up eating influences his cooking. The menu at Link's first restaurant, Herbsaint, is a mix of European and South Louisiana cooking. Link's Cajun heritage is most apparent at one of the city's best and most innovative Cajun restaurants, Cochon, which he operates with chef Steven Stryjewski. Around the corner from Cochon, Link's more casual restaurant, Cochon Butcher, offers small plates, and housemade charcuterie. His empire continues to expand with new restaurants Pêche Seafood Grill and the event space Calcasieu.

Donald Link

EMERIL LAGASSE

Emeril Lagasse has done more to bring the cuisine of New Orleans to the attention of modern diners than any other individual. Though he no longer has quite the omnipresence in the media he once enjoyed, his restaurants in New Orleans—Emeril's, NOLA, and Delmonico—are consistently ranked among the best in the city by locals.

Emeril Lagasse

JOHN BESH

John Besh, a native of south Louisiana, has eight restaurants in New Orleans. August, his flagship, is a consistently rated top restaurant in New Orleans. Lüke, an Alsatian brasserie; the American Sector and the Soda Shop, both in the National WWII Museum; the Italian restaurant, Domenica; the French restaurant, La Provence; the steakhouse, Besh Steak, and the Spanish-influenced seafood destination Borgne round out his culinary dominance in town. Besh demonstrates his commitment to sourcing products locally by raising animals and growing produce for all of his operations.

John Besh

SUSAN SPICER

Susan Spicer came to prominence when she opened the intimate Bistro at Maison de Ville in 1986. Four years later, Spicer opened Bayona in a 200-year-old converted cottage on Dauphine Street in the French Quarter. Mediterranean, Asian, North African, Indian, and other cuisines influence Spicer's cooking both at Bayona and the more casual restaurant, Mondo, in the Lakeview neighborhood. Spicer has led the way for other female chefs in the Crescent City and like the other tastemakers identified here, she has received numerous awards.

Susan Spicer

$$ ✕**Domenica.** Local celebrity-chef John Besh and executive chef Alon
ITALIAN Shaya continue to wow diners, here with rustic Italian cooking, a rar-
Fodor'sChoice ity in New Orleans's culinary landscape. In the renovated Roosevelt
★ Hotel—a 19th-century landmark—Domenica departs from the hotel
lobby's historic, gilded decor and opts instead for sleek black walls
and chain-link curtains, warmed by jewel-box displays of house-cured
meats. Friendly and knowledgeable waiters happily help patrons with
lesser-known ingredients, but it doesn't take a lengthy explanation to
know that the fresh pastas and wood-fired pizzas are a must. $ *Aver-
age main: $24* ⊠ *Roosevelt New Orleans Hotel, 123 Baronne St., CBD*
☏ *504/648–6020* ⊕ *www.domenicarestaurant.com* ✛ *2:A3.*

$$ ✕**Drago's.** Since 1969 the Cvitanovich family restaurant has been a
ITALIAN fixture in Metairie, just a short drive from downtown New Orleans, so
FAMILY when it was revealed the family would open a second location inside the
Hilton Riverside hotel, locals started salivating and the word quickly
spread. ■TIP➔**The charbroiled oysters are the absolute must-order.**
After that you can branch out to authentic Italian pasta dishes, Maine
lobster, and fried seafood entrées. Families love the place—especially
because of the kids' menu—and the warm apple cobbler is the sweet stuff
legends are made of. $ *Average main: $26* ⊠ *Hilton New Orleans Riverside, 2 Poydras St., CBD* ☏ *504/584–3911* ⊕ *www.dragosrestaurant.
com* ⌂ *Reservations not accepted* ✛ *2:B5.*

$$ ✕**Grand Isle.** The rustic interior, reminiscent of 1920s and '30s Louisi-
SOUTHERN ana fish camps, is the perfect backdrop for shrimp gumbo; spicy boiled
shrimp; fresh Gulf fish; cold smoked-and-grilled tuna; and a lemon ice-
box pie that will make you fall in love with New Orleans all over again.
Except for freshwater catfish and Canadian mussels, all the seafood
comes from the Gulf of Mexico and often straight from the fishermen.
Produce and pork are also local. Near Harrah's Casino, Grand Isle is
generally packed, but it's worth the wait (which also gives you an excuse
to spend some time at the elegant mahogany bar). $ *Average main:
$18* ⊠ *575 Convention Center Blvd., CBD* ☏ *504/520–8530* ⊕ *www.
grandislerestaurant.com* ✛ *2:B5.*

$$$$ ✕**The Grill Room.** With its elegant table settings and canvases depicting
AMERICAN the lives of the British nobility, the Grill Room on the second floor of the
Windsor Court has always been a beacon of class and an elegant setting
for special occassions. The Cajun- and Creole-influenced menu might
include a sweet-potato soup with bacon panna cotta, roasted Gulf snap-
per, or foie gras with pickled huckleberries and house-smoked andouille
sausage. The wine cellar, with its extensive collection of vintage red
Bordeaux, remains awe-inspiring, so don't hesitate to ask the knowl-
edgeable staff for recommendations. $ *Average main: $36* ⊠ *Windsor
Court Hotel, 300 Gravier St., 2nd level, CBD* ☏ *504/523–6000* ⊕ *www.
grillroomneworleans.com* ⌂ *Reservations essential* ✛ *2:B4.*

$$ ✕**Lucky Rooster.** Menu categories like "Happy Endings" (desserts) and
ASIAN "Relaxing Times" (the expertly crafted spirits list) cue diners to expect
pan-Asian fare with a lighthearted twist at this trendy dining spot,
the brainchild of executive chef and owner Neal Swidler, whose restaurant consulting group also brought the city casual dining spots
Slice and Juan's Flying Burrito. Dishes to try include crispy shiitake

8

imperial rolls with tamarind-hoisin glaze, red ginger shrimp bao buns, and oversize fortune cookies complete with saucy messages (such as "Beyoncé is your spirit animal"), scrawled by in-house staff. ⑤ *Average main: $22 ☒ 515 Baronne St., CBD ☎ 504/529–5825 ⊕ www. luckyroosternola.com ⊗ Closed Sun. ✛ 2:B3.*

$$$
SOUTHERN

✕ **MiLa.** Chefs Slade Rushing and Allison Vines-Rushing, from Mississippi and Louisiana, respectively, merged the names and cuisines of their home states to produce MiLa. The restaurant defines a new Southern elegance with its comfy-chic atmosphere and its culinary tributes to each chef's childhood memories of Southern cooking. The results on the seasonally updated menu are dishes like oysters Rockefeller "deconstructed" and sweet tea–brined rotisserie duck. Much of the restaurant's produce comes from a farm in Mount Hermon, Louisiana. ⑤ *Average main: $30 ☒ Renaissance Pere Marquette Hotel, 817 Common St., CBD ☎ 504/412–2580 ⊕ www.milaneworleans. com ⊗ Closed Sun. No lunch Sat. ✛ 2:A3.*

$
CAFÉ

✕ **Mother's.** Tourists and locals line up for solid—if unspectacular—down-home eats at this island of blue-collar sincerity amid downtown's glittery hotels. Mother's dispenses baked ham and roast beef po'boys (ask for "debris" on the beef sandwich and the bread will be slathered with meat juices and shreds of meat), home-style biscuits and jambalaya, and chicken and sausage gumbo in a couple of bare-bones—yet charming—dining rooms. Breakfast service is a bit slow, but that doesn't seem to repel the hordes fighting for seats at peak mealtimes. Service is cafeteria style, with a counter or two augmenting the tables. ⑤ *Average main: $10 ☒ 401 Poydras St., CBD ☎ 504/523–9656 ⊕ www. mothersrestaurant.net ⊜ Reservations not accepted ✛ 2:B4.*

THE WAREHOUSE DISTRICT

Next to the CBD, in the sprawling Warehouse District, gallery hoppers and condo dwellers fuel up at trendy bistros and stylish casual eateries.

$$
AMERICAN
FAMILY

✕ **The American Sector.** Celebrity-chef John Besh has dazzled the culinary world with his prowess on the plate and his Southern-boy charm, but his most impressive feat might be this restaurant inside the National World War II Museum—worth visiting even if you skip the exhibits. The menu updates comfort fare like heirloom tomato soup served in a can or a sloppy Joe made from short ribs. This is also a fun spot for kids: the efficient staff wear period garb and children's meals are served in lunch boxes. Accompany your meal with a seasonal milk shake or, if you're of age, a well-made retro cocktail like a Pink Squirrel or Singapore Sling. ⑤ *Average main: $22 ☒ National World War II Museum, 945 Magazine St., Warehouse District ☎ 504/528–1940 ⊕ www.nationalww2museum.org/american-sector ✛ 2:D3.*

$
CARIBBEAN

✕ **Carmo.** Vegan, vegetarian, and gluten-free options abound at this self-proclaimed "tropical café," which playfully references the cuisines of Latin America, Southeast Asia, and the Caribbean. Fresh, local, and organic produce are used to create dishes like *acaraje*, a black-eyed pea fritter stuffed with *vatapa* (a cashew, peanut, and coconut paste) or the Rico sandwich, a breadless creation of grilled plantains, melted cheese, vegan meat, avocado, salsa fresca, and a tangy secret sauce. Try one of the unusual fresh fruit juices: options like *cupuaçu* (a nutrient packed fruit with flavors of pineapple, passion fruit, pear, banana, and chocolate), *acerola* (Amazon cherry), and *graviola* (also known as soursop, tastes like brown sugar and pears) are nearly impossible to find this side of the Amazon. $ *Average main: $12* ✉ *527 Julia St., Warehouse District* ☎ *504/875–4132* ⊕ *www.cafecarmo.com* ⊗ *Closed Sun., no dinner Mon.* ✛ *2:C3.*

$$
CAJUN
Fodor's Choice
★
✗**Cochon.** Chef-owned restaurants are common in New Orleans, but this one builds on owner Donald Link's family heritage as he, working with co-owner Stephen Stryjewski (who received a James Beard Award for his work here), prepares Cajun dishes he learned to cook at his grandfather's knee. The interior may be a bit too hip and noisy for some patrons, but the food makes up for it. The fried boudin with pickled peppers is a must—trust us on this one—then move on to black-eyed pea–and-pork gumbo, and a hearty Louisiana *cochon* (pork) with turnips, cracklings, and cabbage. Despite the pork-centric reputation, all the vegetable sides are excellent. $ *Average main: $20* ✉ *930 Tchoupitoulas St., Warehouse District* ☎ *504/588–2123* ⊕ *www.cochonrestaurant.com* ⟠ *Reservations essential* ⊗ *Closed Sun.* ✛ *2:D4.*

$
SOUTHERN
Fodor's Choice
★
✗**Cochon Butcher.** Around the corner from its big brother Cochon, Butcher packs its own Cajun punch with an upscale sandwich menu that dials up the flavor on local classics. With house-cured meats and olive salad, the muffuletta reveals exactly how delicious Creole-Italian can be, although the pork-belly sandwich also brings customers back. In addition to sandwiches, there are meaty small plates and a rotating selection of wines, beers, and well-made cocktails. There are a few tall tables for dining in, or you can get your sandwich to go. Before leaving, stock up on boudin, bacon pralines, and other to-go Cajun delicacies—all much better souvenirs than anything for sale on Bourbon Street. $ *Average main: $10* ✉ *930 Tchoupitoulas St., Warehouse District* ☎ *504/588–7675* ⊕ *www.cochonbutcher.com* ⟠ *Reservations not accepted* ⊗ *No dinner Sun.* ✛ *2:D4.*

$$$
ITALIAN
✗**Eleven 79.** If the Rat Pack boys were alive today, they'd ask for a corner table at this tiny, softly lit Italian eatery, where garlic rules and red wine is revered. Dean Martin music adds a soft ambience, while candlelit tables serve as the perfect platform for tender pastas bathed in perfectly seasoned sauces. The *panéed* (breaded) veal with asparagus, buffalo mozzarella, roasted red peppers, and lemon sauce is sublime, but make sure to check out the specials. Note that pasta dishes are available as half orders. Every dish is full of flavor; there is no such thing as a bad meal at Eleven 79. Only the bar is open on Mondays. $ *Average main: $30* ✉ *1179 Annunciation St., Warehouse District* ☎ *504/299–1179* ⊕ *www.eleven79.com* ⊗ *Closed Sun. No dinner Mon. No lunch Sat.–Wed.* ✛ *2:D4.*

8

$$$ ✕ **Emeril's.** Celebrity-chef Emeril Lagasse's urban-chic flagship res-
AMERICAN taurant is always jammed, so it's fortunate that the basket-weave-
patterned wood ceiling muffles much of the clatter and chatter. The
ambitious menu gives equal emphasis to Creole and modern American
cooking—try the andouille-crusted drum fish or the barbecue shrimp,
which is one one of the darkest, richest versions of that local specialty.
Desserts, such as the renowned banana cream pie, verge on the gargan-
tuan. Service is meticulous, and the wine list's depth and range mean
that you shouldn't hesitate to ask your server for advice. $ *Average
main: $30* ⊠ *800 Tchoupitoulas St., Warehouse District* ☏ *504/528–
9393* ⊕ *www.emerilsrestaurants.com* ⚱ *Reservations essential* ☉ *No
lunch Sat. and Sun.* ✛ *2:C4.*

$$$ ✕ **Herbsaint.** Chef Donald Link (also of Cochon, Cochon Butcher, and
SOUTHERN Pêche Seafood Grill) turns out food that sparkles with robust flavors
Fodor'sChoice and top-grade ingredients at this casually upscale restaurant. Small
★ plates and starters such as a daily gumbo, charcuterie, and house-made
pastas are mainstays. Don't overlook the rich and flavorful Louisiana
shrimp and fish ceviche. Also irresistible is the muscovy duck leg confit
with dirty rice and citrus gastrique. For dessert, banana brown-butter
tart will ensure return trips. The plates provide most of the color in the
lighthearted, often noisy, rooms. The wine list is expertly compiled and
reasonably priced. ◼ TIP➔ **The restaurant serves an abbreviated "bistro menu" between lunch and dinner.** $ *Average main: $27* ⊠ *701 St.
Charles Ave., Warehouse District* ☏ *504/524–4114* ⊕ *www.herbsaint.
com* ☉ *Closed Sun. No lunch Sat.* ✛ *2:B3.*

$$$ ✕ **La Boca.** Need a break from the bounties of the sea prevalent in New
LATIN AMERICAN Orleans restaurants? Book a table at this classic Argentine steakhouse.
While most steakhouses are clubby, masculine, and hard on the wal-
let, this Warehouse District eatery feels more like a party. The kitchen
coaxes flavor from less expensive cuts, like flank and hanger steaks.
Sides include empanadas, thick rounds of provolone grilled and sprin-
kled with oregano, and house-made pasta, a nod to Argentina's large
Italian population. After dinner at La Boca, you'll walk outside and be
surprised to discover that you're not in Buenos Aires. $ *Average main:
$27* ⊠ *857 Fulton St., Warehouse District* ☏ *504/525–8205* ⊕ *www.
labocasteaks.com* ☉ *Closed Sun. No lunch* ✛ *2:C4.*

$$$ ✕ **Pêche Seafood Grill.** The name implies fish, and that's what you'll find
SEAFOOD at this modern temple to seafood, the brainchild of nearby Cochon
proprietors Donald Link and Stephen Stryjewski. In addition to an airy,
modern space enhanced by exposed beams and a wood-burning grill,
the dining room has a fascinating history: the building was a former
mortuary that claims to have embalmed Confederate president Jefferson Davis on-site. If that doesn't give you something to talk about, the
crowd-satisfying fare will: there's head-on, whole grilled fish; smothered
catfish with pickled greens; and excellent non-fish options. The small
plates offer inventive options such as curried mussels, spicy ground
shrimp with noodles, and catfish with pickled greens. $ *Average main:
$28* ⊠ *800 Magazine St., Warehouse District* ☏ *504/522–1744* ⊕ *www.
pecherestaurant.com* ⚱ *Reservations essential* ☉ *Closed Sun.* ✛ *2:C4.*

CLOSE UP

Food Glossary

Barbecue shrimp. Shrimp baked in the shell in a blend of olive oil and butter, and seasoned with garlic and other herbs and spices.

Béarnaise. A sauce of egg yolk and butter with shallots, wine, and vinegar, used on meat and fish.

Boudin (pronounced boo-dan). A soft Cajun sausage, often spicy, made of pork, rice, and a bit of liver for seasoning.

Bouillabaisse (pronounced *booey-*yah-base). A stew of various fish and shellfish in a broth seasoned with saffron and other spices.

Boulette (pronounced *boo-*let). Minced, chopped, or pureed meat or fish shaped into balls and fried.

Café brûlot (pronounced broo-*loh*). Cinnamon, lemon, clove, orange, and sugar, steeped with strong coffee, then flambéed with brandy and served in special pedestaled cups.

Chicory coffee. The ground and roasted root of a European variety of chicory is added to ground coffee in varying proportions.

Crème brûlée. Literally meaning "burned cream," a custard with a brittle crust of browned sugar.

Dirty rice. In this cousin of jambalaya, bits of meat, such as giblets or sausage, and seasonings are added to white rice before cooking.

Dressed. A po'boy "dressed" contains lettuce, tomato, pickles, and mayonnaise or mustard.

Meunière (pronounced muhn-*yehr*). This method of preparing fish or soft-shell crab entails dusting it with seasoned flour, sautéing it in brown butter, and using the butter with lemon juice as a sauce.

Mirliton (pronounced merl-i-*tawn*). A pale-green member of the squash family, usually identified as a vegetable pear or chayote.

Oysters Bienville (pronounced byen-*veel*). Oysters lightly baked in the shell, topped with a cream sauce flavored with bits of shrimp, mushroom, and green seasonings.

Oysters en brochette (pronounced awn-bro-*shet*). Whole oysters and bits of bacon dusted with seasoned flour, skewered, and deep-fried; traditionally served on toast with lemon and brown butter.

Panéed veal (pronounced pan-*aid*). Breaded veal cutlets sautéed in butter.

Po'boy. A hefty sandwich made with local French bread and any number of fillings: roast beef, fried shrimp, oysters, ham, meatballs in tomato sauce, and cheese are common.

Ravigote (pronounced rah-vee-*gote*). In Creole usage, this is a piquant mayonnaise—usually made with capers—used to moisten crabmeat.

Rémoulade (pronounced ray-moo-*lahd*). A mixture of olive oil, mustard, scallions, cayenne, lemon, paprika, and parsley, served on cold peeled shrimp or lumps of back-fin crabmeat.

Souffléed potatoes. Thin, hollow puffs of deep-fried potato, produced by two fryings at different temperatures.

Sno-balls. Shaved ice topped with flavored syrup.

Tasso. Smokey cured pork often diced fine and added to dishes as a flavoring.

8

$$
SEAFOOD

✕ **Rio Mar.** The seafood-centric menu here explores the flavors of Spain and Latin America. For entrées, try the Serrano ham–wrapped tuna or the stew-like *zarzuela* with chunks of fish and shellfish in a peppery red broth. New chef Miles Prescott has kept the favorites while adding extra layers of flavor. It's all tapas at lunch, when you tick off your selections on a small menu card: options include salty Spanish ham, roasted peppers, Manchego cheese, and marinated seafood. The dining room's low ceiling and tiled floor mean that the atmosphere can get loud and boisterous—but this, and the decor, are very reminiscent of good times in Barcelona. ■ TIP→ **Over 40 Spanish wines are available, along with sherries, cocktails, and sangrias.** ⓢ *Average main: $21 ⊠ 800 S. Peters St., Warehouse District* ☎ *504/525–3474* ⊕ *www. riomarseafood.com* ☉ *Closed Sun. No lunch Sat.* ✛ *2:C4.*

$$$
MODERN
AMERICAN

✕ **Root.** The joke used to be that New Orleans had a thousand restaurants with only one menu. But today you'll fine a dizzying array of culinary creativity, and nowhere pushes the boundaries farther than Root. They serve, for lack of a better word, "molecular gastronomy" cuisine, the kind of food created by chefs who grew up admiring Mr. Science as much as Julia Child. The menu changes frequently, but expect to find dishes like oysters topped with mustard green foam, roasted marrow bones with "face bacon" jam, and scallops perfumed with actual Cohiba cigar smoke. A menu with plates of various sizes helps keep the cost in check. Does it always work? No. Is Root always an adventure? Yes. ⓢ *Average main: $28 ⊠ 200 Julia St., Warehouse District* ☎ *504/252–9480* ⊕ *rootnola.com* ☉ *No lunch weekends* ✛ *2:C4.*

$$
ITALIAN

✕ **Tommy's Cuisine.** The upscale dining rooms here are clubby and festive, the crowd is always interesting, and the menu seamlessly blends Creole and Italian. There are several types of oyster appetizers to choose from, including the signature Oysters Tommy with Romano cheese, pancetta, and roasted red pepper. The mains focus on sophisticated preparations of fish and meat, but make sure to find out the chef's imaginative daily specials before you make your decision. Service is gentlemanly. And the wines span all of Italy. After dinner, head next door to cushy Tommy's Wine Bar. ⓢ *Average main: $22 ⊠ 746 Tchoupitoulas St., Warehouse District* ☎ *504/581–1103* ⊕ *www.tommysneworleans.com* ⌲ *Reservations essential* ☉ *No lunch* ✛ *2:C4.*

THE GARDEN DISTRICT

Although a stroll through this quiet enclave of stately antebellum mansions is an essential part of a New Orleans trip, the dining options here are limited, since most of the area is residential. The handful of recommended restaurants, however, are some of the city's most talked about.

$$$
CREOLE

✕ **Commander's Palace.** No restaurant captures New Orleans's gastronomic heritage and celebratory spirit as well as this grande dame of New Orleans fine dining. Upstairs, the Garden Room's glass walls have marvelous views of the giant oak trees on the patio below. The menu's classics include a spicy and meaty turtle soup; shrimp and tasso Henican (shrimp stuffed with ham, with pickled okra); and a wonderful pecan-crusted Gulf fish. The bread-pudding soufflé might ruin you for other bread puddings. The weekend brunch is a not-to-be-missed New Orleans tradition, complete with live jazz. ■TIP→ **The band takes requests, so come armed with tip money. Jackets are preferred at dinner. Shorts and T-shirts are forbidden, and men must wear closed-toe shoes.** $ *Average main: $35* ⊠ *1403 Washington Ave., Garden District* ☎ *504/899–8221* ⊕ *www.commanderspalace.com* ⌖ *Reservations essential* ✛ *3:D4.*

$$$
AMERICAN
Fodor's Choice
★

✕ **Coquette.** Every neighborhood needs a hangout, and the dwellers of the Garden District's elegant mansions tend to spend their time at this fabulous corner bistro. The long bar downstairs fuels the lively scene, and the window seats here, looking out on Magazine Street, are always in demand. Those seeking a quieter evening head to the upstairs dining room, where chef Michael Stoltzfus has created a menu of seasonal modern-American offerings. The seafood dishes, in particular, are stellar. The relentlessly creative chef changes the menu almost nightly, making every meal here a new adventure. The kitchen opens at 5:30 pm, but the bar gets started at 4:30 pm. $ *Average main: $26* ⊠ *2800 Magazine St., Uptown* ☎ *504/265–0421* ⊕ *www.coquette-nola.com* ⌖ *Reservations essential* ◷ *Closed Tues. No lunch Mon.* ✛ *3:D4*

$$$
CREOLE
Fodor's Choice
★

✕ **Emeril's Delmonico.** Chef Emeril Lagasse bought the century-old Delmonico restaurant in 1998 and converted it into a large, extravagant restaurant serving some of the most ambitious reinterpretations of classic Creole dishes in town. The atmosphere is lush, with high-ceiling dining spaces swathed in upholstered walls and superthick window fabrics, and the food is decadent. House-cured charcuterie is a reliable option, as are crab cakes, rabbit crepes, and sautéed fish meunière. Prime dry-aged steaks with traditional sauces have emerged as a specialty in recent years, but the menu gets more ambitious by the month. Plush and polish are the bywords here, and the service is exemplary. $ *Average main: $29* ⊠ *1300 St. Charles Ave., Lower Garden District* ☎ *504/525–4937* ⊕ *www.emerilsrestaurants.com* ⌖ *Reservations essential* ◷ *No lunch Sat.–Thurs.* ✛ *3:C4.*

$
CAFÉ
FAMILY
Fodor's Choice
★

✕ **Sucré.** Do you have a sweet tooth? If so, make sure to stop in at Sucré, whether it be for a morning coffee and pastry, a late-night snack (the shop is open until midnight on Friday and Saturday and serves alcohol), or perhaps an afternoon gelato—this stylish sweetshop offers a wide array of irresistible confections. The pastel *macarons* (airy French meringue cookies), artisanal chocolates, and gelato hold their own with even the prettiest offerings at a French patisserie. Eat your sweets here, savor them on a stroll down the shop-lined street, or pack some for later. $ *Average main: $8* ⊠ *3025 Magazine St., Garden District* ☎ *504/520–8311* ⊕ *www.shopsucre.com* ⌖ *Reservations not accepted* ✛ *3:D4.*

8

UPTOWN AND CARROLLTON-RIVERBEND

UPTOWN

The homes in this residential zone range from brightly colored shotguns to imposing historic mansions. The restaurants also cover the gamut: there are corner po'boy shops and seafood joints, as well as ambitious bistros. The boutique-lined strip of Magazine Street runs the entire length of Uptown, and along the way you'll discover everything from bakeries and sno-ball stands to family eateries and nationally known dining destinations.

$ ╳ **Ancora.** Every dish on the short menu here shows an obsessive atten-
ITALIAN   tion to detail. The starters prominently feature the sausages and other
FAMILY   cured meats that hang inside a glass-walled room in the back. The main attraction are the pizzas, which follow Neapolitan pizza rules and use only flour, water, yeast, and salt for their dough. They enter an 800°F oven—which was imported from Naples—and emerge a minute later charred and fragrant. Despite the seriousness of the kitchen, the vibe out front is casual and contemporary. This welcoming pizzeria, like many other places on burgeoning Freret Street, suits the needs of neighbors but turns out food worthy of a visitor's attention. ⑤ *Average main: $13* ✉ *4508 Freret St., Uptown* ☎ *504/324–1636* ⊕ *www.ancorapizza.com* ⊘ *Closed Sun. No lunch* ✛ *3:C3.*

$$ ╳ **Atchafalaya.** Even with reservations, expect to wait for weekend brunch
CREOLE   at this Uptown institution, but your tastebuds will thank you later. Locals tend to linger over sultry Creole creations like eggs Tremé (boudin cake with poached eggs, popcorn crawfish, and hollandaise sauce), a DIY bloody Mary bar, and jumping live jazz on Saturdays and Sundays. At dinner the food is just as delicious, but the vibe is more romantic. The shrimp and grits are a standout, but there are plenty of other excellent choices. As a bonus, the expertly cultivated wine list shows plenty of options for under $50. ⑤ *Average main: $20* ✉ *901 Louisiana Ave., Uptown* ☎ *504/891–9626* ⊕ *www.atchafalayarestaurant.com* ⌑ *Reservations essential* ⊘ *No lunch Mon. and Tues.* ✛ *3:D4.*

$ ╳ **Casamento's.** Casamento's has been a haven for Uptown seafood lov-
SEAFOOD   ers since 1919. Family members still wait tables and staff the immacu-
FAMILY   late kitchen in back, while a reliable handful of oyster shuckers ensure that plenty of cold ones are available for the standing-room-only oyster bar. Specialties from the diminutive menu include oysters lightly poached in seasoned milk; fried shrimp, trout, and soft-shell-crab platters; and a must-try fried "oyster loaf" sandwich (two thick slices of white bread stuffed with fresh and greaseless bivalves). Everything is clean, and nothing is superfluous. Even the houseplants have a just-polished look. ⑤ *Average main: $8* ✉ *4330 Magazine St., Uptown* ☎ *504/895–9761* ⊕ *www.casamentosrestaurant.com* ⌑ *Reservations not accepted* ▭ *No credit cards* ⊘ *Closed Sun., Mon., No dinner Tues., Wed. Closed June–Aug.* ✛ *3:D3.*

$$ ╳ **Chiba.** With a chic dining room, late-night hours, and perhaps the
SUSHI   city's best sushi, this Oak Street eatery has quickly become a dining destination in Carrollton. In addition to creative rolls like the Black and Gold (salmon, avocado, tuna, and cucumber topped with black

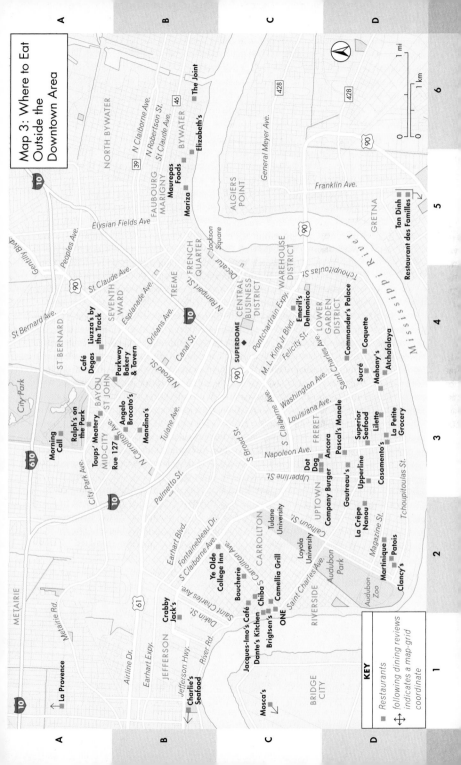

Map 3: Where to Eat Outside the Downtown Area

KEY
- ■ Restaurants
- ✛ following dining reviews indicates a map-grid coordinate

The Joint
Elizabeth's
Maurepas Foods
Mariza
Tan Dinh
Restaurant des Familles
Emeril's Delmonico
Commander's Palace
Coquette
Sucré
Mahony's
Atchafalaya
Pascal's Manale
Superior Seafood
Lilette
La Petite Grocery
Ancora
Upperline
Casamento's
Dot Dog
Gautreau's
Company Burger
La Crêpe Nanou
Martinique
Patois
Clancy's
Boucherie
Ye Olde College Inn
Chiba
Camellia Grill
Jacques-Imo's Café
Dante's Kitchen
Brigtsen's
ONE
Crabby Jack's
Charlie's Seafood
Mosca's
La Provence
Morning Call
Ralph's on the Park
Toups' Meatery
Rue 127
Angelo Brocato's
Mandina's
Café Degas
Liuzza's by the Track
Parkway Bakery & Tavern

NORTH BYWATER
BYWATER
FAUBOURG MARIGNY
ALGIERS POINT
GRETNA
BRIDGE CITY
RIVERSIDE
CARROLLTON
UPTOWN
FRERET
TREME
SEVENTH WARD
ST BERNARD
MID-CITY
BAYOU ST JOHN
FRENCH QUARTER
CENTRAL BUSINESS DISTRICT
WAREHOUSE DISTRICT
LOWER GARDEN DISTRICT
METAIRIE
JEFFERSON

Mississippi River
City Park
Audubon Park
Audubon Zoo
Tulane University
Loyola University
Jackson Square
SUPERDOME
Franklin Ave.
General Meyer Ave.
Elysian Fields Ave
Peoples Ave.
Gentilly Blvd.
St Bernard Ave.
St Claude Ave.
Esplanade Ave.
N Claiborne Ave.
N Robertson St.
St Claude Ave.
Orleans Ave.
Canal St.
N Broad St.
N Carrollton Ave.
Tulane Ave.
Palmetto St.
Earhart Blvd.
Fontainebleau Dr.
S Claiborne Ave.
S Carrollton Ave.
Dakin St.
Saint Charles Ave.
Calhoun St.
Magazine St.
Tchoupitoulas St.
Napoleon Ave.
S Broad St.
S Claiborne Ave.
Washington Ave.
Louisiana Ave.
St Charles Ave.
Felicity St.
M.L. King Jr Blvd.
Pontchartrain Expy.
N Rampart St.
Decatur
Tchoupitoulas St.
Airline Dr.
Earhart Expy.
Jefferson Hwy.
River Rd.
Metairie Rd.
City Park Ave.
Upperline St.
Rue 127 Ave.

10
610
90
39
46
428
428
90
90
61

0   1 km
0   1 mi

and gold roe), the restaurant has developed a following for its pillowy steamed buns stuffed with mouthwatering fillings, lilke duck or chicken katsu. ■TIP➜ Don't miss the "Funk n' Roll" happy hour every Wednesday from 4 to 6 pm, when rolls, appetizers, and steamed buns are a steal at $3 a pop. $ *Average main: $22* ✉ *8312 Oak St., Carrollton-Riverbend* ☎ *504/826–9119* ⊕ *www.chiba-nola.com* ☾ *Closed Sun. No lunch Mon., Tues.* ✛ *3:C2.*

$$$
CREOLE

✗ **Clancy's.** Understatement defines the mood at locally beloved Clancy's, and the classy but neutral decor reflects this, though the scene can get lively. The small bar is usually filled with regulars who know one another—and tourists who wish they were regulars. Most of the dishes are imaginative treatments of New Orleans favorites. Some specialties, like the seasonal smoked soft-shell crab, are exceptional. Other signs of an inventive chef are the expertly fried oysters matched with warm Brie, and a peppermint-ice cream pie. On more festive nights you may yearn for earplugs. ■TIP➜ The expansive wine list has many New World and French options, with many bottles available for under $100. $ *Average main: $28* ✉ *6100 Annunciation St., Uptown* ☎ *504/895–1111* ⊕ *www.clancysneworleans.com* ⊛ *Reservations essential* ☾ *Closed Sun. No lunch Mon.–Wed. and Sat.* ✛ *3:D2.*

$
AMERICAN
FAMILY
Fodor'sChoice
★

✗ **Company Burger.** At the Company Burger you'll have it their way. The amazing signature burger comes with two fresh-ground patties, bread-and-butter pickles, American cheese, and red onions on a freshly baked bun. No lettuce and no tomatoes, but you can load it up with home-made condiments like basil mayonnaise or Creole honey mustard. Other options include lamb or turkey burgers and hot dogs with franks from artisanal butcher Cleaver & Co. A daily burger special adds variety to the menu. Owner Adam Biderman grew up in New Orleans, but first earned burger fame in Atlanta. He's part of the wave of young transplants and returning natives not beholden to local traditions who have reenergized New Orleans since Katrina. $ *Average main: $8* ✉ *4600 Freret St., Uptown* ☎ *504/267–0320* ⊕ *www.thecompanyburger.com* ☾ *Closed Tues.* ✛ *3:C3.*

$
AMERICAN
FAMILY

✗ **Dat Dog.** No one can leave Dat Dog unhappy. The sprawling stand is painted in primary hues, as if the work had been outsourced to a talented kindergarten class, and the Hawaii shirt–clad staff bustles about with the enthusiasm of amateur actors staging a musical. The menu is all about hot dogs, and frank options range from standard German wieners to Louisiana alligator sausages. Even fish eaters and vegetarians have options. The long list of toppings includes guacamole, wasabi, and andouille sauce. Can't decide? Let the kitchen surprise you. And what goes better with a brat than an ice-cold brew? Luckily, the menu offers an exhaustive list of domestic and international beers. There's also a Dat Dog location in Uptown at 3336 Magazine Street. $ *Average main: $7* ✉ *5030 Freret St., Uptown* ☎ *504/899–6883* ⊕ *datdognola.com* ⊛ *Reservations not accepted* ▭ *No credit cards* ✛ *3:C3.*

$$$
MODERN
AMERICAN

✗ **Gautreau's.** This vine-covered neighborhood bistro doesn't have a sign, but that hasn't stopped the national food media from finding it. Lauded chef Sue Zemanick cooks with elegant confidence in a classic French style, but with surprising bursts of understated creativity, evidenced in dishes like seared tuna with peach salsa and fried plantains. At Gautreau's, even the simple roasted chicken satisfies, and everyone should indulge in the caramelized banana split at least once. An older crowd of well-dressed regulars monopolizes most of the tables in this dark, quiet space that once housed a pharmacy, but if you can get a reservation, you'll feel like you've gained admittance to an elite club. $ *Average main: $30* ⊠ *1728 Soniat St., Uptown* ☎ *504/899–7397* ⊕ *www. gautreausrestaurant.com* ⊙ *Closed Sun. No lunch* ✛ *3:D3.*

$$ ✗ **La Crêpe Nanou.** French chic for the budget-minded is the style at FRENCH this welcoming neighborhood bistro, where during peak hours there might be a half-hour wait for a table. Woven café chairs on the sidewalk and awnings that resemble metro-station architecture evoke the Left Bank of Paris, and the Gallic focus is also evident in dishes like the filet mignon, served with a choice of several classic French sauces. Other good options are the pâté maison, mussels and fries, and the lavish dessert crepes. ■ TIP➔ **The cheese plate is filled with fromage from beloved local cheese shop St. James Cheese Company.** Space is a little tight in the oddly configured dining areas, but the whimsical paintings and profuse greenery combine to create an inviting room. $ *Average main: $19* ⊠ *1410 Robert St., Uptown* ☎ *504/899–2670* ⊕ *www.lacrepenanou.com* ⌂ *Reservations not accepted* ⊙ *No lunch Mon.–Sat.* ✛ *3:D2.*

$$ ✗ **La Petite Grocery.** Flower shops sometimes bloom into intimate fine-SOUTHERN dining establishments in New Orleans, and this one, with just-bright-enough lighting and a sturdy mahogany bar, has caught on in a big way with the locals. In the kitchen, chef/owner Justin Devillier draws on contemporary American tastes, using Louisiana raw materials whenever he can. He's been quietly developing a reputation across the country (and scored a nomination for a coveted James Beard Award). Signature items include the blue crab beignets and the braised lamb shank with polenta, though many locals return to the red-leather banquettes for the signature burger and a round of cocktails. $ *Average main: $21* ⊠ *4238 Magazine St., Uptown* ☎ *504/891–3377* ⊕ *www.lapetitegrocery.com* ⌂ *Reservations essential* ⊙ *No lunch Mon.* ✛ *3:D3.*

$$$ ✗ **Lilette.** Proprietor-chef John Harris uses French and Italian culinary MODERN traditions as springboards for Lilette's inspired dishes. Look for tomato AMERICAN soup with gnocchetti; panéed black drum with Israeli couscous, leeks, and tomatoes; and roasted muscovy duck breast with cauliflower, buttered breadcrumbs, and sautéed spinach. For dessert, the goat cheese quenelles with lavender honey are as light as sorbet but more satisfying. The wine list has been thoughtfully chosen. Framed mirrors hang along the maroon walls of the intimate front dining room–cum–bar, and there are also a few tables filling out a second room and a heated patio. $ *Average main: $29* ⊠ *3637 Magazine St., Uptown* ☎ *504/895–1636* ⊕ *www.liletterestaurant. com* ⌂ *Reservations essential* ⊙ *Closed Sun. and Mon.* ✛ *3:D3.*

$ ✗ **Mahony's Po-Boy Shop.** What happens when a fine-dining chef opens DELI a po'boy joint? You get delicious local shrimp, hand-cut french fries, FAMILY and nontraditional menu items like chicken livers with coleslaw or fried oysters "dressed" with rémoulade sauce. Despite the ambitions in the kitchen, this restaurant still feels like a low-key neighborhood hangout.

8

The crowds are equal parts working class and professional, with a good number of families. The po'boy is New Orleans's own version of fast food, but here the waits can sometimes stretch to half an hour. It's wise to avoid peak meal times, or, if you're not in a hurry, order an Abita beer and settle into a seat on the patio. $ *Average main: $8* ✉ *3454 Magazine St., Uptown* ☎ *504/899–3374* ⊕ *www.mahonyspoboys.com* ⚑ *Reservations not accepted* ✛ *3:D3.*

$$ ✕ **Martinique Bistro.** The original chef here was influenced by Caribbean
FRENCH flavors, hence the name of this one-room restaurant with a tropical court-yard. These days, though, the Martinique Bistro is known for its French cooking, including the orange-scented pumpkin bisque, wild mushroom beignets, and oven-roasted, cane-syrup-infused duck breast options on the menu. Make sure to budget for wine—the excellent list is continu-ally updated. Dinner menus change every three months. The corner table in Martinique's courtyard is now a legendary marriage-proposal spot. Friday lunch is seasonable. $ *Average main: $28* ✉ *5908 Magazine St., Uptown* ☎ *504/891–8495* ⊕ *www.martiniquebistro.com* ⚑ *Reservations essential* ☾ *Closed Mon. No lunch Tues.–Thurs.* ✛ *3:D2.*

$$ ✕ **Pascal's Manale.** Barbecue shrimp is an addictive regional specialty that
ITALIAN involves neither a barbecue nor barbecue sauce, and Pascal's is consid-ered the dish's birthplace. The original recipe, introduced a half-century ago, remains unchanged: jumbo shrimp, still in the shell, are cooked in a buttery pool enhanced with just the right amount of Creole spice and pepper. The rest of the menu here is taken up with generally unex-citing regional seafood and Italian-style creations, although the turtle soup and the fried eggplant are good starters, and the uppercrust scene always amuses. Most important, the atmospheric old bar might be the best place in the city to slurp raw oysters. $ *Average main: $24* ✉ *1838 Napoleon Ave., Uptown* ☎ *504/895–4877* ⊕ *www.pascalsmanale.com* ⚑ *Reservations essential* ☾ *Closed Sun. No lunch Sat.* ✛ *3:D3.*

$$$ ✕ **Patois.** Hidden on a quiet residential corner, this bustling bistro could
FRENCH have been transported directly from Provence. The menu continues the
Fodor's Choice French theme, although with a Louisiana attitude. Mussels arrive in a
★ fragrant tomato broth, sautéed sweetbreads are served with a crispy country ham, and the meunière sauce on the Gulf fish gets a bright burst from local citrus. Chef Aaron Burgau developed close connections with growers and fishermen while managing a local farmers' market, so his kitchen is stocked with the best. He knows what New Orleanians like to eat, and his Uptown neighbors, a mix of affluent young and older couples, have rewarded him with nightly full houses. $ *Average main: $26* ✉ *6078 Laurel St., Uptown* ☎ *504/895–9441* ⊕ *www.patoisnola. com* ⚑ *Reservations essential* ☾ *Closed Mon.–Tues. No dinner Sun. No lunch Wed., Thurs., Sat.* ✛ *3:D2.*

$$ ✕ **Superior Seafood.** The menu at this Uptown seafood specialist reads
CREOLE like a greatest hits collection from the New Orleans culinary canon:
FAMILY from po'boys and red beans and rice on the casual end to barbecue shrimp and cornmeal-crusted Gulf fish on the fancier side. Brunch might be the best option here. This cavernous space mimics a Parisian bis-tro, but with a tad too much polish to feel authentic. But who cares about the inside, when the many windows offer views of streetcars

rolling by on St. Charles Avenue. The owners also run the nearby but not terribly exciting Superior Grill (*3636 St. Charles Ave.*). $ *Average main: $18* ✉ *4338 St. Charles Ave., Uptown* ☎ *504/293–3474* ⊕ *www. superiorseafoodnola.com* ✛ *3:D3.*

$$$
CREOLE
Fodor'sChoice
★

✕ **Upperline.** For more than 25 years this gaily colored cottage filled with a museum's worth of regional art has defined New Orleans Creole bistro fare, combining lusty traditional items like dark gumbo or étouffée with enough elegance to be worthy of white tablecloths. Boisterous regulars know their orders before the cocktails even arrive: perhaps fried green tomatoes with shrimp rémoulade, spicy local shrimp with jalapeño cornbread, or duck with ginger-peach sauce. ■ TIP→ Order the $45 "Taste of New Orleans" menu to sample seven classic dishes. Owner and local character JoAnn Clevenger presides over Upperline like the hostess of a party. New chef Dave Bridges has sharpened the focus without forgetting the history. $ *Average main: $27* ✉ *1413 Upperline St., Uptown* ☎ *504/891–9822* ⊕ *www.upperline.com* ⚌ *Reservations essential* ⊗ *Closed Mon. and Tues. No lunch* ✛ *3:D3.*

CARROLLTON-RIVERBEND

With Tulane and Loyola Universities nearby, it's fitting that the Carrollton-Riverbend neighborhood is filled with casual, affordable, and on-trend eateries, particularly on busy Maple Street.

$
SOUTHERN
Fodor'sChoice
★

✕ **Boucherie.** Nathanial Zimet's gutsy, down-home cooking, a unique blend of Louisiana and contemporary Southern styles, fits right in at its cozy location in a converted Uptown home. The menu here is updated monthly, but it always kicks off with small plates, including every iteration of grits imaginable—as fries, cakes, and even crackers. Large plates pack big flavors—smoked scallops, Wagyu brisket, and pulled-pork all deliver. No entrée costs more than $18. Try the Krispy Kreme bread pudding, even if you haven't saved room for it. And explore the beer list, which is one of the most thoughtful in town. $ *Average main: $15* ✉ *8115 Jeannette St., Uptown* ☎ *504/862–5514* ⊕ *www.boucherie-nola.com* ⊗ *Closed Sun. and Mon.* ✛ *3:C2.*

$$$
CREOLE

✕ **Brigtsen's.** Chef Frank Brigtsen's fusion of Creole refinement and Acadian earthiness reflects his years as a Paul Prudhomme protégé, and his dishes here represent some of the best south Louisiana cooking you'll find anywhere. Everything is fresh and filled with deep, complex tastes. The butternut shrimp bisque defines comfort food. Rabbit and duck dishes, usually presented in rich sauces and gravies, are full of robust flavor. But Brigtsen really gets to unleash his creativity on the "Shell Beach Diet," a nightly changing seafood platter. Trompe l'oeil murals add whimsy to the intimate spaces of this turn-of-the-20th-century frame cottage. Ask for a table on the enclosed front sun porch. $ *Average main: $29* ✉ *723 Dante St., Uptown* ☎ *504/861–7610* ⊕ *www.brigtsens.com* ⚌ *Reservations essential* ⊗ *Closed Sun. and Mon. No lunch* ✛ *3:C2.*

$$
SOUTHERN

✕ **Dante's Kitchen.** Ask local chefs where they dine on their day off, and chances are a good number of them will mention Dante's Kitchen. Chef Eman Loubier, a nine-year veteran of Commander's Palace, prepares seasonal menus for those with a sense of adventure. Duck breast is served with kumquats and pickled hot-pepper sauce, pork is paired with Brie-and-pastrami mac and cheese, and every visit demands a helping of

8

root beer–candied sweet potatoes. Desserts, such as the sweet-potato-and-white-chocolate pie, are homey and hearty. An outdoor patio is especially welcoming on cooler nights and at brunch on Saturday and Sunday. Reservations are not accepted for brunch. ■ TIP→ **The famous "chicken roasted under a brick" takes about 40 minutes to prepare, but it's worth the wait.** ⑤ *Average main: $25* ⊠ *736 Dante St., Uptown* ☎ *504/861–3121* ⊕ *www.danteskitchen.com* ⊗ *Closed Tues. No lunch Mon. and Wed.–Fri.* ⊕ *3:C2.*

$$ ✕ **Jacques-Imo's Cafe.** Oak Street might look like any other sleepy urban
CREOLE   thoroughfare by day, but once the sun sets the half-block stretch containing Jacques-Imo's Cafe feels like the center of the universe. Prepare for lengthy waits in the festive bar for a table in the boisterous, swamp-theme dining rooms (fortunately, the bartenders are fast). Although not everyone is a fan, most say the modest-looking but innovative food is worth it: deep-fried roast beef po' boys, alligator sausage cheesecake, Cajun bouillabaisse, and smothered rabbit over grits are among the only-at-Jacques-Imo's specialties. Reservations are required for parties of five or more and not accepted for smaller groups. ⑤ *Average main: $18* ⊠ *8324 Oak St., Carrollton-Riverbend* ☎ *504/861–0886* ⊕ *www.jacques-imos.com* ⊗ *Closed Sun. No lunch* ⊕ *3:C2.*

$$ ✕ **ONE.** Intimate, neighborhoody, and chic all at once, ONE manages to
SOUTHERN   feel casual and upscale at the same time. The interior is sleek and sophisticated, while the kitchen is wide open. Even though the restaurant is pretty much as far uptown as you can go, it's more than worth the trip. Chef Scott Snodgrass and co-owner Lee McCullough are the perfect hosts, and seem to love every minute of it. Typical of Snodgrass's creations are pan-fried flounder atop spaghetti squash gratin and the beef tenderloin with beef rillettes and Stilton cheese. ⑤ *Average main: $23* ⊠ *8132 Hampson St., Carrollton-Riverbend* ☎ *504/301–9061* ⊕ *www. onerestaurantnola.com* ⊗ *Closed Sun. No lunch Sat.–Mon.* ⊕ *3:C2.*

MID-CITY

Most visitors make their way to Mid-City for Jazz Fest but there's lots happening any time of year. The surrounding dining options include hip but unpretentious newcomers as well as neighborhood establishments that have been feeding locals affordably for generations.

$ ✕ **Angelo Brocato's.** Traditional Sicilian gelato, spumoni, cannoli, pastries,
CAFÉ   and candies are the attractions at this quaint little sweetshop, now over a
FAMILY   century old. The crisp biscotti, traditional Sicilian desserts, and the lemon and strawberry ices haven't lost their status as local favorites. The shop closes at 10 pm weekdays (closed Monday), 10:30 pm Fridays and Saturdays, and 9 pm on Sundays. Plan to stand in line and chat with mostly locals. On your way out, look for the brass plaque on the door that marks how high the water reached after the levees failed in 2005. ⑤ *Average main: $4* ⊠ *214 N. Carrollton Ave., Mid-City* ☎ *504/486–1465* ⊕ *www. angelobrocatoicecream.com* ⊗ *Closed Mon.* ⊕ *3:B3.*

$ ✕ **Café Degas.** Dining at Café Degas is like being at a sidewalk café in
FRENCH   Paris, even though the restaurant is completely covered: there's a tree growing through the center of the dining room, and the front windows

overlook picturesque Esplanade Avenue. Employees are matter-of-fact, but in a relaxing, European way. The fare here is a mixture of French-bistro cooking and what you might find at a countryside inn—house-made pâtés, onion soup, steamed mussels, duck in orange sauce, steaks, crème brûlée. Daily specials are always creative and ingenious. An evening here is inevitably romantic. ■ TIP➔ **Every Wednesday evening, diners can enjoy a 3-course meal for just $35.** ⑤ *Average main: $20* ✉ *3127 Esplanade Ave., Mid-City* ☎ *504/945–5635* ⊕ *www.cafedegas. com* ☾ *Closed Mon. and Tues.* ✛ *3:A4.*

$ ✕ **Liuzza's by the Track.** Fried-oyster po'boys drenched in garlic butter, bowls
CREOLE of sweet-corn-and-crawfish bisque, and grilled Reuben sandwiches with succulent corned beef are some of the reasons you might decide to tolerate the poor ventilation in this barroom near the racetrack and Jazz Fest grounds. The Creole chicken and sausage gumbo with shrimp is always good—thin on body, but heavy on spice (the shrimp is cooked to order and can be left out if you have dietary restrictions). But the pièce de résistance here is a barbecue-shrimp po'boy, for which the shrimp are cooked in a bracing lemon-pepper butter with enough garlic to cure a cold. The kitchen closes at 7 pm. ⑤ *Average main: $10* ✉ *1518 N. Lopez St., Mid-City* ☎ *504/218–7888* ⚏ *Reservations not accepted* ☾ *Closed Sun.* ✛ *3:A4.*

$ ✕ **Mandina's.** Although New Orleans has many nationally known res-
CREOLE taurants, the locals tend to frequent their neighborhood favorites. Man-
FAMILY dina's is such a spot, and has been since 1932. Although this Canal Street fixture has expanded over the years, nothing has diminished the full flavors of the shrimp rémoulade, the crawfish cakes, the turtle soup, or, on Monday, tender red beans with Italian sausage. Excellent étouffée, po'boys, fried seafood, and pastas are also on the menu. And if you're looking for the ideal bar and restaurant to spend a football Sunday in, complete with flat-screen TVs and the iciest beers in town, this is also your place. ⑤ *Average main: $16* ✉ *3800 Canal St., Mid-City* ☎ *504/482–9179* ⊕ *www.mandinasrestaurant.com* ✛ *3:B3.*

$ ✕ **Morning Call.** Once upon a time there were two famous French Quar-
CREOLE ter places to get beignets: Café du Monde and Morning Call. Then
FAMILY in 1974, after being open over a century, Morning Call packed up its antique fixtures and relocated to a suburban strip mall. Now this purveyor of fried dough has returned to New Orleans with a location in City Park. The beignets arrive "naked," so you can eat them plain or you can add a dusting of powdered sugar. The dark coffee is laced with chicory (and made using the French drip method). A small menu of savory dishes, like red beans and rice, is offered. It's open 24/7. ⑤ *Average main: $3* ✉ *City Park Casino, 56 Dreyfous St., Mid-City* ☎ *504/300–1157* ⊕ *morningcallcoffeestand.com* ⚏ *Reservations not accepted* ▭ *No credit cards* ✛ *3:A3.*

$ ✕ **Parkway Bakery & Tavern.** Former contractor Jay Nix resurrected more
CAFÉ than just a dilapidated building when he reopened Parkway: he also
FAMILY brought back to life a dormant community spirit. You can find neighbors and regulars from other parts of the city sinking into Parkway's roast beef and grilled-ham po'boys; some simply wander in for a hot dog and beer at the bar, and to take in the New Orleans nostalgia decorating the walls. For dessert, cake, bread pudding, and banana pudding

are all made fresh daily. As it's near the fairgrounds, Parkway jumps during Jazz Fest. ■**TIP→ The famous fried oyster po'boy is available only Monday and Wednesday.** $ *Average main: $8* ⊠ *538 Hagan Ave., Mid-City* ☎ *504/482–3047* ⊕ *www.parkwaypoorboys.com* ⌕ *Reservations not accepted* ⊘ *Closed Tues.* ✛ *3:B4.*

$$$
CREOLE
FAMILY

✕ **Ralph's on the Park.** Seasoned restaurateur Ralph Brennan has matched this beautifully renovated historic building with a menu that mixes contemporary Creole standbys with innovative twists. The culinary staff excels with full-flavored seafood dishes like the fried smoked oysters and a variety of fresh fish. By all means, try the rib eye wrapped scallops. For Sunday brunch, which even has a kids' menu, the lobster and tasso eggs Benedict and the chicken and waffles with boudin balls will remind you that you're way down in Louisiana. The solid wine list is always evolving. The bar, where you can order the full menu, looks out on the oaks of City Park and has become a virtual public clubhouse for nearby residents. $ *Average main: $27* ⊠ *900 City Park Ave., Mid-City* ☎ *504/488–1000* ⊕ *www.ralphsonthepark.com* ⌕ *Reservations essential* ⊘ *No lunch Mon.–Thurs. and Sat.* ✛ *3:A3.*

$$
MODERN
AMERICAN

✕ **Rue 127.** This diminutive bistro, set back from the street, can be hard to find amid the neighboring bars and casual eateries. Inside, the staff greets you with more enthusiasm than polish, but it only takes a minute to realize most customers are regulars, and by the first course you'll understand why they return. Chef Ray Gruezke turns out plates like scallops with cauliflower and sour cream whipped potatoes or seared drum with mussels and lardons with masterful technique. Even earthier dishes, such as a simple roast chicken with baked mac and cheese, are more robust than rustic. $ *Average main: $23* ⊠ *127 N. Carrollton Ave., Mid-City* ☎ *504/483–1571* ⊕ *www.rue127.com* ⊘ *Closed Sun. No lunch Mon. and Sat.* ✛ *3:B3.*

$$
CAJUN

✕ **Toups' Meatery.** No one can say there were misled by a restaurant called a "meatery." On the menu, you'll find meat, meat, and more meat, from foie gras and charcuterie to a lamb neck with chow chow (pickled relish) and tri tip steak with Bordelaise sauce. Chef Isaac Toups, who logged time in Emeril Lagasse's organization, is hardly the only young American chef obsessed with animal flesh, but at this intimate spot with a DIY elegance, he adds a Louisiana edge with items like boudin, cracklins, or sides of dirty rice. And not everything coming out of the kitchen is meat: they do make their own pickles. $ *Average main: $22* ⊠ *845 N. Carrollton Ave., Mid-City* ☎ *504/252–4999* ⊕ *www. toupsmeatery.com* ⊘ *Closed Sun., Mon.* ✛ *3:A3.*

$
CREOLE
FAMILY

✕ **Ye Olde College Inn.** A stalwart neighborhood joint, the age-old College Inn occupies a new building after decades in an older, now razed structure next door. The flat, greasy burgers are still popular, particularly when ordered with french fries and a cold Abita beer, but the diner fare has been joined by options like lemon-thyme chicken and grilled Gulf fish over crawfish étouffée. Many of the vegetables come from the restaurant's two neighboring urban gardens. Despite all the updates, you can still get the veal cutlet that's been on the menu since 1933. $ *Average main: $18* ⊠ *3000 S. Carrollton Ave., Mid-City* ☎ *504/866–3683* ⊕ *www.collegeinn1933.com* ⊘ *Closed Sun., Mon. No lunch* ✛ *3:C2.*

WHERE TO STAY

9

Updated by
Nathalie Jordi

Deciding where to stay in New Orleans has everything to do with what you want from your visit. Do you want to be where the party is? Do you need to be close to the business district and convention center? New Orleans is a fairly compact town, but if you choose to stay Uptown, you'll need to travel a bit to reach the Quarter. Although most hotels favored by visitors are in the French Quarter, Central Business District (CBD), or Warehouse District, there are also good options that are farther afield.

The French Quarter is a destination in itself. With fascinating architecture, vibrant nightlife, shopping, and incredible restaurants, you could spend several days without leaving its confines.

Hotels in the CBD, many of them chains, cater to business travelers as well as tourists; most are larger than those in the French Quarter, and have more amenities. The Warehouse District harbors many hotels in buildings that were originally used to store cotton or other goods. In most cases, thoughtful renovations have let the original purpose of the structures show through, making for an interesting architectural style.

Just across Esplanade Avenue on the north and east of the Quarter is the Faubourg Marigny. Originally a Creole plantation and one of the first "suburbs" of New Orleans, it remains a residential area, with its own nightlife and restaurant scene centered along Frenchmen Street.

To the west, upriver of the city's center, the Garden District and Uptown neighborhoods offer streets lined by the spreading boughs of live oaks, excellent stores, interesting architecture, and more outstanding dining and music venues.

PLANNING

RESERVATIONS

Book your room as far in advance as possible—up to a year ahead for Mardi Gras, Jazz Fest, or other special events.

SERVICES

Most hotels have private baths, central heating, air-conditioning, and private phones. More and more major hotels have added Wi-Fi or in-room broadband Internet service, though many major chains continue to charge for in-room Wi-Fi. Smaller bed-and-breakfasts and hotels may not have all of these amenities; ask before you book your room.

Hotels that do not have pools may have agreements with nearby health clubs or other facilities to allow guests to use club facilities for a nominal fee.

Most hotels have parking available, but this can run you as much as $36 a day. Valet parking is usually available at the major hotels. If you park on the street, keep in mind that New Orleans meter attendants are relentless, and ticketing is prevalent for illegally parked vehicles. The minimum fee for a parking ticket is $20.

PRICES

Properties are assigned price categories based on the rate for a standard double room during high season.

The lodgings we list are the most desirable in each price category, but rates are subject to change. Use Fodors.com to shop around for rooms before booking. Many major hotels occasionally offer Internet special rates. Be aware that room rates may be higher in October (considered peak convention season) and during the July 4 weekend (due to the annual Essence Music Festival). Rates are also high at the end of April and beginning of May during Jazz Fest. Rates are at their peak during Mardi Gras, and major hotels will require either a three- or four-night stay.

WITH KIDS

FAMILY In the listings, look for this symbol, which indicates the property is particularly good for kids.

USING THE MAPS

Throughout the chapter, you'll see mapping symbols and coordinates (✛ 3:F2) at the end of each review. The first number after the ✛ symbol indicates the map number. Following that is the property's coordinate on the map grid.

HOTEL REVIEWS

Listed alphabetically within neighborhood. The following reviews have been condensed for this book. Please go to Fodors.com for full reviews of each property.

THE FRENCH QUARTER

$$
B&B/INN
Andrew Jackson Hotel. A seriously enviable location in the French Quarter comes with plain, comfortable rooms surrounding a courtyard where lush foliage surrounds a prominent fountain. **Pros:** free in-room Wi-Fi; comfortable rooms; balcony views; killer location. **Cons:** basic furnishings; no parking; no restaurant. $ *Rooms from: $169* ⊠ *919 Royal St., French Quarter* ☎ *504/561–5881, 800/654–0224* ⊕ *www.andrewjacksonhotel.com* ⤴ *20 rooms, 2 suites* ⊙| *Breakfast* ✛ *1:D2.*

$
HOTEL
Astor Crowne Plaza. A great location within walking distance of everything that counts in the Quarter and downtown comes with a rooftop pool with spectacular views and a great in-house restaurant. **Pros:** convenient location; large guest rooms and big fitness center; direct access to streetcar. **Cons:** Bourbon Street is right next door, which is too close for some; fees for some Wi-Fi plans. $ *Rooms from: $141* ⊠ *739 Canal St., French Quarter* ☎ *504/962–0500, 888/696–4806* ⊕ *www.astorneworleans.com* ⤴ *693 rooms, 28 suites* ⊙| *No meals* ✛ *1:C3.*

$$$$
B&B/INN
Audubon Cottages. Seven one- and two-bedroom cottages in the heart of the French Quarter are a luxury retreat that supply a wonderful sense of privacy. **Pros:** lovely pool with outdoor lounge and cabanas; lots of personal service; use of the fitness center at the nearby Dauphine Orleans Hotel. **Cons:** you have to climb steps to reach one unit; some courtyards are shared. $ *Rooms from: $400* ⊠ *509 Dauphine St., French Quarter* ☎ *504/586–1516* ⊕ *www.auduboncottages.com* ⤴ *7 cottages* ⊙| *Breakfast* ✛ *1:C2.*

$
HOTEL
Bienville House Hotel. Some of the antique-filled rooms open to a gorgeous sundeck and others have balconies overlooking the courtyard's saltwater pool, and the attractions in the Quarter and the CBD are nearby. **Pros:** close to the Canal Street streetcars and Jackson Square; personalized service. **Cons:** noise can be a problem at night; standard rooms are on the small side; fitness center off-site. $ *Rooms from: $149* ⊠ *320 Decatur St., French Quarter* ☎ *504/529–2345* ⊕ *www.bienvillehouse.com* ⤴ *80 rooms, 3 suites* ⊙| *Breakfast* ✛ *1:D3.*

$
B&B/INN
Bon Maison Guest House. It is possible to find quiet, homey accommodation on Bourbon Street—these pleasantly furnished rooms in the former slave quarters of an 1833 town house face a brick patio filled with tropical plants. **Pros:** on the less touristy end of the Quarter's main drag, within walking distance of French Quarter attractions and lots of restaurants; Wi-Fi and cable TV; warm welcome from hosts. **Cons:** can be difficult to reserve; minimum stay of three nights most of the time; no parking; no breakfast. $ *Rooms from: $131* ⊠ *835 Bourbon St., French Quarter* ☎ *504/561–8498* ⊕ *www.bonmaison.com* ⤴ *2 rooms, 1 suite* ⊙| *No meals* ✛ *1:D2.*

BEST BETS FOR
NEW ORLEANS LODGING

Fodor's offers a selective listing of quality lodging in every price range. Here are our top recommendations by price and experience. The best properties— the ones that provide a remarkable experience in their price range—are designated Fodor's Choice.

Fodor's Choice ★

By Price

Best By Experience

9

$$ 🏨 **Bourbon Orleans Hotel.** The location's about as central as it gets,
HOTEL though the beautiful courtyard and pool provide a welcome retreat from
the loud, 24-hour Bourbon Street action just outside the door. **Pros:** free
Wi-Fi; welcome cocktail; gym; bar and restaurant on-site. **Cons:** lobby
level is often crowded and noisy due to curious passersby; street-facing
rooms can be noisy. ⑤ *Rooms from: $189* ✉ *717 Orleans St., French
Quarter* ☎ *504/523–2222* ⊕ *www.bourbonorleans.com* ⤵ *218 rooms,
28 suites* ⑩ *No meals* ✛ *1:D2.*

$$ 🏨 **Chateau LeMoyne.** Just one block off Bourbon Street, this branch of
HOTEL the Holiday Inn chain is surprisingly distinctive, with large, pleasant,
antique-and-reproduction-filled rooms occupying an 1847 traditional
New Orleans landmark. **Pros:** great location; large pool; affordable rates;
moderately priced authentic Southern breakfast (kids accompanied by
adults eat free). **Cons:** no room service or meals beyond breakfast; beds
are doubles, not queens; some bathrooms are small. ⑤ *Rooms from: $179*
✉ *301 Dauphine St., French Quarter* ☎ *504/581–1303, 800/465–4329*
⊕ *www.hi-chateau.com* ⤵ *160 rooms, 11 suites* ⑩ *No meals* ✛ *1:C3.*

$ 🏨 **Dauphine Orleans.** A great location—within walking distance of the
HOTEL action but removed enough to make this a secluded respite—comes with
a lot of charm. **Pros:** French Quarter architecture; saltwater pool. **Cons:**
some rooms require climbing stairs; some rooms can be noisy. ⑤ *Rooms
from: $149* ✉ *415 Dauphine St., French Quarter* ☎ *504/586–1800,
800/521–7111* ⊕ *www.dauphineorleans.com* ⤵ *107 rooms, 3 suites*
⑩ *Breakfast* ✛ *1:C3.*

$$ 🏨 **Four Points By Sheraton French Quarter.** With a heart-of-the-party
HOTEL Bourbon Street location, the most coveted of the well-kept rooms here
(especially during Mardi Gras) are the ones with balconies overlook-
ing the street. **Pros:** ideal for those who want to be in the center of the
French Quarter; free Wi-Fi. **Cons:** the high-traffic location means the
party outside your front door never ends. ⑤ *Rooms from: $189* ✉ *541
Bourbon St., French Quarter* ☎ *504/524–7611, 800/535–7891* ⊕ *www.
fourpointsfrenchquarter.com* ⤵ *179 rooms, 7 suites* ⑩ *No meals* ✛ *1:C3.*

$$ 🏨 **Hotel Le Marais.** An outpost of the cutting edge in the French Quarter
HOTEL has trendy furnishings and a blacklit lobby that combines urban chic
with a voguish New Orleans vibe. **Pros:** modern furnishings; free in-
room Wi-Fi; quiet despite location near Bourbon Street. **Cons:** not for
those who want a traditional-looking hotel; no in-hotel restaurant.
⑤ *Rooms from: $159* ✉ *717 Conti St., French Quarter* ☎ *504/525–
2300* ⊕ *www.hotellemarais.com* ⤵ *66 rooms* ⑩ *Breakfast* ✛ *1:C3.*

$$$$ 🏨 **Hotel Maison de Ville.** A collection of historic town houses and "bach-
HOTEL elor quarters" make up this charmer with a delightfully secluded vibe
Fodor'sChoice amid the hustle and bustle of the French Quarter. **Pros:** lots of local
★ history; unique rooms; personal and consistent service. **Cons:** tough to
get a reservation; no on-site restaurant. ⑤ *Rooms from: $315* ✉ *727
Toulouse St., French Quarter* ☎ *504/324–4888* ⊕ *www.maisondeville.
com* ⤵ *14 rooms, 1 suite, 1 cottage* ⑩ *Breakfast* ✛ *1:C2.*

$$ 🏨 **Hotel Mazarin.** An enviable French Quarter location combines with
HOTEL loads of charm, including a picture-perfect courtyard with a fountain
Fodor'sChoice and slightly garish guest rooms featuring black marble floors. **Pros:** out-
★ standing breakfast; great location; excellent guest service. **Cons:** rooms

WHERE SHOULD I STAY?

NEIGHBORHOOD	VIBE	PROS	CONS
The French Quarter	The tourist-focused main event is action packed, but still charming. Lodging runs from small inns to luxury hotels.	Lots of visitor attractions and nationally acclaimed restaurants. Everything is within walking distance of your hotel.	Crowded, high-traffic area. If you're sound sensitive, request a room that does not face a main street, or find a hotel some distance from Bourbon.
Faubourg Marigny/ Tremé	Residential area just to the east of the French Quarter with a bohemian feel and fast-growing nightlife scene.	Balanced residential–commercial community. Close to French Quarter nightlife, and with an eclectic nightlife scene of its own. The area is a more peaceful alternative to the Quarter.	Can be confusing to navigate for newcomers. Don't forget your map!
CBD and Warehouse District	The Warehouse District is also known as New Orleans's arts district. It's a great area for visitors who want to stay in luxurious high-rise hotels or smaller boutique properties.	Good retail and restaurants, and some of the best galleries and museums in the city. Within walking distance of the French Quarter.	Crowded; traffic can be a problem for pedestrians.
Garden District	Residential, upscale, and fashionable, this neighborhood is a slower-paced alternative to staying downtown.	Beautiful and right on the historic St. Charles Ave. streetcar line. Traffic here is not as heavy as downtown. Excellent shopping opportunities on Magazine St.	Far from the French Quarter and tourist attractions; must drive or take public transportation.
Mid-City	This is primarily an urban–residential area, with few lodging options.	Many local businesses and mid-price owner-operated restaurants. Home to City Park, one of the largest urban parks in the country.	More challenging for tourists to navigate—some distance from tourist attractions. You'll need a car; public transportation is not convenient.

facing the street can be noisy; no tubs. ⑤ *Rooms from: $169* ✉ *730 Bienville St., Downtown* ☎ *504/581–7300, 800/535–9111* ⊕ *www. hotelmazarin.com* ⌇ *102 rooms, 3 suites* ⦿| *Breakfast* ✛ *1:C3.*

$$ 🖼 **Hotel Monteleone.** One of the grand old hotels of New Orleans, the HOTEL Monteleone, dates back to 1886 and oozes sophistication, romance, **Fodor'sChoice** and history. **Pros:** great location in the French Quarter; Royal Street ★ shopping; fabulous bar. **Cons:** the lobby and entrance can get crowded. ⑤ *Rooms from: $219* ✉ *214 Royal St., CBD* ☎ *504/523–3341, 800/ 535–9595* ⊕ *www.hotelmonteleone.com* ⌇ *600 rooms, 55 suites* ⦿| *No meals* ✛ *1:C3.*

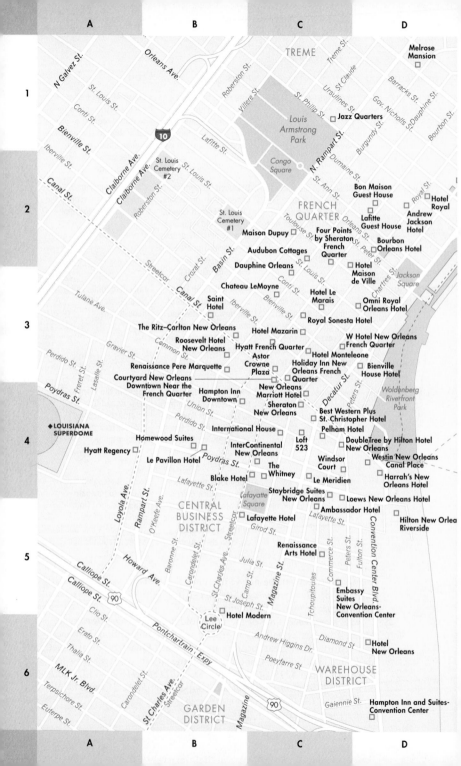

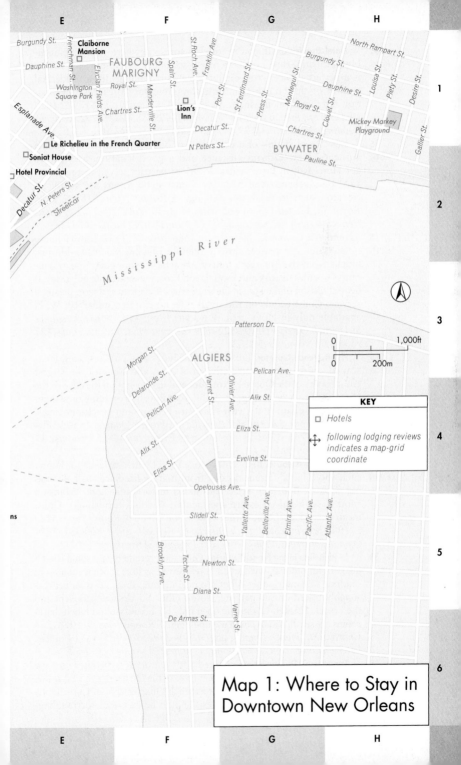

Map 1: Where to Stay in Downtown New Orleans

$$ **Hotel Provincial.** If you're looking for somewhere that's memora-
HOTEL bly authentic, this inn that's nicely secluded yet close to the action
is a perfect choice. **Pros:** quaint; quiet surroundings (in a residential
section of the French Quarter); complimentary breakfast; destina-
tion restaurant. **Cons:** suites are pricey. **$** *Rooms from: $179* ⊠ *1024
Chartres St., French Quarter* ☎ *504/581–4995, 800/535–7922* ⊕ *www.
hotelprovincial.com* ➵ *93 rooms, 6 suites* ⫟⊙⫟ *Breakfast* ⊹ *1:E2.*

$$ **Hotel Royal.** Think of a cool big-city boutique hotel, mix in some
HOTEL authentic New Orleans elegance and a good location, and you've
got Hotel Royal. **Pros:** central location; pastries served in the courtyard on weekends and Monday. **Cons:** some rooms are small; no
elevator, steps to reach upper floors. **$** *Rooms from: $189* ⊠ *1006
Royal St., French Quarter* ☎ *504/524–3900, 800/776–3901* ⊕ *www.
frenchquarterhotelgroup.com* ➵ *43 rooms* ⫟⊙⫟ *No meals* ⊹ *1:D2.*

$ **Hotel Villa Convento.** This intimate, four-story 1833 Creole town house
HOTEL on a quaint, quiet street close to the Old Ursuline Convent—but just
blocks from the Quarter's tourist attractions, shopping, and restaurants—exudes history and local flavor. **Pros:** located in the quieter residential section of the French Quarter; true New Orleans flavor; personal
service. **Cons:** rooms on the small side; no children under 10; Wi-Fi
available only in lobby area. **$** *Rooms from: $145* ⊠ *616 Ursulines
St., French Quarter* ☎ *504/522–1793* ⊕ *www.villaconvento.com* ➵ *25
rooms* ⫟⊙⫟ *No meals* ⊹ *1:E2.*

$$$ **Hyatt French Quarter.** Luxury here includes airy public spaces, land-
HOTEL scaped courtyards, an attractive pool area, and some of the largest
guest rooms in the Quarter. **Pros:** airy and light; right on the edge of the
Quarter but set back from the hubbub of Bourbon Street. **Cons:** slight
feeling of a chain hotel; very noisy at check-in and check-out times.
$ *Rooms from: $299* ⊠ *800 Iberville St., French Quarter* ☎ *504/586–
0800, 800/766–3782* ⊕ *frenchquarter.hyatt.com* ➵ *254 rooms, 11
suites* ⫟⊙⫟ *No meals* ⊹ *1:C3.*

$ **Lafitte Guest House.** In this four-story 1849 French-style manor house,
B&B/INN each room has different details, from marble fireplaces to balconies
overlooking Bourbon. **Pros:** feels like a historic mansion; "Mansion
rooms" with balconies are spectacular; updated furnishings. **Cons:**
located on a high-traffic corner of Bourbon Street. **$** *Rooms from: $149*
⊠ *1003 Bourbon St., French Quarter* ☎ *504/581–2678, 800/331–7971*
⊕ *www.lafitteguesthouse.com* ➵ *14 rooms* ⫟⊙⫟ *Breakfast* ⊹ *1:D2.*

$$ **Le Richelieu in the French Quarter.** Guests appreciate the personal friend-
HOTEL liness of an old-fashioned small hotel as well as luxe touches such as an
outdoor saltwater pool—all at a moderate rate. **Pros:** great value; reasonably priced on-site parking; close to the Old Ursuline Convent and
the French Market. **Cons:** café open only for breakfast and lunch; bathrooms are small; rooms could use updating. **$** *Rooms from: $160* ⊠ *1234
Chartres St., French Quarter* ☎ *504/529–2492, 800/535–9653* ⊕ *www.
lerichelieuhotel.com* ➵ *69 rooms, 17 suites* ⫟⊙⫟ *No meals* ⊹ *1:E2.*

$$ **The Maison Dupuy.** Seven restored 19th-century town houses just two
HOTEL blocks from Bourbon Street surround one of the Quarter's prettiest court-
yards. **Pros:** quiet, yet still close to French Quarter action. **Cons:** lobby
can be cramped at check-in; guests should be aware of surroundings

if walking late at night. $ *Rooms from: $189* ✉ *1001 Toulouse St., French Quarter* ☎ *504/586-8000, 800/535-9177* ⊕ *www.maisondupuy.com* ✎ *187 rooms, 13 suites* ⦿ *No meals* ✛ *1:C2.*

$$
B&B/INN
☷ **Melrose Mansion.** A few minutes from the French Quarter, this renovated Victorian mansion turns on the grandeur with antique furnishings, hardwood floors, cathedral ceilings, and large chandeliers—and lots of luxurious, modern conveniences. **Pros:** private and luxurious, with lots of pampering; renovated property; breakfast included; access to pool and gym is complimentary. **Cons:** one night's stay is charged prior to arrival. $ *Rooms from: $209* ✉ *937 Esplanade Ave., French Quarter* ☎ *504/944-2255, 800/650-3323* ⊕ *www.melrosemansion.com* ✎ *11 rooms, 3 suites* ⦿ *Multiple meal plans* ✛ *1:D1.*

$$$
HOTEL
☷ **New Orleans Marriott Hotel.** This centrally located skyscraper boasts fabulous views of the Quarter, downtown, and the river. **Pros:** good location; stunning city and river views. **Cons:** typical chain hotel; inconsistent service; lacks charm; daily charge for Wi-Fi in the rooms (access is free from the lobby). $ *Rooms from: $239* ✉ *555 Canal St., French Quarter* ☎ *504/581-1000, 800/228-9290* ⊕ *www.neworleansmarriott.com* ✎ *1,274 rooms, 55 suites* ⦿ *No meals* ✛ *1:C4.*

$$$
HOTEL
☷ **Omni Royal Orleans Hotel.** One of the more elegant options on Bourbon Street, this large white-marble landmark is a replica of the grand 1800s St. Louis Hotel, with columns, gilt mirrors, and magnificent chandeliers. **Pros:** old-world grandeur; central location. **Cons:** can be crowded in the lobby and pool areas; some rooms are small. $ *Rooms from: $299* ✉ *621 St. Louis St., French Quarter* ☎ *504/529-5333, 800/843-6664* ⊕ *www.omnihotels.com* ✎ *345 rooms, 16 suites* ⦿ *No meals* ✛ *1:D3.*

$$$$
HOTEL
Fodor'sChoice
★
☷ **Ritz-Carlton New Orleans.** One of the city's most iconic hotels sits regally on Canal Street, with luxurious rooms and suites occupying what was once the Maison Blanche department store. **Pros:** great location for either business or pleasure; outstanding modern New Orleans fare at M Bistro; afternoon tea in Davenport Lounge is one of the most civilized traditions in the city. **Cons:** sometimes feels a like a chain; rates are some of the highest in town. $ *Rooms from: $309* ✉ *921 Canal St., French Quarter* ☎ *504/524-1331* ⊕ *www.ritzcarlton.com* ✎ *527 rooms, 38 suites* ⦿ *No meals* ✛ *1:B3.*

$$$
HOTEL
Fodor'sChoice
★
☷ **Royal Sonesta Hotel New Orleans.** Adding a touch of class to its Bourbon Street environs, this French Quarter favorite is soothing from the moment you step into the marbled lobby, where lush plants enhance a cool, serene atmosphere. **Pros:** outstanding service; bustling, cavernous lobby; great balcony views of the Quarter. **Cons:** consistent high occupancy can lead to slow elevator service; rooms

---

CLIMBERS BEWARE!

One of the best Mardi Gras parade-viewing spots in town is the **Royal Sonesta Hotel** balcony. To keep revelers from climbing up from the street below, the staff greases all the support poles with petroleum jelly. The media turns out in droves, and the hotel turns the event into a party. For many New Orleanians, this odd event signifies the true beginning to Mardi Gras weekend. Festivities start at 10 am the Friday before Mardi Gras.

9

facing Bourbon are noisy. ⑤ *Rooms from: $249* ⊠ *300 Bourbon St., French Quarter* ☎ *504/586–0300, 800/766–3782* ⊕ *www.sonesta. com/royalneworleans* ⟿ *482 rooms, 35 suites* ✛ *1:C3.*

$$

HOTEL

🏨 **The Saint Hotel.** In the 1909 Beaux-Arts Audubon Building, up-to-the-minute decor wows in a lobby glittering with chandeliers, atmospheric photos of Mardi Gras, and acres of sheer tulle curtains, and compact, white-and-cobalt rooms are crisply outfitted with high-end bedding and cushy amenities. **Pros:** on the Canal streetcar line and parade route; a few blocks from French Quarter action; marble baths; free Wi-Fi. **Cons:** may be too edgy and stark for some guests; part of Marriott's boutique line lacks traditional New Orleans ambience and charm. ⑤ *Rooms from: $199* ⊠ *931 Canal Street, French Quarter* ☎ *504/522–5400* ⊕ *www.thesainthotelneworleans.com* ⟿ *166 rooms* ⦿ *No meals* ✛ *1:B3.*

$$$

B&B/INN

Fodor's Choice

★

🏨 **Soniat House.** Many regular New Orleans visitors consider these three meticulously restored town houses from the 1830s to be the city's finest hotel, with elegant rooms where contemporary artwork complements the polished hardwood floors, Oriental rugs, and American and European antiques. **Pros:** very refined; expert service; afternoon wine service is as civilized as it gets; use of off-site New Orleans Athletic Club included in rates. **Cons:** breakfast is delicious, but it costs extra, and menu options are limited; several rooms are accessible by steps only. ⑤ *Rooms from: $245* ⊠ *1133 Chartres St., French Quarter* ☎ *504/522–0570, 800/544–8808* ⊕ *www.soniathouse.com* ⟿ *18 rooms, 12 suites* ⦿ *No meals* ✛ *1:E2.*

$$$$

HOTEL

🏨 **W Hotel New Orleans French Quarter.** The many pluses here include one of the best locations in the Quarter, rooms designed with funky jazz and voodoo themes, and balconies that overlook either are courtyard or Chartres Street. **Pros:** beautiful courtyard and pool; excellent service. **Cons:** small driveway area can get crowded with valet activity; lines at check in and check out. ⑤ *Rooms from: $349* ⊠ *316 Chartres St., French Quarter* ☎ *504/581–1200, 888/627–8260* ⊕ *www. wfrenchquarter.com* ⟿ *97 rooms, 6 suites* ⦿ *No meals* ✛ *1:C3.*

$$$

HOTEL

🏨 **The Westin New Orleans Canal Place.** Views from this large convention hotel are enviable: two-story arched lobby windows overlook the French Quarter and rooms tower over the great bend in the Mississippi River. **Pros:** luxurious rooms and suites; fabulous views of the Mississippi River and the French Quarter; rooftop pool; close to shopping. **Cons:** lobby is on the 11th floor and can be a bit cumbersome to access; hotel has a big-box chain feel; groups can overwhelm common spaces; daily charge for Internet access. ⑤ *Rooms from: $249* ⊠ *100 Iberville St., French Quarter* ☎ *504/566–7006, 800/996–3426* ⊕ *www.starwoodhotels.com/westin* ⟿ *438 rooms, 40 suites* ⦿ *No meals* ✛ *1:D4.*

Haunted Hotels

In New Orleans reminders of human mortality are never far from view. Because most of the city is at or below sea level, graves were built aboveground, and walled cemeteries are common tourist destinations. As a port city, New Orleans has always been a boisterous place, where pirates, prostitutes, gamblers, and characters of all manner could find a comfortable home. The city's reputation as a home for voodoo is well founded; it is the birthplace of legendary voodoo priestess Marie Laveau. Not surprisingly, many of the city's hotels are purportedly home to restless spirits. Guests at the **Dauphine Orleans** (⌂ *415 Dauphine St., French Quarter* ☎ *504/586–1800 or 800/521–7111*) report seeing a dancing woman in the courtyard and the spirit of a patron roaming the grounds, a reminder of the days when there was a brothel here. The grandfather clock in the lobby of the **Hotel Monteleone** (⌂ *214 Royal St., French Quarter* ☎ *504/523–3341 or 800/535–9595*) is said to be haunted by the ghost of its maker, and in the Garden District's **Columns Hotel**

(⌂ *3811 St. Charles Ave., Uptown* ☎ *504/899–9308 or 800/445–9308*) a former owner—who died in 1898—is occasionally still seen by guests. Hurricane Katrina was only the most recent catastrophe to befall New Orleans; yellow fever was a scourge on the city in the 18th and 19th centuries. The **Lafitte Guest House** (⌂ *1003 Bourbon St., French Quarter* ☎ *504/581–2678 or 800/331–7971*) is only one hotel in which victims of the disease still linger. Of course you can't talk about the haunted hotels of New Orleans without mentioning the **Bourbon Orleans Hotel** (⌂ *717 Orleans, French Quarter* ☎ *504/523–2222*). Once a ballroom, and then convent, the storied building is said to house apparitions of former tenants, like the Confederate soldier roaming the sixth and seventh floors, and the dancer seen swaying underneath the crystal chandelier in the hotel's ballroom. There are a number of tour operators that cater to those with an interest in the supernatural, but if you stay at the right hotel, you may not need their services.

9

FAUBOURG MARIGNY AND TREMÉ

FAUBOURG MARIGNY

$$
B&B/INN
Claiborne Mansion. One of the most beautiful places to stay in Faubourg Marigny, the Claiborne Mansion has enormous rooms with high ceilings, canopy beds, polished hardwood floors, and rich fabrics. **Pros:** big rooms; very private and relaxing; within walking distance of several great restaurants and jazz clubs. **Cons:** limited parking on the premises. ⓢ *Rooms from: $150* ⌂ *2111 Dauphine St., Faubourg Marigny* ☎ *504/949–7327* ⊕ *www.clairbornemansion.com* ⤳ *2 rooms, 5 suites* ⦿ *Breakfast* ✛ *1:E1.*

$
B&B/INN
Lion's Inn. With a swimming pool and hot tub in the private garden and elegant, Old South room decor, it's easy to feel you're in a traditional Louisiana mansion, though the many nightspots and restaurants on Frenchmen Street are nearby. **Pros:** gracious owners; private courtyard; lovely neighborhood feel. **Cons:** a 10-minute walk to the

Quarter or Frenchmen Street means that you may want to take a cab at night. ⑤ *Rooms from: $125* ✉ *2517 Chartres St., Faubourg Marigny* ☎ *800/485–6846, 504/945–2339* ⊕ *www.lionsinn.com* ↩ *10 rooms* ⟋⊙⟍ *Breakfast* ✛ *1:F1.*

TREMÉ

$

B&B/INN

⊡ **Jazz Quarters New Orleans.** These charming guesthouses and suites, surrounded by meticulous gardens and furnished with antiques, were once a part of the historic Tremé plantation, and are located within walking distance of the French Quarter. **Pros:** not widely known, even among frequent New Orleans visitors; quaint, intimate surroundings. **Cons:** a bit pricey and, while improving, the neighborhood is not the best place to walk around after dark. ⑤ *Rooms from: $135* ✉ *1129 St. Philip St., Tremé* ☎ *504/523–1372, 800/523–1060* ⊕ *www. jazzquarters.com* ↩ *9 guest houses* ⟋⊙⟍ *Breakfast* ✛ *1:C1.*

CBD AND THE WAREHOUSE DISTRICT

CBD

$$

HOTEL

⊡ **The Ambassador Hotel.** Bastions of real character in the otherwise corporate CBD, these guest rooms have hardwood floors, oversize windows, and high ceilings, and are furnished with four-poster iron beds, armoires, and local jazz prints. **Pros:** distinctive decor; urban-chic atmosphere. **Cons:** some first-floor rooms let in too much noise from street and lobby area. ⑤ *Rooms from: $151* ✉ *535 Tchoupitoulas St., CBD* ☎ *504/527–5271, 800/455–3417* ⊕ *www.ambassadorneworleans.com* ↩ *165 rooms* ⟋⊙⟍ *Breakfast* ✛ *1:C5.*

$$

HOTEL

⊡ **Best Western Plus St. Christopher Hotel.** A former office complex from the 1890s offers rooms with exposed brick and basic furnishings, just a block from the French Quarter. **Pros:** good location for the Convention Center and the French Quarter; free Wi-Fi. **Cons:** generic breakfast room—and breakfast; bar only open Thursday to Saturday. ⑤ *Rooms from: $179* ✉ *114 Magazine St., CBD* ☎ *800/645–9312, 504/648–0444* ⊕ *www.stchristopherhotel.com* ↩ *108 rooms* ⟋⊙⟍ *Breakfast* ✛ *1:C4.*

$

⊡ **The Blake Hotel New Orleans.** Sizable rooms decorated with contemporary furnishings are on one of the Big Easy's best Carnival corners, the intersection of Poydras Street and St. Charles Avenue, just a block from Lafayette Square. **Pros:** convenient location on the St. Charles streetcar line; pet-friendly. **Cons:** busy intersection; can be noisy. ⑤ *Rooms from: $129* ✉ *500 St. Charles Ave., CBD* ☎ *504/522–9000, 888/211–3447* ⊕ *www.blakehotelneworleans.com* ↩ *124 rooms* ⟋⊙⟍ *No meals* ✛ *1:C4.*

$$

HOTEL

FAMILY

⊡ **Courtyard New Orleans Downtown Near the French Quarter.** A wraparound wrought-iron balcony overlooking St. Charles Avenue, a stunning six-story atrium, and some nods to period charm distinguish this family-friendly, CBD hotel. **Pros:** central CBD location. **Cons:** significant street noise at all hours; balcony rooms are in high demand during Mardi Gras. ⑤ *Rooms from: $219* ✉ *124 St. Charles Ave., CBD* ☎ *504/581–9005, 800/321–2211* ⊕ *www.marriott.com* ↩ *140 rooms* ⟋⊙⟍ *No meals* ✛ *1:C3.*

$

HOTEL

⊡ **DoubleTree by Hilton Hotel New Orleans.** Open, airy rooms done in country French decor are close to family-friendly adventures as well as the river, the Canal Place mall, and the French Quarter. **Pros:** close to the French Quarter and Riverfront attractions; across the street from the Insectarium. **Cons:** some rooms could use an update; restaurant is average at best; chain hotel vibe. $ *Rooms from: $149* ✉ *300 Canal St., CBD* ☎ *504/581–1300, 800/222–8733* ⊕ *www.doubletree.com* ⌁ *364 rooms, 4 suites* ¶○¶ *No meals* ✛ *1:C4.*

$$
HOTEL
FAMILY
⌁ **Embassy Suites New Orleans-Convention Center.** If your primary destination is the Convention Center (three blocks away) or the restaurants, galleries, and museums in the Warehouse District, these suites with bedrooms and separate parlors are a great choice. **Pros:** spacious, well-maintained rooms; friendly service; room service available from the Sugar House restaurant. **Cons:** lackluster restaurant; a significant distance from the French Quarter. $ *Rooms from: $199* ✉ *315 Julia St., CBD* ☎ *504/525–1993, 800/362–2779* ⊕ *www.embassyneworleans.com* ⌁ *346 suites, 24 rooms* ¶○¶ *Breakfast* ✛ *1:C5.*

$$
HOTEL
⌁ **Hampton Inn Downtown.** A converted office building with large, comfortable, and pleasant rooms is an oasis in the midst of the bustling CBD. **Pros:** spacious rooms; particularly nice breakfast; free Wi-Fi; convenient to French Quarter (but be careful when walking at night). **Cons:** rooms that face the street can be noisy; typical chain hotel. $ *Rooms from: $159* ✉ *226 Carondelet St., CBD* ☎ *504/529–9990, 800/426–7866* ⊕ *www.neworleanshamptoninns.com* ⌁ *185 rooms* ¶○¶ *Breakfast* ✛ *1:B4.*

$$
HOTEL
Fodor's Choice
★
⌁ **Harrah's New Orleans Hotel.** Location, location, location—directly across the street from Harrah's New Orleans Casino, near the Convention Center and Riverfront attractions, close to the Warehouse District, the CBD, and the French Quarter. **Pros:** above-average service; stylish rooms. **Cons:** the hustle and bustle of this part of town mean peace and quiet can be in short supply; casino marketing is ever present. $ *Rooms from: $189* ✉ *228 Poydras St., at Fulton St., CBD* ☎ *504/533–6000, 800/847–5299* ⊕ *www.harrahsneworleans.com* ⌁ *450 rooms, 94 suites* ¶○¶ *No meals* ✛ *1:D4.*

$$
HOTEL
FAMILY
⌁ **Hilton New Orleans Riverside.** The superb river views are hard to beat, and the French provincial decor comes with all the modern amenities—as well as proximity to shops and the casino. **Pros:** well-maintained facilities; hotel runs like a well-oiled machine; great security. **Cons:** the city's biggest hotel; typical chain service and surroundings; groups can overwhelm lobby. $ *Rooms from: $199* ✉ *2 Poydras St., CBD* ☎ *504/561–0500, 800/445–8667* ⊕ *www3.hilton.com/en/hotels/louisiana/hilton-new-orleans-riverside-MSYNHHH/index.html* ⌁ *1,600 rooms, 60 suites* ¶○¶ *No meals* ✛ *1:D5.*

$$
HOTEL
FAMILY
⌁ **Homewood Suites by Hilton New Orleans.** A stay in these huge apartment-like suites with high ceilings and big windows means that you'll be just three blocks from the Superdome and near Warehouse District museums and restaurants. **Pros:** friendly; huge rooms; near Lafayette Square's live music offerings. **Cons:** no in-hotel restaurant or room service; about a half mile from French Quarter. $ *Rooms from: $199* ✉ *901 Poydras St., CBD* ☎ *504/581–5599* ⊕ *www.homewoodsuitesneworleans.com* ⌁ *166 suites* ¶○¶ *Breakfast* ✛ *1:B4.*

$$
HOTEL
⌁ **The Hyatt Regency New Orleans.** The most luxurious of the bigger accommodation options in the city, this 32-story business and convention hotel has a cavernous lobby, a mega-ballroom, acres of meeting

9

space, and spacious and well-appointed guest rooms, with natural stone baths and iPod docking stations. **Pros:** next door to the Superdome; excellent service and amenities; close to Tulane University Hospital and the New Orleans BioInnovation Center. **Cons:** lacks New Orleans charm; in a high-traffic area complicated by construction of the Loyola streetcar line; not pedestrian friendly. $ *Rooms from: $179* ✉ *601 Loyola Ave., CBD* ☎ *504/561–1234, 888/591–1234* ⊕ *neworleans. hyatt.com* ⬎ *1,193 rooms, 95 suites* ♥♥ *No meals* ✛ *1:A4.*

$$ ⚏ **InterContinental New Orleans.** The modern rose-granite structure
HOTEL overlooking St. Charles Avenue has large, well-lighted guest rooms, with traditional furnishings that include quilted spreads and matching draperies. **Pros:** polished service; club-level rooms are among the best in town; perfect location for Mardi Gras; streetcar is just out front. **Cons:** located on one of the city's busiest downtown streets, which can be noisy; large big-box hotel. $ *Rooms from: $211* ✉ *444 St. Charles Ave., CBD* ☎ *504/525–5566, 800/445–6563* ⊕ *www.intercontinental. com* ⬎ *479 rooms, 31 suites* ♥♥ *No meals* ✛ *1:C4.*

$ ⚏ **International House.** Contemporary style pairs with creature comforts
HOTEL in guest rooms attractively decorated in a contemporary New Orleans style. **Pros:** great downtown location near the French Quarter; ideal if you want sophisticated surroundings; sceney hotel bar. **Cons:** small rooms; hotel faces busy downtown street with heavy traffic. $ *Rooms from: $149* ✉ *221 Camp St., CBD* ☎ *504/553–9550, 800/633–5770* ⊕ *www.ihhotel.com* ⬎ *117 rooms, 5 suites* ♥♥ *No meals* ✛ *1:C4.*

$ ⚏ **Lafayette Hotel.** For those who prefer a quieter neighborhood, the
HOTEL elegance of St. Charles Avenue is laid out before you in these spacious, sunny, and comfortable guest quarters that date back to 1916. **Pros:** streetcar stops right outside the front door; within walking distance of Riverfront and French Quarter attractions; pet-friendly. **Cons:** not a great area for walking late at night. $ *Rooms from: $119* ✉ *600 St. Charles Ave., CBD* ☎ *504/524–4441, 800/366–2743* ⊕ *www. thelafayettehotel.com* ⬎ *24 rooms, 20 suites* ♥♥ *No meals* ✛ *1:B5.*

$$$ ⚏ **Le Meridien.** This hip property, once the W Hotel New Orleans, is being
HOTEL transformed into a Le Meridien (also a Starwood brand). $ *Rooms from: $299* ✉ *333 Poydras St., CBD* ☎ *504/525–9444, 888/627–8389* ⊕ *www.whotels.com* ⬎ *410 rooms* ♥♥ *No meals* ✛ *1:C4.*

$$ ⚏ **Le Pavillon Hotel.** One of the most regally sumptuous hotels in town
HOTEL offers up romantic spaces, attentive service, and high-ceilinged, traditionally furnished guest rooms in history-filled surroundings from 1907. **Pros:** elegant French ambience; attentive staff; lovely restaurant. **Cons:** guest rooms could use some updating; not a fit if you're after something contemporary; on a busy street. $ *Rooms from: $189* ✉ *833 Poydras St., CBD* ☎ *504/581–3111, 800/535–9095* ⊕ *www.lepavillon. com* ⬎ *219 rooms, 7 suites* ♥♥ *No meals* ✛ *1:B4.*

$$$ ⚏ **Loews New Orleans Hotel.** Claims to be the friendliest large hotel in the
HOTEL city stand up quite well; there's also stellar service, a Brennan-family restaurant, and bright, oversize rooms. **Pros:** well managed; accessible to everything that counts downtown; reliable service; excellent restaurant and lounge. **Cons:** some amenities need an upgrade; about a 10-minute walk to the French Quarter. $ *Rooms from: $289* ✉ *300 Poydras St.,*

CBD ☎ 504/595–3300, 800/235–6397 ⊕ www.loewshotels.com/en/ New-Orleans-Hotel ⇶ 285 rooms, 12 suites ⍾⃝ No meals ⊹ 1:C4.

$$ ⚏ **Loft 523.** One of the few options for chic, loft-style digs in New
HOTEL Orleans—and a great choice at that—is so subtle from the outside that you may have trouble finding it among the surrounding buildings. **Pros:** sexy setting; inviting lounge; top-shelf amenities. **Cons:** some guests may be put off by the trendiness of it all; no restaurant. ⑤ Rooms from: $199 ⊠ 523 Gravier St., CBD ☎ 504/200–6523 ⊕ www.loft523.com ⇶ 16 rooms, 2 penthouses ⍾⃝ No meals ⊹ 1:C4.

$ ⚏ **Pelham Hotel.** A 19th-century building with homey accommodations
HOTEL is close to CBD sights like the Riverwalk and the casino and offers a less hectic alternative to the convention hotels. **Pros:** centrally located, but far from heavily traveled tourist streets; free Wi-Fi. **Cons:** rooms can be small and some lack windows; no on-site fitness area; noise from downtown traffic. ⑤ Rooms from: $149 ⊠ 444 Common St., CBD ☎ 504/522–4444, 800/659–5621 ⊕ www.thepelhamhotel.com ⇶ 60 rooms ⍾⃝ No meals ⊹ 1:C4.

$$ ⚏ **Renaissance Pere Marquette Hotel.** On floors named after renowned jazz
HOTEL musicians, large, quiet rooms have soothing colors, comfortable fabrics, and oversize marble bathrooms. **Pros:** amazing on-site bar and restaurant; excellent service. **Cons:** location is not especially pedestrian friendly; additional fee for Wi-Fi unless you are in the lobby. ⑤ Rooms from: $239 ⊠ 817 Common St., CBD ☎ 504/525–1111, 800/372–0482 ⊕ www. renaissancehotels.com ⇶ 268 rooms, 4 suites ⍾⃝ No meals ⊹ 1:B3.

$$$ ⚏ **The Roosevelt Hotel New Orleans.** From its glittering lobby to each beau-
HOTEL tiful, traditionally furnished guest room, one of the truly iconic New
Fodor's Choice Orleans hotels offers a grand experience. **Pros:** exquisite lobby, especially
★ when the holiday decorations are up; location near downtown and French Quarter; outstanding bar and restaurants; streetcar just outside. **Cons:** pricey fees for parking and in-room Wi-Fi. ⑤ Rooms from: $269 ⊠ 123 Baronne St., CBD ☎ 504/648–1200 ⊕ www.therooseveltneworleans. com ⇶ 504 rooms, 135 suites ⍾⃝ No meals ⊹ 1:B3.

$$ ⚏ **Sheraton New Orleans Hotel.** Executive rooms come with many special
HOTEL amenities, but even the regular guest rooms here are spacious and well appointed, with contemporary finishes and lots of extras. **Pros:** large hotel with lots of rooms; experienced staff; great service; central location. **Cons:** typical corporate convention property; lacks the warmth of some of its competitors; can be crowded during peak season. ⑤ Rooms from: $220 ⊠ 500 Canal St., CBD ☎ 504/525–2500, 800/253–6156 ⊕ www. sheratonneworleans.com ⇶ 1,100 rooms, 53 suites ⍾⃝ No meals ⊹ 1:C4.

$$ ⚏ **Staybridge Suites New Orleans French Quarter/Downtown.** One of the few
HOTEL genuinely good value options for extended-stay business travelers, families, or friends staying together, this all-suites hotel is well located and comfortable. **Pros:** spacious rooms; a good-size pool. **Cons:** a bit generic; no restaurant; located on a very busy intersection in the CBD. ⑤ Rooms from: $208 ⊠ 501 Tchoupitoulas St., CBD ☎ 504/571–1818, 800/541–4998 ⊕ www.staybridge.com ⇶ 182 suites ⍾⃝ Breakfast ⊹ 1:C4.

$ ⚏ **The Whitney, A Wyndham Historic Hotel.** This stylish European-style
HOTEL hostelry, with top-notch service and eminently comfortable rooms, is a great choice if you're looking to stay away from the Bourbon

9

Street bustle. **Pros:** free Wi-Fi; near the Convention Center, the French Quarter, and the Superdome. **Cons:** it's at one of the busiest downtown intersections in the city; narrow lobby can be difficult to navigate when the hotel is busy. $ *Rooms from: $139* ✉ *610 Poydras St., CBD* ☎ *504/581–4222, 800/996–3426* ⊕ *www.wyndham.com* ⮌ *93 rooms, 23 suites* ⦿ *No meals* ✛ *1:C4.*

$$$$
HOTEL
Fodor'sChoice
★

⌂ **Windsor Court Hotel.** A classic luxury hotel with plush carpeting, marble vanities, and mirrored dressing areas set in spacious guest rooms is just four blocks from the French Quarter. **Pros:** old-world elegance; superior service; location near the French Quarter but not in the thick of it. **Cons:** location close to casino can mean traffic outside. $ *Rooms from: $355* ✉ *300 Gravier St., CBD* ☎ *504/523–6000, 800/262–2662* ⊕ *www.windsorcourthotel.com* ⮌ *58 rooms, 266 suites, 1 penthouse* ⦿ *No meals* ✛ *1:C4.*

THE WAREHOUSE DISTRICT

$$
HOTEL

⌂ **Hampton Inn and Suites–Convention Center.** Convention Center lodgings with character can be hard to come by, but here, two century-old warehouses have been converted into a French colonial–style hotel with large, airy rooms that are comfortable, architecturally distinctive, and moderately priced. **Pros:** architecturally stunning; minutes from Convention Center. **Cons:** extremely busy area; can be daunting to both pedestrians and drivers; no restaurant on site. $ *Rooms from: $189* ✉ *1201 Convention Center Blvd., Warehouse District* ☎ *504/566–9990, 800/292–0653* ⊕ *www.neworleanshamptoninns.com* ⮌ *288 rooms* ⦿ *Breakfast* ✛ *1:D6.*

$
HOTEL

⌂ **Hotel Modern.** One of the most idiosyncratic and genuinely charming hotels in the city delivers a bit of attitude along with its eclectic selection of rooms of all shapes and sizes, from postage stamp to spacious, all comfortable and done up in an mix of modern and antique. **Pros:** on the St. Charles streetcar line and parade route; hip vibe; excellent service; on-site restaurant and bar. **Cons:** hallways can be cramped; you're a 15-minute walk from the French Quarter; some rooms are tiny, with small windows; not a traditional New Orleans stay. $ *Rooms from: $129* ✉ *936 St. Charles Ave., Warehouse District* ☎ *504/962–0900, 800/684–9525* ⮌ *135 rooms* ⦿ *No meals* ✛ *1:B5.*

$$
HOTEL

⌂ **Renaissance Arts Hotel.** Art lovers looking to stay close to downtown should check out this circa-1910 warehouse-turned-hotel, where huge windows now make for great views from comfortable, spacious, well-designed rooms furnished with a minimalist bent. **Pros:** modern, well-appointed facilities; beautiful artwork. **Cons:** not suitable for those who want a traditional New Orleans hotel or to spend lots of time in the French Quarter; daily fee for Wi-Fi. $ *Rooms from: $189* ✉ *700 Tchoupitoulas St., Warehouse District* ☎ *504/613–2330, 800/431–8634* ⊕ *www.marriott.com* ⮌ *210 rooms, 7 suites* ⦿ *No meals* ✛ *1:C5.*

THE GARDEN DISTRICT

$$
HOTEL

⌂ **Avenue Plaza Resort.** A haven of real local charm off the French Quarter grid offers spacious suites with kitchens and an impressive courtyard and pool. **Pros:** Garden District location; reasonable on-site parking. **Cons:** not convenient to French Quarter or CBD; lobby is small and can get crowded during busy times. $ *Rooms from: $143* ✉ *2111 St. Charles Ave., Garden District* ☎ *504/566–1212, 800/439–6493* ⊕ *www.avenueplazahotel.com* ⟿ *264 suites* ❑ *No meals* ✛ *2:B6*.

$$
B&B/INN
Fodor's Choice
★

🏠 **Grand Victorian Bed & Breakfast.** This real escape from the New Orleans hoopla more than lives up to its lofty name with lavishly appointed, romantic rooms that evoke old Louisiana through period pieces and distinctive private baths. **Pros:** a block and a half from Commander's Palace Restaurant; elegant; rooms are exquisitely appointed; possibly the best bed-and-breakfast value in the area; on the streetcar line. **Cons:** limited parking; not within easy walking distance of French Quarter or the CBD. $ *Rooms from: $210* ✉ *2727 St. Charles Ave., Garden District* ☎ *504/895–1104, 800/977–0008* ⊕ *www.gvbb.com* ⟿ *8 rooms* ❑ *Breakfast* ✛ *2:B5*.

$
B&B/INN

🏠 **St. Charles Guest House.** Simple and affordable, this 125-year-old bed-and-breakfast enjoys an ideal location in the Garden District. **Pros:** very affordable rates; within walking distance of the St. Charles streetcar line; pool; well run. **Cons:** furnishings and surroundings are in need of an update; no elevator or restaurant; credit cards not accepted. $ *Rooms from: $85* ✉ *1748 Prytania St., Garden District* ☎ *504/523–6556* ⊕ *www.stcharlesguesthouse.com* ⟿ *30 rooms, 24 with bath* ▬ *No credit cards* ❑ *Breakfast* ✛ *2:B6*.

$$
HOTEL

🏠 **Sully Mansion.** The stunning, art-filled setting, guest rooms with high ceilings and tall windows, and the personal attention you receive from the responsive owners set this B&B apart. **Pros:** old-world charm; individualized attention to guests. **Cons:** it's a mile or so from the French Quarter. $ *Rooms from: $215* ✉ *2631 Prytania St., Garden District* ☎ *504/891–0457, 800/364–2414* ⊕ *www.sullymansion.com* ⟿ *8 rooms, 2 suites* ❑ *Breakfast* ✛ *2:C5*.

UPTOWN

$$
B&B/INN
Fodor's Choice
★

🏠 **Chimes Bed and Breakfast.** Elegant and charming guest rooms, in a main house and a converted carriage house, are homey, well-equipped, and have private entrances. **Pros:** everything sparkles; just three blocks from the streetcar and Magazine Street; laptop and printer for guest use. **Cons:** noise carries easily from room to room; 3 miles from the French Quarter, which might be too far for some. $ *Rooms from: $158* ✉ *1146 Constantinople St., Uptown* ☎ *504/899–2621* ⊕ *www.chimesneworleans.com* ⟿ *5 rooms* ❑ *Breakfast* ✛ *2:C4*.

$
HOTEL

🏠 **Columns Hotel.** This white-columned 1883 Victorian hotel drips with local charm and is listed on the National Register of Historic Places—guests especially enjoy the wide and lovely veranda. **Pros:** exquisite architecture; the veranda's perfect for watching the St. Charles parades during Mardi Gras; on the streetcar line. **Cons:** rooms are large but need updating; second-floor rooms feel a bit stale (try to book on the third floor); transportation necessary to French Quarter and CBD. $ *Rooms from: $130* ✉ *3811 St. Charles Ave., Uptown* ☎ *504/899–9308, 800/445–9308* ⊕ *www.thecolumns.com* ⟿ *20 rooms* ❑ *Breakfast* ✛ *2:C4*.

$$
HOTEL

🏠 **Indigo Hotel.** Large windows frame a trendy-looking property, a new addition to a tree-lined avenue in the historic Garden District with bright, airy, and fresh contemporary rooms. **Pros:** close to the streetcar line; quiet residential neighborhood. **Cons:** conspicuously modern

9

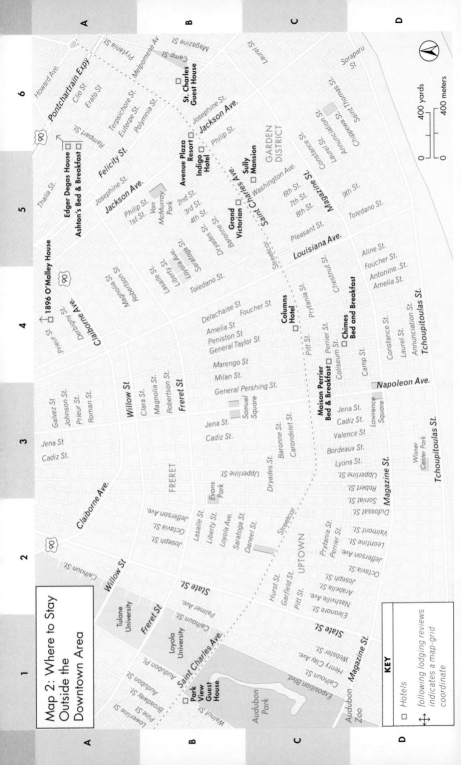

Map 2: Where to Stay Outside the Downtown Area

KEY

□ Hotels

↕ *following lodging reviews indicates a map-grid coordinate* ↔

in a historic neighborhood; somewhat soulless. $ *Rooms from: $186* ⊠ *2203 St. Charles Ave., Uptown* ☎ *877/834–3613* ⤢ *132 rooms, 10 suites* ❍ *No meals* ✢ *2:B5.*

$$
B&B/INN
☷ **Maison Perrier Bed & Breakfast.** Keeping up a tradition of Southern hospitality and historic elegance, this 1890s Victorian mansion is filled with antiques, gorgeous local art, and many extra comforts. **Pros:** personalized service; lovely residential setting; local Abita beer on draft for guests. **Cons:** not well located if you prefer to spend most of your time in the French Quarter; no elevator. $ *Rooms from: $199* ⊠ *4117 Perrier St., Uptown* ☎ *504/897–1807, 888/610–1807* ⊕ *www.maisonperrier. com* ⤢ *9 rooms* ❍ *Breakfast* ✢ *2:C4.*

$$
B&B/INN
☷ **Park View Guest House.** This Victorian guesthouse, steps from the streetcar and Audubon Park, adds to the delightful choices of smaller Uptown lodgings. **Pros:** great park views; easy access to public golf course; close to St. Charles streetcar line; good restaurants nearby. **Cons:** not walkable to downtown or the French Quarter. $ *Rooms from: $159* ⊠ *7004 St. Charles Ave., Uptown* ☎ *504/861–7564, 888/533–0746* ⊕ *www.parkviewguesthouse.com* ⤢ *21 rooms* ❍ *Breakfast* ✢ *2:B1.*

MID-CITY

$
B&B/INN
☷ **1896 O'Malley House.** Best suitable for those seeking a less touristy New Orleans experience, this elegant bed-and-breakfast near the intersection of Canal Street and North Carrollton Avenue offers rooms furnished with beautiful antiques and equipped with heavy cypress doors, hardwood floors, and plush draperies at the oversize windows. **Pros:** complimentary snacks, wine, and beer available; an iPad loaded with information about New Orleans is located in each room; walking distance to entertainment and restaurants; good base for Jazz Fest. **Cons:** roughly 3 miles from the French Quarter and the Garden District; not for guests wanting to be in the middle of the action. $ *Rooms from: $135* ⊠ *120 S. Pierce St., Mid-City* ☎ *504/488–5896, 866/226–1896* ⊕ *www.1896omalleyhouse.com* ⤢ *8 rooms* ❍ *Breakfast* ✢ *2:A4.*

$$
B&B/INN
☷ **Ashton's Bed & Breakfast.** Few details have been missed in this sumptuous 1861 mansion, where distinctively appointed guest rooms have a range of beds, including iron, Shaker, and four-poster. **Pros:** exquisitely decorated and spacious rooms; nice location not far from New Orleans City Park; convenient to Jazz Fest. **Cons:** if you don't have a car, you need to take a taxi or city bus to reach the French Quarter. $ *Rooms from: $199* ⊠ *2023 Esplanade Ave., Mid-City* ☎ *504/942–7048, 800/725–4131* ⊕ *www.ashtonsbb.com* ⤢ *8 rooms* ❍ *Breakfast* ✢ *2:A6.*

$$
B&B/INN
Fodor's Choice
★
☷ **Edgar Degas House.** Art buffs will love that this was once home to French impressionist Edgar Degas; plus, the 1852 mansion retains its original floor plan and colors, and the spacious second-floor rooms have chandeliers that hang from 14-foot ceilings. **Pros:** meticulously maintained and expertly operated; luxe amenities and extras; on the National Register of Historic Places; close to Jazz Fest. **Cons:** not in the middle of the action; if you don't have a car, you'll be taking the city bus on Esplanade Avenue to the Quarter, or cabbing it at night. $ *Rooms from: $199* ⊠ *2306 Esplanade Ave., Mid-City* ☎ *504/821–5009, 800/755–6730* ⊕ *www.degashouse.com* ⤢ *9 rooms* ❍ *Breakfast* ✢ *2:A6.*

9

NIGHTLIFE AND
THE ARTS

COCKTAIL CULTURE

In the early 1800s the Creole apothecary Antoine Amadie Peychaud ran a pharmacy in the French Quarter. He concocted a cherry-colored bitters that is still an essential ingredient of the Sazerac, New Orleans's favorite cocktail.

(above) Ingredients for New Orleans's official cocktail, the Sazerac. (top right) Tales of the Cocktail festival. (bottom right) The Museum of the American Cocktail.

According to legend, Peychaud mixed his bitters with brandy, water, and sugar, then served the drink in a traditional French eggcup called a "coquetier." Soon English speakers mangled the French word and called the drink a "cocktail." It's a good story, except that Peychaud was three years old when the word "cocktail" first appeared in print. But even if the cocktail wasn't invented in New Orleans, no other city has embraced it with more passion. From Peychaud's now-famous bitters to the iconic Hurricane and beyond, New Orleans is home to many of the greatest inventions in cocktail history. In recent years a new generation of bartenders has reinvigorated the Crescent City's cocktail culture with elaborate techniques and farm-fresh ingredients. —by Todd A. Price

NEW ORLEANS'S OFFICIAL DRINK

Legislators were concerned giving the state of Louisiana an official cocktail would cause people to associate the state with drinking. Apparently the city of New Orleans was already a lost cause, though, and on June 2008 the Sazerac became the official cocktail of New Orleans. It's the only city in the country to have an officially legislated drink.

COCKTAIL EVENTS AND EXHIBITS

Drink & Learn: The Cocktail Tour. Culinary historian and Louisiana native Elizabeth Pearce leads an informative two-hour walking tour dedicated to the city's cocktail culture. The $50 ticket includes four drinks. ⊠ *French Quarter* ⊕ *www.drinkandlearn.com.*

The Museum of the American Cocktail. As of this writing the museum is closed and in the process of moving into a new space in Central City, near the CBD, that it will share with the Southern Food and Beverage Musuem. The extensive collection of rare spirits, books, Prohibition-era literature and music, vintage cocktail shakers, glassware, tools, gadgets, and all manner of cocktail memorabilia and photographs culled from the collections of museum founders and patrons should be installed in its new home by the summer of 2014, but check the website for details. ⊠ *1504 Oretha Castle Haley Blvd., CBD* ☎ *504/569–0405* ⊕ *www.museumoftheamericancocktail.org.*

New Orleans Original Cocktail Tour. This 2½-hour Gray Line walking tour leads you through the saloons and wine cellars of the French Quarter, with stops for libations. ⊠ *Warehouse District* ☎ *504/569–1401* ⊕ *www.graylineneworleans.com/cocktail-tour.html.*

New Orleans Wine and Food Experience. Serious wine drinkers skip the beach for this four-day celebration of Bacchus

over Memorial Day weekend. Events include vintner dinners at local restaurants and the two-day Grand Tasting, where nearly 75 restaurants serve food and 1,000 different wines are poured. ☎ *504/529–9463* ⊕ *www.nowfe.com.*

NOLA Brewing Tour. Every Friday, hundreds of people show up at New Orleans's only craft brewery (the name stands for New Orleans Lager and Ale) to learn how beer gets made, with unlimited free suds. The 90-minute free tour starts at 2 pm. Go early. ⊠ *3001 Tchoupitoulas St., Garden District* ☎ *407/222–0449 (marketing and sales)* ⊕ *www.nolabrewing.com.*

Old New Orleans Rum Distillery. Founded in 1995, this craft distillery is the oldest maker of rum in the continental United States. Tours start with a cocktail and end with a tasting of four different rums; they cost $10. Complimentary transportation from the French Quarter is available during the week. ⊠ *2815 Frenchmen St., Gentilly* ☎ *504/945–9400* ⊕ *www.oldneworleansrum.com.*

Tales of the Cocktail. Each July Tales of the Cocktail, billed as "the most spirited event of the summer," brings thousands of experts and enthusiasts together for an internationally acclaimed, five-day celebration dedicated to the artistry and science of making drinks. ☎ *504/948–0511* ⊕ *www.talesofthecocktail.com.*

TOP FIVE ICONIC NEW ORLEANS COCKTAILS

Sazerac: Rye whiskey, Peychaud's bitters, and sugar served in a rocks glass rinsed with absinthe or Herbsaint, a local absinthe substitute

Claim to Fame: Official drink of New Orleans

Best Places to Try One: Column's Hotel Victorian Lounge Bar or French 75

Ramos Gin Fizz: Gin, cream, orange flower water, and lemon and lime juice shaken with an egg white and topped with club soda

Claim to Fame: Huey P. Long's favorite eye-opener

Best Place to Try One: Sazerac Bar at the Roosevelt Hotel

Hurricane: Blend of rum, grenadine, and tropical juices

Claim to Fame: The start of many a lost weekend

Best Place to Try One: Pat O'Brien's

Vieux Carré: Brandy, rye whiskey, sweet vermouth, Bénédictine, and a dash each of Peychaud's and Angostura bitters

Claim to Fame: A perfectly balanced tribute to the French Quarter

Best Place to Try One: Carousel Bar at the Hotel Monteleone, where it was invented

Pimm's Cup: Pimm's No. 1 topped with lemon-lime soda and garnished with a cucumber

Claim to Fame: A British thirst quencher embraced by the Crescent City

Best Place to Try One: Napoleon House Bar and Café

There are many iconic images that come to mind when people think of New Orleans nightlife, including the neon glitz of Bourbon Street and the lone jazzman playing his horn beneath an old French Quarter gas lamp. But this is only the start of what New Orleans nightlife is all about. Whether you're looking for the simple pleasures of a perfectly constructed cocktail with a balcony view or something more adventurous, you've come to the right place.

NIGHTLIFE

Updated by
Cameron Todd

No American town places such a premium on pleasure as New Orleans. From swank hotel lounges and refined jazz halls to sweaty dance clubs and raucous Bourbon Street bars, this city is serious about frivolity—and famous for it. Partying is more than an occasional indulgence in this city; it's a lifestyle. The bars and clubs that pulse with music are the city's lifeblood, and are found in every neighborhood. Like stars with their own gravity, they draw people through their doors to belly up to the bars or head feet first onto the dance floors. Blues, jazz, funk, R&B, rock, roots, Cajun, and zydeco—there are many kinds of music and nightlife experiences to be had in New Orleans. On any day or night of the year, the city is brimming with musical possibilities.

The French Quarter and Faubourg Marigny are the easiest places to find great music and nightspots. The venues are numerous and all within easy walking distance of one another. In the nearby Warehouse District, New Orleans institutions like Howlin' Wolf, Mulate's, and Circle Bar have been joined by scores of new bars, clubs, and restaurants. Moving upriver through the Garden District and Uptown, you'll find some of the most famous music spots in the city, such as Tipitina's and Maple Leaf. Bywater, Mid-City, and Tremé are residential neighborhoods with fewer commercial strips, but they too have their crown jewels, like Vaughan's, Bullet's, and Rock 'n' Bowl.

10

PLANNING

HOURS

Bars tend to open in the early afternoon and stay open well into the morning hours. Live music usually begins around 6 in a handful of clubs that host early sets, but **things really get going between 9 and 11 pm.** Bear in mind that many venues operate on "New Orleans time," meaning that if a show is advertised for 10 pm then it might kick off closer to 11.

If you're a night owl, plenty of clubs have **late-night sets,** some not starting until 1 am.

WHAT TO WEAR

Dress codes are as rare as snow in this city. On any given night in the French Quarter, and especially during the Carnival season, you'll see everything from tuxedoes to tutus, T-shirts to fairy wings, and everything in between. Wear whatever is easiest to dance in.

COVER CHARGE VS DRINK MINIMUMS

Many bars on Bourbon Street entice visitors by presenting bands with no cover charge. They make their money by imposing a **one- or two-drink minimum,** with draft beer or soft drinks costing $5 to $8 apiece. In general, prices for beer, wine, and cocktails range from $4 to $9, unless you land in a good neighborhood dive bar, and then the prices can drop by as much as half. Music clubs generally charge a flat cover of between $5 and $20, with the high-end prices usually reserved for national touring artists, holidays, and special occasions.

TIPPING THE BAND

Bring cash to live-music clubs; **many bands play for tips alone.** Expect the hat (or the bucket, or the old coffee can, or the empty goldfish bowl) to be passed around once per set.

SAFETY

Although much of New Orleans is safe, especially in the French Quarter, it's always a good idea to **keep an eye out and be aware of your surroundings,** especially late at night, or if it's readily apparent that you've been hitting the Hurricanes a little too hard. Pickpockets and muggers do exist, but an ounce of prevention in the form of awareness goes a long way toward avoiding any kind of incident. In the French Quarter and downtown it's usually fine to walk from place to place, but if you're traveling through outlying neighborhoods late at night it's best to take a car or taxi.

EVENT INFO

A great source for concert, event, and local information is **WWOZ,** the jazz and heritage community radio station, which broadcasts worldwide over the Internet at ⊕ *www.wwoz.org.* Local musicians, music historians, and personalities make up the all-volunteer corps of DJs, and they broadcast live 24/7 out of the French Quarter.

For more detailed event listings, check out **Gambit Weekly** (⊕ *www.bestofneworleans.com*), the alternative weekly available free in many bars, cafés, and stores. **The Times-Picayune** (⊕ *www.nola.com*), the city's main newspaper, publishes an entertainment supplement every Friday called Lagniappe. The monthly **OffBeat** (⊕ *www.offbeat.com*) magazine has in-depth coverage of local music and venues and is available at many hotels, stores, and restaurants.

FRENCH QUARTER

The old neighborhood, with its Spanish architecture and narrow, French-named streets, is the hub of the Crescent City and remains the beating heart of New Orleans's nightlife. Live music comes at you from all directions—from bars, clubs, concert halls, restaurants, and even from the streets themselves, and many of the neighborhood's restaurants, shops, cafés, and galleries stay open late to accommodate the night crowd. Although mostly fueled by tourists, the French Quarter remains the city's premiere nightlife destination because of its diversity and convenience.

BARS

Bar Tonique. An eclectic spot on North Rampart Street, this brick-walled room with private nooks and opening to a beautiful outdoor courtyard looks like a cross between a dive and a lounge on the Riviera. The book-length drinks menu, with everything from pre-Prohibition classics to modern creations, reads like a history of the cocktail. The talented staff can turn out any of those offerings with aplomb. ⊠ *820 N. Rampart St., French Quarter* ☎ *504/324–6045* ⊕ *www.bartonique.com.*

Bombay Club. A longtime favorite and a rather swanky place for the French Quarter, with leather chairs and dark paneling, covers cocktail history with an encyclopedic menu that starts with drinks from the mid-19th century. Although there is no formal dress code, men are encouraged to wear jackets. Tucked away from the street in the Prince Conti Hotel, this lair hosts piano players and jazz combos nightly. ⊠ *Prince Conti Hotel, 830 Conti St., French Quarter* ☎ *504/586–0972* ⊕ *www.thebombayclub.com.*

Cane and Table. With its elegant, understated Caribbean decor, dim lighting, and low volumes, this rum house is a refreshing relief from the general chaos of the neighborhood. The friendly barkeeps boast "ProtoTiki Cocktails" (specialty rum drinks with modern twists), but there's a sophisticated list of Spanish wines to choose from as well. The space offers a large marble bar, newly renovated courtyard out back, and small tables for intimate dining. Come for the cocktails and atmosphere, but don't miss out on the food: the menu is comprised of Caribbean and traditional Southern combinations, and the dishes are inventive and intensely flavorful. ⊠ *1113 Decatur St., French Quarter* ☎ *504/581–1112* ⊕ *www.caneandtablenola.com.*

Carousel Bar. A favorite New Orleans drinking destination since 1949, the revolving bar has served the likes of Tennessee Williams, Truman Capote, and Ernest Hemingway. A recent renovation added extra space for a second bar, more tables, and a stage that hosts free shows by local musicians Wednesday through Saturday. ⊠ *Hotel Monteleone, 214 Royal St., French Quarter* ☎ *504/523–3341* ⊕ *www.hotelmonteleone.com.*

10

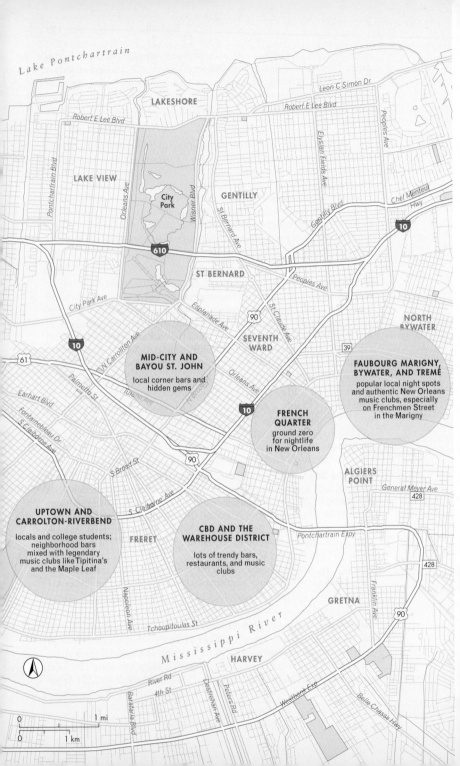

Lake Pontchartrain

LAKESHORE

Leon C Simon Dr

Robert E Lee Blvd

Robert E Lee Blvd

LAKE VIEW

Pontchartrain Blvd

Orleans Ave

City Park

Wisner Blvd

GENTILLY

Peoples Ave

St Bernard Ave

Elysian Fields Ave

Gentilly Blvd

Chef Menteur Hwy

610

10

ST BERNARD

Peoples Ave

City Park Ave

Esplanade Ave

90

St Claude Ave

SEVENTH WARD

NORTH BYWATER

39

10

61

N Carrollton Ave

Tulane Ave

Palmetto St

MID-CITY AND BAYOU ST. JOHN
local corner bars and hidden gems

Orleans Ave

10

FAUBOURG MARIGNY, BYWATER, AND TREMÉ
popular local night spots and authentic New Orleans music clubs, especially on Frenchmen Street in the Marigny

Earhart Blvd

Fontainebleau Dr

S Claiborne Ave

S Broad St

FRENCH QUARTER
ground zero for nightlife in New Orleans

ALGIERS POINT

General Meyer Ave

428

90

UPTOWN AND CARROLTON-RIVERBEND
locals and college students; neighborhood bars mixed with legendary music clubs like Tipitina's and the Maple Leaf

FRERET

S Claiborne Ave

CBD AND THE WAREHOUSE DISTRICT
lots of trendy bars, restaurants, and music clubs

Pontchartrain Expy

428

Napoleon Ave

Tchoupitoulas St

Mississippi River

GRETNA

Franklin Ave

90

HARVEY

River Rd

4th St

Barataria Blvd

Destrehan Ave

Peters Rd

Westbank Expy

Belle Chasse Hwy

0   1 mi

0   1 km

Cat's Meow. Before you see it, you'll hear this Bourbon Street landmark, New Orleans's most popular karaoke bar. Given an ideal corner location, the bar's tall doors and windows open onto two streets, beckoning undergrads, conventioneers, and bachelorette parties to dance on the floor and grab the mic. High energy MCs and DJs keep the night spinning along, but get on the sign-up sheet early if you want a chance at French Quarter fame. ✉ *701 Bourbon St., French Quarter* ☎ *504/523–2788* ⊕ *www.catskaraoke.com.*

> ### ONE FOR THE ROAD
>
> Although bottles and glasses are officially banned on the street, New Orleans is one of the few places where it's legal to carry a drink in public. Ready to move on? Ask the bartender for a "go cup."

Chart Room. Unpretentious even by New Orleans standards, this little dive not far from Canal Street draws a good number of locals from the Quarter and beyond for the inexpensive drinks and the wide-open doorways that offer table seating just off the sidewalk. ✉ *300 Chartres St., French Quarter* ☎ *504/522–1708.*

Cosimo's. Few tourists make their way to this hip neighborhood hangout, which is in a far corner of the Lower Quarter. A short flight of stairs leads to a pool and dart room. Quirky wagon-wheel ceiling fans, ample windows, and a friendly vibe make it a low-key place to wind down. Food options include pizzas, burgers, and sandwiches. ✉ *1201 Burgundy St., French Quarter* ☎ *504/522–9715.*

Crescent City Brewhouse. The only microbrewery in the French Quarter (and one of two in the city), this convivial pub and restaurant makes four specialty beers on the premises and one seasonal selection. The atmosphere can get a little touristy, but oysters on the half shell, live jazz in the evenings, and a second-floor riverview balcony make a visit more than worthwhile. ✉ *527 Decatur St., French Quarter* ☎ *504/522–0571* ⊕ *www.crescentcitybrewhouse.com.*

Fodor's Choice ★ **French 75.** This is a must-visit for any who love to submerge themselves in old-time elegance. Adjoining Arnaud's, the classic New Orleans Creole restaurant, this dark-wood bar is complete with leather-backed chairs and imposing columns. The bartenders work magic with their encyclopedic knowledge of cocktails and arsenal of ingredients. Be sure to venture upstairs to the Germaine Wells Mardi Gras Museum (free), a slightly bizarre showcase for memorabilia and ball gowns worn by the original owner's daughter. ✉ *813 Bienville St., French Quarter* ☎ *504/523–5433* ⊕ *www.arnaudsrestaurant.com/french-75.*

Kerry Irish Pub. This well-worn favorite has a pool table, a jukebox stocked with the Pogues and Flogging Molly, and, of course, Guinness on draft. A small stage at the back hosts Irish musicians, singer-songwriters, and R&B or jazz musicians nightly with no cover charge. It's one of the last venues for Irish music in the Quarter. ✉ *331 Decatur St., French Quarter* ☎ *504/527–5954* ⊕ *www.kerryirishpub.com.*

Lafitte's Blacksmith Shop. Perhaps the most photographed building in the Quarter after the St. Louis Cathedral, this 18th-century blacksmith shop was once a front for the eponymous pirate's less legitimate business

10

ventures—or so says local legend. Today, it's an atmospheric piano bar with a rustic, candlelit interior and a small outdoor patio shaded by banana trees. Despite the addition of a few flat-screen TVs, a drink here just after sundown, when the place is lit by candles, lets you slip back in time for an hour or so. ⊠ *941 Bourbon St., French Quarter* ☎ *504/593–9761* ⊕ *www.lafittesblacksmithshop.com.*

Molly's at the Market. Grab a perch almost any time of day at one of the best-known and most popular bars along the far stretch of Decatur Street. Expect perfect pints of Guinness, generously poured cocktails, and gregarious bartenders. From a window seat watch the crowds of shop-goers, sightseers, and all-day revelers. Everyone from politicians to punk rockers eventually drifts though the doors. ⊠ *1107 Decatur St., French Quarter* ☎ *504/525–5169* ⊕ *www.mollysatthemarket.net.*

Fodor's Choice
★

Napoleon House Bar and Café. It's a living shrine to what may be called the semiofficial New Orleans school of decor: faded grandeur. Chipped wall paint, diffused light, and a tiny courtyard with a trickling fountain and lush banana trees create a timeless escapist mood. The house specialty is a Pimm's Cup (here they top Pimm's No. 1 with lemonade and 7-Up). This vintage restaurant and watering hole has long been popular with writers, artists, and other free spirits, although today most customers are tourists. But even locals who don't venture often into the French Quarter will make an exception for Napoleon House. ⊠ *500 Chartres St., French Quarter* ☎ *504/524–9752* ⊕ *www.napoleonhouse.com.*

Old Absinthe House. Over its 200-year history, this low-key oasis with its famous marble absinthe fountain has served guests including Oscar Wilde, Mark Twain, Franklin Roosevelt, and Frank Sinatra. It's now mostly frequented by tourists and casual local characters who appreciate a good brewski or cocktail to go. Thousands of business cards stapled to the wall serve as interesting wallpaper. ⊠ *240 Bourbon St., French Quarter* ☎ *504/524–0113* ⊕ *www.ruebourbon.com/oldabsinthehouse.*

Pat O'Brien's. Sure, it's touristy, but there are reasons Pat O's has been a must-stop on the New Orleans drinking trail since Prohibition. There's plenty of room to spread out, from the elegant side bar and piano bar that flank the carriageway entrance to the lush (and in winter, heated) patio. Friendly staff, an easy camaraderie among patrons, and a signature drink—the pink, fruity, and extremely potent Hurricane, which comes with a souvenir glass—make this French Quarter stalwart a pleasant afternoon diversion. Expect a line on weekend nights, and if you don't want your glass, return it for the deposit. ⊠ *718 St. Peter St., French Quarter* ☎ *504/525–4823* ⊕ *www.patobriens.com.*

Patrick's Bar Vin. Dapper Patrick Van Hoorebeek holds court at his wine bar in a clubby atmosphere of dark wood and red upholstery. Wines by the glass are the specialty, but there's also an excellent selection of cocktails and beers, including Van Hoorebeek's own Belgium brew. Major oenophiles can rent personal wine lockers. Only a few steps from Bourbon Street, Bar Vin feels like another world. It opens at noon on Friday to catch the lunch crowd. ⊠ *730 Bienville St., French Quarter* ☎ *504/200–3180* ⊕ *www.patricksbarvin.com.*

GAY NIGHTLIFE

Bourbon Pub. It's impossible to miss this 24-hour video bar at the corner of St. Ann and Bourbon, especially in early evenings, when the doors are open and the dance crowd spills into the street. There's usually a cover charge on Friday and Saturday nights after 10 pm; Sunday afternoon is devoted to vintage videos by assorted gay icons. ⊠ *801 Bourbon St., French Quarter* ☎ *504/529–2107* ⊕ *www.bourbonpub.com.*

Café Lafitte in Exile. A Bourbon Street stalwart attracts a somewhat older and very casual group of gay men. The recently renovated second floor has a pool table, pinball machine, and wraparound balcony with a bird's-eye view of the street scene below. Sunday afternoon, when the oldies spin and the paper-napkin confetti flies, is especially popular. ⊠ *901 Bourbon St., French Quarter* ☎ *504/522–8397* ⊕ *www.lafittes.com.*

Corner Pocket. Filmmaker John Waters reportedly counts the Pocket as a New Orleans favorite, and with skinny, tattooed strippers on the bar and an inebriated drag queen emceeing the show, it's easy to see why. Sleazy fun on a good night, but keep your wits about you. ⊠ *940 St. Louis St., French Quarter* ☎ *504/568–9829* ⊕ *www.cornerpocket.net.*

Golden Lantern. The Lower Quarter has become a lot more upscale since this neighborhood gay haunt's heyday, but the officially named Tubby's Golden Lantern soldiers on. The bartender's whims determine the music, the drinks are strong, and happy hour runs noon to 8 pm Mondays and Tuesdays and 8 am to 8 pm every other day. The bar is best known as ground zero for the annual Southern Decadence drag parade, when a throng gathers out front for the kickoff. ⊠ *1239 Royal St., French Quarter* ☎ *504/529–2860* ⊕ *www.tubbysbarneworleans.com.*

Good Friends. With its tasteful decor and reasonable volume level, this is a slightly more upscale, sedate alternative to the blasting disco bars down the street. The Queen's Head Pub on the second floor, open weekends, has darts, a wraparound balcony, and respectable martinis. Brush up on your show tunes at the popular Sunday afternoon piano sing-along. ⊠ *740 Dauphine St., French Quarter* ☎ *504/566–7191* ⊕ *www.goodfriendsbar.com.*

Napoleon's Itch. The only gay bar in New Orleans that's also attached to a large hotel, this narrow space is in the heart of St. Ann–and–Bourbon gay central; it's a must-visit during the annual Southern Decadence festival. The comfy sofas and handsome bartenders are a plus, and the crowd tends to be a bit dressier than at similar venues. ⊠ *Bourbon Orleans Hotel, 734 Bourbon St., French Quarter* ☎ *504/237–4144* ⊕ *www.napoleonsitch.com.*

10

Oz. A spacious dance club that mainly attracts young gay men also draws straight men and women, largely because of the scarcity of good dance floors in the French Quarter. It's open around the clock and tends to peak very late. ⊠ *800 Bourbon St., French Quarter* ☎ *504/593–9491* ⊕ *www.ozneworleans.com.*

Parade Disco. High-energy disco rules at this dance club above the Bourbon Pub. If it gets to be too much, a quieter back bar and a balcony offer retreat. The crowd is mostly male and young, but women are welcome. ⊠ *801 Bourbon St., above Bourbon Pub, French Quarter* ☎ *504/529–2107* ⊕ *www.bourbonpub.com.*

MUSIC CLUBS

Davenport Lounge. Swanky digs in the Ritz Carlton Hotel are home to namesake Jeremy Davenport, an old school crooner in the mold of Sinatra and Crosby. With a hot trumpet, Davenport plays Thursday through Saturday and draws a mixed crowd of visitors and locals to the swinging dance floor. Other musicians perform on Wednesdays. ✉ *The Ritz Carlton New Orleans, 921 Canal St., French Quarter* ☎ *504/524–1331* ⊕ *www.ritzcarlton.com.*

Fritzel's European Jazz Pub. An old-school gem in the midst of Bourbon Street's many venues with bad cover bands, this Dixieland music club, built in the style of the old jazz halls, has tight rows of seating close to the stage and floating barmaids. Drinks cost a little more, but there's never a cover charge. Shows nightly. ✉ *733 Bourbon St., French Quarter* ☎ *504/586–4800* ⊕ *www.fritzelsjazz.net.*

House of Blues. Despite its name, blues rarely makes the bill at this Decatur Street link of a national chain. The mid-size venue embraces rock, country, soul, funk, and world music, and it's one of the city's most reliable destinations for national touring acts. The adjoining restaurant hosts a popular gospel brunch. The **Parish,** a more intimate offshoot upstairs from the main house, books edgier and up-and-coming groups. ✉ *225 Decatur St., French Quarter* ☎ *504/310–4999* ⊕ *www.houseofblues.com.*

Irvin Mayfield's Jazz Playhouse. Serious music lovers converge on this intimate lounge with a modern aesthetic. Irvin Mayfield, one of the city's great musicians and winner of both Grammy and Billboard awards, was determined to bring topflight jazz back to Bourbon Street, where loud rock and blues cover bands are the norm. He succeeded, providing an incredible lineup of local talent for multiple sets every day with no cover and shows starting between 5 pm and midnight. ✉ *Royal Sonesta Hotel, 300 Bourbon St., French Quarter* ☎ *504/553–2299* ⊕ *www.irvinmayfield.com.*

Margaritaville Café. Ever-popular with tourists and Jimmy Buffett fans (but often mocked by locals), Margaritaville books regional blues and roots rock with sets starting as early as 11 am and going into the night. Whimsical island-themed decor includes an airplane emerging from a wall and a tire swing bar. Yes, you can order a salt-rimmed signature drink with a "Cheeseburger in Paradise." ✉ *1104 Decatur St., French Quarter* ☎ *504/592–2565* ⊕ *www.margaritavilleneworleans.com.*

One Eyed Jack's. This former Toulouse Street theater hosts touring modern rock acts as well as local up-and-comers, '80s nights, and even the occasional female arm-wrestling competition. The 19th-century saloon interior provides an appropriately decadent backdrop for Fleur de Tease, a resident burlesque troupe. ✉ *615 Toulouse St., French Quarter* ☎ *504/569–8361* ⊕ *www.oneeyedjacks.net.*

Palm Court Jazz Café. Banjo player Danny Barker immortalized this restaurant in his song "Palm Court Strut." Traditional New Orleans jazz is presented in a timeless setting with tile floors, exposed-brick walls, and a handsome mahogany bar. There are decent creature comforts here; regional cuisine is served, and you can sit at the bar and rub elbows with local musicians. A wide selection of records and CDs are on sale. ✉ *1204 Decatur St., French Quarter* ☎ *504/525–0200* ⊕ *www.palmcourtjazzcafe.com.*

FAMILY
Fodor's Choice
★ **Preservation Hall.** At this cultural landmark founded in 1961, a cadre of distinguished New Orleans musicians, most of whom were schooled by an ever-dwindling group of elder statesmen, nurture the jazz tradition that flowered in the 1920s. There is limited seating on benches—many patrons end up squatting on the floor or standing in back—and no beverages are served, although you can bring your own drink in a plastic cup. Nonetheless, legions of satisfied music lovers regard an evening at this all-ages venue as an essential New Orleans experience. Cover charge is $15 (cash only), and $20 for Friday and Saturday performances. The price can be a bit higher for special appearances. A limited number of $30 VIP tickets guarantee you a seat and let you skip the line. ⊠ *726 St. Peter St., French Quarter* ☎ *504/522–2841* ⊕ *www. preservationhall.com.*

FAUBOURG MARIGNY, BYWATER, AND TREMÉ

FAUBOURG MARIGNY

Frenchmen Street in the Marigny is the hottest music strip in town, and is also known for its food and street life. Much of Frenchmen's activity is within a three-block area (between Decatur and Dauphine streets), where fun seekers crawl bars and people-watch on the sidewalk. Some clubs along this strip charge a $5–$10 cover for music, but many charge nothing at all. Along St. Claude Avenue a diverse cluster of bars and clubs offers everything from brass-band jams to death metal to experimental, avant-garde indie rock.

BARS

AllWays Lounge & Theatre. This lounge/theater combo has become one of the centerpieces of the local indie, avant-garde, and art scenes. Bringing to mind 1930s Berlin, the lounge has a black-and-red color scheme and frayed-at-the-edges art deco aesthetic. Musicians, burlesque dancers, clowns, artists, and jacks-of-all-trades take to the stage here most nights of the week. Meanwhile, in the back of the house, the 100-seat AllWays Theatre hosts weekend plays and other performances. ⊠ *2240 St. Claude Ave., Faubourg Marigny* ☎ *504/218–5778* ⊕ *www. theallwayslounge.net.*

Checkpoint Charlie's. This bustling corner bar draws young locals who shoot pool and listen to blues and rock, whether live or from the jukebox—24 hours a day, seven days a week. Weekends often feature hard rock, punk, and metal bands. There's also a paperback library, a menu of bar grub, and even a fully functioning Laundromat if you don't mind clean clothes that smell like smoke. ⊠ *501 Esplanade Ave., Faubourg Marigny* ☎ *504/281–4847.*

The Maison. This historic building—with a sprawling three-story floor plan, interior balconies, a terrific kitchen, plus multiple bars, stages, and dance floors—has become one of Frenchmen Street's most popular destinations. Live music every night of the week (normally with no cover) makes it inviting, and the managers skillfully weave local and touring DJs and electronic music into their lineup of parties and events. ⊠ *508 Frenchmen St., Faubourg Marigny* ☎ *504/371–5543* ⊕ *www. maisonfrenchmen.com.*

10

Continued on page 206

by Alison Fensterstock
and Jennifer Odell

Above and opposite, French Quarter jazz clubs, Maison Bourbon and Preservation Jazz Hall.

NEW ORLEANS NOISE

The late local R&B star Ernie K-Doe once said, "I'm not sure, but I think all music comes from New Orleans." He wasn't far off. The Crescent City has crafted American music for hundreds of years— from Jelly Roll Morton's Storyville jazz piano to the siren sound of Louis Armstrong's genre-defining trumpet; from Little Richard's first French Quarter rock 'n' roll recording session to Lil Wayne's hip-hop domination.

Right, New Orleans' musical legend, Louis Armstrong.

THE SOUNDS OF THE BIG EASY

JAZZ

The roots of New Orleans jazz reach back to the 17th century, when slaves sang traditional songs in Congo Square. As their African and Caribbean polyrhythms blended with European styles, new sounds were born.

In the Storyville red-light district in 1895, cornetist Buddy Bolden played what is considered to be the first jazz. It was a march-meets-syncopation sound that drew from the city's numerous fraternal and societal brass marching bands, from ragtime, and from blues.

Pianist Jelly Roll Morton, who also got his start playing in Storyville's bordellos, helped transition ragtime into jazz with his more flamboyant playing style. In 1915 he published the first jazz composition, "Jelly Roll Morton Blues."

But it was the cornet and trumpet players of the day who really sounded off. Joe "King" Oliver, Louis Armstrong's mentor, changed his cornet's sound by holding a plunger over the bell. Sidney Bechet revolutionized soloing with his radical fingering. Louis Armstrong made jazz a phenomenon with his skill, improvisational style, and showmanship. These men were the originators of New Orleans Dixieland, which rapidly spread across the nation and was itself transformed—here and elsewhere—through the decades.

Today, young New Orleans musicians benefit from the work of contemporary jazz players and educators like pianist Ellis Marsalis. His students have included Terence Blanchard, Donald Harrison, Jr., and Nicholas Payton, as well as his own talented sons: Wynton (trumpet), Branford (sax), Delfeayo (trombone), and Ellis III (drums).

LISTEN TO: King Oliver, Louis Armstrong, Sidney Bechet, Jelly Roll Morton, Kid Ory, Donald Harrison, Jr., Nicholas Payton, Trombone Shorty, Christian Scott.

GO TO: Preservation Hall and Palm Court Jazz Café (traditional; French Quarter). Snug Harbor and the Blue Nile (contemporary; Faubourg Marigny).

EXPERIENCE IT: during ranger-led talks and walks at the Jazz National Historic Park (www.nps.gov/jazz).

Far left, clockwise from left, jazz at Bourbon Street, Jelly Roll Morton, Louis Armstrong. Below right, Zydeco accordionist. Left, Soul Rebel Brass Band.

BRASS BANDS

To lay down those 2/4 and 4/4 rhythms, traditional New Orleans Dixieland was greatly influenced by the format of the city's brass bands: trumpet or coronet for melody; clarinet for countermelody and harmony; trombone to emphasize the chord-change notes; banjo (later replaced by guitar); tuba (later, the piano); and drums.

In the 1970s and '80s, young brass bands like Rebirth and Dirty Dozen updated the traditional rollicking drum-and-horn street parade sound with funk and hip-hop. Now they're the elder statesmen of a thriving scene.

LISTEN TO: Hot 8, Stooges, Rebirth, Soul Rebels.
GO SEE: Rebirth at the Maple Leaf (Tues., Uptown); Soul Rebels at Le Bon Temps Roulé (most Thurs., Uptown).
EXPERIENCE IT: at the Backstreet Cultural Museum (www.backstreetmuseum. org), with artifacts from the Mardi Gras Indian, brass band, and second-line traditions.

CAJUN AND ZYDECO

Most purveyors of plaintive French-language balladry and squeeze-box and fiddle-driven dancehall rhythms play a few hours outside of the city. But some bands, like the Grammy-nominated Lost Bayou Ramblers, do make their way into *la ville*. The same is true of zydeco, accordion and washboard-driven music that evolved from the rural black-Creole sounds and urban R&B.

LISTEN TO: Cajun—Beausoleil, Feufollet, Pine Leaf Boys, Les Freres Michot, Savoy Family Cajun Band. Zydeco—Clifton Chenier, Chubby Carrier, Terrance Simien, Rockin' Dopsie Jr.
GO TO: For Cajun, Mulate's the Original Cajun (Warehouse District); dba (the Marigny). For zydeco, Bruce Daigrepont's Sunday *fais do do* at Tipitina's (Uptown). Every Thursday Rock 'n' Bowl (Mid-City) books Cajun, zydeco, and swamp pop.
EXPERIENCE IT: at mid-June's Louisiana Cajun-Zydeco Festival (www.jazzand heritage.org/cajun-zydeco) in the French Quarter.

Above, performers at Congo Square, New Orleans, Jazz Fest. Below, Allen Toussaint. Top right, Dr. John. Below right, Partners-N-Crime.

SOUL AND R&B

In the 1950s and '60s, producers like Allen Toussaint and Dave Bartholomew laid the groundwork for rock 'n' roll with funky, groove-based R&B that captured the gritty, fun-loving rhythm of New Orleans.

LISTEN TO: Professor Longhair, Fats Domino, Irma Thomas, Ernie K-Doe, Allen Toussaint, Neville Brothers, Dr. John, Guitar Lightnin' Lee, Little Freddie King.

GO SEE: Veterans like Al "Carnival Time" Johnson and Ernie Vincent still perform around town, most often at festivals, but occasionally at the Rock 'n' Bowl, dba, or neighborhood bars.

BOUNCE AND HIP-HOP

The danceable, hard-driving party rap known as bounce originated in New Orleans housing projects and neighborhood bars in the late 1980s. In the 1990s, No Limit and Cash Money Records put New Orleans hip-hop on the map.

LISTEN TO: Big Freedia, Truth Universal, Partners-N-Crime, Mystikal, Juvenile, Lil' Wayne

GO SEE: Big-name acts like Juvenile and Mystikal play at the House of Blues (the Quarter) or the Arena (CBD). Look for bounce performers at small rock venues around town and hip-hop artists at Dragon's Den in the Marigny.

SECOND LINES AND JAZZ FUNERALS

Second line parade in the French Quarter.

If you encounter a marching band parading down the streets of New Orleans, chances are it's a second line, a type of parade historically associated with jazz funerals. The term second line refers specifically to the crowd that marched behind the "first line" of the brass band and family of the deceased. During the early 20th century, the New Orleans second line served an important community function; African Americans were not allowed to buy insurance, so they formed mutual-aid societies—called Social Aid and Pleasure Clubs—to help members through tough times. The tradition continues to this day; different Social Aid and Pleasure Clubs parade in all neighborhoods of the city every weekend of the year, outside of the hottest summer months. If you get wind of an authentic second line, go, but use caution. Stick to the safer-looking streets, and be prepared to make an exit if things start to get edgy.

The website www.blogofneworleans.com posts routes and schedules for the weekend's second lines.

Sylvester Francis has spent the better part of a lifetime documenting second-line parades and jazz funerals; his **Backstreet Cultural Museum** (*1116 St. Claude Ave., Tremé, 504/522-4806, www.backstreetmuseum.org*) is a repository of second-line mementos and tons of photographs. Open Tuesday through Saturday.

"Uncle" Lionel Batiste of the Tremé Brass Band.

JAZZ AND HERITAGE FESTIVAL

Above, crowds and performers at Jazz Fest. Opposite page, Mr. Okra vending truck.

A sprawling, rollicking celebration of Louisiana music, food, and culture, Jazz Fest is held annually the last weekend in April and the first weekend in May at the historic Fair Grounds Race Course. The grounds reverberate with rock, Cajun, zydeco, gospel, rhythm and blues, hip-hop, folk, world music, country, Latin, and, yes, traditional and modern jazz. Throw in world-class arts and crafts, exhibitions and lectures, and an astounding range of local food, and you've got a festival worthy of America's premiere party town.

Over the years, Jazz Fest lineups have come to include mainstream performers—Bruce Springsteen, Tom Petty, and Eric Clapton topped the bill in recent years—but at its heart the festival is about the hundreds of Louisiana musicians who live, work, and hone their chops in the Crescent City. Many New Orleans musicians are still recovering from the effects of Hurricane Katrina, and Jazz Fest is their chance to show a huge, international audience that the music survives.

HISTORY

Veterans of the first Jazz Fest, which took place in 1970 in what's now Armstrong Park, talk about it with the same awe and swagger of those who rolled in the mud at Woodstock in 1969. The initial lineup included such legendary performers as Mahalia Jackson, Duke Ellington, Fats Domino, The Meters, and the Olympia Brass Band, who played for a small audience of about 350 people, approximately half the number of performers and production staffers it took to put the event on. In 2006 the first post-Katrina festival drew an estimated 300,000 to 350,000 people from all over the world and showcased the talents of some 6,000 performers, artisans, and chefs. Many of the musicians who performed at the first Jazz Fest came back to play the emotional 2006 festival. In 2014 the festival welcomed more than 430,000 attendees.

Official Logo of Jazz and Heritage Festival.

MUSIC

Each of the 12 stages has its own musical bent. The Congo Square stage hosts hip-hop and world music, the Fais-Do-Do stage specializes in Cajun and zydeco performers, fans of traditional jazz head for the Economy Hall Tent, and everyone spends at least a few minutes in the Gospel Tent soaking up the exuberant testimony.

FOOD

Cooks from all over Louisiana turn out dishes both familiar (shrimp po'boys and jambalaya) and exotic (alligator sausage, anyone?). Favorites include gumbo, soft-shell-crab, cochon de lait po'boys, and Crawfish Monica, a creamy pasta dish. Beer and wine are available, but hard liquor is taboo.

CRAFTS

Craft areas at Jazz Fest include Contemporary Crafts, near the Gospel Tent, which sells wares from nationwide artists; the Louisiana Marketplace, near the Fais-Do-Do stage and Louisiana Folklife Village, which showcase area folk art; and a Native American Village, which spotlights indigenous culture. Surrounding the Congo Square stage are stands with African and African-influenced artifacts items. ■TIP→ **Many artists have a spot for only part of the fest; ask about their schedule before putting off any purchases.**

A tent beside Economy Hall sells CDs by festival performers, as well as other New Orleans and Louisiana artists; nearby is the official merchandise, including limited-edition Jazz Fest posters, which range in price from about $70 for a numbered silkscreen to several hundred dollars for a signed and numbered remarque print. In the Books Tent, local authors sign works on Louisiana music and culture. ■TIP→ **You don't need to bring a lot of cash. ATMs are located throughout the site.**

JAZZ FEST TIPS

■ Book hotels as early as possible.

■ Thursdays on the second weekend are the least-packed day, and a local favorite.

■ You can purchase a full program once you arrive at the festival, with detailed schedules and maps, or tear the "cubes" out of the *Gambit* weekly paper, *Offbeat* monthly, or the *Times-Picayune's* weekly Lagniappe pullout. Free iPhone apps are also available.

■ Don't stress out trying to catch all the big names; inevitably, the obscure local musicians provide the most indelible Jazz Fest memories.

■ For a break from the heat and sun (plus air-conditioned indoor restrooms), visit the Grandstand, which hosts exhibits, cooking demonstrations (often with free samples), musician interviews, and an oyster bar.

■ Longtime fest goers bring flags to let friends know where they're located. These make great markers when trying to find your friends in the crowd.

■ Cool, casual, and breathable fabrics, along with a wide-brim hat and plenty of sunscreen, are your best bets for the long day outdoors. Wear comfortable shoes, and ones that can get dirty. The grounds are a racetrack, after all, and by the end of Jazz Fest the ground is a mix of dust, straw, mud, and crawfish shells.

Mimi's. A popular locals hangout, this two-story nightspot perches over the corner of Franklin and Royal streets with a wraparound balcony and big windows that stay open most evenings. Downstairs is a bar with table seating, couches, and a pool table, while upstairs is home to a tapas-styled kitchen and the dance floor where bands and DJ's play nightly. DJ Soul Sister's always-packed Saturday night Hustle should be on everyone's list. ⊠ *2601 Royal St., Faubourg Marigny* 🕾 *504/872–9868* ⊕ *www. mimisinthemarigny.net.*

Phoenix. It bills itself as a "Leather/ Levi Neighborhood Alternative Bar," and that's a pretty apt description. The downstairs bar is a popular Marigny nightspot, with a calendar of special events and themed parties, including the International Mr. Leather Contest. The upstairs bar, called The Eagle, is notorious for its "anything goes" atmosphere. ⊠ *941 Elysian Fields Ave, Faubourg Marigny* 🕾 *504/945–9264* ⊕ *www.neworleansphoenix.com.*

> **FRENCHMEN STREET PERSONALITIES**
>
> Street life on Frenchmen can be as entertaining as anything going on inside the clubs and bars. Street artists and brass bands gather on corners and in doorways on most weekends and turn intersections and sidewalks into impromptu, open-air galleries, boutiques, and dance parties. A poet selling custom love sonnets typed up on a vintage typewriter, and a shopping cart turned mechanical bull with built-in music and smoke machine are just some of the rarities you'll encounter on an average night.

R Bar. Behind the tinted windows of this corner bar, find a red-vinyl-clad hipster hangout and stylish social hub with a throwback ambience. In addition to crawfish boils on Friday afternoons (during season), the place runs offbeat specials—on Monday night, for example, 10 bucks gets you a shot and a haircut—and it's prime real estate on costume holidays like Mardi Gras and Halloween. ⊠ *Royal St. Inn, 1431 Royal St., Faubourg Marigny* 🕾 *504/948–7499* ⊕ *www.royalstreetinn.com.*

Yuki Izakaya. At this traditional Japanese izakaya—a tapas-like bar where the snacks pair perfectly with the list of beer, sakes, and shochus—options for eats range from the exotic, like octopus balls or beef tongue, to grilled chicken and deep-fried mashed potato balls. Expect a large bar crowd and loud house music on weekends. ⊠ *525 Frenchmen St., Faubourg Marigny* 🕾 *504/943–1122.*

MUSIC CLUBS

Fodor'sChoice
★

d.b.a. At this southern outpost of a popular pair of bars in Brooklyn and Manhattan's East Village, the selection of drinks—including international and craft beers on tap, bourbon and aged Scotches, and obscure tequilas, all listed on chalkboards above the bar—is reason enough to visit. Live music most nights and the Marigny's best people-watching in a narrow cypress-lined room make it a neighborhood favorite. ⊠ *618 Frenchmen St., Faubourg Marigny* 🕾 *504/942–3731* ⊕ *www.dbabars.com/dbano.*

Snug Harbor. This intimate club with a sometimes steep cover charge is one of the city's best rooms to soak up modern jazz. It is the home base of such esteemed talent as vocalist Charmaine Neville, who plays every

Monday, and pianist-patriarch Ellis Marsalis (father of Wynton and Branford). The dining room serves good local food but is best known for its burger. ✉ *626 Frenchmen St., Faubourg Marigny* ☎ *504/949–0696* ⊕ *www.snugjazz.com.*

Fodor's Choice ★

The Spotted Cat. Jazz, old time, and swing bands perform nightly at this rustic club right in the thick of the Frenchmen Street action. Sets start at 4 pm on weekdays and 3 pm on the weekends. Drinks cost a little more at this cash-only destination, but there's never a cover charge and the entertainment is great—from the popular bands to the cadres of young, rock-step swing dancers. ✉ *623 Frenchmen St., Faubourg Marigny* ⊕ *www.spottedcatmusicclub.com.*

BYWATER

Perhaps the edgiest local scene in New Orleans can be found in Bywater, home to a dozen low-key bars. Past the corner of Royal and Franklin streets a smattering of watering holes cater to a varied crowd. As an added incentive to explore this neighborhood, local idol Kermit Ruffins (of *Treme* fame) plays in Bywater and the Seventh Ward some nights.

BARS

Fodor's Choice ★

Bacchanal Fine Wine & Spirits. In the far reaches of Bywater, Bacchanal is part wine shop, part bar, part music club—and one hundred percent neighborhood hangout. Among the wine racks in the old New Orleans building are two big round tables, as well as seating in the courtyard and a spacious new bar upstairs that serves beer and liquor. You can have a bottle uncorked on the premises or order by the glass. The kitchen supplies gourmet cheeses plates and small, tasty dishes that go well with the wine selections—osso buco, mussels, and confit chicken leg are among the best. Local bands play seven nights a week. ✉ *600 Poland Ave., Bywater* ☎ *504/948-9111* ⊕ *www.bacchanalwine.com.*

BJ's Lounge. This gritty corner bar is a beloved neighborhood joint. Sometimes it hosts music, like Little Freddie King (most Fridays) and King James and the Special Men (Mondays), who blow the top off the place. ✉ *4301 Burgundy Street, Bywater.*

Country Club New Orleans. For a non-touristy, out-of-the-way experience, check out this "restaurant, lounge, pool, Jacuzzi, cabana bar" in a handsome 19th-century Bywater mansion. A mixed crowd enjoys this elegant retreat from the hustle and bustle of the city with its lounge area, front patio, and restaurant. The clothing-optional outdoor pool and deck bar hidden away behind lush vegetation and high walls is especially popular with the gay crowd. Pool access requires a small fee, and towels and lockers are available. ✉ *634 Louisa St., Bywater* ☎ *504/945-0742* ⊕ *www.thecountryclubneworleans.com.*

Mariza. Inspired by the aperitif bars of Italy, this casually sophisticated Bywater destination was opened by the husband and wife team behind celebrated restaurant Iris. Although you could make a meal from the menu, everything about Mariza—from the large selection of small bites, the aperitifs and thoughtful wines by the glass list, and a graceful modern decor dominated by the bar—encourages the fashionable neighbors to linger for hours. ✉ *Rice Mill Lofts, 2900 Chartres St., Bywater* ☎ *504/598-5700* ⊕ *www.marizaneworleans.com.*

10

MUSIC CLUBS

Vaughan's. Jazz trumpeter Kermit Ruffins's legendary Thursday sets (served up with free red beans and rice late in the evening) are the big draw at this ramshackle place in Bywater's farthest reaches. At other times, it's an exceptionally friendly neighborhood dive. ⊠ *800 Lesseps St., at Dauphine St., Bywater* ☎ *504/947–5562.*

TREMÉ

Tremé, which has found new popularity in the wake of the HBO series, is one of the oldest musical neighborhoods in the nation. Largely residential, Tremé is home to some great local nightclubs and music venues. Be careful traveling after dark, however, as the neighborhood remains rough.

MUSIC CLUBS

Bullet's Sports Bar. For a real taste of New Orleans, drop by on a Tuesday night, when Kermit Ruffins is playing. Not just the soul of the city, but the soul food, too, emerges as Kermit and friends serve up their famous barbecue and fixin's in between sets. Featured in the HBO series *Treme*, Bullets has become something of a New Orleans hot spot, but remember that if the neighborhood around the bar looks a little scary, that's because it *is* a little scary. Use caution when traveling here, but be prepared for a warm and welcoming musical experience when you arrive. ⊠ *2441 A.P. Tureaud Ave., Tremé.*

Candlelight Lounge. This small, old school joint draws the crowds on Wednesday nights to hear the Treme Brass Band. Uncle Lionel Batiste, the club's legendary fixture, has sadly passed away, but the lively music and smoky, local atmosphere are still the same. We recommend taking a cab out here. ⊠ *925 N. Robertson St., Tremé* ☎ *504/906–5877.*

CBD AND WAREHOUSE DISTRICT

CBD

The Central Business District (CBD) is mostly quiet at night, but closer to Canal Street and the French Quarter are some terrific nightspots.

BARS

Handsome Willy's. Sandwiched between a forlorn stretch of the Interstate 10 overpass and the Medical District, this friendly lounge—named for a dapper repeat customer of the notorious brothel that used to be on the site—offers daily drink and menu specials, happy hour cookouts on the back patio, and on Thursday, Friday, and often Saturday, a rotating cast of DJs. It's not on many tourist maps, but it's casually hip and worth seeking out. ⊠ *218 S. Robertson St., CBD* ☎ *504/525–0377.*

Loa. In voodoo tradition, *loa* are the divine spirits, and this bar just off the lobby of the chic International House Hotel certainly strives for an extraordinary experience with its modern upscale decor. Well-heeled downtown professionals mingle with an international crowd gathering for the evening and sipping on inventive, high-end cocktails created by master bartender Alan Walter. A new aperitif hour from 4 to 5 Thursday through Saturday includes a tasting of one of Alan's signature cocktails. ⊠ *International House Hotel, 221 Camp St., CBD* ☎ *504/553–9550* ⊕ *www.ihhotel.com.*

Rusty Nail. Nestled in between the overhead highway and a series of converted 18th-century warehouses, this discreet neighborhood bar can be difficult to find. With live music most nights of the week, a great selection of scotches, a gorgeous renovated patio, frequent visits by food trucks, and even the occasional play reading, it's worth firing up the GPS to get here. ⊠ *1100 Constance St., CBD* ☎ *504/525–5515* ⊕ *www.therustynail.biz.*

The Sazerac Bar. One of the most famous bars in Louisiana, this art deco gem and slinger of fine libations has a lineage that dates back to the mid-19th century. Drawn to the signature Sazerac cocktails and Ramos Gin Fizzes, a famous and intriguing clientele has graced this hotel bar over the years, including Governor Huey P. Long, who in the 1930s built a 90-mile highway between New Orleans and the state capital, so, many believe, he could get directly to the hotel lounge for his signature drink. ⊠ *Roosevelt Hotel, 123 Baronne St., CBD* ☎ *504/648–1200* ⊕ *www. therooseveltneworleans.com.*

Victory. In the city's drab business district hides another entry in the growing list of craft cocktail bars. Named for Daniel Victory, an owner and one of the city's best mixologists, it draws a young professional crowd to its dimly lit, vaguely industrial space for drinks that push the boundaries of traditional cocktails. A cozy new room in the back is available for private parties and intimate sipping. ⊠ *339 Baronne St., CBD* ☎ *504/522–8664* ⊕ *victorycocktails.com.*

CASINOS

Harrah's New Orleans Casino. Commanding the foot of Canal Street and anchoring a cluster of restaurants and clubs, this beaux arts–style casino is the largest in the South. Try your luck at one of the 3,800 slot machines, 20 poker tables, and every other game of chance that you can imagine. There's an upscale steak restaurant run by local celebrity-chef John Besh and a club in the middle of the gaming floor. Valet parking available. ⊠ *228 Poydras St., CBD* ☎ *504/533–6000, 800/427–7247* ⊕ *www.harrahsneworleans.com.*

MUSIC CLUBS

Club Ampersand. New Orleans has very few dedicated electronic music dance clubs; this converted bank building is one of the biggest and nicest. It features two levels, a large dance floor, VIP Suite, a balcony, courtyard, and several cozy sitting rooms, one of which used to be the bank's vault. Regularly featuring local DJs, the venue also boasts performances by many of the most famous names in electronic and hip-hop music. ⊠ *1100 Tulane Ave., CBD* ☎ *504/587–3737* ⊕ *www. clubampersand.com.*

WAREHOUSE DISTRICT

With the many apartment buildings built from converted 19th-century warehouses and cotton mills as backdrop, the Warehouse District has turned into a great draw for locals and visitors alike with numerous bars, restaurants, and clubs that cater to hip professionals. It's also home to the contemporary-art scene, with dozens of galleries arranged through the district that host their own series of parties and celebrations.

10

Enjoying New Orleans Music with Your Kids

Bourbon Street's entertainment options are largely off-limits to children, but younger music fans need not feel excluded. Dozens of options exist outside of barrooms and traditional clubs, and several of the most prestigious clubs offer all-ages shows.

Preservation Hall and **Palm Court Jazz Café**, both legendary jazz venues, welcome underage patrons. **Tipitina's** and **Howlin' Wolf** occasionally host all-ages shows as well *(see listings in this chapter)*. Around **Jackson Square**, talented street musicians perform most days of the week, and the **French Market** hosts a regular series of concerts as well as a separate busking stage for local and visiting performers to play for tips. The **Louisiana Music**

Factory, an excellent New Orleans music and record store, regularly hosts in-store performances *(see Shopping)*. And kids are always welcome at the free shows staged by the National Park Service's **New Orleans Jazz Historical Park**, both at the park's visitor center *(see the French Quarter)* and the Tuesday through Saturday afternoon shows in the French Market.

BARS

Bellocq. Pre-Prohibition drinks are all the rage, but this Lee Circle lounge goes deeper into the past with a menu focused on the cobbler: a popular 19th-century refresher of aperitif wine mixed with crushed ice and fresh fruit. The louche location, attached to the super-contemporary Hotel Modern, captures the faded grace of a bordello in Storyville, New Orleans's once legal red-light district. ⊠ *Hotel Modern, 936 St. Charles Ave., Warehouse District* ☎ *504/962–0900* ⊕ *www.thehotelmodern. com/bellocq.*

Ernst Cafe. Ernst has been operating as a bar since the first years of the 20th century, and the classic interior and upstairs balcony provide a welcome respite for conventioneers, lawyers from nearby firms, and service-industry folks finishing shifts at surrounding hotels. The classic menu includes local bar-food staples like fried green tomatoes, po'boys, wraps, and burgers. ⊠ *600 S. Peters St., Warehouse District* ☎ *504/525–8544* ⊕ *www.ernstcafe.net.*

MUSIC CLUBS

Circle Bar. Like something out of a Tim Burton film, this teetering old Victorian house that straddles the concrete jungles of downtown and the Warehouse District hides one of the coolest indie rock clubs in the city. Around 10 pm, scenesters descend on the recently renovated venue, but earlier in the evening this is a laid-back haunt. Pull on your hipster skinny pants, so that you can squeeze into the room that holds what might be the world's tiniest stage. ⊠ *1032 St. Charles Ave., Warehouse District* ☎ *504/588–2616* ⊕ *www.circlebarneworleans.com.*

Howlin' Wolf. This New Orleans favorite has long been a premier venue and anchor of the Warehouse District club and music scene. With a great corner location in a converted warehouse, they host larger rock, funk, blues, Latin, and hip-hop shows nearly every night on the main stage. Meanwhile, the side bar called The Den books intimate events and popular weekly parties like Brass Band Sundays. ⊠ *907 S. Peters St., Warehouse District* ☎ *504/529–5844* ⊕ *www.thehowlinwolf.com.*

Mulate's. Across the street from the Convention Center, this large venue seats 400, and the dance floor quickly fills with couples twirling and two-stepping to authentic Cajun bands from the countryside. Regulars love to drag first-timers to the floor for impromptu lessons. The home-style Cajun cuisine is acceptable, but what matters is nightly music. ⊠ *201 Julia St., Warehouse District* ☎ *504/522–1492* ⊕ *www.mulates.com.*

Republic. Part of the new generation of music venues in the Warehouse District, this rock club retains the rough-timbered feel of the cotton-and-grain warehouse it used to be. The club books touring rock bands as well as local acts, and DJs take over the sound system late at night for popular dance parties. ⊠ *828 S. Peters St., Warehouse District* ☎ *504/528–8282* ⊕ *www.republicnola.com.*

THE GARDEN DISTRICT

Near downtown and right on the streetcar line, the Garden District is relatively easy to reach and offers numerous options for dining and going out, especially along St. Charles Avenue, which is the main thoroughfare. Running parallel, just a few blocks toward the river, Magazine Street is another corridor rich with restaurants, bars, and nightspots. St. Charles Avenue tends to offer a more upscale and elegant version of nightlife, with historic venues and a touch of haute couture, while Magazine Street caters to a younger crowd of students and young professionals looking for vibrant neighborhood hangouts, beer gardens, and sidewalk cafés.

BARS

The Avenue Pub. Beer lovers from around the globe make a beeline to this 24-hour neighborhood joint with pressed-tin ceilings. With the best beer selection in New Orleans, the bar hosts a regular schedule of tastings and special events. The whiskey offerings also rank among the top in town. Sip your pint on the wraparound balcony upstairs, where you can watch streetcars roll past on St. Charles Avenue. ⊠ *1732 St. Charles Ave., Garden District* ☎ *504/586–9243* ⊕ *www.theavenuepub.com.*

Bridge Lounge. Youngish professionals love to kick back here, often with their dogs in tow. The drinks are good, the low light flattering, and the owners' oenophilia is reflected in the extensive list of wines by the glass. ⊠ *1201 Magazine St., Garden District* ☎ *504/299–1888* ⊕ *www.bridgeloungenola.com.*

The Bulldog. The post-college set claims most of the seats on the beautiful brick patio here with its views of the bustle on Magazine Street and a fountain made from dozens of beer taps. The dog-friendly venue bills itself as "Uptown's International Beer Tavern," and it backs up the boast with 50 different brews on tap and more than 100 selections in

10

bottles. Solid bar food keeps patrons fueled up, but during crawfish season, boiled mudbugs from the seafood market across the street are the preferred meal. ⊠ *3236 Magazine St., Garden District* ☎ *504/891–1516* ⊕ *bulldog.draftfreak.com.*

Garden District Pub. Just down the block from some of Magazine Street's best boutiques, you'll find this neighborhood haunt that, with its exposed brick walls and a copper-top bar, exudes the ambience of a 19th-century pub, complete with Sazeracs and absinthe on a terrific drink menu. It's a great place to end a day of exploring or to get the evening started while mingling among the neighborhood denizens. ⊠ *1916 Magazine St., Garden District* ☎ *504/267–3392* ⊕ *www.gardendistrictpub.com.*

Parasol's Restaurant & Bar. Roast beef po'boy devotees genuflect at the mention of this friendly hole-in-the-wall, which for more than 60 years has served the sloppy sandwiches along with Guinness on tap. The annual St. Patrick's Day block party at Parasol's spills out into the surrounding neighborhood of the Lower Garden District; it's grown so large that police have to erect barricades to keep traffic out—or keep the revelers in. ⊠ *2533 Constance St., Garden District* ☎ *504/302–1543* ⊕ *www.parasolsbarandrestaurant.com.*

Tracey's. This cavernous sports bar and neighborhood pub comes with a backstory. The owners used to manage Parasol's, a nearby dive famous for its roast beef po'boys. When new owners at Parasol's forced them out, they took their recipe and most of their regulars around the corner to this larger location on Magazine Street. And, well, now the neighborhood has two great bars with stellar roast beef po'boys. ⊠ *2604 Magazine St., Garden District* ☎ *504/897–5403* ⊕ *www.traceysnola.com.*

UPTOWN AND CARROLLTON-RIVERBEND

UPTOWN

Uptown is rich in clubs, although they are far less concentrated than the ones downtown. They tend to be tucked down residential side streets or scattered along one of the main drags, and they mostly cater to the large populations of college students and young professionals who dwell in this part of town. Many are local institutions and ever-popular destinations for music lovers drawn to the beats of funk, brass, blues, and rock.

BARS

Fodor'sChoice ★ **Columns Hotel's Victorian Lounge Bar.** An Old Fashioned or a Sazerac on the expansive front porch, shaded by centuries-old oak trees, overlooking the St. Charles Avenue streetcar route, and crowded with Uptown gentry decked out in preppy attire, ranks as one of New Orleans's most traditional experiences. Built in 1883 as a private home, the Columns has been the scene of TV ads, movies, and plenty of weddings. The interior scenes of Louis Malle's *Pretty Baby* were filmed here. The Victorian Lounge, with its restored period decor and a fireplace, has a decaying elegance marred only by the television above the bar. Live jazz combos play Monday through Friday. ⊠ *3811 St. Charles Ave., Uptown* ☎ *504/899–9308* ⊕ *www.thecolumns.com.*

Cooter Brown's. This rambling tavern across from the Mississippi River levee boasts 400 different bottled beers and 45 on tap. That, along with the excellent cheese fries and an oyster bar, makes it a favorite haunt of students from nearby Tulane and Loyola universities, along with nostalgic alums. ⊠ *509 S. Carrollton Ave., Uptown* ☎ *504/866–9104* ⊕ *www.cooterbrowns.com.*

Cure. A pioneer on the revitalized Freret Corridor, one of the city's first serious cocktail bars adds a touch of urban chic to a historic neighborhood. A doorman welcomes guests into a converted fire station with 20-foot ceilings and a lovely patio. Knowledgeable bartenders use a breathtaking arsenal of liquor to push the boundaries of what a drink can be. Take note that even in August, men must wear long pants on Thursday, Friday, and Saturday, and baseball caps are not allowed at any time. ⊠ *4905 Freret St., Uptown* ☎ *504/302–2357* ⊕ *www.curenola.com.*

Delachaise. A long, slender room with plush banquettes in a charming sliver of a building on a busy stretch of St. Charles Avenue looks as if it were air-dropped straight from Paris. Offering a carefully chosen (and reasonably priced) selection of beer, spirits, and wines by the glass, the menu also includes upscale small plates, such as frogs' legs, frites fried in duck fat, and Puerto Rican *mofongo* (fried plantains). ⊠ *3442 St. Charles Ave., Uptown* ☎ *504/895–0858* ⊕ *www.thedelachaise.com.*

F&M Patio Bar. For college kids and grown-ups reliving their youth, an all-nighter in New Orleans isn't complete until you've danced on top of a pool table at this classic hangout. There's a loud jukebox, a popular photo booth, and a late-night kitchen (it gets going around 7 pm and keeps serving until early morning). The tropical patio can actually be peaceful at times. You'll need to get here by car or taxi. ⊠ *4841 Tchoupitoulas St., Uptown* ☎ *504/895–6784* ⊕ *www.fandmpatiobar.com.*

The Kingpin. Deep-red walls and a velvet Elvis lend this Uptown spot a touch of kitsch, but the friendly atmosphere, a jukebox stocked with vintage soul and modern rock, and a young, fun crowd really draw people back nightly. It's a frequent destination for food trucks and a favored place to cheer on the city's beloved Saints. ⊠ *1307 Lyons St., Uptown* ☎ *504/891–2373* ⊕ *www.kingpinbar.com.*

10

Publiq House. This spacious corner bar, with its high ceilings and Victorian chandeliers, resembles a vintage movie theater, and has something going on every night of the week, be it live local music, bingo, or trivia. The Brass-a-holics play each Thursday. With fairly priced craft cocktails and beers on tap, food trucks lined up outside, and free popcorn, it's easy to see why this place is so popular with the locals. ⊠ *4528 Freret St., Uptown* ☎ *504/826–9912* ⊕ *www.publiqhouse.com.*

St. Joe's. A young Uptown professional crowd packs this narrow bar known for its blueberry mojitos and religious-themed decor. The narrow front bar has more crosses than a Catholic church; the back patio, strung with Chinese lanterns and decorated with statues of Asian deities, is a "Caribbean Zen temple," in the owner's words. ⊠ *5535 Magazine St., Uptown* ☎ *504/899–3744.*

Sovereign Pub. No need to book a ticket to the UK, when this cozy bar so faithfully recreates a British pub. Even the daily newspapers come from the other side of the pond. Of course, you can be guaranteed a well-poured pint and warm company. ⊠ *1517 Aline St., Uptown* ☎ *504/899–4116.*

MUSIC CLUBS

Le Bon Temps Roulé. Local acts from a wide range of genres—including the Soul Rebels with their standing Thursday night gig—shake the walls of this ramshackle Magazine Street nightspot. The music normally gets started after 10 pm. Pool tables and a limited bar-food menu keep the crowd, which includes plenty of students from nearby Tulane and Loyola universities, occupied until the show starts. ⊠ *4801 Magazine St., Uptown* ☎ *504/895–8117.*

Tipitina's. Rub the bust of legendary New Orleans pianist Professor Longhair, or "Fess," inside this Uptown landmark named for one of the late musician's popular songs. The old concert posters on the walls read like an honor roll of musical legends, both local and national. The mid-size venue still boasts an eclectic and well-curated calendar, particular during the weeks of Jazz Fest. The long-running Sunday afternoon Cajun dance party still packs the floor. Although the neighborhood isn't dangerous, it's enough out of the way to require a cab trip. ⊠ *501 Napoleon Ave., Uptown* ☎ *504/895–8477* ⊕ *www.tipitinas.com.*

CARROLLTON-RIVERBEND

Farther uptown than Uptown, the Carrollton-Riverbend area is a favorite among students at Loyola and Tulane universities and is home to citywide favorites like the famous Maple Leaf club, which hosts live music every night of the week. Around the corner, Carrollton Station is a more laid-back option, with bands on weekends and some weeknights. Uptown bars tend to warm up with after-work crowds and then go late into the night.

BARS

Oak Wine Bar and Bistro. The dark windows give no hint of the sleek, modern lounge inside. A sophisticated spot for grown-ups to mingle over glasses of wine and gourmet nibbles draws professionals from Uptown and the nearby suburbs. Jazz and folk musicians perform Thursday through Saturday. ⊠ *8118 Oak St., Carrollton-Riverbend* ☎ *504/302–1485* ⊕ *www.oaknola.com.*

MUSIC CLUBS

Carrollton Station. This cozy neighborhood bar keeps unfolding the farther back you go—from the front bar to the stage to the backyard. The regular schedule of live music emphasizes local roots, rock, and acoustic acts. It's two blocks off the Carrollton streetcar line and close to the Oak Street commercial district. ⊠ *8140 Willow St., Carrollton-Riverbend* ☎ *504/865–9190* ⊕ *www.carrolltonstation.com.*

Fodor's Choice ★ **Maple Leaf.** The phrase "New Orleans institution" gets thrown around a lot, but this place deserves the title. It's wonderfully atmospheric, with pressed-tin walls and a lush tropical patio, and it's also one of the city's best venues for blues, New Orleans–style R&B, funk, zydeco, and jazz. On Sunday afternoons, the bar hosts the South's longest-running poetry reading. Rebirth Brass Band's standing Tuesday gig is a show everyone should see, and Joe Krown starts his set around 10:30 pm. It's a long haul from the French Quarter, but worth the trip, especially if combined with a visit to one of the restaurants clustered near this commercial stretch of Oak Street. ⊠ *8316 Oak St., Carrollton-Riverbend* ☎ *504/866–9359* ⊕ *www.mapleleafbar.com.*

MID-CITY AND BAYOU ST. JOHN

MID-CITY

A quick streetcar ride up Canal from downtown, this mostly residential area around City Park is almost like a small town: it's got neighborhood joints unknown to most tourists. The area has lots to offer if you know where to look. Venues are spread out, so a car or taxi is recommended at night.

BARS

Finn McCool's Irish Pub. Run by devoted soccer fans from Belfast, this popular and expansive neighborhood bar beams in European games via satellite. Pool and darts tournaments are a regular feature as well, and the kitchen serves delicious barbecue and burgers. On Monday night, there's a popular and competitive trivia quiz. If you happen to be in town for St. Patrick's Day, don't miss their rollicking day-long festival. ⊠ *3701 Banks St., Mid-City* ☎ *504/486–9080* ⊕ *www.finnmccools.com.*

Twelve Mile Limit. This smoke-free neighborhood joint might be off the beaten path, but it's worth the trip for its unlikely combination of an innovative cocktail menu and . . . barbecue. This place compares favorably to swanky wine and cocktail bars like Cure or The Delachaise, yet it offers a decidedly down-home vibe with its pulled pork and brisket, its run-down exterior (a contrast with the nicely done interior), and reasonable prices. ⊠ *500 Telemachus St., Mid-City* ☎ *504/488–8114.*

MUSIC CLUBS

Banks Street Bar and Grill. This comfortable Mid-City nightspot has become one of the city's most reliable venues for local music, with live shows—sometimes several a night—every day of the week. The bill of fare leans toward blues and funk. ⊠ *4401 Banks St., Mid-City* ☎ *504/486–0258* ⊕ *www.banksstreetbarandgrill.com.*

Chickie Wah Wah. Right on the Canal Street streetcar line, this neighborhood music club is unassuming from the outside but hosts some of the city's most popular acts. With happy hour and early evening music sets, a covered patio, a delicious menu of designer pub grub, and a clean, smoke-free environment, this destination is a favorite among low-key New Orleanians who aren't into the late nights. ⊠ *2828 Canal St., Mid-City* ☎ *504/304–4714* ⊕ *www.chickiewahwah.com.*

FAMILY **Rock 'n' Bowl.** Down-home Louisiana music, rockabilly, R&B, and New Orleans swing in a bowling alley? Go ahead, try not to have fun. This iconic venue has a terrific lineup of music Wednesday through Saturday. Thursday is Cajun, Zydeco, and Swamp Pop Night, when some of the best musicians from rural Louisiana take the stage. The new Front Porch Grill serves burgers made from grass-fed Louisiana beef. ⊠ *3000 S. Carrollton Ave., Mid-City* ☎ *504/861–1700* ⊕ *www.rocknbowl.com.*

10

BAYOU ST. JOHN

Winding around the bayou and the surrounding blocks, you'll find one of the city's prettiest and quietest neighborhoods. A few solid bars offer entertainment and cheap cocktails, but if you want to really do like the locals, get a go-cup and sit along the water.

BARS

Bayou Beer Garden. Claim a seat on the sprawling multilevel outdoor patio at this low-key neighborhood pub and sip a pint from the great selection of beers. Multiple TVs show the big games, and live bands play Thursday through Saturday. Although not worthy of a special trip, it's a terrific stopover on any visit to Mid-City. ⊠ *326 N. Jefferson Davis Parkway, Mid-City* ☎ *504/302–9357* ⊕ *www.bayoubeergarden.com.*

Pal's. Tucked away in a quiet residential neighborhood, this hipster hang-out updated a neighborhood bar with the kind of carefully designed rundown vibe that might make Tom Waits smile. All the details are there, down to the soft porn on the restroom walls. ⊠ *949 N. Rendon St., Bayou St. John* ☎ *504/488–7257* ⊕ *www.palslounge.com.*

THE ARTS

For a relatively small city, New Orleans has a remarkably active and varied performing-arts community. While there are many traditional performance venues around town, one of the most exciting movements in recent years is the fringe theater action along Saint Claude Avenue, in the Bywater neighborhood. The annual Fringe Theater Festival brings pop-up performances, but there are also some permanent venues as well.

CLASSICAL MUSIC

Philharmonic orchestral and chamber groups thrived in New Orleans during the 19th century. As jazz achieved society status during the 20th century, classical music took a backseat; however, many professional and amateur players ensure that the scene stays active.

Friends of Music. This organization brings superior performers from all over the world to Tulane University's Dixon Hall. Concerts take place approximately once a month, and tickets usually cost $30 to $35. ⊠ *Willow St. entrance, Tulane University, Uptown* ☎ *504/895–0690* ⊕ *www.friendsofmusic.org.*

Louisiana Philharmonic Orchestra. The always good, sometimes excellent LPO has returned to the beautifully renovated Mahalia Jackson Theater for the Performing Arts and continues to perform at Tulane and Loyola university auditoriums and at local churches. There's also a concert series in parks around town during the spring months. ⊠ *1010 Common St., Suite 2120, CBD* ☎ *504/523–6530* ⊕ *www.lpomusic.com.*

New Orleans Center for Creative Arts (*NOCCA*). Wynton Marsalis and Harry Connick Jr. are just two of the better-known alumni of this prestigious high school. NOCCA hosts some fine student and faculty shows at its modern Faubourg Marigny campus, and its Center Stage Series presents top-notch performances by visiting jazz, classical, dance, and theater artists. The focus is on emerging talent, and tickets usually sell out fast. ⊠ *2800 Chartres St., Bywater* ☎ *504/940–2787* ⊕ *www.nocca.com.*

Trinity Artist Series. Gratifying concerts of all types—solo, choral, orchestral, and chamber—fill the vaulted interior of Trinity Episcopal Church most Sunday evenings. Organized by local organist Albinas Prizgintas, the series features both local and regional artists, though the occasional star passes through. Admission is free, and a relaxed, enjoyable evening is assured. And if you're fortunate enough to be in town the right weekend in late March or early April, don't miss "Bach Around the Clock," a 29-hour performance marathon that features everything from the eponymous composer's fugues and variations to classic rock hits arranged for organ. Check Albinas's website for dates. ⊠ *1329 Jackson Ave., Garden District* ☎ *504/522–0276* ⊕ *www.albinas.org.*

DANCE

Local dance performances can be found at arts venues like the Contemporary Arts Center, NOCCA, and Tulane and Loyola universities' auditoriums.

New Orleans Ballet Association. The city's prestigious dance organization has returned to the lavishly renovated Mahalia Jackson Theater with a full schedule of performances and events. Performances also take place at other venues, including Freda Lupin Memorial Hall at NOCCA. ⊠ *1419 Basin St., Tremé* ☎ *504/522–0996* ⊕ *www.nobadance.com.*

FILM

Generous state tax breaks and scenic architecture have made New Orleans a popular place to film movies, which has given the Big Easy another nickname: "Hollywood South."

New Orleans Film Festival. Cinephiles can get their film fix during this juried festival in October, which brings an influx of indie and film culture to town and commands screens at venues throughout the city. The film society, which presents the annual fest, also hosts screenings year-round, a French film fest, and filmOrama in April—a week-long spring showcase of new foreign and independent films. ☎ *504/309–6633* ⊕ *www. neworleansfilmsociety.org.*

The Theatres At Canal Place. This first-run and art-house minimultiplex has five screens of premium viewing in the upscale Canal Place shopping center, on the edge of the French Quarter. A recent renovation added deluxe leather seating as well as a full-service gourmet café and bar that offers wait service for in-theatre dining and cocktails. ⊠ *Canal Place, 333 Canal St., French Quarter* ☎ *504/581–2540* ⊕ *www. thetheatres.com.*

10

Zeitgeist Multidisciplinary Arts Center. Working with volunteer staff and a shoestring budget, Zeitgeist founder and filmmaker Rene Broussard established this funky and eclectic space as a venue for experimental theater. It later developed into the city's center for alternative cinema, although it continues to stage live performances as well. ⊠ *1618 Oretha Castle Haley Blvd., Uptown* ☎ *504/827–5858* ⊕ *www.zeitgeistinc.net.*

OPERA

New Orleans has long had a love affair with opera. The first grand opera in North America was staged here, and in the mid-19th century New Orleans had three full-time opera companies. Through the

20th century the city continued to produce famous singers, including Norman Treigle, Phyllis Treigle, Ruth Falcon, and Jeanne-Michelle Charbonnet.

New Orleans Opera Association. Returning to the Mahalia Jackson Theater for the Performing Arts and the Placido Domingo Stage, the October-through-April opera season generally showcases three operas, as well as a small handful of special events. Opera on Tap is an innovative series bringing performances to area pubs. ☎ 504/529–3000 ⊕ www.neworleansopera.org.

THEATER

New Orleans has a diverse theater scene, from touring Broadway productions at the Mahalia Jackson Theatre to original works performed by local companies.

AllWays Lounge & Theatre. From contemporary burlesque to Brecht's *Threepenny Opera*, the AllWays provides an enticing array of avante-garde theater and performance art. It's hip, sly, and always provocative. ⊠ 2240 St. Claude Ave., Faubourg Marigny ☎ 504/218–5778 ⊕ www.theallwayslounge.net.

Saenger Theatre. Reopened for the 2013 season after a massive, multi-year renovation and restoration effort, the Saenger hosts a Broadway in New Orleans series as well as national headliners. The theater, built in 1927, has impressive ceiling decorations, a chandelier that came from a château near Versailles, and Italian baroque touches. ⊠ 143 N. Rampart St., Tremé ☎ 504/525–1052 ⊕ www.saengernola.com.

The Shadowbox Theatre. This intimate theater is the perfect setting for alternative productions, and it attracts not only intelligent productions from local companies but touring artists from around the country, including the occasional Broadway hit. ⊠ 2400 St. Claude Ave., Bywater ☎ 504/298–8676 ⊕ www.theshadowboxtheatre.com.

Southern Repertory Theater. This well-established theater company specializes in original and first-rate contemporary theater productions. They stage premieres by regional and international playwrights and are the city's only year round professional theater. Performances are held in the Contemporary Arts Center. ⊠ 900 Camp St., Warehouse District ☎ 504/522–6545 ⊕ www.southernrep.com.

SHOPPING

Updated
by Susan
Granger

The shopping scene in New Orleans is as eclectic as the city's music, food, and culture, and in local boutiques and specialty stores you'll find everything from rare antiques to novelty T-shirts, artwork, jewelry, fashion, and foods that represent the city's varied flavors. Up and down Magazine Street and throughout the French Quarter you spot old-world influences intersecting with modern trends, making it easy for even the pickiest shopper to find something.

New Orleanians have a deep love for the Crescent City and its various cultural components. For shoppers, this translates into pride-centric merchandise, from jewelry and clothing bearing city emblems, such as the fleur-de-lis—a French symbol associated with New Orleans since its early days—to Mardi Gras masks, black-and-gold Saints symbols, and humorous statements about political issues and local personalities. Residents strongly support local entrepreneurs, which means they favor homegrown stores selling locally made goods.

Make sure to pay attention to some of the city's artwork. Posters, for example, designed around Jazz Fest and other special events, often become collector's items. In the thriving arts districts you'll find contemporary works by local artists alongside renowned names in the art world. The sounds of New Orleans—Dixieland to contemporary jazz, rhythm and blues, Cajun, zydeco, rap, hip-hop, and the unique bounce beat—are available in music stores, such as Louisiana Music Factory and Peaches Records, and at live-music venues including Preservation Hall, Snug Harbor, and House of Blues. Independent bookstores and major chains stock a plethora of local books on photography, history, cooking, and lore. Clothing stores focus on items that wear well in New Orleans's often intense heat and humidity, with styles ranging from the latest runway fashions to vintage frocks and styles by local designers.

WHAT'S WHERE

The Crescent City's main shopping areas are the **French Quarter,** with narrow, picturesque streets lined with antiques shops, art galleries, and gift, fashion, and home decor stores; the **Central Business District (CBD)** and the **Warehouse District,** best known for contemporary art galleries and cultural museums; and **Magazine Street,** the city's 6-mile boutique strip filled with designer clothing, accessories, locally made jewelry, and antiques shops, art galleries, and specialty stores. Magazine Street stretches from the **Central Business District** to the Uptown area. Nearby, the **Carrollton-Riverbend** neighborhood is another hot spot for finding women's clothing, jewelry, and bookstores.

PRIDE IN BLOOM

The fleur-de-lis, historically an emblem of French royalty, has long been a symbol of New Orleans. Since Hurricane Katrina, however, locals have elevated the fleur-de-lis into a badge of courage and a symbol of pride and recovery. You can find creative examples all over the city, worked into jewelry, artwork, candles, glassware, T-shirts, and even tattoos.

FRENCH QUARTER

Browsing through the French Quarter is as much a cultural experience as a shopping excursion. Royal Street, known for its antiques stores, is great for a stroll and some window-shopping. Along both Royal and Chartres streets, you'll find clusters of high-end fine-art galleries displaying traditional, contemporary, and New Orleans–centric works. Many stores sell decorative Carnival masks that range from simple feather and ceramic styles that go for about $10 to handcrafted, locally made varieties that carry much heftier price tags. Jewelry stores feature curated selections of estate and antique jewelry alongside new creations. Souvenir shops are around every corner, especially as you approach the heavily trafficked areas near the river. If your energy lags, plenty of cafés, coffee shops, candy stores, and bistros will provide a boost.

SHOPPING CENTERS AND MARKETS

French Market. Vendors have been selling their wares on this spot since 1791, making it one of the oldest public marketplaces in the country. Today, the French Market includes a large flea market, small produce stands, and retail shops. For the daily flea market, dozens of vendors set up tables inside and outside the covered pavilion, selling jewelry, handbags, T-shirts, and curios as well as vintage and used items, clothing, and collectibles. The market generally is open daily from about 7 to 7, but hours can vary depending on the weather. ✉ *1200 block of N. Peters St., French Quarter* ☎ *504/522–2621* ⊕ *www.frenchmarket.org.*

Jax Brewery. A historic building that once was a factory for Jax beer now holds a mall filled with local shops and a few national chain stores, such as Chico's, along with a food court and balcony overlooking the Mississippi River. Shops carry souvenirs, clothing, books, artwork, and more, with an emphasis on New Orleans–themed items. The mall is open daily. During summer days, it serves as an air-conditioned refuge. ✉ *600 Decatur St., French Quarter* ☎ *504/566–7245* ⊕ *www.jacksonbrewery.com.*

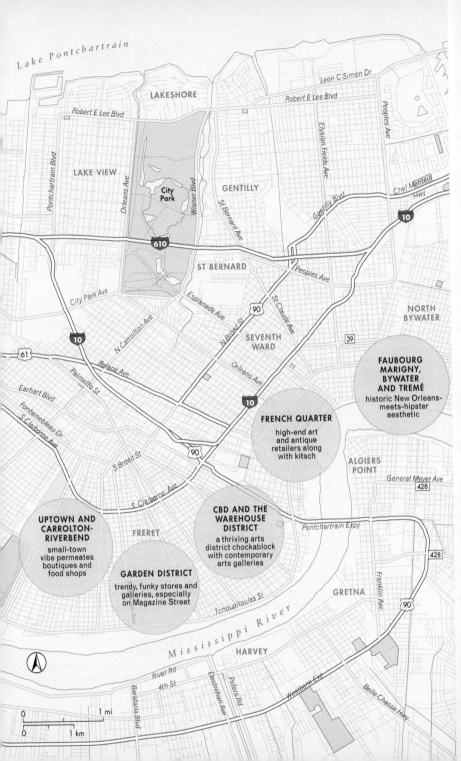

ANTIQUES AND COLLECTIBLES

Brass Monkey. This small but charming shop specializes in Limoges boxes with design motifs ranging from small red beans—a favorite food in New Orleans—to baby carriages. It also has antique walking sticks, Venetian glass, and English Staffordshire porcelain. ⊠ *407 Royal St., French Quarter* ☎ *504/561–0688.*

French Antique Shop. One of the largest collections of European crystal and bronze chandeliers in the country glitters over gilded mirrors, 18th- and 19th-century hand-carved marble mantels, French and Continental furniture, porcelain, and objets d'art in this shop, which originally opened in 1947 and is run by a second generation of the founding family. ⊠ *225 Royal St., French Quarter* ☎ *504/524–9861* ⊕ *www.gofrenchantiques.com.*

Greg's Antiques. This giant, 8,000-square-foot retail wonderland is filled with interesting antiques, light fixtures, salvaged items, and art. The antiques come from England, France, and Belgium, and are high quality but affordable. The store's selection of salvaged elements, mostly from old New Orleans houses, and art from emerging local artists, allows shoppers to take home a unique part of the city. The shop also rents bicycles by the hour, day, and week. ⊠ *1209 Decatur St., French Quarter* ☎ *504/202–8577* ⊕ *www.gregsantiques.net.*

Harris Antiques. Locals as well as visitors are drawn to this shop for its two floors of 19th-century paintings, 18th- and 19th-century French and English furniture, trumeau mirrors, estate jewelry, bronze sculptures, and chandeliers. ⊠ *233 Royal St., French Quarter* ☎ *504/523–1605* ⊕ *www.harrisantiques.com.*

James H. Cohen & Sons Inc. Pick up a piece of history in this shop, opened in 1898, which sells many one-of-a-kind antique firearms, swords, and currency, including coins from as early as 319 BC. There also are obsolete bank notes, jewelry made from rare coins, and collectibles such as antique telescopes and opera glasses. ⊠ *437 Royal St., French Quarter* ☎ *504/522–3305, 800/535–1853* ⊕ *www.cohenantiques.com.*

Keil's Antiques. Leave yourself plenty of time to browse through the three floors of 18th- and 19th-century French and English furniture, chandeliers, estate jewelry, art, statuary, and other furnishings. The shop, run by the fourth generation of the family that founded it in 1899, is a favorite stop for interior designers. ⊠ *325 Royal St., French Quarter* ☎ *504/522–4552* ⊕ *www.keilsantiques.com.*

DO YOU VOODOO?

Voodoo souvenirs are available all over the French Quarter, and include dolls with pins, special hex or prayer candles, and gris-gris bags. Pick yours with care. Gris-gris bags, for example, are not created equal; they are crafted according to your needs: attracting love, bringing good luck, ending bad luck, or providing protection from the evil eye. They are prepared with an even number of items, and you have to add something personal to the mix. Follow the instructions that come with the bag for best results.

Fodor's Choice
★

Lucullus. The entire store is focused on the art of food—preparing it, serving it, and eating it—and is filled with French tables, English china, cooking and serving utensils, linens, lighting, food-related art, snuff boxes, and more, including oddities like Lady Sarah Churchill's picnic set. Items are mainly from the 18th and 19th centuries. The shop is owned by Patrick Dunne, author of *Epicurean Collector*. ⊠ *610 Chartres St., French Quarter* ☎ *504/528–9620* ⊕ *www.lucullusantiques.com.*

> ### SHOPPING TOUR
>
> If you want a personal guide, local art-and-antiques shopping consultant **Macon Riddle** (☎ *504/899-3027* ⊕ *www. neworleansantiquing.com*) conducts half- and full-day personalized shopping expeditions by appointment. She can sometimes gain access to antiques warehouses that are not normally open to the public.

Fodor's Choice
★

M.S. Rau. Historically significant items, such as furniture and other pieces from royal families, are spotlighted among 18th- and 19th-century French, American, and English furniture, sterling silver, cut glass, statuary, fine art, and jewelry in this 30,000-square-foot store, which opened in 1912. ⊠ *630 Royal St., French Quarter* ☎ *504/523–5660, 866/349–0705* ⊕ *www.rauantiques.com.*

Moss Antiques. Specialties include French and English antiques from the early 19th century, including period jewelry, wooden boxes, furniture with inlaid woods, porcelain oyster plates, sculpture, objets d'art, walking sticks, and silver services. ⊠ *411 Royal St., French Quarter* ☎ *504/522–3981* ⊕ *www.mossantiques.com* ☉ *Closed Sun.*

Royal Antiques. French, English, and Continental antique furniture and Biedermeier pieces can be found alongside chandeliers, sconces, trumeau mirrors, accessories, and estate jewelry in this 114-year-old shop. ⊠ *309 Royal St., French Quarter* ☎ *504/524–7033* ⊕ *www.royalantiques.com.*

Vintage 329. An essential stop for memorabilia collectors carries items autographed by celebrities, including a framed photo signed by Gene Autry, a music sheet autographed by Fred Astaire and Ginger Rogers, a guitar signed by the Allman Brothers band, posters from performances, costume jewelry, first-edition signed books, and more. New items arrive every week. ⊠ *329 Royal St., French Quarter* ☎ *504/525–2262* ⊕ *www.vintage329.com.*

Waldhorn & Adler. Founded in 1881, one of the city's oldest antiques stores specializes in French, Italian, and English furniture from the 18th, 19th, and early 20th centuries. It also carries new and estate jewelry. ⊠ *343 Royal St., French Quarter* ☎ *504/581–6379* ⊕ *www. waldhornadlers.com* ☉ *Closed Mon.*

Whisnant Galleries. Antique weapons and armor are the real eye-catchers here and range from the Gothic to art-deco periods, but the shop also carries a large selection of antique gilded furniture, lighting, and mirrors; paintings from the 18th, 19th, and 20th centuries; African and ethnic art and jewelry; religious items; objets d'art; and statuary. ⊠ *343 Royal St., French Quarter* ☎ *504/524–9766* ⊕ *www. whisnantgalleries.com.*

Antiques shops are one of New Orleans's specialties.

ART GALLERIES

Fodor's Choice
★ **A Gallery for Fine Photography.** The rare books and photographs here include works from emerging local artists like Josephine Sacabo and Jerry N. Uelsmann; luminaries such as E.J. Bellocq, Ansel Adams, and Henri Cartier-Bresson; and more-contemporary giants, including Annie Leibovitz, Walker Evans, Helmut Newton, and Herman Leonard. ⊠ *241 Chartres St., French Quarter* ☎ *504/568–1313* ⊕ *www.agallery.com.*

Angela King Gallery. Gallery owner Angela King renovated an 1850s jewelry store into a modern gallery that exhibits oil paintings, prints, and metal and cast-glass sculptures from about 25 contemporary artists. ⊠ *241 Royal St., French Quarter* ☎ *504/524–8211* ⊕ *www. angelakinggallery.com.*

Artist's Market. This co-op of regional artists showcases a wide variety of works, including handmade masks, photography focusing on New Orleans personalities and scenes, ceramics, blown-glass, paintings, wrought-iron architectural accents, turned-wood bowls and vases, prints, jewelry, beads, and more. ⊠ *1228 Decatur St., French Quarter* ☎ *504/561–0046* ⊕ *www.artistsmarketnola.com.*

Elliott Gallery. Pioneers of modern and contemporary art are represented, with a large selection of prints and paintings by Marc Chagall, Picasso, and others. ⊠ *540 Royal St., French Quarter* ☎ *504/523–3554* ⊕ *www.elliottgallery.com.*

Great Artists' Collective. More than 50 regional artists display their works in this double-shotgun house in the middle of the French Quarter. You'll find paintings, metalwork mirrors, a vast array of earrings, blown glass, ceramics, wood sculptures, handmade clothing, hats, ironwork, masks, vignettes in oyster shells, and more. ✉ *815 Royal St., French Quarter* ☎ *504/525–8190* ⊕ *www. greatartistscollective.com.*

Harouni Gallery. David Harouni, a favored artist among locals and businesses, offers his take on neo-Expressionism in his paintings of faces, figures, and streetscapes, created in this gallery-studio space. ✉ *933 Royal St., French Quarter* ☎ *504/299–4393* ⊕ *www. harouni.com.*

Kurt E. Schon, Ltd. In the hushed atmosphere of an art museum, this gallery, with its well-educated staff, showcases high-end European paintings from the 18th and 19th centuries. ✉ *510 St. Louis St., French Quarter* ☎ *504/524–5462* ⊕ *www. kurteschonltd.com* ⊙ *Closed Sun.*

La Belle Galerie & the Black Art Collection. Global themes from Russian art to African-American experiences in music, history, and culture are portrayed through limited-edition graphics, photographs, posters, paintings, furniture, ceramics, textiles, and sculpture. ✉ *309 Chartres St., French Quarter* ☎ *504/529–5538.*

Michalopoulos. Local artist James Michalopoulos showcases his abstract visions of New Orleans's architecture, street scenes, and personalities in oil paintings, lithographs, prints, posters, and serigraphs. ✉ *617 Bienville St., French Quarter* ☎ *504/558–0505* ⊕ *www.michalopoulos.com.*

Rodrigue Studios. One of Louisiana's most successful artists, George Rodrigue, who passed away in 2013, is best known for his series featuring the Blue Dog, which has become a local icon. But it's the images of his Cajun ancestors in stylized Acadiana settings that got the most praise from art critics. His work is available in original paintings and signed and numbered silk-screen prints, mixed media, and sculpture. ✉ *730 Royal St., French Quarter* ☎ *504/581–4244* ⊕ *www.georgerodrigue.com.*

BOOKS

Dauphine Street Books. New and used books focus on local history, the arts, modern fiction, and out-of-print works. Bibliophiles will delight in its selection of antique books and rare titles. ✉ *410 Dauphine St., French Quarter* ☎ *504/529–2333* ⊙ *Closed Wed.*

Fodor's Choice
★

Faulkner House Books. Named for William Faulkner, who rented a room here in 1925, this bookstore is designated a National Literary Landmark. It specializes in first editions, rare and out-of-print books, mostly by Southern authors, but also carries new titles. The store keeps thousands of additional books at an off-site warehouse and hosts an annual Words & Music Festival that salutes Faulkner and new Southern writers and musicians. ✉ *624 Pirate's Alley, French Quarter* ☎ *504/524–2940* ⊕ *www.faulknerhouse.net.*

Librairie Book Shop. Set up like a library with well-stocked shelves of old, new, and hard-to-find volumes, this spot carries one of the Quarter's largest selections of books, posters, and postcards of local lore. ✉ *823 Chartres St., French Quarter* ☎ *504/525–4837.*

CLOTHING

Cajun Clothing Co. A smaller version of the locally owned Perlis boutique on Magazine Street carries clothing for men, women, and children, with a focus on polo shirts, boxers, and ties with crawfish logos, as well as everything from Hawaiian shirts to boxer shorts printed with images of Tabasco products. ✉ *Jax Brewery, 600 Decatur St., Suite 104, French Quarter* ☎ *504/523–6681* ⊕ *www.perlis.com.*

Fodor's Choice ★ **Fleurty Girl.** Owned by the ebullient Lauren Thom, Fleurty Girl—its title a play on the fleur-de-lis—is a place to go for New Orleans–centric T-shirts, other apparel, home decor, and gifts. The store is known for its T-shirts displaying the humorous catchphrases and iconography of local "Yat" culture and pride for the New Orleans Saints. There's affordable jewelry, children's books, colorful rain boots, Carnival-themed gear, and fleurs-de-lis in every imaginable form. There's also a location in the Garden District, at 3117 Magazine Street. ✉ *632 St. Peter St., French Quarter* ☎ *504/304–5529 French Quarter* ⊕ *www.fleurtygirl.net.*

Fodor's Choice ★ **Trashy Diva Boutique.** New Orleans–based designer Candice Gwinn puts a retro-romantic spin on the women's fashions she creates. Inspired by styles from the 1940s to the 1950s, the Trashy Diva line includes dresses, blouses, skirts, coats, jewelry, and upscale shoes with vintage flair but modern fit. There are several Trashy Diva boutiques. The lingerie shop, located at 831 Chartres Street, features corsets and romantic evening wear, while a shoe store (839 Chartres St.) sells retro-inspired footwear styles. Trashy Diva shoe, clothing, and lingerie boutiques also are located in the 2000 block of Magazine Street. ✉ *537 Royal St., French Quarter* ☎ *504/581–4555* ⊕ *www.trashydiva.com* ✉ *2048 Magazine St., Lower Garden District* ☎ *504/299–8777.*

United Apparel Liquidators. Label-loving locals as well as celebrities in town shooting movies are known to shop this designer clothing liquidator. The tiny boutique is busting with deeply discounted apparel, shoes, and accessories by major designers, such as Marni, Balenciaga, Michael Kors, Phillip Lim, and Prada. Contemporary lines, such as Serfontaine Denim, Steven Alan, Yigal Azrouel, and Alexander Wang, also fill the racks. The stylish, friendly, and eminently helpful sales staff has created a loyal cult of frequent shoppers, and many of them visit the store several times a week. ✉ *518 Chartres St., French Quarter* ☎ *504/301–4437* ⊕ *www.shopual.com.*

Violet's. Girly girls rule at this boutique, which caters to the softer side of feminine dresses, skirts, sexy blouses, handbags, jewelry, and accessories, with styles ranging from contemporary to retro romantic. ✉ *808 Chartres St., French Quarter* ☎ *504/569–0088.*

The Voluptuous Vixen. Owner Jaclyn McCabe sources hip, trendy apparel, undergarments, and accessories designed to fit and flatter fuller figures sizes 12 and up. Word about the boutique has gotten out, and Hollywood stylists have come calling when they need a dress that rocks a woman's shape even when she's not stick-thin. ✉ *818 Chartres St., French Quarter* ☎ *504/529–3588* ⊕ *www.thevoluptuousvixen.com.*

GLUTTONY TO GO

There are lots of treats to sample while you're in the Big Easy, but you don't have to eat them all while you're here. Many of the city's famous tastes come in easy-to-pack (or ship) forms. In the French Quarter you can pick up classic pralines at **Aunt Sally's Praline Shop** or **Laura's Candies**. Don't forget beignet mix and chicory coffee to re-create the breakfasts you've enjoyed at **Café du Monde**. All of the city's bookstores and many gift shops are stocked with a variety of cookbooks by local chefs and tomes about local tastes. In the Garden District, **Sucré** sells artisanal chocolates featuring New Orleans flavors, such as Bananas Foster and chicory.

FOOD

Aunt Sally's Praline Shop. Satisfy your sweet tooth with an array of pralines made while you watch. The traditional version is concocted from cane sugar spiked with pecans, but newer treatments include chocolate and other ingredients. You also can buy prepackaged tomato gravy, muffuletta mix, and Bourbon Street glaze, as well as art and books about New Orleans, zydeco CDs, and logo cups and aprons. ⊠ *French Market, 810 Decatur St., French Quarter* ☎ *504/524–3373, 800/642–7257* ⊕ *www.auntsallys.com.*

Café du Monde. This open-air café and New Orleans landmark serves café au lait (half coffee, half hot milk) and beignets (holeless doughnuts sprinkled liberally with powdered sugar). Take-home products from the café include prepackaged chicory coffee and beignet mix, coffee mugs, and posters depicting the spot. The café's store across the street also sells logo T-shirts, aprons, and other souvenirs. ⊠ *800 Decatur St., French Quarter* ☎ *504/525–4544, 800/772–2927* ⊕ *www. cafedumonde.com* ⊠ *Riverwalk Marketplace, 1 Poydras St., Suite 27, CBD* ☎ *504/587–0841.*

Evans Creole Candy Factory. The smell of candy being made on-site will draw you in to this shop, established in 1900. You'll find a variety of pralines, pecan logs, and New Orleans's own Cuccia Chocolates, as well as coffee and gift baskets. ⊠ *848 Decatur St., French Quarter* ☎ *504/522–7111, 800/637–6675* ⊕ *www.evanscreolecandy.com.*

Laura's Candies. In the candy-making business since 1913, this shop sells sweet pralines as well as chocolate specialties—including its signature Mississippi mud, made with milk or dark chocolate laced with caramel. ⊠ *331 Chartres St., French Quarter* ☎ *504/525–3880, 800/992–9699* ⊕ *www.laurascandies.com.*

New Orleans School of Cooking and Louisiana General Store. Learn how to make a roux and other Louisiana cooking techniques at this school located in a renovated 1800s molasses warehouse. Lessons are spiced with history and tales about the state's famous cuisine. The store also stocks all kinds of regional spices, condiments, sauces, snacks, gift baskets, and cookbooks. ⊠ *524 St. Louis St., French Quarter* ☎ *504/525–2665, 800/237–4841* ⊕ *www.neworleansschoolofcooking.com.*

Tabasco Country Store. Named for the famous Louisiana-produced hot sauce, this store also offers spices, cookbooks, New Orleans–themed clothing and aprons, kitchen accoutrements, ties, posters, pewter items, and more. ✉ *537 St. Ann St., French Quarter* ☎ *504/539–7900* ⊕ *www. Nolacajunstore.com.*

HOUSEWARES

Cameron Jones for Your Home. Contemporary furniture, local art, home accessories, rugs, art glass, lighting, and a cadre of gift items here have a distinctly West Coast attitude melded with New Orleans flair. ✉ *1305 Decatur St., French Quarter* ☎ *504/524–3119* ⊕ *www.cjaccents.com* ⊙ *Closed Sun.*

JEWELRY AND ACCESSORIES

Currents Fine Jewelry. Owners Terry and Sylvia Weidert create a variety of chic, art deco–inspired designs in 14- and 18-karat gold and platinum. ✉ *627 Royal St., French Quarter* ☎ *504/522–6099* ⊙ *Closed Sun.*

Dashka Roth Contemporary Jewelry and Judaica. The handmade, contemporary jewelry on display here are the works of designer Dashka Roth and 80 other artists. The store sells necklaces, rings, and bracelets as well as contemporary Judaica, including kiddush cups, mezuzahs, menorahs, and dreidels. The boutique is closed for all Jewish holidays. ✉ *332 Chartres St., French Quarter* ☎ *504/523–0805, 877/327–4523* ⊕ *www.dashkaroth.com* ⊙ *Closed Sat.*

Fodor'sChoice ★ **Fifi Mahony's.** Anyone with a passion for playing dress up and a flair for the dramatic will love this place, filled with custom wigs, wild accessories, makeup, and hair products. The shop provides essential resources for Mardi Gras and Halloween costume accoutrements as well as ample creative advice. ✉ *934 Royal St., French Quarter* ☎ *504/525–4343* ⊕ *www.fifimahonys.com.*

NOLA Couture. Preppy motifs and New Orleans pride are the twin hallmarks of this line of locally designed accessories. You'll find belts, neckties, pet leashes, wallets, hats, headbands, bags, glassware, and totes emblazoned with tiny Crescent City symbols—fleur de lis, sno-balls, pelicans, hurricane swirls, street cars—all in repeat patterns. They're the perfect gift for the prepster in your life. There is also a location Uptown, at 2928 Magazine Street. ✉ *542 St. Peter St., French Quarter* ☎ *504/875–3522* ⊕ *www.nolacouture.com.*

Quarter Smith. Gemologist and gold- and silversmith Ken Bowers designs contemporary jewelry in gold, silver, and platinum and carries a selection of antique pieces. ✉ *535 St. Louis St., French Quarter* ☎ *504/524–9731* ⊕ *www.quartersmith.com* ⊙ *Closed Sat.–Mon.*

Sterling Silvia. Silvia and Juan Asturias operate this business near the French Market, where Silvia's fleur-de-lis and flower-inspired jewelry designs share space with other silver jewelry from Chile, Mexico, Indonesia, Russia, Thailand, and elsewhere. There are also coral pieces, gift items, ceramic dolls, and more. The shop has a second location Uptown, at 4861 Magazine Street. ✉ *41 French Market Pl., French Quarter* ☎ *504/299–9225, 504/299–9229* ⊕ *www.sterlingsilvia.com.*

DID YOU KNOW?

Royal Street is known for its high-end galleries. A stroll here provides a nice shopping contrast to the kitschy souvenir shops that line many other French Quarter streets.

St. Louis

MASKS

Mask Gallery. Artist Dalili fabricates his intricate but wearable masks out of leather at a workstation in the front of the store. There also are masks made by other local artists, as well as Venetian and feather versions, pewter sculptures, jewelry, and figurines. ⊠ *636 Royal St., French Quarter* ☎ *504/523–6664, 888/278–6672* ⊕ *www.neworleansmask.com.*

Serendipitous Masks. With masks mingled with elaborately dressed dolls, the layout of this shop evokes the playroom of royalty. The masks are made by local artists using exotic feathers, jewels, ceramics, and leather. ⊠ *831 Decatur St., French Quarter* ☎ *504/522–9158* ☉ *Closed Tues. and Wed.*

Yesteryear's. Elaborate feather masks made by owner Teresa Latshaw and other artists comprise most of the inventory, but voodoo dolls and folklore objects are also available. ⊠ *626 Bourbon St., French Quarter* ☎ *504/523–6603.*

MUSIC

Peaches Records. This locally owned music shop specializes in vinyl records as well as CDs, with a focus on New Orleans rap, hip-hop, and bounce. But you'll also find jazz, gospel, classic soul, and a few music accessories. Live shows are sometimes presented in the café at the front of the store. ⊠ *408 N. Peters St., French Quarter* ☎ *504/282–3322* ⊕ *www.peachesrecordsneworleans.com.*

NOVELTIES AND GIFTS

Erzulie's Authentic Voudou. If the food, music, and architecture of New Orleans haven't cast their spell on you, then this voodoo shop might. Altars display good-luck charms and other ritual items, as well as spell kits, elixirs and potions, body-care products, voodoo dolls, gris-gris bags, and gift items. Tarot readings also are available. ⊠ *807 Royal St., French Quarter* ☎ *504/525–2055, 866/286–8368* ⊕ *www.erzulies.com* ☉ *Closed Tues. and Wed.*

Esoterica Occult Goods. Calling itself "the one-stop shop for all your occult needs," this store is a place to pick up potions, gris-gris goods, jewelry, spell kits, incense, and altar and ritual items, as well as books on magic and the occult arts. Tarot reading and astrological consultations are available by appointment. ⊠ *541 Dumaine St., French Quarter* ☎ *504/581–7711, 866/581–7711* ⊕ *www.onewitch.com.*

Forever New Orleans. It's all about the Crescent City in this small shop filled with New Orleans–themed items, including glassware adorned with pewter fleur-de-lis, affordable jewelry that boasts local icons, stationery, tiles, clocks, ceramics, framed crosses, charms, bottle stoppers, frames, candles, cookbooks, and more. This is a place to pick up upscale souvenirs and gifts. ⊠ *700 Royal St., French Quarter* ☎ *504/586–3536.*

HEALTHY JAVA

Local coffee brands like Community, French Market, Luzianne, and Café Du Monde add up to 30% chicory to their coffee. Chicory is caffeine-free and reportedly helps control blood sugar, reduce cholesterol, and boost bone-mineral density, and may be healthful for your liver.

MARDI GRAS SHOPPING BLITZ

The best way to experience the joys of Carnival is to go in costume. To assemble the perfect getup, start at the top, with a custom-made wig from Fifi Mahony's on Royal Street in the French Quarter. Feel free to turn to the store's expert staff for all manner of advice, from how to properly apply glitter eye shadow and false eyelashes to how to pull off Lady Gaga's platinum bow-tied hairdo. For the rest of your outfit, stroll down to the French Market, where you can find cheap sunglasses, feather boas, and all sorts of other accessories, or continue to the **Artist's Market**, where there are masks you'll want to keep long after Mardi Gras has faded into Lent. For a one-stop costume experience, travel to Magazine Street and **Funky Monkey** for costumes, stockings, wigs, and accessories, or the **Encore Shop**, where you can choose from affordable ball gowns, suits, and more. Mardi Gras is all about having fun. So dress the part, enjoy the sardonic humor of the Carnival krewes, and have a ball.

Idea Factory. Wood becomes art at the hands of craftspeople who carve functional clocks, clipboards, and jewelry boxes as well as more whimsical whirligigs, hand-carved board games, puzzles, kaleidoscopes, and toys, proving that not all playthings need to be plugged in. ⊠ *924 Royal St., French Quarter* ☎ *504/524–5195, 800/524–4332* ⊕ *www. ideafactoryneworleans.com.*

Nadine Blake. New Orleans native Nadine Blake worked in interior design in New York before moving home and setting up shop. Her delightful store reflects her varied travels and eclectic interests with quirky gifts, gorgeous design books, handmade note cards, vintage furniture, and a slew of cool whatnots. ⊠ *1036 Royal St., French Quarter* ☎ *504/529–4913* ⊕ *www.nadineblake.com.*

Rendezvous Inc. A throwback to the days of Southern belles, this shop on Jackson Square has linens and lace ranging from christening outfits for babies to table runners, napkins, women's handkerchiefs, and more. It also offers a charming array of antiques and reproductions such as perfume bottles, tea sets, fleur-de-lis, and crosses. ⊠ *522 St. Peters St., French Quarter* ☎ *504/522–0225.*

Santa's Quarters. It's Christmas year-round at this shop, which displays a diverse range of traditional and novelty ornaments and decorations, Santa Clauses of all kinds, and a host of Louisiana-themed holiday items. ⊠ *1027 Decatur St., French Quarter* ☎ *504/581–5820, 800/626–8717* ⊕ *www.santasquarters.com.*

What's New. Everything in this store carries a New Orleans theme, making it a great place to buy souvenirs people will actually want to keep, including fleur-de-lis–clad flasks, decorative pillows, nightlights with shades made from photographs of city scenes, glassware, ceramics, jewelry, and other works by local artists. ⊠ *French Market, 824 Decatur St., French Quarter* ☎ *504/586–2095* ⊕ *www.whatsnew-nola.com.*

11

SPA AND BEAUTY

Bourbon French Parfums. Opened in 1843, this old-world-style shop offers about three dozen fragrances for men and women, including a 200-year-old formula for men's cologne. It will custom blend perfumes for individuals based on assessments of body chemistry, personality, and scent preferences. The shop also sells perfume bottles and toiletries. ⊠ *805 Royal St., French Quarter* ☎ *504/522–4480, 800/476–0303* ⊕ *www. neworleansperfume.com.*

Fodor's Choice ★ **Hové Parfumeur, Ltd.** A must-visit for perfume lovers, this store has been creating fragrances since 1931. Scented oils, soaps, sachets, and potpourri have been made on-site for four generations and are sold all over the world. There are 52 fragrances for men and women, bath salts, anti-aging treatments, massage and body oils, and antique shaving and dressing-table accessories, as well as new and antique perfume bottles. ⊠ *434 Chartres St., French Quarter* ☎ *504/525–7827* ⊕ *www.hoveparfumeur.com.*

TOYS

FAMILY **Little Toy Shop.** For more than 50 years this has been the stop for a mix of New Orleans souvenirs, miniature die-cast metal cars (from the Model T to the Hummer), character lunch boxes, puppets, plastic animals, and collectible Madame Alexander dolls. There is a second location in the French Quarter at 513 St. Ann Street. ⊠ *900 Decatur St., French Quarter* ☎ *504/522–6588* ⊠ *513 St. Ann St., French Quarter* ☎ *504/523–1770.*

FAUBOURG MARIGNY AND BYWATER

Stores in these neighborhoods reflect the area's bohemian spirit, selling unique and locally made products. The shops on or around Frenchmen Street are easily walkable, but it may be wise to bring along a map or knowledgeable local while exploring the Bywater, where businesses are sparser. There are plenty of cafés and restaurants in the area in which to refuel during shopping trips.

BYWATER

MUSIC

Louisiana Music Factory. A favorite resource for New Orleans and regional music—new and old—has records, tapes, CDs, DVDs, sheet music, and books as well as listening stations, music-oriented T-shirts, original art, and a stage that hosts frequent live concerts. ⊠ *421 Frenchmen St., Faubourg Marigny* ☎ *504/586–1094* ⊕ *www.louisianamusicfactory.com.*

CBD AND WAREHOUSE DISTRICT

This area between the French Quarter and Magazine Street shopping districts is filled with boutique hotels, locally owned shops, and national chain stores, and (in the Warehouse District) museums and art galleries displaying a variety of work from local, regional, and nationally known artists. Julia Street in particular is a cornucopia of art galleries, many of them artist owned.

The *Times-Picayune* and *Gambit* newspapers publish detailed listings of exhibition openings. The events are generally accompanied by wine, hors d'oeuvres, and sometimes music. Because many of the galleries are artist owned, days of operation can vary. It's best to confirm gallery hours; many owners are happy to set up appointments to view their art.

CBD

SHOPPING CENTERS AND MARKETS

Canal Place. This high-end shopping center focuses on national chains, including Saks Fifth Avenue, Michael Kors, Anthropologie, Banana Republic, Coach, J.Crew, Lululemon, and BCBG Max Azria. But the mall also includes quality local shops, such as the artists co-op RHINO ("Right Here in New Orleans"), Jean Therapy denim boutique, Wehmeier's Belt Shop, and Saint Germain shoes. A highlight is the Mignon Faget jewelry store, which carries the local designer's full line of upscale, Louisiana-inspired creations. ⊠ *333 Canal St., CBD* ☎ *504/522–9200* ⊕ *www. theshopsatcanalplace.com.*

> ### A RELAXING SCENT
>
> Take home the scents of New Orleans with soaps, sprays, candles, and perfumes in sweet olive or vetiver. The latter was a staple in proper Creole households, where it was used to keep moths away from fabrics and add a pleasant scent to bed linens and clothing stored in armoires. Oil extracted from the roots of the grassy plant is popular among aromatherapy enthusiasts, who claim the scent relieves stress and increases energy.

ART GALLERIES

RHINO Contemporary Crafts Co. The name stands for Right Here In New Orleans, which is where most of the artists involved in this upscale co-op live and work. You'll find original paintings in varying styles, metalwork, sculpture, ceramics, glass, functional art, jewelry, fashion accessories, and artwork made from found objects. The gallery also holds art classes for children and adults. ⊠ *Shops at Canal Place, 333 Canal St., CBD* ☎ *504/523–7945* ⊕ *www.rhinocrafts.com.*

CLOTHING

Fodor's Choice ★ **Rubensteins.** One of the city's premier men's stores has been selling high-end suits, tuxedos, casual wear, and made-to-measure apparel since 1924. Brands range from Brioni and Zegna to Ralph Lauren, Prada, and Hugo Boss. ⊠ *102 St. Charles Ave., CBD* ☎ *504/581–6666* ⊕ *www. rubensteinsneworleans.com.*

JEWELRY AND ACCESSORIES

Adler's. This century-old, locally owned jewelry store carries upscale watches, engagement rings, gemstone jewelry, wedding gifts, top-of-the-line china, silver, crystal, and more. ⊠ *722 Canal St., CBD* ☎ *504/523–5292, 800/925–7912* ⊕ *www.adlersjewelry.com.*

Clock and Watch Shop. Master clockmaker Josef Herzinger repairs and restores all types of new, vintage, and antique watches and clocks at his two-story shop. The store also sells more than 15 brands of new watches and clocks, ranging from miniature and mantle styles to large grandfather clocks. ⊠ *824 Gravier St., CBD* ☎ *504/523–0061, 504/525–3961* ⊕ *www.clockwatchshop.com* ☯ *Closed weekends.*

Meyer the Hatter. One of the South's largest hat stores has been in operation for more than a hundred years and is run by a fourth generation of the Meyer family. A favorite of locals and out-of-towners, the shop carries a large selection of fedoras, tweed caps, Kangols, cowboy hats, and just about any type of topper you can put on your head. ⊠ *120 St. Charles Ave., CBD* ☎ *504/525–1048, 800/882–4287* ⊕ *www. meyerthehatter.com* ⊘ *Closed Sun.*

WAREHOUSE DISTRICT

SHOPPING CENTERS AND MARKETS

The Outlet Collection at Riverwalk Marketplace. Built in what was once the International Pavilion for the 1984 World's Fair, the Riverwalk Marketplace is set to reopen in 2014 as an upscale outlet mall with shops such as Neiman Marcus Last Call, Johnston & Murphy Factory Store, and outlets for Kenneth Cole, Forever 21, Carter's Babies and Kids, Chico's, and other brands. Outside the mall is Spanish Plaza, the scene of frequent outdoor concerts and special events. ⊠ *1 Poydras St., Warehouse District* ☎ *504/522–1555* ⊕ *www.riverwalkmarketplace.com.*

ART GALLERIES

Ariodante. Mostly local and Gulf Coast artists are represented in this gallery, featuring high-end and reasonably priced contemporary crafts and fine art, including jewelry, blown glass, sculpture, furniture, photography, paintings, ceramics, and decorative accessories. ⊠ *535 Julia St., Warehouse District* ☎ *504/524–3233* ⊕ *www.ariodantegallery.com* ⊘ *Closed Sun.*

Fodor's Choice
★

Arthur Roger Gallery. One of the most respected local galleries has compiled a must-see collection of local contemporary artwork by Lin Emery, Jacqueline Bishop, and Willie Birch, as well as national names such as glass artist Dale Chihuly and filmmaker-photographer John Waters. ⊠ *432–434 Julia St., Warehouse District* ☎ *504/522–1999* ⊕ *www. arthurrogergallery.com.*

Callan Contemporary. This sleek gallery specializes in contemporary sculpture and paintings from both local and internationally renowned artists, including Pablo Atchugarry, Eva Hild, Raine Bedsole, Keysook Geum, Adrian Deckbar, and Sibylle Peretti. ⊠ *518 Julia St., Warehouse District* ☎ *504/525–0518* ⊕ *www.callancontemporary.com* ⊘ *Closed Sun. and Mon.*

George Schmidt Gallery. History, particularly New Orleans's rich past, is the passion of artist George Schmidt. His gallery displays and sells paintings and narrative art, from small-scale monotypes to mural-size depictions of historic moments. He also sells signed and numbered prints of his work. ⊠ *626 Julia St., Warehouse District* ☎ *504/592–0206* ⊕ *www.georgeschmidt.com* ⊘ *Closed Sun. and Mon.*

Jean Bragg Gallery of Southern Art. Aficionados call it one of the city's best sources for collectible pottery from Newcomb and George Ohr, but the gallery also carries 19th- and 20th-century Louisiana paintings. Exhibits of works by contemporary artists are presented each month. ⊠ *600 Julia St., Warehouse District* ☎ *504/895–7375* ⊕ *www. jeanbragg.com* ⊘ *Closed Sun.*

Jonathan Ferrara Gallery. Cutting-edge art with a message is the focus of this gallery's monthly exhibits. Contemporary paintings, photography, mixed-media artworks, sculpture, and glass and metalwork by local

If you're in town for Mardi Gras, buy a mask at one of the city's many costume shops.

and international artists are displayed. ✉ *400-A Julia St., Warehouse District* ☎ *504/522–5471* ⊕ *www.jonathanferraragallery.com.*

LeMieux Gallery. Gulf Coast artists from Louisiana to Florida display art and high-end crafts here alongside work by the late New Orleans abstract artist Paul Ninas. ✉ *332 Julia St., Warehouse District* ☎ *504/522–5988* ⊕ *www.lemieuxgalleries.com* ☾ *Closed Sun.*

FAMILY **New Orleans ArtWorks at New Orleans Glassworks and Printmaking Studio.** One of the South's largest glassblowing and printmaking studios has a viewing room where visitors can watch glassblowers at work. The gallery also displays and sells functional and decorative art and sculptures. ✉ *727 Magazine St., Warehouse District* ☎ *504/529–7277* ⊕ *www.neworleansglassworks.com* ☾ *Closed Sun.*

Octavia Art Gallery. This gallery space features a number of established, midcareer, and emerging local and international artists who work in a variety of mediums. The gallery also shows works by 20th century masters such as Andy Warhol, Keith Haring, and Alex Katz. ✉ *454 Julia St., Warehouse District* ☎ *504/309–4249* ⊕ *www.octaviaartgallery.com* ☾ *Closed Sun. and Mon.*

Ogden Museum of Southern Art. You don't have to pay admission to enter the museum's Center for Southern Craft and Design store, where you can buy ceramics, glasswork, decorative pieces, books, scarves, and jewelry by Southern artists. The museum is filled with contemporary and folk paintings, mixed-media, photography, and sculpture. ■TIP→ Live music and after-hours events are held on Thursday. ✉ *925 Camp St., Warehouse District* ☎ *504/539–9600* ⊕ *www.ogdenmuseum. org* ☾ *Closed Tues.*

Søren Christensen. More than 30 local, national, and international artists working in a diverse range of mediums and aesthetics showcase at this gallery. Popular artists include Gretchen Weller Howard, Michael Marlowe, Steven Seinberg, and Luc Leestemaker. ⊠ *400 Julia St., Warehouse District* ☎ *504/569–9501* ⊕ *www.sorengallery.com* ⊘ *Closed Sun. and Mon.*

FOOD AND WINE AND SPIRITS

Wine Institute of New Orleans. Walk around with a glass and sample this shop's more than 120 wines, available to taste for a fee by the ounce, half glass, or full glass using the Enomatic serving systems (the machines resemble fountain soda or beer taps). Buy the wines you like by the bottle, or just continue to taste to your heart's content—just make sure you keep tabs on your credit card tally, as it's easy to get carried away. Owner Bryan Burkey offers regular wine-tasting events and classes at this venue best known as WINO. ⊠ *610 Tchoupitoulas St., Warehouse District* ☎ *504/324–8000* ⊕ *www.winoschool.com.*

THE GARDEN DISTRICT AND MAGAZINE STREET

A winding, 6-mile strip of kitsch, commerce, funk, and fashion, Magazine Street is a shopper's mecca, a browser's paradise, and a perch for prime people-watching. It meanders from Uptown through the Garden District to downtown. Young professionals, college students, and hipsters flock to the area's funky vintage shops, cafés, boutiques, restaurants, and casual bars. Clothing stores here run the gamut, offering everything from on-trend casual wear to vintage and consignment goods to high-end apparel. The street houses mostly locally owned stores, but there are also a few chains like American Apparel, Design Within Reach, and Free People. Antiques and home furnishing shops also are peppered throughout.

City buses provide transportation to and along Magazine Street, and streetcars travel St. Charles Avenue, which is a short walk away. Walking the 6-mile length of Magazine is possible, but some blocks have more stores than others, and you're best off making a plan and deciding beforehand where you want to focus. If you're looking for a concentrated clothes-shopping destination, try the blocks farther west, between Nashville Avenue and Jefferson Avenue, where there are a number of stores carrying designer labels. Between Jackson Avenue and Felicity Street, to the east, you'll find a stretch of shops selling eco-friendly attire and accessories, men's wear, and home decor. The blocks between Louisiana Avenue and Washington Avenue are filled with popular restaurants, bars, and boutiques. Detailed maps are available from the Magazine Street Merchants Association.

Magazine Street Merchants Association. The Magazine Street Merchants Association publishes a free brochure with maps and descriptions of the myriad stores, galleries, restaurants, and shops that line the city's boutique strip; it's available in hotels and stores, or you can request one from the association's website. ☎ *866/679–4764, 504/342–4435* ⊕ *www.magazinestreet.com.*

ANTIQUES AND COLLECTIBLES

Antiques Magazine. Lighting is the specialty here, with nearly 200 lighting fixtures hanging from the ceiling, some dating back to the 1850s. The store also carries Victorian furniture, rare oyster plates, and accessories. ⊠ *2028 Magazine St., Garden District* ☎ *504/522–2043* ☾ *Closed Sun.*

As You Like It Silver Shop. Everything you'd want in silver is available here, with a bounty of discontinued, hard-to-find, and obsolete American sterling-silver tea services, trays, and flatware. Victorian pieces, art-nouveau and art-deco items, and engraved pillboxes round out the selection. The store also offers monogramming, repair, and sterling silver pattern identification. ⊠ *3033 Magazine St., Garden District* ☎ *800/828–2311* ⊕ *www.asyoulikeitsilvershop.com* ☾ *Closed Sun.*

Blue Harp Antiques. An eclectic selection of furniture, jewelry, and collectibles fill this delightful store, where you'll find solid wood antiques, glassware, lighting, and small knickknacks. For things a little too big for your suitcase, the friendly staff will ship. ⊠ *2023 Magazine St., Garden District* ☎ *504/952–5651.*

La Belle Nouvelle Orleans. Elaborate stained-glass windows are mounted to the ceiling because the rest of the ample space is devoted to European antique furniture, artwork, porcelain, sculpture, and oddities from the 18th to 20th centuries. An open-air patio outfitted with garden benches, fountains, and other outdoor decor is linked to the main showroom by a warehouse-type gallery stacked almost floor to ceiling with furniture, salvaged doors, and other architectural items. ⊠ *2112 Magazine St., Garden District* ☎ *504/581–3733* ⊕ *www.labellenouvelle.com* ☾ *Closed Sun.*

Magazine Antique Mall. If you are easily overwhelmed, you should take a deep breath before you walk into this expansive shop, where every possible inch of counter and shelf space is filled with antiques and vintage goods. You will find an array of costume and fine jewelry, vintage photographs, antique clocks, home decor, glassware, clothing, silver, furniture, collectible china and ceramics, and a variety of other collectibles from a number of vendors. ⊠ *3017 Magazine St., Garden District* ☎ *504/896–9994.*

ART GALLERIES

Derby Pottery. Fragments of wrought ironwork and other architectural details form the inspiration for many of Mark Derby's beautiful pottery pieces, from mugs and vases to handmade Victorian reproduction tiles. His clocks and plaques, fashioned from reproductions of New Orleans's historic art deco water-meter covers, have earned cult popularity, and his reproductions of letter tiles found on Crescent City street corners

LOOKING FOR LAGNIAPPE

Lagniappe (pronounced lan-yap), or a little something extra, is a tradition in New Orleans, whether it's getting a free taste of fudge at the candy store, free whipped cream on your latte, or an unexpected balloon animal from the clowns who entertain visitors on Jackson Square.

can be spotted all over town. ⊠ *2029 Magazine St., Garden District* ☎ *504/586–9003* ⊕ *www.derbypottery.com* ⊗ *Closed Sun.*

Thomas Mann Gallery I/O. Handmade jewelry by local artist Thomas Mann, known for his "technoromantic" pins, earrings, bracelets, and necklaces (often featuring industrial-style hearts), is showcased here alongside work by a changing slate of other artists. The result is an eclectic mix of contemporary jewelry, housewares, sculpture, and unique gifts—the "I/O" stands for "Insight-full Objects." ⊠ *1810 Magazine St., Garden District* ☎ *504/581–2113, 800/875–2113* ⊕ *www. thomasmann.com* ⊗ *Closed Sun.*

BOOKS

Garden District Book Shop. This small store at the Rink boutique shopping center is packed with works of history, fiction, and cookbooks by local, regional, and national authors; it was the first stop on novelist Anne Rice's book tours when she lived in New Orleans. Autographed copies and limited editions of her titles are usually in stock, and the store hosts frequent author events. ⊠ *The Rink, 2727 Prytania St., Garden District* ☎ *504/895–2266* ⊕ *www.gardendistrictbookshop.com.*

CLOTHING

Funky Monkey. Popular with local college students, the clothing exchange mixes new, used, and vintage apparel for men and women with hipster T-shirts, handmade costumes, and lots of quirky accessories, all at affordable prices. ⊠ *3127 Magazine St., Garden District* ☎ *504/899–5587.*

Green Serene. This is store for women who love stylish clothes that reflect their values sells only clothing and accessories made with environmentally friendly practices. Owner Jamie Menutis has an expert eye for sourcing chic, affordable dresses, shirts, skirts, and pants made with organic cotton, soy silk, hemp, alpaca, and other eco-fabrics, including—and this is something you should really feel—surprisingly soft recycled plastics. Cool, locally made tote bags, candles, and other accessories also keep with the green theme. ⊠ *2041 Magazine St., Garden District* ☎ *504/252–9861.*

Storyville. This T-shirt shop has its own collection of "Storyville Originals" but also solicits the work of local designers and holds online design contests. Shirts depict everything from fleurs-de-lis to local catchphrases to Louisiana State University–theme gear. ⊠ *3029 Magazine St., Garden District* ☎ *504/304–6209* ⊕ *www.storyvilleapparel.com.*

FOOD

Sucré. Elaborate cakes on display in the window lure Magazine Street strollers inside this pastel-painted café and confectionery. The sweets live up to their colorful environs: the artisanal chocolates, pillowy marshmallows, French macarons, and other treats crafted by executive pastry chef Tariq Hanna and his team are among the best in the city. You can buy chocolates individually, mix and match to create your own box, or purchase a pre-assembled box organized by theme. ⊠ *3025 Magazine St., Garden District* ☎ *504/520–8311* ⊕ *www.shopsucre.com.*

HOUSEWARES

Loisel Vintage Modern. Take a step back to the atomic age in this retro furniture and accessories store, which carries vintage sofas, chairs, tables, clocks, lamps, and housewares from the 1940s to the 1970s. ⊠ *2855 Magazine St., Garden District* ☎ *504/899–2444* ⊕ *www. loiselvintagemodern.com.*

Fodor's Choice ★   **perch.** Eclectic, feminine, and contemporary, this store's collection of home furnishings is the sort you'd find in a high-end home decor magazine. If you love the look but don't have the decorating gene, the staff provides interior design services. ⊠ *2844 Magazine St., Garden District* ☎ *504/899–2122* ⊕ *www.perch-home.com* ☾ *Closed Sun. and Mon.*

Spruce Eco-Studio. Even if you aren't looking for environmentally friendly furniture and accessories, this chic home decor store is worth a visit for its well-curated collection of Jonathan Adler ceramics and lamps, John Robshaw bedding, and Greenform outdoor items. The owner has a sharp eye for design, but also an environmental consciousness that makes going green seem smart and easy. ⊠ *2043 Magazine St., Garden District* ☎ *504/265–0946* ⊕ *www.sprucenola.com* ☾ *Closed Mon.*

JEWELRY

Gogo Jewelry. You can't help but be in a good mood after spending a few minutes in this store surrounded by Gogo Borgerding's brightly colored jewelry designs. Her vibrant cuff bracelets, made of sterling silver and anodized aluminum, are the store's signature. The boutique also carries her sterling silver necklaces, rings, and other items, as well as work by a few other artists. A quirky blend of kitsch and high-end, the shop also features offbeat items like paint-by-numbers sets and taxidermy. ⊠ *2036 Magazine St., Suite A, Garden District* ☎ *504/529–8868* ⊕ *www.ilovegogojewelry.com* ☾ *Closed Sun.*

SPA AND BEAUTY

Fodor's Choice ★   **Aidan Gill for Men.** Merging the attentiveness of a spa with the old-world charm of a barbershop, this high-end men's salon caters to guys who prefer getting a hot-towel shave and a haircut while enjoying a whiskey. The front of the store is devoted to manly diversions, with shaving sets, contemporary and New Orleans–theme cuff links, pocket knives, wallets, bow ties (a specialty), grooming products for face and hair, and gifts. The store has a second location on Fulton Street in the Warehouse District. ⊠ *2026 Magazine St., Garden District* ☎ *504/587–9090* ⊕ *www.aidangillformen.com* ⊠ *550 Fulton St., CBD* ☎ *504/566–4903.*

UPTOWN AND MAGAZINE STREET, WITH CARROLLTON-RIVERBEND

Clothing boutiques, home decor stores, contemporary art galleries, and trendy restaurants, many housed in turn-of-the-century cottages, are scattered throughout the area near Tulane and Loyola universities. Reflecting the neighborhood's family-friendly vibe, you'll find something for every age: toys and novelties, locally made jewelry, books, artwork, and Crescent City–centric T-shirts. The Uptown end of Magazine Street, a popular haunt for college students, is a main shopping drag. On Maple Street boutiques cover about six blocks, from Carrollton Avenue to Cherokee Street, and in the Riverbend they dot the streets behind a shopping center on Carrollton Avenue. Oak Street, a burgeoning boutique corridor and one of the city's up-and-coming dining destinations, has several of the city's newest cafés and restaurants, serving up everything from barbecue to sushi.

UPTOWN

ANTIQUES AND COLLECTIBLES

Kevin Stone Antiques & Interiors. Unusual European antiques, most from the 17th, 18th, and early 19th centuries, fill this shotgun house; the collection includes many large, very ornate pieces from the Louis XIV and XV eras. The inventory ranges from small decorative bowls and sconces to grand pianos and armoires. ⊠ *3420 Magazine St., Uptown* ☎ *504/891–8282, 504/458–7043* ⊕ *www.ksantiquer.com.*

ART GALLERIES

Carol Robinson Gallery. This two-story Uptown house is home to contemporary paintings and sculpture by U.S. artists, with a special nod to those from the South, including Jere Allen, David Goodman, Nell C. Tilton, and Jean Geraci. ⊠ *840 Napoleon Ave., at Magazine St., Uptown* ☎ *504/895–6130* ⊕ *www.carolrobinsongallery.com.*

Cole Pratt Gallery. Contemporary paintings and sculptures by more than 40 Southern artists are displayed in this modern space. Opening receptions are held the first Saturday of every month. ⊠ *3800 Magazine St., Uptown* ☎ *504/891–6789* ⊕ *www.coleprattgallery.com.*

Nuance/Louisiana Artisans Gallery. Local and regional handblown-glass artists are represented in this Riverbend neighborhood studio, which also carries an eclectic mix of jewelry, pewter, ceramics, lamps, T-shirts, and more. ⊠ *728 Dublin St., Uptown* ☎ *504/865–8463* ⊕ *www. nuanceglass.com* ⊗ *Closed Sun.*

BOOKS

Octavia Books. The building's contemporary architecture gets attention, and the attractive layout inside invites leisurely browsing. The collection includes a strong selection of architecture, art, and fiction as well as books of local interest. The store hosts frequent book signings. ⊠ *513 Octavia St., Uptown* ☎ *504/899–7323* ⊕ *www.octaviabooks.com.*

CLOTHING

Jean Therapy. Popular for its diverse range of denim brands—the store carries more than 100 styles of jeans for men and women—this busy store also offers a small collection of tops, jackets, and accessories, as well as T-shirts emblazoned with New Orleans–proud slogans and local lingo. ⊠ *5505 Magazine St., Uptown* ☎ *504/897–5535* ⊕ *www. jeantherapy.com* ⊠ *Canal Place, 333 Canal St., CBD* ☎ *504/558–3966.*

Perlis. The bottom floor of this venerable New Orleans retail institution is devoted to outfitting men with classic suits (white linen and seersucker are very popular), sportswear, shoes, ties, and accessories, as well as the store's signature crawfish-logo polo shirts. Upstairs is filled with dressy, casual, and formal wear for women. ⊠ *6070 Magazine St., Uptown* ☎ *504/895–8661, 800/725–6055* ⊕ *www.perlis.com.*

FOOD AND WINE

Blue Frog Chocolates. Chocolates and other confections from all over the world are sold from an old-fashioned display case, and truffles, cocoa, and a host of other sweet treats are also on offer. Many of the candies come in novel shapes; chocolate-covered almonds, for example, form flower petals for sweet bouquets. ⊠ *5707 Magazine St., Uptown* ☎ *504/269–5707* ⊕ *www.bluefrogchocolates.com.*

Southern Food & Beverage Museum gift shop. The Southern Food and Beverage Museum, which documents and celebrates Southern culinary heritage, is moving into a new location in 2014. The gift shop will feature food-related and New Orleans–centric items, a large selection of Southern cookbooks, cooking utensils, and both vintage and modern cocktail tools and books. ⊠ *1504 Oretha Castle Haley Blvd., Uptown* ☎ *504/569–0405* ⊕ *southernfood.org.*

St. James Cheese Company. Inspired by cheese shops in Europe, the stock here includes massive wheels and wedges of Gruyère, Brie, cheddar, blue, and exotic cheeses from around the globe. Owners Danielle and Richard Sutton pride themselves on the select inventory, which also includes specialty meats and a variety of great foodie gifts, such as cutting boards, preserves, pastas, cutlery, crackers, and more. Sandwiches and salads are served daily, making this a popular, and crowded, spot at lunchtime. ⊠ *5004 Prytania St., Uptown* ☎ *504/899–4737* ⊕ *www.stjamescheese.com.*

JEWELRY AND ACCESSORIES

Fleur D'Orleans. Silver jewelry adorned with the fleur-de-lis is the main attraction here, but you'll also find items that carry other New Orleans icons such as crowns, masks, hearts, and architectural details. In addition to jewelry, the store sells handbags, handmade paper, glassware, wood and ceramic boxes, batik scarves, ironwork, and more. ⊠ *3701-A Magazine St., Uptown* ☎ *504/899–5585* ⊕ *www.fleurdorleans.com* ☾ *Closed Sun.*

Jezebel's Art and Antiques. Inside this Magazine Street cottage is an impressive collection of new, antique, and estate jewelry by famous designers as well as more-affordable reproductions and pieces by local artists. The store also carries new and vintage furs, coats, and hats. ⊠ *4606 Magazine St., Uptown* ☎ *504/895–7784* ⊕ *www.jezebels.com* ☾ *Closed Sun.*

Fodor's Choice ★ **Mignon Faget.** Mignon Faget is the New Orleans's most famous jewelry designer, and her sterling silver and 14k gold collections reflect her love and fascination with botany, nature, architecture, and New Orleans culture. Elements of bamboo, fleurs-de-lis, honey bees, red beans, and iron balconies have all been inspirations. Faget studied sculpture at Sophie Newcomb College at Tulane University and started out as a fashion designer in 1969, but she quickly gave up clothing to focus exclusively on jewelry. Her work has been featured in museums and shops around the world, but her biggest fan club remains right here in New Orleans, where her pieces are instantly recognized. In addition to her boutique on Magazine Street, she has a gallery at Canal Place in the French Quarter. ⊠ *3801 Magazine St., Uptown* ☎ *504/891–2005* ⊕ *www.mignonfaget.com.*

Mon Coeur. Handmade jewelry crafted by Janet Bruno-Small from antique and vintage pieces is a specialty, but the showroom also has an assortment of distinctive pieces by contemporary designers as well as antique and estate jewelry. ⊠ *3952 Magazine St., Uptown* ☎ *504/899–0064* ⊕ *www.moncoeurfinejewelry.com* ⊙ *Closed Sun.*

LINGERIE

Basics Underneath. The ladies here are focused on ridding the world of sagging bra straps and overflowing cups. With a sharp eye for measurement, the staff specializes in finding the right fit for intimates, whether it's something to wear under work clothes or a bra for a more romantic occasion. The store also carries sleepwear, swimwear, and gifts. ⊠ *5513 Magazine St., Uptown* ☎ *504/894–1000* ⊕ *www.basicsunderneath.com* ⊙ *Closed Sun.*

NOVELTIES AND GIFTS

Aux Belles Choses. This dreamy cottage of French and English delights has richly scented soaps, vintage and new linens, antique enamelware, collectible plates, and decorative accessories. ⊠ *3912 Magazine St., Uptown* ☎ *504/891–1009* ⊕ *www.abcneworleans.com.*

Dirty Coast. T-shirts and bumper stickers brandishing the phrase "Be a New Orleanian. Wherever you are" deeply resonated with displaced residents after Hurricane Katrina. Since then, locals leave it to this shop's shirts, stickers, and hats to satirize ("New Orleans: So far behind, we're ahead") and celebrate local culture in a clever way with eye-catching designs. The store has a second location at 329 Julia Street in the Warehouse District. ⊠ *5631 Magazine St., Uptown* ☎ *504/324–3745* ⊕ *www.dirtycoast.com.*

Hazelnut. Founded by stage and television actor Bryan Batt (he played Salvatore Romano on *Mad Men*) and his partner, Tom Cianfichi, this jewel box of a shop carries gorgeous home accessories and gifts, including New Orleans–themed toile pillows, decorative items, stemware, tableware, accent furniture, frames, and more. ⊠ *5515 Magazine St., Uptown* ☎ *504/891–2424* ⊕ *www.hazelnutneworleans.com.*

Orient Expressed Imports. Imported porcelain, vases, ceramics, jewelry, and the store's own line of smocked children's clothing are popular gift items. The shop also has a showroom of home furnishings, including accent furniture, lamps, and antique accessories. ⊠ *3905 Magazine St., Uptown* ☎ *504/899–3060* ⊕ *www.orientexpressed.com* ⊙ *Closed Sun.*

Scriptura. Fitting tributes to the arts of writing and communication are evident in the Italian leather address books, fancy journals, hand-decorated photo albums, specialty papers, custom stationery, handmade invitations, and high-quality fountain pens sold here. ⊠ *5423 Magazine St., Uptown* ☎ *504/897–1555* ⊕ *www.scriptura.com* ⊙ *Closed Sun.*

SHOES

Victoria's Shoes. Jimmy Choo, Giuseppe Zanotti, Hoss Intropia, and Marni are just a few of the high-end brands available here. The boutique also carries handbags and jewelry. ⊠ *4858 Magazine St., Uptown* ☎ *504/265–8010.*

TOYS

FAMILY **Magic Box.** This toy store loved by both children and adults sells the kind of items you won't find in big box places. While the shop carries popular toys by LEGO and Playskool, the emphasis is on independent brands. You'll find everything from baby toys to play items for older children to party games for adults. The staff goes above and beyond with customer service, offering shipping and assembly. ✉ *5508 Magazine St., Uptown* ☎ *504/899–0117* ⊕ *www.magicboxneworleans.com* ⊘ *Closed Mon.*

CARROLLTON-RIVERBEND

ART GALLERIES

Highwater Gallery. This hidden gem slightly off Oak Street's main drag features fair-trade folk art, as well as mixed media, textile works, stained glass, paintings, and sculpture from local artists. A highlight is proprietor Forrest Bacigalupi's handmade jewelry made of mixed media ranging from antiques to animal bones. ✉ *7800 Oak St., Carrollton-Riverbend* ☎ *504/309–5535* ⊕ *www.artskinetic.com* ⊘ *Closed weekends.*

BOOKS

FAMILY **Maple Street Book Shop.** Local and national authors stop here frequently to catch up on literary trade news, give readings, and autograph their works. The popular store's motto is "Fight the Stupids." Its focus is on New Orleans and Louisiana literature, but you'll also find most new titles of note in its well-stocked stacks. The store also carries children's books and frequently hosts storytellers. A rare- and used-books section is located in an adjacent house. ✉ *7523–7529 Maple St., Carrollton-Riverbend* ☎ *504/866–4916* ⊕ *www.maplestreetbookshop.com.*

CLOTHING

Angelique. This upscale women's clothing store provides on-trend apparel, shoes, and accessories from contemporary labels such as Diane von Furstenburg, Badgley Mischka, Theory, Red Valentino, and Alice & Olivia. An Angelique shoe boutique is located at 5421 Magazine Street, and a children's store is at 5519 Magazine Street. ✉ *7725 Maple St., Carrollton-Riverbend* ☎ *504/866–1092* ⊘ *Closed Sun.*

C. Collection. Geared toward fashion-forward college students, this store resembles a sorority-house closet jammed with hip, flirty, affordable clothes, shoes, handbags, and accessories, ranging from casual to dressy, by brands such as Kensie and Tulle. ✉ *8141 Maple St., Carrollton-Riverbend* ☎ *504/861–5002* ⊕ *www.ccollectionnola.com* ⊘ *Closed Sun.*

Encore Shop. This resale shop supports the local symphony orchestra by selling high-quality, previously owned designer clothes, from casual to formal wear, as well as shoes, handbags, and jewelry. The shop takes consignment as well as donated items. ✉ *7814 Maple St., Carrollton-Riverbend* ☎ *504/861–9028* ⊘ *Closed Sun. and Mon.*

Gae-Tana's. Racks are filled with a mix of natural fabrics and stylish-but-comfortable clothing, as well as the latest trendy styles. The combination makes this a favorite stop for fashion-conscious mature women as well as college students looking for skirts, jeans, shorts, dresses, blouses, casual shoes, handbags, and jewelry. ✉ *7732 Maple St., Carrollton-Riverbend* ☎ *504/865–9625* ⊕ *www.gaetanas.com* ⊘ *Closed Sun.*

CLOSE UP

Museum Shops

11

For souvenirs that go beyond the typical T-shirt or snow globe, visit the gift shops inside New Orleans's many museums and cultural institutions. The stores, which help support the organizations' missions, are often open to shoppers without paying museum admission. The gift shop in the **New Orleans Museum of Art** (✉ *1 Collins C. Diboll Circle, Mid-City*), for example, has a wealth of books on art, photography, and Louisiana cooking, as well as scarves, puzzles, and locally made crafts, such as jewelry by New Orleans designer Mignon Faget. The **Ogden Museum of Southern Art** (✉ *925 Camp St., Warehouse District*) includes the beautifully curated Center for

Southern Craft and Design store, where you'll find ceramics, glasswork, jewelry, and books on and by Southern artists. The **Historic New Orleans Collection**'s (✉ *533 Royal St., French Quarter*) gift shop is the place to find such items as a reproduction of a 1916 Louisiana railroad map or a NOVA documentary DVD on Hurricane Katrina. The **Aquarium of the Americas** (✉ *1 Canal St., French Quarter*), the **Audubon Insectarium** (✉ *423 Canal St., French Quarter*), and the **Audubon Zoo** (✉ *6500 Magazine St., Uptown*), all part of the Audubon Nature Institute, have gift shops stocked with colorful, quirky, educational, and fun items for children and adults.

Swap. You're as likely to find designer duds by Diane von Furstenberg and Dolce & Gabbana as Ann Taylor and J.Crew on the racks of this upscale consignment store. New consignors come in every day, adding fresh inventory. A children's store, Swap for Kids (7722 Maple St.), is next door, selling children's clothing and accessories, maternity apparel, strollers, diaper bags, and high-end accessories. ✉ *7716 Maple St., Carrollton-Riverbend* ☎ *504/304–6025* ⊕ *www.swapboutique.com* ⊘ *Closed Sun.*

Yvonne LaFleur. Though the clothes are stylish and contemporary, this beloved local boutique's approach is decidedly old-world elegance. Owner Yvonne LaFleur custom designs hats for all occasions, and her store is always infused with the soft scent of her signature perfume line. The romantic fashions here run the gamut, from casual dresses and flirty skirts to lingerie, ball gowns, and a whole room filled with bridal dresses in a variety of styles. ✉ *8131 Hampson St., Carrollton-Riverbend* ☎ *504/866–9666* ⊕ *www.yvonnelafleur.com* ⊘ *Closed Sun.*

JEWELRY

Symmetry Jewelers. Designer Tom Mathis creates custom wedding and engagement rings and other in-house designs and performs jewelry, and the shop also offers a variety of contemporary jewelry by local, national, and international artists. ✉ *8138 Hampson St., Carrollton-Riverbend* ☎ *504/861–9925, 800/628–3711* ⊕ *www.symmetry-jewelers.com* ⊘ *Closed Sun. and Mon.*

MID-CITY

This neighborhood isn't known as a shopping destination. However, the store inside the New Orleans Museum of Art (NOMA) is worth a stop for anyone interested in art-related gifts or souvenirs. Small wine shops in the area also provide perfect companions for picnics in City Park or along Bayou St. John. A streetcar runs along Canal Street and then down North Carrollton Avenue, ending at City Park Avenue, near the park and art museum.

NOVELTIES AND GIFTS

Goorin Brothers. From fedoras to flat caps, you'll find hats of every style and shape at this national chain with a local sensibility, including straw toppers perfect for strolling the streets of the French Quarter. The Magazine Street location (2127 Magazine St.) includes a custom hat shop for those looking for a personal fit. ⊠ *709 Royal St., French Quarter* ☎ *504/523–4287* ⊕ *www.goorin.com.*

New Orleans Museum of Art. Stocked with art and photography books, children's items, puzzles, jewelry, and locally made crafts, this gift shop is well worth a visit, even if you're not browsing the museum's exhibits. The shop has its own cookbook, as well as items created exclusively for it by local favorite jewelry designer Mignon Faget. You don't have to pay museum admission to enter the shop; just say you are shopping at the front desk, and you will receive a special pass. ⊠ *1 Collins C. Diboll Circle, Mid-City* ☎ *504/658–4100* ⊕ *www.noma. org* ☉ *Closed Mon.*

SIDE TRIPS FROM
NEW ORLEANS

WELCOME TO
SIDE TRIPS FROM NEW ORLEANS

TOP REASONS
TO GO

★ **Take a swamp tour:**
Get to know the wetlands
surrounding New Orleans
and Baton Rouge on a
boat ride. The area is
home to alligators, snakes,
nutrias, and more.

★ **Visit quirky Abita
Springs:** Head to the home
of the Abita brewery for
an afternoon day trip,
and check out the Abita
Mystery House museum.

★ **Jam to Cajun and
zydeco music:** Ensembles
of fiddles, accordions, and
guitars produce eminently
danceable folk music, with
songs sung in a mélange of
English and Cajun French.
Zydeco, closely related
to Cajun music, adds
washboard and drums to
the mix to create an R&B-
infused jumping rhythm.

★ **Marvel at plantation
homes:** Stately homes
will have you reenact-
ing your favorite scenes
from *Gone With the
Wind*; some are beauti-
fully preserved, others in
ruins alongside bayous,
testifying to the clash
between old and new.

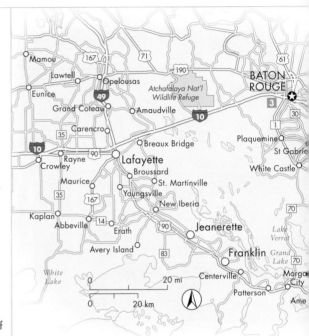

1 Abita Springs. This
quirky town is an easy day
trip from New Orleans. Part
of the drive is on a 30-mile
causeway over the water.

2 Plantation Country.
Take a journey into the
past and see some of
the South's most beauti-
ful antebellum homes.
Within an hour's drive of
New Orleans you will see
dozens of plantation homes
in various states of repair
scattered along either side
of the Mississippi, heading
west toward the state's
capital, Baton Rouge. The
views these days also
include sights of the heavy
industry that is scattered
along the river west of
New Orleans.

GETTING ORIENTED

Baton Rouge, the state's capital and second-largest city, is about an hour west of New Orleans. Plantation homes are scattered between the two cities, within a two-hour drive if you take the scenic Great River Road. Lafayette, about two hours west of New Orleans via Interstate 10, is a good post for exploring Cajun Country. Smaller Cajun towns surround the small city in all directions.

3 Cajun Country. French Louisiana, spread across the bayous, rice fields, and canebrakes to the west of New Orleans, is famous for two things: its food (jambalaya and blackened fish) and its music (Cajun and zydeco). You'll also find excellent antiques shopping, and many natural and historical sights. Here you'll find much of what the Big Easy has to offer, but in a family-friendly, small-town setting.

Updated by
Nathalie Jordi

New Orleans has never been a typical old Southern city. But look away to the west of town, and you can find the antebellum world conjured by the term *Dixieland*, which was coined here in the early 19th century. Anyone with an interest in the history of the Old South or a penchant for a picturesque drive along country roads should spend at least half a day along the winding Great River Road, where the romantic ruins of plantation homes alternate with the occasional restored manor.

Popular day trips include tours of the swamps and brackish, slow-moving bayous that surround New Orleans and were once the highways of the Choctaw, Chickasaw, Chitimacha, and Houma. Two centuries ago Jean Lafitte and his freebooters easily hid in murky reaches of swamp, which were covered with thick canopies of subtropical vegetation; it's said that pirate gold is still buried here. The state has a wild alligator population of about 1.5 million, and most of them laze around in these meandering tributaries and secluded backwaters of south Louisiana.

A variety of tour companies take groups to swampy sites a half-hour to two hours away from the city center. Guides steer you by boat through still waters, past ancient gnarled cypresses with gray shawls of Spanish moss, explaining the state's flora and fauna and the swamp traditions of the trappers who settled here. *For swamp tour operators, see Cajun Encounters.*

South Louisiana, the center of the Cajun population, is decidedly French in flavor. In small communities along the coast and in the upland prairie Cajun French is still spoken, although just about everyone also speaks English. After a hard day's work fishing or working crawfish ponds, rural residents of Cajun Country often live up to the motto *Laissez les bons temps rouler!*, or "Let the good times roll!"

PLANNING

WHEN TO GO

Spring and summer are full of small-town, family-friendly festivals celebrating local food and culture. In late September and October temperatures cool off, making this a good time for plantation explorating and swamp tours (however, it's also the tail end of hurricane season). In December plantation homes are decked out for the holidays, and seasonal bonfires glow along the river.

ABOUT THE RESTAURANTS

Part of the considerable charm of the region west of New Orleans is the Cajun food, popularized in the 1970s and early 1980s by Cajun chef Paul Prudhomme, a native of Opelousas. This is jambalaya, crawfish pie, and filé gumbo country, and nowhere else on earth is Cajun food done better than where it originated. Cajun food is often described as the robust, hot-peppery country kin of Creole cuisine. It's a cuisine built upon economy—heavy on the rice and the sauces, lighter on the meats—and strongly influenced by African as well as French cooking traditions. Indigenous sea creatures turn up in étouffées, bisques, and pies, and on almost every Acadian menu are jambalaya, gumbo, and blackened fish. Alligator meat is a great favorite, as are sausages like andouille and boudin (stuffed with a spicy pork-and-rice dressing). Cajun food is very rich, and portions tend to be ample. Biscuits and grits are breakfast staples, and many an evening meal ends with bread pudding.

Cajun cuisine extends beyond Cajun Country itself and into many of the restaurants along River Road. North of Baton Rouge, however, in St. Francisville, more typical Southern fare prevails. Here you will still find po'boys and sometimes gumbo, but barbecue is more common than boudin. *For descriptions of many Cajun foods, see Chapter 8.*

ABOUT THE HOTELS

Some of the handsome antebellum mansions along River Road are also bed-and-breakfasts, allowing visitors to roam the stately rooms during the day and then live out the fantasy of spending the night there in a big four-poster or canopied bed. The greatest concentration of accommodations in Cajun Country is in Lafayette, which has an abundance of chain properties as well as some B&Bs. Charming B&Bs are also abundant in other nearby towns, including St. Francisville, which is considered one of the best B&B towns in the South.

For expanded hotel reviews, visit Fodors.com.

12

ABITA SPRINGS

45 miles north of New Orleans.

Tiny Abita Springs, north of Lake Pontchartrain, is notable for three things: artesian spring water, Abita beer, and an oddball institution known as the Abita Mystery House. It's a fun day trip from New Orleans.

EXPLORING

Abita Brewing Company. Head out to Abita Springs to see where this popular beer is made—the area has long been known for its artesian spring water, which is used in brewing. Free hour-long tours run Wednesday, Thursday, and Fridays at 2 pm, and Saturdays at 11 am, noon, 1 pm, and 2 pm (tours are occasionally canceled, so call to confirm). Note that closed-toe shoes need to be worn on all tours. ⊠ *166 Barbee Rd., Abita Springs* ☎ *985/893–3143* ⊕ *www.abita.com.*

Abita Mystery House. Artist John Preble's strange vision—sort of a Louisiana version of the Watts Towers of Los Angeles—is an obsessive collection of found objects (combs, old musical instruments, paint-by-number art, and taxidermy experiments gone horribly awry) set in a series of ramshackle buildings, including one covered in broken tiles. This museum is truly odd and entertaining, but not for clutter-phobes. Ask Preble if you can see his studio, where he creates paintings of green-eyed Creole beauties. ⊠ *22275 Hwy. 36, at Grover St., Abita Springs* ☎ *985/892–2624* ⊕ *www.abitamysteryhouse.com* ⊡ *$3* ☺ *Mon.–Sun. 10–5.*

WHERE TO EAT

$ ✕ **Abita Brew Pub.** Albita's original brew building is now the setting for
AMERICAN   meals chosen from a surprisingly lengthy menu of pasta, salads, burgers, and entrées like jambalaya, barbecued ribs, and cornmeal-crusted catfish. These dishes all go well with the beer—a full selection of Abita on tap, including seasonal brews. ⑤ *Average main: $17* ⊠ *72011 Holly St., Abita Springs* ☎ *985/892–5837* ⊕ *www.abitabrewpub.com* ☺ *Closed Mon.*

PLANTATION COUNTRY

A parade of plantations unfolds along the Great River Road leading west from New Orleans, and another group of fine old houses dots the landscape north of Baton Rouge, around the town of St. Francisville. Louisiana plantation homes range from the grandiose Nottoway on River Road to the humbler, owner-occupied Butler Greenwood near St. Francisville. Some sit upon an acre or two; others, such as Rosedown, are surrounded by extensive, lush grounds.

The River Road plantations are closely tied to New Orleans's culture and society: it was here that many of the city's most prominent families made their fortunes generations ago, and the language and tastes are historically French. The St. Francisville area, on the other hand, received a heartier injection of British-American colonial culture during the antebellum era, evidenced in the landscaped grounds of homes such as Rosedown and the restrained interior of Oakley House, where John James Audubon, the ornithologist and painter, once lived. Baton Rouge, the state capital, provides a midpoint between the River Road plantations and St. Francisville and has some interesting sights of its own.

GETTING HERE AND AROUND

AIR TRAVEL

Baton Rouge Metropolitan Airport, 7 miles north of downtown, is served by American, Delta, United, and U.S. Airways. New Orleans International Airport is off Interstate 10, 20 minutes from Destrehan Plantation.

Airport Information Baton Rouge Metropolitan Airport (*BTR*). ✉ *9430 Jackie Cochran Dr.* ☎ *225/355–0333* ⊕ *www.flybtr.com.*

BUS TRAVEL

Greyhound Southeast Lines has frequent daily service from New Orleans to Baton Rouge and Lafayette, and limited service to surrounding areas.

Bus Information Greyhound Southeast Lines ☎ *800/231–2222* ⊕ *www.greyhound.com.*

CAR TRAVEL

From New Orleans the fastest route to the River Road plantations is Interstate 10 west to Interstate 310 to Exit 6, River Road. Alternatives to the Great River Road are to continue on either Interstate 10 or U.S. 61 west; both have signs marking exits for various plantations. Route 18 runs along the west bank of the river, Route 44 on the east.

Interstate 10 and U.S. 190 run east–west through Baton Rouge. Interstate 12 heads east, connecting with north–south Interstate 55 and Interstate 59. U.S. 61 leads from New Orleans to Baton Rouge and north. Ferries across the Mississippi cost $1 per car; most bridges are free. Route 1 travels along False River, which is a blue "oxbow lake" created ages ago when the Mississippi changed its course and cut off this section. The drive along Interstate 10 will take a little more than an hour from New Orleans to Baton Rouge. Expect the drive to take two hours if you take either Route 18 or 44, which wind around the river.

TIMING

Don't try to visit every plantation listed here—your trip will turn into a blur of columns. If you can, spend the night at one of the plantations, such as Oak Alley or Nottoway, and then tour the region. Oak Alley and Laura plantations are just a few miles from each other and provide a nice contrast in architectural styles and approaches. St. Francisville is a weekend trip in its own right. If you're visiting from New Orleans and are pressed for time, then Destrehan, one of the state's oldest plantations, might fit the bill; it's 23 miles from the city.

TOURS

Allons à Lafayette. Guided tours of the River Road plantations and swamp tours are available from this company, based in Lafayette. Tours of Cajun areas are also available. ☎ *800/264–5465* ⊕ *www. allonsalafayette.com.*

Cajun Encounters Tour Co. From Cajun Encounters you can get guided tours to Oak Alley and Laura Plantations, as well as personal tours of Honey Island Swamp. ☎ *866/928–6877, 504/834–1770* ⊕ *www. cajunencounters.com.*

VISITOR INFORMATION

Contacts **Baton Rouge Area Convention and Visitors Bureau** ✉ *359 Third St., Baton Rouge* ☎ *225/383–1825, 800/527–6843* 🌐 *www.visitbatonrouge.com.* **Louisiana Visitor Information Center** ✉ *900 N. Third St., Baton Rouge* ☎ *225/342–7317* 🌐 *www.louisianatravel.com.* **West Feliciana Parish Tourist Commission** ✉ *11157 Ferdinand St., St. Francisville* ☎ *225/635–4224, 800/789–4221* 🌐 *www.stfrancisville.us.*

THE GREAT RIVER ROAD

Between New Orleans and Baton Rouge beautifully restored antebellum plantations along the Mississippi are filled with period antiques, evoking tales of Yankee gunboats and the ghosts of former residents. Industrial plants share the scenery now, and the man-made levee, constructed in the early 20th century in an attempt to keep the mighty Mississippi on a set course, obstructs the river views that plantation residents once enjoyed. Still, you can park your car and climb up on the levee to survey a stretch of the wide, muddy river.

Between the Destrehan and San Francisco plantations you will drive through what amounts to a deep bow before the might of the Mississippi: the Bonnet Carré Spillway is a huge swath of land set aside specifically to receive the river's periodic overflow, thus protecting New Orleans, 30 miles downriver.

The Great River Road is also called, variously, Route or LA 44 and 75 on the east bank of the river and Route or LA 18 on the west bank. "LA" and "Route" are interchangeable; we use Route throughout this chapter. Alternatives to the Great River Road are Interstate 10 and U.S. 61; both have signs marking exits for various plantations. All the plantations described are listed on the National Register of Historic Places, and some of them are B&Bs. Plantation touring can take anywhere from an hour to two days, depending upon how many houses you want to see—and how much talk of moonlight and magnolias you'd like to hear.

EXPLORING

Destrehan Plantation. The oldest plantation left intact in the lower Mississippi Valley is a simple West Indies–style house, built in 1787 by a free man of color and typical of the homes built by the earliest planters in the region. The plantation is notable for the hand-hewn cypress timbers that were used in its construction and for the insulation in its walls, made of *bousillage,* a mixture of horsehair, Spanish moss, and mud. A costumed guide leads you on a 45-minute tour through the house, which is furnished with period antiques. You are free to explore the grounds, where there are several smaller structures and massive oak trees borne down by their weighty old branches. Demonstrations of crafts such as indigo dying, candle making, or open-hearth cooking bring the period to life, and an annual fall festival with music, crafts, and food is held during the second weekend in November. ✉ *13034 River Rd., Destrehan* ✣ *23 miles west [upriver] of New Orleans* ☎ *985/764–9315, 877/453–2095* 🌐 *www.destrehanplantation.org* 🎟 *$18* ⏲ *Daily 9–4.*

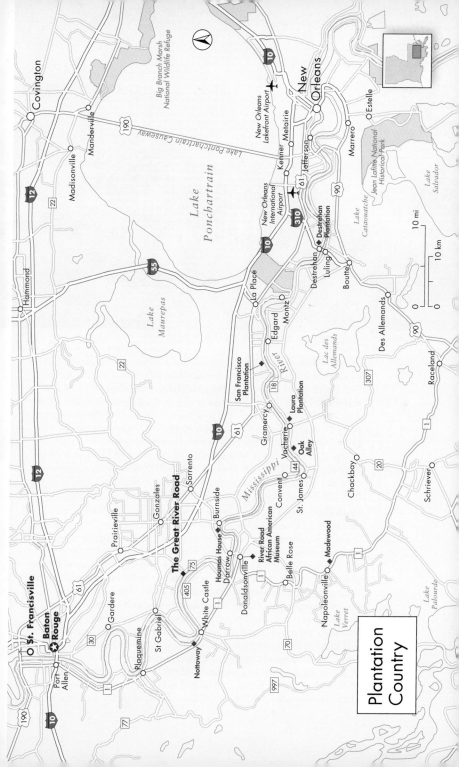

Nottoway Plantation, our Fodor's Choice pick for best plantation home.

Houmas House. Majestic 200-year-old oaks surround this classic Louisiana plantation house, with grand white pillars and all. It's actually two buildings of quite different styles joined together. In 1770 Alexander Latil built the smaller rear house in the French–Spanish Creole style that was becoming popular in New Orleans. The Greek Revival mansion was added to the grounds in 1828 by Wade Hampton, who eventually connected the two structures with an arched carriageway. ⊠ *40136 Hwy. 942, ½ mile off Rte. 44, Darrow ⊹ 58 miles west of New Orleans* ☎ *225/473–7841, 225/473–9380* ⊕ *www.houmashouse. com* ⊠ *Guided home and garden tour $20, self-guided garden tour $10* ☉ *Daily 9–7, closed on Christmas and New Year's.*

Laura Plantation. This is a more intimate and better-documented presentation of Creole plantation life than any other property on River Road. The narrative of the guides is built on first-person accounts, estate records, and original artifacts from the Locoul family, who built the simple, Creole-style house in 1805. Laura Locoul, whose great-grandparents founded the estate, wrote a detailed memoir of plantation life, family fights, and the management of slaves. The information from Laura's memoir and the original slave cabins and other outbuildings (workers on the plantation grounds lived in the cabins into the 1980s) provide rare insights into slavery in south Louisiana. The plantation gift shop stocks a large selection of literature by and about slaves and slavery in southern Louisiana and the United States. Senegalese slaves at Laura are believed to have first told folklorist Alcee Fortier the tales of Br'er Rabbit; his friend Joel Chandler Harris used the stories in his Uncle Remus tales. ⊠ *2247 Hwy. 18 (aka River Rd.), Vacherie ⊹ 57*

12

miles west of New Orleans ☎ *225/265–7690, 888/799–7690* ⊕ *www.lauraplantation.com* ✉ *$20* ☽ *Daily 10–4.*

Madewood. This galleried, 21-room Greek Revival mansion with massive white columns was designed by architect Henry Howard and completed in 1854. The house has an enormous freestanding staircase and 25-foot-high ceilings, and is best experienced with an overnight stay in the bed-and-breakfast. Guests can arrange a tour with the owners; call for appointments. Bayou Lafourche is across the road. ✉ *4250 Rte. 308, 2 miles south of town, Napoleonville* ✛ *20 miles south of Houmas House, 74 miles west of New Orleans* ☎ *985/369–7151* ⊕ *www.madewood.com* ✉ *$15 tour, by appointment only.*

Fodor'sChoice
★
Nottoway. The South's largest plantation house is a dramatic monument to antebellum grandeur. Built in 1857, the mansion is of Italianate style, with 64 rooms, 22 columns, and 200 windows. The crowning achievement of architect Henry Howard, it was saved from destruction during the Civil War by a Northern officer (a former guest of the owners, Mr. and Mrs. John Randolph). An idiosyncratic, somewhat rambling layout reflects the individual tastes of the original owners and includes a grand ballroom, famed in these parts for its crystal chandeliers and hand-carved columns. You can stay here overnight, and a formal restaurant serves breakfast, lunch, and dinner daily. The plantation is 2 miles north of its namesake, the town of White Castle (you'll understand how the town got its name when you see the vast white planation, which looks like a castle). ✉ *31025 Hwy. 1, White Castle* ✛ *33 miles northwest of Madewood, 70 miles west of New Orleans* ☎ *225/545–2730, 866/527–6884* ⊕ *www.nottoway.com* ✉ *$20* ☽ *Daily 9–4.*

Oak Alley. The most famous of all the antebellum homes in Louisiana is a darling of Hollywood, having appeared in such major movies as *Interview with the Vampire* and *Primary Colors*, as well as smaller movies and television productions. Built between 1837 and 1839 by Jacques T. Roman, a French-Creole sugar planter from New Orleans, Oak Alley is an outstanding example of Greek Revival architecture. The 28 gnarled oak trees that line the drive and give the columned plantation its name were planted in the early 1700s by an earlier settler. A guided tour introduces you to the grand interior of the manor, furnished with period antiques. Be sure to take in the view from the upper gallery of the house and to spend time exploring the expansive grounds. A number of late-19th-century cottages behind the main house provide simple overnight accommodations, and a restaurant is open daily for breakfast (8:30–10:30) and lunch (11–3). ✉ *3645 River Rd. (Rte. 18), Vacherie* ✛ *3 miles west of Laura Plantation, 60 miles west of New Orleans* ☎ *225/265–2151, 888/279–9802* ⊕ *www.oakalleyplantation.com* ✉ *$18* ☽ *Weekdays 9:30–4:30, weekends 9:30–5.*

River Road African American Museum. The contributions of African-Americans in Louisiana's rural Mississippi River communities come to light through exhibits that explore their cuisine, the Underground Railroad, free people of color, and the rural roots of jazz. ✉ *406 Charles St., Donaldsonville* ☎ *225/474–5553* ⊕ *www.africanamericanmuseum.org* ✉ *$5* ☽ *Wed.–Sat. 10–5, Sun. 1–5.*

San Francisco Plantation. An intriguing variation on the standard plantation styles, with galleries resembling the decks of a ship, gave rise to the term for an architectural style, Steamboat Gothic. The house, completed in 1856, was once called St. Frusquin, a pun on a French slang term, *sans fruscins,* which means "without a penny in my pocket"—the condition its owner, Valsin Marmillion, found himself in after paying exorbitant construction costs. Valsin's father, Edmond Bozonier Marmillion, had begun the project. According to lore his design for the house was inspired by the steamboats he enjoyed watching along the Mississippi. Upon his father's death, Valsin and his German bride, Louise von Seybold, found themselves with a plantation on their hands. Unable to return to Germany, Louise brought German influence to south Louisiana instead. The result was an opulence rarely encountered in these parts: ceilings painted in trompe l'oeil, hand-painted toilets with primitive flushing systems, and cypress painstakingly rendered as marble and English oak. Tour guides impart the full fascinating story on the 45-minute tour through the main house. An authentic one-room schoolhouse and a slave cabin have been installed on the grounds, which you can tour at your leisure. Louisiana novelist Frances Parkinson Keyes used the site as the model for her novel *Steamboat Gothic.* ✉ *2646 River Rd., Garyville* ✛ *18 miles west of Destrehan Plantation, 35 miles west of New Orleans* ☎ *985/535–2341, 888/322–1756* ⊕ *www.sanfranciscoplantation.org* ✍ *$15* ☯ *Nov.–Mar., daily 9:40–4; Apr.–Oct., daily 9:40–4:40.*

WHERE TO EAT

$

SOUTHERN

✕ **B&C Seafood.** This small shop and restaurant serves some of the tastiest seafood gumbo around River Road (and there's plenty of competition). Try it with a dash of hot sauce and a sprinkle of filé, or sample the alligator and garfish po'boys. Finish with a scoop of rich, dense bread pudding. The shop carries fresh and frozen catfish, crawfish, alligator, and turtle meat harvested from the nearby swamps. You can buy seafood packed to travel. ⑤ *Average main: $10* ✉ *2155 Rte. 18, beside Laura Plantation, Vacherie* ☎ *225/265–8356* ☯ *Closed Sun.*

$$$$

CAJUN

✕ **Latil's Landing Restaurant.** Set in the rear wing of Houmas House Plantation, Latil's Landing Restaurant is furnished with period antiques and reproductions that put you in the mood for its "nouvelle Louisiana" food, a mélange of traditional ingredients with more contemporary cooking techniques and flavors. Try the roasted oysters with local Creole cream-cheese sauce, the foie gras beignets, or the duck with praline sauce. ⑤ *Average main: $35* ✉ *Houmas House Plantation, 40136 Hwy. 942, Darrow* ☎ *225/473–7841, 888/323–8314* ⌖ *Reservations essential* ☯ *No dinner Sun.–Tues.*

$

SOUTHERN

✕ **Spuddy's Cajun Foods.** Midway between Laura and Oak Alley plantations, downtown Vacherie is short on sights but long on flavor, thanks in no small part to this down-home lunchroom. Photos and murals on the walls tell tales of local history, while po'boys, jambalaya, and fried catfish fill the tables. You can also pick up some house-made sausage as an edible souvenir. ⑤ *Average main: $10* ✉ *2644 Hwy. 20, Vacherie* ☎ *225/265–4013* ⌖ *Reservations not accepted* ☯ *Dinner served on Fri. only, until 7:30. Closed Sun.*

12

$ ✕**Wayne Jacob's Smokehouse Restaurant.** LaPlace is known as the andou-
CAJUN ille capital of the world, and the spicy, smoky, Cajun-style sausage is
deservedly popular here. In this butcher shop that doubles as a functional, straightforward restaurant, you can get andouille in burgers,
in gumbo, made into chips for dipping, or worked into white beans
and rice. A jazz brunch on Sunday expands the offerings to include
omelets, pancakes, and other comforting fare. Although reservations
aren't mandatory here, they are a good idea. $ *Average main: $10*
⊠ *769 W. Fifth St., LaPlace* ☎ *985/652–9990* ⊕ *www.wjsmokehouse.
com* ☾ *No dinner Sat.–Wed.*

WHERE TO STAY

$$$$ **Houmas House B&B.** Experience the luxurious and beautiful grounds
B&B/INN of this plantation house in one of 22 rooms in newly built cottages that
face a row of oak trees about a block away from the plantation house.
$ *Rooms from: $350* ⊠ *40136 Highway 942, Darrow* ☎ *225/473–
9380* ⊕ *www.houmashouse.com* ⥱ *22 rooms* ⏐◎⏐ *Breakfast.*

$$$ **Madewood B&B.** Expect gracious hospitality, lovely antiques, and
B&B/INN canopied beds in both the 21-room main house and Charlet House,
a smaller structure on the plantation grounds that holds three of the
inn's eight rooms for guests. **Pros:** quiet; beautiful; staying here is like
stepping back in time—though with Wi-Fi and other modern ameni-
ties. **Cons:** some may find it too quiet; no TV; dinner is a group affair.
$ *Rooms from: $259* ⊠ *4250 Rte. 308, Napoleonville* ☎ *985/369–7151*
⊕ *www.madewood.com* ⥱ *8 rooms* ⏐◎⏐ *Some meals.*

$$$$ **Nottoway B&B.** At the largest antebellum plantation in the South, you
B&B/INN can wander around the grounds at night, sit on the upstairs balcony and
watch the ships go by on the river, and in other ways enjoy Southern life.
Pros: sleeping in history. **Cons:** with so many rooms and a busy schedule
of tours and events, this isn't the place to get away from it all. $ *Rooms
from: $229* ⊠ *31025 Hwy. 1, White Castle* ☎ *225/545–8632, 866/428–
4748* ⊕ *www.nottoway.com* ⥱ *40 rooms, 2 suites* ⏐◎⏐ *Breakfast.*

$$$ **Oak Alley B&B.** These 100-year-old one- and two-bedroom cottages
B&B/INN on Oak Alley Plantation's grounds, just beyond the shadow of the big
house, combine country charm (brass beds and antiques or reproductions) with practical and useful amenities. **Pros:** spectacular sunrise
views from the levee in front of the plantation; serene quiet; charming
rooms with comfortable beds and amenities. **Cons:** few nearby options
for supplies and food (although the chef can make dinners ahead of
time, to be delivered to your cottage during the day). $ *Rooms from:
$150* ⊠ *3645 River Rd. (Rte. 18), Vacherie* ☎ *225/265–2151, 800/442–
5539* ⊕ *www.oakalleyplantation.com* ⥱ *6 cottages* ⏐◎⏐ *Breakfast.*

BATON ROUGE

80 miles northwest of New Orleans via I–10.

Hemmed in as it is by endless industrial plants, Baton Rouge may not
look like much from the road. Yet government-history enthusiasts will
want to stop here on their way through the south Louisiana countryside. The state capital has several interesting and readily accessible
sights, including the attractive capitol grounds and an educational

San Francisco Plantation stands out for its over-the-top "Steamboat Gothic" exterior.

planetarium. This is the city from which the colorful, cunning, and often corrupt Huey P. Long ruled the state; it is also the site of his assassination. Even today, nearly 80 years after Long's death, legends about the controversial governor and U.S. senator abound.

The parishes to the north of Baton Rouge are quiet and bucolic, with gently rolling hills, high bluffs, and historic districts. John James Audubon lived in West Feliciana Parish in 1821, tutoring local children and painting 80 of his famous bird studies. In both terrain and traits, this region is more akin to north Louisiana than to south Louisiana—which is to say, the area is very Southern.

EXPLORING

TOP ATTRACTIONS

FAMILY **Louisiana Arts & Science Museum and Irene W. Pennington Planetarium.** Housed in a 1925 Illinois Central railroad station near the Old State Capitol, this idiosyncratic but high-quality collection brings together a contemporary-art gallery and an Egyptian tomb exhibit featuring a mummy from 300 BC. Also here are a children's museum and a kid-friendly planetarium. The planetarium presents regular shows, as does the ExxonMobil Space Theater. The museum hosts traveling exhibits, and houses the nation's second-largest collection of sculptures by 20th-century Croatian artist Ivan Mestrovic, many of which adorn the entrance hall. ⊠ *100 S. River Rd.* ☎ *225/344–5272* ⊕ *www.lasm.org* 🎟 *$7.25, $9 with planetarium show* ⏱ *Tues.–Fri. 10–3, Sat. 10–5 (planetarium 10–8), Sun. 1–4.*

Louisiana State Museum–Baton Rouge. This museum showcases the history of Louisiana through two permanent exhibits. "Grounds for Greatness: Louisiana and the Nation" relates Louisiana events to the rest of U.S. and world history, from the Louisiana Purchase to World War II. "Louisiana Experience: Discovering the Soul of America" takes the visitor on a road-trip-like exhibit that courses through the different regions of the state. Rotating exhibits in the museum's gallery explore the arts, culture, and history of the region. ✉ *660 N. 4th St.* ☎ *225/342–5428* ⊕ *www.crt.state.la.us/museum* ✑ *Free* ⊙ *Tues.–Sat. 9–5.*

Rural Life Museum and Windrush Gardens. Run by Louisiana State University, this outdoor teaching and research facility aims to represent the rural life of early Louisianians. Three major areas—the Barn, the Working Plantation, and Folk Architecture—contain more than 32 rustic 19th-century structures spread over 25 acres. A visitor center adjoins the Barn, which holds a collection that includes old farm tools, quilts, 19th-century horse-drawn carriages, slave items, and much more. The plantation section's buildings include a gristmill, a blacksmith's shop, and several outbuildings. The gardens were created by the late landscape designer Steele Burden. ✉ *4650 Essen La., off I–10* ☎ *225/765–2437* ⊕ *www.rurallife.lsu.edu* ✑ *$9* ⊙ *Daily 8–5.*

Shaw Center for the Arts. This arts facility houses the Louisiana State University (LSU) Museum of Art, the LSU Museum Store, the Manship Theatre, Hartley/Vey Studio and Workshop Theatres, LSU School of Art Glassell Gallery, two sculpture gardens, and a rooftop terrace with great views of the Mississippi River. On-site restaurants include Tsunami Sushi, Capital City Grill, PJ's Coffee, and Stroubes Chophouse. ✉ *100 Lafayette St.* ☎ *225/389–7171* ⊕ *www.shawcenter.org* ✑ *Museum: $5* ⊙ *Center: Mon. 9–4, Tues.–Sat. 9 am–11 pm, Sun. 11–5. Museum: Tues., Wed., Fri., and Sat. 10–5, Thurs. 10–8, Sun. 1–5. Museum store: Tues.–Sat. noon–8, Sun. 1–5.*

USS *Kidd* & Veterans Memorial Museum. This World War II survivor has been restored to its V-J Day configuration. A self-guided tour takes in more than 50 inner spaces of this ship and also the separate **Nautical Center** museum. Among the museum's exhibits are articles from the United States' 175 Fletcher-class destroyers, a collection of ship models, and a restored P-40 fighter plane hanging from the ceiling. The Louisiana Memorial Plaza lists more than 7,000 Louisiana citizens killed during combat, including the 127 citizens killed in the Iraq and Afghanistan wars. An A-7E Corsair plane pays tribute to the veterans of the Vietnam War. ✉ *305 S. River Rd. (Government St. at the levee)* ☎ *225/342–1942* ⊕ *www.usskidd.com* ✑ *$8* ⊙ *Daily 9–5.*

HUEY'S "DEDUCT" BOX

One of the biggest mysteries about Huey P. Long is what happened to his "deduct box." The deduct box was where Long kept his political contributions—cash—from individuals and corporations. State employees, no matter how high or low, also gave a portion of their salary to Long. The box had a number of homes, and the best known was at the Roosevelt Hotel. But when Long was assassinated in 1935, the location of the deduct box went to the grave with him. Many still think it's within the walls of the hotel.

WORTH NOTING

Old Governor's Mansion. This Georgian-style house was built for Governor Huey P. Long in 1930, and eight governors have since lived there. The story goes that Long instructed the architect to design his home to resemble the White House, representing Long's unrealized ambition to live in the real one. Notable features on the guided tour include Long's bedroom and a secret staircase. This historic house museum also houses the Foundation for Historical Louisiana headquarters and functions as a venue for special events. ✉ *502 North Blvd.* ☎ *225/387–2464* ⊕ *www. oldgovernorsmansion.org* 🎫 *$7* ⊙ *Tues.–Fri. 10–4.*

Old State Capitol. When this turreted Gothic Victorian castle was constructed between 1847 and 1852, it was declared by some a masterpiece, by others a monstrosity. No one can deny that the restored building is colorful and dramatic. In the entrance hall a stunning pink, gold, and green spiral staircase winds toward a stained-glass atrium. The building now holds the Louisiana Center for Political and Governmental History, an education and research facility with audiovisual exhibits. The "assassination room," an exhibit covering Huey Long's final moments, is a major draw. The Ghost of the Castle Exhibit is a 12-minute video that tells the history of the building, as narrated by an actress playing Sarah Morgan, whose father donated the land on which the building was built. ✉ *100 North Blvd., at River Rd.* ☎ *225/342–0500, 800/488–2968* ⊕ *www.louisianaoldstatecapitol.org* 🎫 *Free* ⊙ *Tues–Sat. 9–4.*

State Capitol Building. Still called the "New State Capitol," this building has housed the offices of the governor and Congress since 1932. It is a testament to the personal influence of legendary Governor Huey Long that the funding for this massive building was approved during the Great Depression, and that the building itself was completed in a mere 14 months. You can tour the first floor, richly decked with murals and mosaics, and peer into the halls of the Louisiana legislature. Huey Long's colorful personality—and autocratic ways—eventually caught up with him: he was assassinated in 1935, and the spot where he was shot (near the rear elevators) is marked with a plaque. At 34 stories, this is America's tallest state capitol; an observation deck on the 27th floor affords an expansive view of the Mississippi River, the city, and the industrial outskirts. ✉ *900 N. 3rd St.* ☎ *225/342–7317* 🎫 *Free* ⊙ *Daily 8–4:30 (tower until 4).*

WHERE TO EAT AND STAY

$$$
SOUTHERN
✕ **Juban's.** This upscale bistro with a lush courtyard and walls adorned with art is about 3 miles from the LSU campus. Tempting main courses of seafood, beef, and veal dishes, as well as roasted duck and quail highlight the menu. The Hallelujah Crab (soft-shell stuffed with seafood and topped with "creolaise" sauce) is a specialty, and Juban's own mango tea is delicious. The warm bread pudding makes a memorable end to meals here. 💲 *Average main: $30* ✉ *Acadian Perkins Shopping Center, 3739 Perkins Rd.* ☎ *225/346–8422* ⊕ *www.jubans.com* ⊙ *No lunch Mon. and Sat. No dinner Sun.*

$$
SEAFOOD
✕ **Mike Anderson's.** Locals praise the seafood at this busy spot, and it is true that the food is good, fresh, served in large portions, and consistent. The fried seafood platter—shrimp, oysters, crawfish tails, catfish, and stuffed crab served with onion rings, hush puppies, and a choice of salad

or various coleslaws—is your best bet. ⑤ *Average main: $20* ⊠ *1031 W. Lee Dr.* ☏ *225/766–7823* ⊕ *www.mikeandersons.com.*

$$$ **Hilton Baton Rouge Capitol Center.** A fitness center, a full-service spa,
HOTEL and many other amenities make this historic riverside landmark a popular choice for business people and conventioneers. **Pros:** spectacular view of the river; near all the downtown sites. **Cons:** generic business-like surroundings; can get crowded when conventions are in town. ⑤ *Rooms from: $139* ⊠ *201 Lafayette St.* ☏ *225/344–5866* ⊕ *www. hiltoncapitolcenter.com* ⥱ *290 rooms, 8 suites* |◯| *No meals.*

$$$$ **Marriott Baton Rouge.** This high-rise hotel has somewhat formal rooms
HOTEL and public spaces with traditional furnishings, and rooms on the top four floors come with such perks as Continental breakfast and afternoon hors d'oeuvres and cocktails. **Pros:** accommodating to large groups; full-service hotel; lots of comforts. **Cons:** not that close to downtown sights. ⑤ *Rooms from: $179* ⊠ *5500 Hilton Ave.* ☏ *225/924–5000, 800/627– 7468* ⊕ *www.marriott.com* ⥱ *299 rooms* |◯| *Multiple meal plans.*

$$$ **The Stockade B&B.** It's named for the Civil War–era military prison that
B&B/INN once occupied the site, though you definitely won't feel like a prisoner in this pleasant, tile-roofed, contemporary brick house on the winding, oak-lined Highland Road. **Pros:** Southern hospitality and country elegance. **Cons:** the downtown sights can feel far away. ⑤ *Rooms from: $135* ⊠ *8860 Highland Rd.* ☏ *225/769–7358, 888/900–5430* ⊕ *www. thestockade.com* ⥱ *6 rooms* |◯| *Breakfast.*

ST. FRANCISVILLE

25 miles north of Baton Rouge on U.S. 61.

A cluster of plantation homes all within a half-hour drive, a lovely, walkable historic district, renowned antiques shopping, and a wealth of comfortable B&Bs draw visitors and locals from New Orleans to overnight stays in St. Francisville. The town is just a two-hour drive from New Orleans, so it's also possible to make this a day trip.

St. Francisville's historic district, particularly along Royal Street, is dotted with markers identifying basic histories of various structures, most of them dating to the late 18th or early 19th century. The region's Anglo-Protestant edge, in contrast to the staunchly French-Catholic tenor of the River Road plantations, is evident in the prominent **Grace Episcopal Church,** on a hill in the center of town and surrounded by a peaceful, Spanish moss–shaded cemetery. A smaller (and older) Catholic cemetery is directly across a small fence from the Episcopal complex.

EXPLORING

OFF THE BEATEN PATH

Angola Museum. The 18,000 acres that make up the notorious Angola prison are a half-hour drive from St. Francisville, at the dead end of Highway 66. With a prison population of about 5,200 inmates, this is one of the largest prisons in the United States. Nicknamed "The Farm," Angola was once a working plantation, with prisoners for field hands. Now, it produces 4 million pounds of vegetables each year that feed 11,000 inmates across the state. The prison has been immortalized in countless songs and several films and documentaries, including *Dead Man Walking* and *Angola Prison Rodeo—the Wildest Show in* *the South.* The latter film is based on the prison's biannual rodeo in April and October, which offers visitors a rare look inside the grounds of the prison. Inmates set up stands where they sell their arts and crafts during the rodeo. A small museum outside the prison's front gate houses a fascinating, eerie, and often moving collection of photographs documenting the people and events that have been a part of Angola. Items such as makeshift prisoner weapons and the electric chair used for executions until 1991 are also on display. ⊠ *Hwy. 66* ☎ *225/655–2592* ⊕ *www.angolamuseum.org* 🎫 *Free* ☉ *Mon.–Fri. 8–4:30, Sat. 8–4, every Sun. in Oct. 8–4.*

The Myrtles. A 110-foot gallery with Wedgwood-blue cast-iron grillwork makes a lovely setting for the weddings and receptions frequently held at the Myrtles. The house, built around 1796, has elegant formal parlors with rich molding and faux-marble paneling. Because the upper floor is used as a bed-and-breakfast, the scope of the daytime guided tour is limited. The house is reputedly haunted, and the fun mystery tours, held at night, are more of a draw than the day tours (reservations are a good idea). The Carriage House Restaurant, beside the house, serves lunch and dinner. ⊠ *7747 U.S. 61, about 1 mile north of downtown St. Francisville* ☎ *225/635–6277, 800/809–0565* ⊕ *www.myrtlesplantation.com* 🎫 *$10 day tours, $12 mystery tours* ☉ *Daily 9–5; mystery tours Fri. and Sat. nights at 6, 7, and 8.*

OFF THE
BEATEN
PATH

Audubon State Historic Site and Oakley Plantation House. John James Audubon did a major portion of his *Birds of America* studies in this 100-acre park, and the three-story Oakley Plantation House is where Audubon tutored the young Eliza Pirrie, daughter of Mr. and Mrs. James Pirrie, owners of Oakley. The simple, even spartan, interior contrasts sharply with the extravagances of many of the River Road plantations and demonstrates the Puritan influence in this region. The grounds, too, are reminiscent of the English penchant for a blending of order and wilderness in their gardens. You must follow a short path to reach the house from the parking lot. A state-run museum at the start of the path provides an informative look at plantation life as it was lived in this region 200 years ago. ⊠ *11788 L.A. Highway 965, 2 miles south of St. Francisville off U.S. 61* ☎ *225/635–3739, 888/677–2838* ⊕ *www.crt.state.la.us/parks/iaudubon.aspx* 🎫 *Park and plantation $8* ☉ *Tues.–Sat. 9–5, guided tours 10–4 pm on the hour.*

Fodor'sChoice
★

Rosedown Plantation and Gardens. The opulent, beautifully restored house at Rosedown dates from 1835. The original owners, Martha and Daniel Turnbull, spent their honeymoon in Europe; Mrs. Turnbull fell in love with the gardens she saw there and had the land at Rosedown laid out even as the house was under construction. She spent the rest of her life lovingly maintaining some 28 acres of exquisite formal gardens. The state of Louisiana owns Rosedown, and the beauties of the restored manor, including 90% of the original furniture, can be appreciated during a thorough one-hour tour led by park rangers. Be sure to allow ample time for roaming the grounds after the tour. ⊠ *12501 Highway 10, off U.S. 61* ☎ *225/635–3332, 888/376–1867* ⊕ *www.crt.state.la.us/parks/irosedown.aspx* 🎫 *$10* ☉ *Daily 9–5. Closed on major holidays.*

WHERE TO EAT AND STAY

$$
CAJUN
✕ **Carriage House Restaurant.** Located in the shadow of the Myrtles Plantation, the Carriage House is a boon to overnighters in the St. Francisville area. The dining room is elegant and intimate. The contemporary cuisine draws from a wealth of culinary traditions, with a mix of classic Southern cuisine and a dash of Creole. The baked oysters Bienville and the buttery barbecue shrimp are both delicious, and the Sunday brunch is a favorite. Ⓢ *Average main: $20* ⊠ *Myrtles Plantation, 7747 U.S. 61* ☎ *225/635–6278* ⊕ *www.themyrtlesrestaurant.com* ☾ *Closed Tues. Lunch 11 am–2 pm, dinner 5–9 pm. Only brunch on Sun., 11 am–2 pm.*

$
AMERICAN
✕ **The Magnolia.** This low-key and unassuming restaurant turns into a St. Francisville hot spot on Friday and Saturday nights. During the day, locals and tourists flock to "The Mag" for sandwiches, pizza, steaks, and Southern and Mexican dishes. At night, go for cocktails or dinner; on Friday evenings there's a live band. Ⓢ *Average main: $15* ⊠ *5689 Commerce St.* ☎ *225/635–6528* ⊕ *www.themagnoliacafe.net* ☾ *No dinner Sun.–Wed.*

$
SOUTHERN
✕ **Roadside BBQ & Grill.** Looking for Southern barbecue? Here it is— ribs, pork, and chicken, all perfectly grilled. If you're not in the mood for 'cue, they also have hamburgers, salads, and fried seafood po'boys. There's a seafood buffet for lunch on Sunday. A children's menu is also available. Ⓢ *Average main: $8* ⊠ *Colonial Dr. and U.S. 61, 9 miles south of St. Francisville* ☎ *225/658–9669* ☾ *Closed Mon. No dinner Tues. and Sun.*

$$$
B&B/INN
▥ **Barrow House & Printer's Cottage.** Fittingly located on St. Francisville's historic Royal Street, these two old houses hold some of the most comfortable bed-and-breakfast accommodations in the area, with antique furnishings in most of the rooms. **Pros:** good location in downtown St. Francisville; comfortable atmosphere; friendly staff. **Cons:** if you don't like antiques, you may feel as if you're in a museum or your grandmother's home. Ⓢ *Rooms from: $150* ⊠ *9779 Royal St.* ☎ *225/635–4791* ⊕ *www.topteninn.com* ⟿ *3 rooms, 4 suites* ⵏⵔ *Breakfast.*

$$$$
B&B/INN
▥ **The Myrtles.** If you don't mind a deep legacy of hauntings, you'll enjoy these character-filled guest rooms on the second floor of the plantation house and a couple of outlying buildings, all filled with antiques and most with four-poster beds. **Pros:** historical property oozes atmosphere; ghost hunters' paradise; next door to Carriage House Restaurant. **Cons:** feels like it's in the middle of nowhere; easily spooked travelers might want to stay elsewhere. Ⓢ *Rooms from: $200* ⊠ *7747 U.S. 61* ☎ *225/635–6277, 800/809–0565* ⊕ *www.myrtlesplantation.com* ⟿ *14 rooms, 2 suites* ⵏⵔ *Breakfast.*

CAJUN COUNTRY

French Louisiana, lying amid the bayous, rice fields, and canebrakes to the west of New Orleans, has become famous in the rest of the country for its food—"jambalaya and a crawfish pie and filé gumbo," as Hank Williams put it—and its rollicking Cajun and zydeco music. The Cajun culture has its roots far from these parts in the present-day Canadian provinces of Nova Scotia and New Brunswick, where French settlers

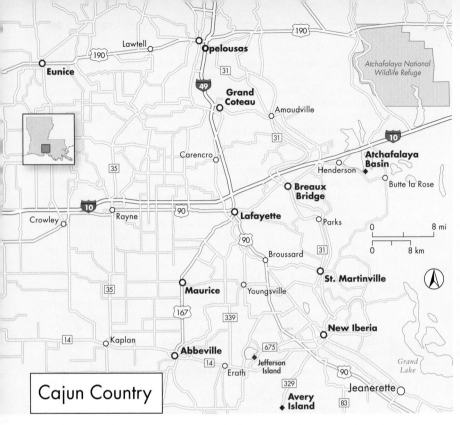

Cajun Country

colonized a region they called l'Acadie at the start of the 17th century. After the British seized control of the region in the early 18th century, the French were expelled. Henry Wadsworth Longfellow described their exile in his epic poem "Evangeline." Many Acadians eventually settled in 22 parishes of southwestern Louisiana. Their descendants are called "Cajun," a corruption of "Acadian"; some continue the traditions of the early French settlers, living by fishing and fur trapping.

Cajun culture is decidedly rural, rooted in a smattering of tiny towns and in the swamps and bayous that wind among them. Driving from one village to the next, antiques shoppers and nature lovers alike will find a whole lot to love. Live oaks with ragged gray buntings of Spanish moss form canopies over the bottle-green bayous. Country roads follow the contortions of the Teche (pronounced *tesh*), the state's longest bayou, and meander through villages where cypress cabins rise up out of the water on stilts and moored fishing boats and canoe-like pirogues scarcely bob on the sluggish waters. At the centers of these same villages are wonderful bakeries, historic churches, fresh oyster bars, and regional antiques for sale in small, weathered shops.

Many visitors to this region are surprised to hear the dialect for the first time. Cajun French is an oral tradition in which French vocabulary and grammar encounter the American accent, and it differs significantly from what is spoken in France. English is also spoken throughout Cajun Country, but you will hear Gallic accents and see many signs that read "Ici on parle français" (French spoken here).

GETTING HERE AND AROUND

BUS TRAVEL

Greyhound has numerous daily departures from New Orleans to Lafayette. The trip takes three to three and a half hours.

Bus Information Greyhound ☎ *800/231–2222* ⊕ *www.greyhound.com.*

CAR TRAVEL

Interstate 10 runs east–west across the state and through New Orleans. Take Interstate 10 west to the Lafayette exit, 136 miles from New Orleans. The interstate route takes about two hours and 15 minutes. Return to New Orleans via U.S. 90, down through Houma, for scenic stopovers. This route will take close to three hours.

TRAIN TRAVEL

Amtrak connects New Orleans and Lafayette via the *Sunset Limited*. Trains make the three- to four-hour scenic trip each way once daily.

Train Amtrak ☎ *800/872–7245* ⊕ *www.amtrak.com.*

VISITOR INFORMATION

Contacts Lafayette Convention and Visitors Commission ☎ *337/232–3737, 800/346–1958* ⊕ *www.lafayettetravel.com.* **St. Martin Parish Tourist Commission** ☎ *888/565–5939* ⊕ *www.cajuncountry.org.* **St. Landry Parish Tourist Commission** ☎ *877/948–8004* ⊕ *www.cajuntravel.com.*

LAFAYETTE

136 miles west of New Orleans.

Lafayette (pronounced lah-fay-*ette*), with a population of about 120,000 (the largest city in Cajun Country), is a major center of Cajun life and lore. It's an interesting and enjoyable city, with some worthwhile historical and artistic sights. The simulated Cajun villages at **Vermilionville** and **Acadian Village** provide evocative introductions to the traditional Cajun way of life. Excellent restaurants and B&Bs make Lafayette a good jumping-off point for exploring the region. In recent years the city has had an infusion of new restaurants and nightclubs—particularly downtown.

EXPLORING

Alexandre Mouton House and Lafayette Museum. Built in 1800 as the *maison dimanche,* or "Sunday house" (town house used when attending church services), of town founder Jean Mouton, this galleried town house with a mid-19th-century addition now preserves local history. It was later home to Alexandre Mouton (1804–1885), the first democratic governor of Lousiana. The older section is an excellent example of early Acadian architecture and contains artifacts used by settlers. The main museum displays Civil War–era furnishings and memorabilia and an exhibit on Mardi Gras. ✉ *1122 Lafayette St.* ☎ *337/234–2208* 🎫 *$5* 🕙 *Tues.–Sat. 10–4.*

Lafayette Courthouse. The courthouse contains an impressive collection of more than 2,000 historical photographs of life in the Lafayette area. There are images of famous politicians such as Dudley LeBlanc and Huey Long working the stump and scenes from the great flood of 1927. ⊠ *800 S. Buchanan St.* ☎ *337/233–0150* ☺ *Weekdays 8:30–4:30.*

FAMILY **Lafayette Natural History Museum and Planetarium.** This sparkling natural-history museum includes changing exhibitions and lots of fun hands-on science for kids. The most popular permanent attraction is the planetarium, outfitted with high-definition digital equipment. ⊠ *433 Jefferson St.* ☎ *337/291–5544* ⊕ *www.lafayettesciencemuseum.org* ⊠ *$5* ☺ *Tues.–Fri. 9–5, Sat. 10–6, Sun. 1–6.*

> ## MURALS
>
> There are several outdoor murals by the local artist Robert Dafford in the center of Lafayette, including a 100-foot-wide Louisiana swamp scene titled *"Till All That's Left is a Postcard,"* which is across from Dwyer's Café. Another work, titled *"Ex-Garage"* and full of splashy cars and TVs with vignettes of Cajun life, is on the Jefferson Tower Building. The reflections in the bumpers of the cars reveal area musicians and traditions.

St. John the Evangelist Cathedral. This Dutch Romanesque structure with Byzantine touches was completed in 1916 (construction began in 1912). In the cemetery behind the church are aboveground tombs that date back to 1820; interred here are town founder Jean Mouton, Civil War hero General Alfred Mouton, General Alfred Gardiner, and Cidalese Arceneaux. Next to the cathedral is a nearly 500-year-old St. John Oak, one of the charter members of the silent but leafy Louisiana Live Oak Society. ⊠ *515 Cathedral St.* ☎ *337/232–1322* ⊕ *www.saintjohncathedral.org* ☺ *Museum: Mon.–Thurs. 9–noon and 1–4; Fri. 9–noon.*

OUTSIDE DOWNTOWN

Acadian Cultural Center. A unit of the National Park Service, the center traces the history of the area through numerous audiovisual exhibits of food, music, and folklore. Be sure to watch the introductory film, which is a dramatization of the Explusion of the Acadians (1755–1764), when the British deported the descendants of French settlers in the maritime provinces of Canada to the 13 colonies. Clips from the 1929 silent movie *Evangeline* (a fictional account based on the Longfellow poem of an Acadian girl's search for her lost love) are incorporated in the film; film buffs will love it. Ranger-guided boat tours of Bayou Vermilion take place March through June and September through November in a traditional Cajun boat. ⊠ *501 Fisher Rd.* ☎ *337/232–0789* ⊕ *www.nps.gov/jela* ⊠ *Free* ☺ *Mon.–Fri. 9 am–4:30 pm, Sat. 8:30 am–noon.*

OFF THE
BEATEN
PATH

Acadian Village. Most of the structures at this re-creation of an early-19th-century bayou settlement were moved here to create an representative "village." They actually represent a broad range of Acadian architectural styles, and the rustic general store, blacksmith shop, and chapel are replicas. The park is on 10 wooded acres, with a meandering bayou crisscrossed by wooden footbridges. Each house is decorated

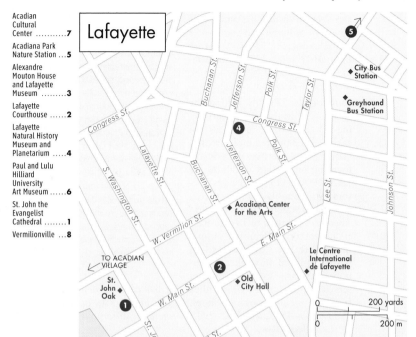

with antique furnishings. The weeks in December before Christmas bring "Noel Acadian au Village," with later hours, musicians, food, and buildings covered in lights. ✉ *200 Greenleaf Dr., south of downtown* ☎ *337/981–2364, 800/962–9133* ⊕ *www.acadianvillage.org* 💲 *$8* ⊗ *Mon.–Sat. 10 am–4 pm.*

Acadiana Center for the Arts. This multicultural arts center hosts art exhibits, musical performances, lectures, and children's programs. Film screenings are occasionally held at the in-house movie theater. ✉ *101 W. Vermilion St.* ☎ *337/233–7060* ⊕ *www.acadianacenterforthearts. org* ⊗ *Tues.–Sat. 10–5.*

FAMILY **Acadiana Park Nature Station.** Naturalists are on hand in the interpretive center at this three-story cypress structure, which overlooks a 42-acre park of natural forest. Discovery boxes help children get to know the wildflowers, birds, and other outdoorsy things they'll see on the 3-mile nature trail. Free guided trail tours are offered on Saturday and Sunday by request. There is a guided evening hike on the last Saturday of the month ($3 per person). ✉ *1205 E. Alexander St.* ☎ *337/291–8448* ⊕ *www.naturestation.org* 💲 *Free* ⊗ *Weekdays 8–5, weekends 11–5.*

Paul and Lulu Hilliard University Art Museum. Inside a gleaming glass-clad box built in 2003, this museum on the campus of the University of Louisiana at Lafayette features world-class works, including a collection of folk art and pieces by Deborah Butterfield and Robert Rauschenberg. ✉ *710 E. St. Mary Blvd.* ☎ *337/482–2278* ⊕ *museum. louisiana.edu* ✍ *$5* ⊗ *Tues.–Thurs. 9–5, Fri. 9–noon, Sat. 10–5.*

FAMILY **Vermilionville.** Directly behind the Acadian Cultural Center, this living-history village re-creates the early life of the region's Creoles, Cajuns, and Native Americans, focusing on the late 1800s to the early 1900s. On select days visitors can see a blacksmith demonstration or watch weavers at work. There are exhibits in 19 Acadian-style structures, including a music hall where live Cajun or zydeco music is played on weekend afternoons. A large rustic restaurant serves Cajun classics. Check ahead for live cooking demonstrations from the on-site cooking school. ✉ *300 Fisher Rd., off Surrey St.* ☎ *337/233–4077, 866/992–2968* ⊕ *www.vermilionville.org* ✍ *$10* ⊗ *Tues.–Sun. 10–4.*

> ## CREOLE VS. CAJUN
>
> Cajun cuisine relies on locally available ingredients, including pork, seafood, smoked meats, yams, and rice. Creole cuisine is more cosmopolitan, incorporating French, Spanish, Italian, African, and French Caribbean influences. Most Cajun and Creole dishes include the "holy trinity" of sautéed celery, bell pepper, and garlic or onion as a base, but Creole dishes, like their French counterparts, are defined by their sauces. Examples include shrimp Creole, crawfish bisque, and oysters Rockefeller.

WHERE TO EAT

$$$ ✗ **Café Vermilionville.** This 19th-century inn with crisp white linens and
CAJUN old-brick fireplaces serves French and Cajun dishes to a well-dressed crowd. Among the specialties are Gulf fish Acadien and grilled duck breast. This is a favorite spot for special occasions among Lafayette residents. ⑤ *Average main: $30* ✉ *1304 W. Pinhook Rd.* ☎ *337/237–0100* ⊕ *www.cafev.com* ⊗ *No lunch weekends.*

$$ ✗ **Crawfish Time.** From roughly December through June, when Louisiana
SOUTHERN crawfish are in season, local families pack in to partake in the outrageous abundance. In the simple, stripped-down room filled with big tables, crawfish, oysters, and a few sides like sausage links and boiled potatoes, plus cold beer, make up the menu. Use the drive-through window to create your own crawfish picnic. ⑤ *Average main: $20* ✉ *2019 Verot School Rd.* ☎ *337/988–2645* ⊕ *www.lacrawfishtime. com* ⊗ *Closed June–Nov. No lunch.*

$ ✗ **Johnson's Boucaniere.** This *boucaniere* (Cajun French for smokehouse)
SOUTHERN is run by the next generation of the same family that operated the iconic Johnson's Grocery in Eunice, LA, which closed in 2005. It's a laid-back, friendly place with a refreshing blend of tradition and modern style. Music from young local bands plays over the sound system (their CDs line the shelves next to barbecue sauces for sale); customers sit on the covered porch and dig into boudin, sandwiches, and the heartily recommended barbecue, which is smoked in-house and rubbed with Cajun-style seasonings. ⑤ *Average main: $7* ✉ *1111 St. John St.* ☎ *337/269–8878* ⊕ *www.johnsonsboucaniere.com* ⊗ *Closed Mon.*

Dropping in on a jam session is a must-do in Cajun country.

$$
CAJUN
Fodor's Choice
★

✕ **Prejean's.** In this cypress house decorated with swamp trees and a large stuffed alligator at the entrance, people gather at tables with red-and-white-check cloths to chow down on some local classics: crawfish and alligator sausage cheesecake, Cajun-style venison, or any of the kitchen's four distinctive gumbos. Grilled seafood provides some lighter options. At breakfast, try the house rendition of eggs Benedict, made here with boudin patties, poached eggs, and crawfish étouffée over a biscuit. There's live Cajun music, and usually dancing, nightly. ⑤ *Average main: $18* ✉ *3480 N.E. Evangeline Throughway* ☎ *337/896–3247* ⊕ *www.prejeans.com.*

$
CAJUN

✕ **T-Coon's Café.** This often-busy diner serves a hearty Cajun breakfast and lunch, which include daily specials such as smothered rabbit, short-rib fricassee, or crawfish omelets. The Southern fare also includes fried chicken and seafood dishes. ⑤ *Average main: $8* ✉ *1900 W. Pinhook Rd.* ☎ *337/233–0422* ⊕ *www.tcoons.com* ☾ *No dinner.*

WHERE TO STAY

$$$
B&B/INN

🛏 **Bois des Chênes Inn.** In the 19th-century Mouton Plantation, in a quiet residential area of Lafayette, an upstairs suite has early Acadian antiques, while downstairs the Louisiana Empire and the Victorian suites both have queen-size beds. **Pros:** nice owners; pretty grounds; glass of wine and tour of the house included in rates. **Cons:** rooms can be a little stuffy. ⑤ *Rooms from: $150* ✉ *338 N. Sterling St.* ☎ *337/233–7816* ⊕ *www.boisdeschenes.com* ⇄ *5 rooms* ⑽ *Breakfast.*

$$
B&B/INN

🛏 **Buchanan Lofts.** These nine rooms inside a refurbished warehouse are like seriously stylish apartments—each has a different layout, but they're all quite spacious, with floor-to-ceiling windows, lots of exposed brick, and streamlined, minimalist furnishings. **Pros:** close to everything downtown; huge rooms filled with stylish furnishings. **Cons:** not much local character. ⑤ *Rooms from: $140* ✉ *403 S. Buchanan St.* ☎ *337/534–4922* ⊕ *www.buchananlofts.com* ⤺ *9 rooms* ❧❍❦ *No meals.*

$$$
B&B/INN
⛬ **Juliet Boutique Hotel.** A sense of privacy prevails in these nicely located rooms in downtown Lafayette, where fine linens and a pool are among the many amenities. **Pros:** room service is a nice perk; extremely comfortable beds. **Cons:** some rooms have structural poles; some guests may not like the shuttered bathroom windows opening into the rooms; checkout can take a while. ⑤ *Rooms from: $129* ✉ *800 Jefferson St.* ☎ *337/261–2225* ⊕ *www.ascendcollection.com/hotel-lafayette-louisiana-LA250* ⤺ *20 rooms* ❧❍❦ *No meals.*

$$
B&B/INN
⛬ **T'Frere's House.** Built in 1880 of native cypress and handmade bricks, Acadian-style "Little Brother's House" is furnished with French and Louisiana antiques; additional accommodations are in an Acadian-style cottage behind the main house. **Pros:** charming decor; owners like to feed their guests well. **Cons:** it feels a bit far from everything; not a good option if you're on a diet. ⑤ *Rooms from: $105* ✉ *1905 Verot School Rd.* ☎ *337/984–9347, 800/984–9347* ⊕ *www.tfreres.com* ⤺ *8 rooms* ❧❍❦ *Breakfast.*

NIGHTLIFE AND THE ARTS

Pick up a copy of the *Times of Acadiana* or the trendier *Independent* to find listings for *fais-do-dos,* zydeco dances, and other events. These free weeklies are available online and in hotels, restaurants, and shops.

Blue Moon Saloon. This cottage doesn't look like much from the street, but after you pay your cover at the garden gate, you'll soon find yourself on a large covered deck packed with a young crowd dancing to the hottest local Cajun, zydeco, and roots music acts. The owner also rents out a whole two-bedroom house, which sleeps six and includes a full kitchen, and a library/study; it costs $350 a night. ✉ *215 E. Convent St.* ☎ *337/234–2422* ⊕ *www.bluemoonpresents.com.*

El Sid-o's. This family-run zydeco club hosts music on Friday and Saturday nights. Sid Williams manages the club, and his brother's band, Nathan and the Zydeco Cha-Chas, performs frequently—as does Nathan's son's band—Lil Nathan and the Zydeco Big Timers. ✉ *1523 N. St. Antoine* ☎ *337/235–0647.*

Randol's. This good Cajun restaurant is also a "salle de danse," with music and dancing nightly. ✉ *2320 Kaliste Saloom Rd.* ☎ *337/981–7080, 800/962–2586* ⊕ *www.randols.com.*

Scotty's Icehouse. The beers are cold and the music from local bands is hot at this nightspot near the University of Louisiana at Lafayette's campus. ✉ *1043 Johnston St.* ☎ *337/534–8612.*

FESTIVALS

ArtWalks. Downtown galleries are open and the streets are hopping during this popular event, which is held on the second Saturday of each month. ☎ *337/291–5566* ⊕ *www.downtownlafayette.org.*

Downtown Alive!. For the last thirty years, on Friday evenings from mid-March through June and from September through November, dancing crowds converge on downtown Lafayette, where bands play on an open-air stage. ✉ *Jefferson St. at Main St.* ☎ *337/291–5566* ⊕ *www.downtownlafayette.org.*

Festival Acadiens et Creoles. This huge music-and-food fest is held in mid-October. The admission's free, the food is outstanding, and the music is the best thing about it all. ☎ *337/232–3737, 800/346–1958* ⊕ *www.festivalsacadiens.com.*

Festival International de Louisiane. Taking place on the last weekend of April, this free music festival may rival the New Orleans Jazz and Heritage Festival; it fills the streets with entertainers, artisans, and chefs from French-speaking nations and communities. ☎ *337/232–8086* ⊕ *www.festivalinternational.com.*

Mardi Gras. The biggest bash in this neck of the woods is in February or March, depending on when Lent occurs. Up to a dozen different parades take to the streets over five days, culminating on "Fat Tuesday," and a festival atmosphere fills the city. ⊕ *www.gomardigras.com.*

SHOPPING

ANTIQUES

Sans Souci Fine Crafts Gallery. If you are looking for authentic Louisiana crafts, you've come to the right place. Pottery; furniture; items made out of gourds, metal, and wood; and cornhusk dolls and jewelry are all created by members of the Louisiana Crafts Guild, which is housed here. ✉ *219 E. Vermilion St.* ☎ *337/266–7999* ⊕ *www.louisianacrafts.org* ⊘ *Closed Sun. and Mon.*

FOOD

Don's Specialty Meats & Grocery. Fill your cooler with boudin, crackling, stuffed pork chops, quail, and a variety of sausages. There's another location at 104 Hwy. 726 in Carencro, also just outside Lafayette. ✉ *730 I–10 S. Frontage Rd., Scott* ☎ *337/234–2528, 337/896–6370 (Carencro)* ⊕ *www.donsspecialtymeats.com.*

Poupart's Bakery. The fresh French bread and pastries baked here are outstanding. The shop also sells specialty sauces and preserves, as well as king cakes, available during the carnival season. ✉ *1902 West Pinhook Rd.* ☎ *337/232–7921* ⊕ *www.poupartsbakery.com* ⊘ *Closed Mon.*

GRAND COTEAU

11 miles north of Lafayette.

The tiny village of Grand Coteau ("Big Hill") may be the most serene place in south Louisiana. Nestled against a sweeping ridge that was a natural levee of the Mississippi River centuries ago, the town is oriented around a core of grand and beautiful religious institutions. Covering the hill itself is a peaceful cemetery, behind the stately St. Charles College, a Jesuit seminary. When the Mississippi overflowed its banks during the cataclysmic flood of 1927, the water stopped at the base of Grand Coteau's ridge, and the town was preserved. Today the entire town center is listed on the National Register of Historic Places, with dozens of historical structures including Creole cottages, early Acadian-style homes, and the grand Academy and Convent of the Sacred Heart. Martin Luther King Drive (Route 93) is the main thoroughfare. Antiques stores line the main street.

EXPLORING

Academy and Convent of the Sacred Heart. A magnificent avenue of pines and moss-hung oaks leads to the entrance of the first international branch of Sacred Heart schools (founded in 1821), and the site of the only Vatican-certified miracle to occur in the United States. The miracle occurred when nuns at the convent said novenas to St. John Berchmans, a 15th-century Jesuit priest, on behalf of Mary Wilson, a very ill novice. St. John Berchmans subsequently appeared to Mary twice, and she was suddenly and unexpectedly cured. St. John Berchmans was canonized in 1888. You may enter a shrine on the exact site of the miracle and (by appointment only) tour a museum with artifacts dating from the school's occupation by Union troops during the Civil War. ✉ *1821 Academy Rd., end of Church St.* ☏ *337/662–5275* ⊕ *www.sshcoteau.org* ☾ *Weekdays 9–3.*

SHOPPING

Kitchen Shop. One of Grand Coteau's historic cottages houses a collection of regional cookbooks and cooking supplies, in addition to gifts and other merchandise, including prints and greeting cards by famed local photographer John Slaughter. In the tearoom, scones, cookies, and a specialty pecan torte called gateau-na-na are served. ✉ *296 Martin Luther King Dr., at Cherry St.* ☏ *337/662–3500* ☾ *Closed Mon.*

> ### WEEKEND ANTIQUES HUNTING
>
> Antiques lovers will want to stop in **Washington,** a short, 2-mile diversion from the main route if you're traveling from Opelousas to Ville Platte. Settled in 1720, Washington has many buildings on its main street that are on the National Register of Historic Places. More than 10 antiques stores cluster within walking distance of one another. Most of these stores are open only Friday to Sunday.

OPELOUSAS

15 miles north of Grand Coteau.

In the heart of St. Landry Parish, Opelousas is the third-oldest town in the state—Poste de Opelousas was founded in 1720 by the French as a trading post with the Opelousas Indians. It's a sleepy spot with a historic central square, a provincial museum, and several excellent zydeco clubs in town and on its outskirts. Look for two murals located in a pocket park–parking lot adjacent to the St. Landry Bank & Trust Co. building. One depicts the history of the area and historical monuments in St. Landry Parish, and the other depicts the legend of the Seven Brothers Oak, which is located south of Washington, a charming nearby town.

Opelousas Tourist Information Center. At the intersection of Interstate 49 and U.S. 190, look for the Opelousas Tourist Information Center, where you can get plenty of information, arrange for tours of historic homes,

CLOSE UP

Cajun and Zydeco Music

It's 9 am on a typical Saturday morning in the Cajun prairie town of Mamou, and Fred's Lounge (⇨ *Nightlife and the Arts in Eunice*) is already so full that people are spilling out the door. Inside, Cajun singer Donald Thibodeaux gets a nod from the radio announcer, squeezes his accordion, and launches into a bluesy rendition of "Pine Grove Blues." Oblivious to the posted warning that says "This is not a dancehall," the packed bar begins to roll. Fred's Lounge may not be a "formal" dance hall, but plenty of dancing is done here; it gets especially lively during Mamou's Mardi Gras and July 4 celebrations. And every Saturday morning for more than 40 years, live Cajun radio shows have been broadcast from the late Fred Tate's lounge. Things get revved up at 8 am and keep going until 1 pm, and the show is aired on Ville Platte's KVPI radio (1050 AM).

Music has been an integral expression of Cajun culture since early Acadian immigrants unpacked stringed instruments and gathered in homes for singing and socializing. *"Fais-do-do"* (pronounced *fay*-doh-doh) is what mothers would murmur to put their babies to sleep as the fiddlers tuned up before one of these house parties (or as those mothers were getting ready to leave). With the growth of towns, most of the fais-do-dos were supplanted by dance halls, but the name fais-do-do stuck. Accordions,

steel guitars, and drums were added and amplified to be heard over the noise of crowded barrooms.

Cajun music went through some lean years in the 1940s and '50s, when the state attempted to eradicate the use of the Cajun-French language, but today Cajun music is enjoyed at street festivals and restaurants such as Randol's and Prejean's, which serve equal portions of seafood and song. These places not only keep the music and dance tradition alive, but also serve as magnets for Cajun dance enthusiasts from around the world.

Zydeco, the dance music of rural African Americans of south Louisiana, is closely related to Cajun music, but with a slightly harder, rock-influenced edge. The best place to find the music is in one of the roadside dance halls on weekends. Modern zydeco and Cajun music both feature the accordion, but zydeco tends to be faster and uses heavy percussion and electric instruments; electric guitars and washboards (called a *frottoir*), largely absent from Cajun music, are staples of zydeco. Zydeco bands often play soul- and rhythm and blues–inflected tunes sung in Creole French.

Dance is the universal language of Cajun Country, but don't worry if you're not fluent—there's always someone happy to lead you around the floor and leave you feeling like a local.

and see memorabilia pertaining to Jim Bowie, the Alamo hero who spent his early years in Opelousas. ⊠ *828 E. Landry St.* ☎ *337/948–6263* ⊘ *Weekdays 8–4:30, Sat. 9–4.*

EXPLORING

Louisiana Orphan Train Museum. Between 1854 and 1929, more than 2,000 orphans from New York were transplanted via train to Louisiana. The museum, housed in an old depot building, has more than 200 photos and articles of clothing of the orphans who made the journey.

✉ *223 S. Academy St.* ☎ *337/948–9922* ⊕ *www.laorphantrain.com*
✍ *$5* ⊙ *Tues.–Fri. 10–3, Sat. 10–2.*

Opelousas Museum and Interpretive Center. This museum traces the history of Opelousas from prehistoric times to the present. There's an exhibit on the town's brief stint as state capital, during the Civil War, and a collection of more than 400 dolls. The museum is also home to the Louisiana Video Library and the Southwest Louisiana Zydeco Festival archives, and rotates exhibits of artists every three months. ✉ *315 N. Main St.* ☎ *337/948–2589* ✍ *Free* ⊙ *Weekdays 8–4:30, Sat 10–3.*

WHERE TO EAT

$ ✕ **Palace Café.** On the town square, you can step back in time at this
DINER old-style diner. Be sure to get the biscuits at breakfast, and try one of the six different types of gumbo at lunch or dinner. $ *Average main: $10* ✉ *135 W. Landry St.* ☎ *337/942–2142* ⊙ *Closed Sun.*

NIGHTLIFE AND THE ARTS

The roads surrounding Opelousas are *the* place to catch authentic, sweaty zydeco music.

Slim's Y-Ki-Ki. This long, low, somewhat musty dance hall is a legend among zydeco lovers: it's been here since the 1940s. All the big regional acts perform here, and during festival times the club is packed wall-to-wall with dancers. ✉ *8410 Hwy. 182* ☎ *337/942–6242* ⊕ *www.slimsykiki.com.*

Southwest Louisiana Zydeco Music Festival. The town of Plaisance, on the outskirts of Opelousas, holds this event in a melon patch on the Saturday before Labor Day. A parade, jam session, and breakfast are all part of the festivities. ☎ *337/942–2392* ⊕ *www.zydeco.org.*

Zydeco Hall of Fame. Known for generations as Richard's, this classic zydeco dance hall has a long history. Its schedule can be sporadic, but when the sign lights up, the zydeco faithful pour in. ✉ *11154 U.S. 190, Lawtell.*

EUNICE

20 miles southwest of Opelousas.

As home to some of Cajun music's most prominent proponents and establishments, tiny Eunice lays claim to some heft within the Cajun music world. Saturday is the best time to visit: spend the morning at a jam at the **Savoy Music Center;** at midday move on to see Tante Sue de Mamou at **Fred's Lounge;** end the day at the variety show *Rendez-Vous des Cajuns,* in Eunice's **Liberty Theatre.**

Courir de Mardi Gras. The area surrounding Eunice is the major stomping ground for an annual event, Courir de Mardi Gras, French for Fat Tuesday Run, which takes place on Mardi Gras Day. Costumed horseback riders dash through the countryside, stopping at farmhouses along the way to shout, "*Voulez-vous recevoir cette bande de Mardi Gras* (Do you wish to receive the Mardi Gras krewe)?" The answer is always yes, and the group enlarges and continues, gathering food for the street festivals that wind things up.

CLOSE UP

Evangeline

In all of Acadiana, St. Martinville is the spot where you can sense most vividly the tragic aspect of the Cajun story, whether in the tiny cemetery behind the main church, or at the bayou-side Evangeline Oak. Henry Wadsworth Longellow's epic poem "Evangeline" (1847) is based on historic documents that chronicle a couple's tragic separation during the "Grand Dérangement" of 1655, when the Acadians were expelled from Nova Scotia by the British. Evangeline Bellefontaine and Gabriel Lajeneusse are taken from each other on their wedding day. Arriving in Louisiana, Evangeline discovers that Gabriel had been there but has gone on to live in the Ozarks. After years of searching for him, Evangeline finds Gabriel on his deathbed in Philadelphia.

Many believe the two represent real-life counterparts Emmeline Labiche and Louis Arceneaux, though those names themselves are based

on another fictional version of the legend. According to the oft-told tale, the real-life lovers met for the last time under the **Evangeline Tree** at Evangeline Boulevard at Bayou Teche. Louis arrived in St. Martinville, a major debarkation port for the refugees, but it was many years before Emmeline came. Legend has it that the two saw each other by chance just as she stepped ashore. He turned deathly pale with shock and told her that, having despaired of ever seeing her again, he was betrothed to another. A film version, *Evangeline*, was filmed in St. Martinville in 1929; clips from it are incorporated in the film presentation at the Jean Lafitte National Historical Park Acadian Cultural Center in Lafayette. Its star, Dolores Del Rio, posed for the bronze statue of Evangeline that the cast and crew donated to St. Martinville; it's in the cemetery behind the church of St. Martin de Tours, near the final resting place of Emmeline Labiche.

EXPLORING

Eunice Depot Museum. This museum, in a former railroad depot, contains modest displays on Cajun culture, including music and Mardi Gras celebrations. ⊠ *220 S. C. C. Duson Dr.* ☎ *337/457–6540, 337/457–2565* 🖃 *Free* ⊘ *Tues.–Sat. 8–5.*

Prairie Acadian Cultural Center. Part of the Jean Lafitte National Historical Park, this impressive center has well-executed exhibits tracing the history and culture of the Prairie Acadians, whose lore and customs differ from those of the Bayou Acadians south of Lafayette. Food, crafts, and music demonstrations are held on Saturday. ⊠ *250 W. Park Ave.* ☎ *337/457–8499* ⊕ *www.nps.gov/jela/prairie-acadian-cultural-center-eunice.htm* 🖃 *Free* ⊘ *Wed.–Fri. 9:30–4:30, Sat. 9:30–6.*

Fodor'sChoice ★ **Savoy Music Center and Accordion Factory.** Part music store, part Cajun accordion workshop, proprietor Marc Savoy's factory turns out about five specialty accordions a month for people around the world. On Saturday morning, accordion players and other instrumentalists head here for jam sessions, and musicians from all over the area drop in. ⊠ *U.S. 190, 3 miles east of town* ☎ *337/457–9563* ⊕ *www.savoymusiccenter. com* 🖃 *Free* ⊘ *Tues.–Fri. 9–noon and 1:30–5, Sat. 9–noon.*

Savoy Family Band jamming in their famous store.

NIGHTLIFE AND THE ARTS

Fred's Lounge. This place is hopping on Saturday from about 8 am until about 2 pm, or for as long as the Cajun band jams and dancers crowd the tiny dance floor. A regular radio broadcast (on KVPI 1050 AM) captures the event. Drive north from Eunice on Route 13 to reach the tiny town of Mamou. ⊠ *420 6th St., Mamou* ☎ *337/468–5411* 🎬 *Free.*

Rendez-Vous des Cajuns. In addition to showcasing the best Cajun and zydeco bands, this two-hour variety program presents local comedians and storytellers and even a "Living Recipe Corner." The show, mostly in French, has been dubbed the Cajun Grand Ole Opry; it's held every Saturday at 6 pm in a 1924 movie house and is broadcast on local radio and TV. ⊠ *Liberty Center for the Performing Arts, 200 W. Park Ave., at 2nd St.* ☎ *337/457–7389* 🎬 *$5.*

BREAUX BRIDGE

10 miles northeast of Lafayette, 20 miles southeast of Grand Coteau.

During the first full weekend in May the Crawfish Festival draws more than 100,000 visitors to this little dyed-in-the-wool Cajun town on Bayou Teche. The town has attracted a small arts community that includes renowned Louisiana photographer Debbie Fleming Caffery, and has traded its honky-tonks for B&Bs, antiques shops, and restaurants.

Chamber of Commerce. You can pick up a city map and information at the Chamber of Commerce, at the foot of the bridge that gives Breaux Bridge its name, about ½ mile south of Interstate 10. ⊠ *314 E. Bridge St.* ☎ *337/332–5406* ⊕ *www.chamber.breauxbridgelive.com.*

WHERE TO EAT AND STAY

$ ✕**Café des Amis.** The culinary heart of downtown Breaux Bridge is in
CAJUN this historic, renovated storefront that's a block from Bayou Teche.
Locals and visitors gather here to enjoy hospitality that is second only
to the food. Soak in the ambience over cocktails or coffee at the bar,
or take a table and try the extraordinary turtle soup or the crawfish
corn bread. Breakfast here should be savored, from the java and fresh-
squeezed orange juice to the *oreille de cochon* (pastry-wrapped boudin)
and *couche-couche* (corn-bread-based cereal). Saturday mornings bring
the extremely popular Zydeco Breakfast, featuring a band and dancing.
⑤ *Average main: $15* ✉ *140 E. Bridge St.* ☎ *337/332–5273* ⊕ *www.*
cafedesamis.com ⊙ *Closed Mon. No dinner Sun. and Tues.*

$ ✕**Poche's.** Order your authentic Cajun cooking at the counter of this
CAJUN butcher shop and lunch room, then eat in or take away. The daily specials will always stick to your ribs. Boudin, sausage, cracklings, and
stuffed chicken are just a few of the items available for takeout. ⑤ *Av-*
erage main: $8 ✉ *33015-A Main Hwy., 2 miles from center of Breaux*
Bridge ☎ *337/332–2108* ⊕ *www.poches.com.*

$$ 🛏**Bayou Cabins.** These cozy one- and two-bedroom cabins are right on
B&B/INN a main drag, but with their homey decor and shaded by the property's
many trees, and some featuring porches facing Bayou Teche, they feel
rustic and have personality galore. **Pros:** socializing with guests and
locals in the café. **Cons:** you can hear the busy road nearby. ⑤ *Rooms*
from: $100 ✉ *100 W. Mills Ave.* ☎ *337/332–6158* ⊕ *www.bayoucabins.*
com ⇔ *14 rooms* ⊙ *Restaurant closed Mon. and Tues.* ⍟❘ *Breakfast.*

$$ 🛏**Maison des Amis.** In this 19th-century house on the bank of Bayou
B&B/INN Teche each room has a queen-size bed covered with luxurious linens
Fodor'sChoice and pillows and its own bathroom with a claw-foot tub. **Pros:** bayou
★ views; steps from downtown Breaux Bridge. **Cons:** breakfast is provided
at nearby restaurants, where you may have to wait. ⑤ *Rooms from:*
$110 ✉ *111 Washington St.* ☎ *337/507–3399* ⊕ *www.maisondesamis.*
com ⇔ *4 rooms* ⍟❘ *Breakfast.*

NIGHTLIFE

La Poussière. This ancient Cajun honky-tonk has live music on Saturday and Sunday. ✉ *1301 Grand Point Ave.* ☎ *337/332–1721* ⊕ *www.*
lapoussiere.com.

ATCHAFALAYA BASIN

5 miles northeast of Breaux Bridge, 12 miles east of Lafayette.

The Atchafalaya Basin is an eerily beautiful 800,000-plus-acre swamp
wilderness, the storybook version of mystical south Louisiana wetlands.
Boating enthusiasts, bird-watchers, photographers, and nature lovers
are drawn by vast expanses of still water, cypresses rising out of the
marsh and dripping with Spanish moss, and blue herons taking flight.
The basin is best viewed from one of the tour boats on its waters, but
it's possible to explore around its edges on the 7 miles of Henderson's
Levee Road (also known as Route 5; off Interstate 10, Exit 115), which
provides several opportunities to cross the levee and access swamp
tours, bars, and restaurants on the other side.

ST. MARTINVILLE

15 miles south of Breaux Bridge.

St. Martinville, along winding Bayou Teche, is the heart of Evangeline country. It was founded in 1761 and became a refuge for Acadians expelled from Nova Scotia as well as royalists who escaped the guillotine during the French Revolution. Known as Petit Paris, this little town was once the scene of lavish balls and operas, and you can still roam through the original old opera house on the central square. St. Martinville is tucked away from the state's major highways and misses much of the tourist traffic. It's a tranquil and historically interesting stop, although neighboring towns are better for dining and nightlife. The St. Martinville Tourist Information Center is across the street from the Acadian Memorial and African American Museum.

EXPLORING

Acadian Memorial. A video introduction, a wall of names of Acadian Louisiana refugees, and a huge mural relate the odyssey of the Acadians. Behind the small heritage center containing these memorials, an eternal flame and the coats of arms of Acadian families pay tribute to their cultural and physical stamina. ⊠ *121 S. New Market St.* ☎ *337/394–2258* ⊕ *www.acadianmemorial.org* ⌦ *$3, includes admission to African American Musuem* ⊙ *Daily 10–4:30.*

African American Museum. This museum traces the African and African American experience in southern Louisiana. Videos, artifacts, and text panels combine to create a vivid, disturbing, and inspiring portrait of a people. It is an ambitious and refreshing balance to the sometimes sidelined references to slavery and its legacy. ⊠ *121 New Market St.* ☎ *337/394–2273* ⌦ *$3, includes admission to Acadian Memorial* ⊙ *Daily 10–4:30.*

Longfellow-Evangeline State Historic Site. Shaded by giant live oaks draped with Spanish moss, this 157-acre park has picnic tables and pavilions and early Acadian structures. The on-site museum traces the history of the Acadians and their settlement along the Bayou Teche in the early 1800s. The modest house was built in 1815 of handmade bricks, and it contains Louisiana antiques. A one-hour tour includes many interesting details about life on the plantation. ⊠ *1200 N. Main St. (Rte. 31), ½ mile north of St. Martinville* ☎ *337/394–3754, 888/677–2900* ⊕ *www. crt.state.la.us/parks* ⌦ *$4* ⊙ *Tues.–Sat. 9–5.*

St. Martin de Tours. The mother church of the Acadians and one of the country's oldest Catholic churches, this 1836 building was erected on the site of an earlier church. Inside is a replica of the Lourdes grotto and a baptismal font said to have been a gift from Louis XVI. Emmeline Labiche, who may have inspired Henry Wadsworth Longellow's poem "Evangeline," is buried in the small cemetery behind the church. ⊠ *133 S. Main St.* ☎ *337/394–6021.*

WHERE TO STAY

$$$
B&B/INN

⌂ **Old Castillo Bed and Breakfast.** Comfortable rooms, with hardwood floors and the odd early Louisiana antique, occupy a two-story redbrick building that in the early 1800s was an inn for steamboat passengers and a gathering place for French royalists. **Pros:** right by a number of attractions; friendly staff; delicious breakfast. **Cons:** downstairs rooms are a bit noisy; decor is a little dated. $ *Rooms from: $125* ✉ *220 Evangeline Blvd.* ☎ *337/394–4010, 800/621–3017* ⊕ *www.oldcastillo. com* ⇥ *7 rooms* ◉ *Breakfast.*

NEW IBERIA

14 miles south of St. Martinville.

The hub of lower Cajun Country is second only to Lafayette as an arts-and-culture draw. Grand homes of sugarcane planters dominate the residential section of Main Street, just off Bayou Teche, pointing to a glorious past as the center of a booming sugar industry. Park downtown or stay in one of the numerous B&Bs and you can easily walk to the bayou, restaurants, art galleries, and shops in the historic business district. Downtown stretches eight blocks east and west on Main Street (Route 182) from the intersection of Center Street (Route 14). The Shadows-on-the-Teche plantation home is at this intersection and is a good place to park.

EXPLORING

Bayou Teche Museum. The story of New Iberia's Spanish colonial roots and the role of Bayou Teche in helping nurture Cajun culture are on display in this small, well-produced museum, housed in a historic building that was once a grocery. Interactive exhibits cover the area's history, its colorful characters, and its culture. The museum's interior layout is based on the snakelike curves of Bayou Teche itself. ✉ *131 Main St.* ☎ *337/606–5977* ⊕ *www.bayoutechemuseum.org* 🖼 *$4* ◷ *Thurs.–Sat. 10–4.*

Shadows-on-the-Teche. One of the South's best-known plantation homes was built on the bank of the bayou for the wealthy sugar planter David Weeks in 1834. In 1917 his descendant William Weeks Hall conducted one of the first historically conscious restorations of a plantation home, also preserving truckloads of documents that helped explain day-to-day life here. The result is one of the most fascinating tours in Louisiana. Weeks Hall willed the property to the National Trust for Historic Preservation in 1958, and each year the trust selects a different historical topic to emphasize. Surrounded by 2 acres of lush gardens and moss-draped oaks, the two-story rose-hued house has white columns, exterior staircases sheltered in cabinet-like enclosures, and a pitched roof pierced by dormer windows. The furnishings are 85% original to the house. ✉ *317 E. Main St.* ☎ *337/369–6446* ⊕ *www. shadowsontheteche.org* 🖼 *$10* ◷ *Mon.–Sat. 9–5.*

WHERE TO EAT AND STAY

$$

CAJUN

× **Clementine.** The cuisine is as artful as the namesake, folk artist Clementine Hunter, and might be called nouveau Cajun: it's inspired by local ingredients and traditions, but subtly seasoned and beautifully presented. Local grouper is seared and served in a red curry sauce, and the richness of roast duck is complemented by the tang of a honey-and-raspberry glaze. Changing art exhibits by locals are introduced at bimonthly openings featuring wine and hors d'oeuvres. Clementine

Alligators Up Close: Swamp Tours

The bayous, swamps, and rivers of south Louisiana's wetlands present a tantalizingly unfamiliar landscape to many visitors, and the best way to get better acquainted is by boat. Tour operators offer convenient departure times and hotel pickups in New Orleans. Most tour operators use pontoon boats, but—depending on the size of the group—a bass boat might be used. Anticipate from one to two hours on the water and 45 minutes to two hours' commute time to and from New Orleans. Prices are generally around $20 per person. Expect to see nutrias, a member of the rodent family that resembles a beaver in appearance and size; egrets (a white, long-necked heron with flowing feathers); turtles; and the occasional snake. During the warmer months, alligator sightings are common. Many of the guides use either chicken or marshmallows to attract them. Plant life includes Spanish moss, cypress, water oaks, and water hyacinths (a member of the lily family). In the summer months be prepared for the heat and humidity—and don't forget the insect repellent and a hat.

Cajun Country Swamp Tours. These tours are led by guide Walter "Butch" Guchereau, who was born, raised, and still lives on the banks of Bayou Teche in Breaux Bridge. An experienced outdoorsman with a degree in zoology and biology, Guchereau uses Cajun crawfish skiffs for his tours to make them environmentally unobtrusive. His son Shawn also leads tours. ⊠ *1226 N. Berard St., Breaux Bridge* ☎ *337/319–0010* ⊕ *www.cajuncountryswamptours. com* ⊙ *Tours daily.*

McGee's Landing. Pontoon boats take passengers out daily for 1½-hour tours of the Atchafalaya Basin. McGee's is a 25-minute drive east of Lafayette. Tour times are contingent upon the presence of at least four passengers. The company also organizes canoe, kayak, and airboat trips. ⊠ *1337 Henderson Levee Rd., Henderson* ⊹ *From I–10, Exit 115 at Henderson; 1 block south of the highway turn left on Rte. 352 and follow it more than 2 miles east over Bayou Amy; turn right atop the levee onto Levee Rd.* ☎ *337/228–2384* ⊕ *www.mcgeeslanding.com* ⊠ *Tour $20* ⊙ *Tours daily 10, 1, and 3. Additional tour at 5 during daylight saving time.*

hosts live music on Friday and Saturday nights. $ *Average main: $22* ✉ *113 E. Main St.* ☎ *337/560–1007* ⊕ *www.clementinedowntown.com* ⊙ *Closed Sun. and Mon. No lunch Sat.*

$$$ ⚏ **Bayou Teche Guest Cottage.** There could scarcely be a better way to
B&B/INN appreciate the Queen City of the Teche than to spend a night in this simple, two-room, 18th-century cottage on the bank of the bayou, down the road from downtown attractions. **Pros:** pretty views; full kitchen with refrigerator; good location to explore New Iberia. **Cons:** depending on what you expect from a bed-and-breakfast, you'll either find it charming or a bit worn around the edges. $ *Rooms from: $125* ✉ *100 Teche St.* ☎ *337/364–1933* ⊕ *www.bayoutechecottage.com* ⟆ *1 cottage* ▤ *No credit cards* ❏ *Breakfast.*

$$$ ⚏ **Le Rosier.** Guest rooms in the restored service wing of this 19th-
B&B/INN century house across from the Shadows-on-the-Teche plantation are small and simple, but all have access to a balcony overlooking the plant-filled courtyard. **Pros:** easy walk into town; beautiful courtyard; good for groups. **Cons:** walls are thin; rooms on the small side. $ *Rooms from: $130* ✉ *314 E. Main St.* ☎ *337/367–5306* ⊕ *www.lerosier.com* ⟆ *5 rooms* ❏ *Breakfast.*

AVERY ISLAND

9 miles southwest of New Iberia.

The Louisiana coastline is dotted with "hills" or "domes" that sit atop salt mines, and Avery Island is one of these. They are covered with lush vegetation, and because they rise above the surface of the flatlands, they are referred to as islands.

Avery Island is the birthplace of Tabasco sauce, which pleases the Cajun palate and flavors many a Bloody Mary.

EXPLORING

FAMILY **Jungle Gardens.** This 170-acre garden has trails through stands of wisteria, palms, lilies, irises, and ferns and offers a lovely perspective on southern Louisiana wilderness. Birdlife includes ducks and geese, and there's also a 1,000-year-old statue of Buddha. These gardens belonged to Edward Avery McIlhenny, the son of the Tabasco company's founder, who brought back plants from his travels: lotus and papyrus from Egypt, bamboo from China. You can park your car at the beginning of the trails and strike out on foot, or drive through the gardens and stop at will. ✉ *Rte. 329* ☎ *337/369–6243* ⊕ *junglegardens.org* 🎟 *$8 Jungle Gardens and Bird City; $1 toll to enter Avery Island* ⊙ *Daily 9–5.*

Bird City. The bird sanctuary on the southeast edge of Jungle Gardens is sometimes so thick with egrets that it appears to be blanketed with snow. The largest egret colony in the world (20,000) begins nesting here in February or March, and offspring remain until the following winter. Herons and other birds find refuge here as well. ✉ *Rte. 329.*

Tabasco Factory. Tabasco was invented by Edmund McIlhenny in the mid-1800s, and the factory is still presided over by the McIlhenny family. Tabasco is sold all over the world, but it is aged, distilled, and bottled only here, on Avery Island (these days the peppers themselves

PARLEZ-VOUS CAJUN FRANÇAIS?

12

It's not uncommon while traveling through Cajun country to hear French—the Cajun version. Here are a few words that might help you enjoy and understand the lingo.

Allons: Let's go!

Bayou: A sluggish body of water, larger than a creek but smaller than a river.

C'est la vie: Such is life.

Cher: Dear

Cochon de lait: A pig roast; literally, a suckling pig.

Étouffée: French for "smothered"— the term applies to a stew, usually made with seafood, in which a roux and the "holy trinity" (celery, garlic or onion, and bell pepper) is used.

Fais-do-do: A dance. French for "Go to sleep," which was what parents would whisper to their children so they could go dancing.

Lagniappe: A little something extra.

Laissez les bons temps rouler: Let the good times roll.

Roux: Flour browned in fat and used as a thickener in many Cajun dishes such as gumbo.

are mostly grown in Central and South America). You can take a factory tour, which lasts about 20 minutes and highlights the bottling process. The Jungle Gardens and Bird City are adjacent. ⊠ *Rte. 329* ☎ *337/365–8173, 800/634–9599* ⊕ *www.tabasco.com* ✉ *Tour free; $1 toll to enter Avery Island* ☉ *Daily 9–4.*

ABBEVILLE

15 miles south of Lafayette.

Abbeville has a number of historic buildings and two pretty village squares anchoring the center of downtown. It's a good stop for pleasant walks and for oysters on the half shell, a local obsession. The town sponsors the annual Giant Omelet Festival each November, when some 5,000 eggs go into the concoction. Abbeville is also the base for Steen's Cane Syrup.

Vermilion Parish Tourist Commission. You can pick up information about the town of Abbeville and the entire parish at the Vermillion Parish Tourist Commission. Many buildings in Abbeville's 20-block Main Street district are on the National Register of Historic Places. ⊠ *1907 Veterans Memorial* ☎ *337/898–6600* ⊕ *www.mostcajun.com.*

EXPLORING

St. Mary Magdalen Catholic Church. This fine Romanesque Revival building built in 1915 has stunning stained-glass windows. ⊠ *300 Père Megret St.* ☎ *337/893–0244* ⊕ *www.stmarymagdalenparish.org* ☉ *Mon.–Sat. 8–4; Masses Sat. 4:30, Sun. 7, 9:30, 11, and 5:30.*

WHERE TO EAT

$$
SEAFOOD
✕ **Dupuy's Oyster Shop.** This small and simply furnished restaurant has been serving family-harvested oysters in the same location since 1869. Seafood platters feature seasonal specials. Steaks, pastas, and regional

specialties like boudin balls and po'boys all round out the menu. $ *Average main: $16* ⊠ *108 S. Main St.* ☎ *337/893–2336* ⊕ *www. dupuysoystershop.com* ⊗ *Closed Sun. and Mon. No lunch Sat.*

$　× **Richard's Seafood Patio.** You cross the Vermilion River on a vintage
CAJUN　drawbridge and continue down a winding country road to find this classic Cajun "seafood patio," a no-frills dining room serving immense quantities of boiled crawfish, shrimp, and crabs. There's a full menu of fried and grilled items—and cold beer. Richard's opens at 5 pm and fills up almost immediately, so expect a wait. $ *Average main: $15* ⊠ *1516 S. Henry St.* ☎ *337/893–1146* ⊗ *Closed Sun.*

MAURICE

10 miles north of Abbeville, almost 11 miles south of Lafayette.

Maurice is considered the gateway to Vermilion Parish, and lies between Lafayette and Abbeville. Many overlook this small town, but it's worth the stop for Hebert's Specialty Meats' world-famous turducken and the Maurice Flea Market.

WHERE TO EAT

$　× **Hebert's Specialty Meats.** A visit to Cajun country is not complete
CAJUN　without stopping at Hebert's. This butcher shop is one of several contenders claiming to be the place that invented turducken—a turkey stuffed with a duck that's been stuffed with a chicken. You can grab a link of hot boudin to eat on the spot, or fill a cooler with andouille, deboned chicken, and other regional delicacies for later. $ *Average main: $10* ⊠ *8212 Maurice Ave. (aka Rte. 167)* ☎ *337/893–5062* ⊕ *www.hebertsmaurice.com.*

SHOPPING

Maurice Flea Market. From fine antiques to slightly rusted kitchen utensils, this is a treasure-hunter's paradise. Be prepared to spend more than an hour at this store. ⊠ *9004 Maurice Ave. (Rte. 167)* ☎ *337/898–2282* ⊗ *Closed Sun.–Tues.*

TRAVEL SMART
NEW ORLEANS

GETTING HERE AND AROUND

New Orleans fills an 8-mile stretch between the Mississippi River and Lake Pontchartrain. Downtown includes the French Quarter, the Central Business District (CBD), Warehouse District, Tremé, and the Faubourg Marigny. Uptown includes the Garden District, Audubon Park, and Tulane and Loyola universities, as well as the Carrollton and Riverbend neighborhoods.

It's best to know your location relative to the following thoroughfares: Canal Street (runs from the river toward the lake), St. Charles Avenue (runs uptown from Canal), Interstate 10 (runs west to the airport, east to Slidell), and LA Highway 90 (takes you across the river to the West Bank). To get to the CBD from Interstate 10, exit at Poydras Street near the Louisiana Superdome. For the French Quarter, look for the Orleans Avenue/Vieux Carré exit.

Canal Street divides the city roughly into the uptown and downtown sections (though the CBD and Warehouse District, considered part of downtown, actually lie just upriver from Canal). Keeping a visual on the Superdome is the surest way to know where the CBD is; the French Quarter lies just to the northeast of it over Canal Street.

Streets that start in the French Quarter and cross over Canal Street change names as they go upriver. For example, Decatur Street becomes Magazine Street and Royal Street becomes St. Charles Avenue. Addresses begin at 100 on either side of Canal Street, and begin at 400 in the French Quarter at the river.

▌ AIR TRAVEL

Flying time is 3 hours from New York, 2 hours and 30 minutes from Chicago, 1 hour and 40 minutes from Dallas, and 4 hours and 20 minutes from Los Angeles. Book early for popular times such as Mardi Gras and Jazz Fest.

Airline Security Issues Transportation Security Administration ⊕ www.tsa.gov.

AIRPORTS

The major gateway to New Orleans is Louis Armstrong New Orleans International Airport (MSY), 15 miles west of the city in Kenner. There's an airport exit off Interstate 10. Plan for about 30–45 minutes of travel time from downtown New Orleans to the airport (more at rush hour). An alternative route is Airline Drive, which will take you directly to the airport from Tulane Avenue or the Earhart Expressway. Be prepared for stoplights and possible congestion.

Airport Information Louis Armstrong New Orleans International Airport ☎ 504/303–7500 ⊕ www.flymsy.com.

GROUND TRANSPORTATION
SHUTTLE BUSES

Shuttle-bus service to and from the airport and downtown hotels is available through Airport Shuttle New Orleans, the official ground transportation of Louis Armstrong International Airport. You can purchase shuttle tickets at the Airport Shuttle desk across from baggage claim areas 3, 6, and 12. To return to the airport, call 24 hours in advance of flight time. The cost one way to the CBD is $20 per person, and the trip takes about 40 minutes.

Jefferson Transit also runs a bus between the airport, the CBD, and Mid-City, although it goes to the CBD only on weekdays. The trip costs $2 in exact change ($1.50 from Carrollton and Tulane avenues) and takes about 45 minutes. From the airport you can catch the E-2 line on the second level near the Delta counter in the median (look for the sign and a bench). Departures for the airport are every 10 to 15 minutes during peak hours and every 30 to 35 minutes in the middle of the day from Elks Place and Tulane Avenue across from the main branch of the New Orleans Public Library, and from the corner of Tulane and Carrollton avenues. The last bus leaves at 6:52 from Tulane and Elks Place, 9:49 pm from Tulane and Carrollton.

Contacts Airport Shuttle New Orleans ☎ *504/522–3500, 866/596–2699* ⊕ *www.airportshuttleneworleans.com.* **Jefferson Transit** ☎ *504/818–1077* ⊕ *www.jeffersontransit.org/e2airport.php.*

TAXIS

A cab ride to or from the airport and uptown or downtown costs $33 for up to two passengers. For groups of three or more, the rate is $14 per person. Pickup is on the lower level, outside the baggage-claim area. There may be an additional charge for extra baggage. *See Taxi Travel for taxi companies and contact information.*

▮ BIKE TRAVEL

Biking is a good options for getting around New Orleans, especially in Faubourg Marigny.

Contacts Bicycle Michael's. Rentals begin at $25 for half a day. ⊠ *622 Frenchmen St., Faubourg Marigny* ☎ *504/945–9505* ⊕ *www. bicyclemichaels.com.* **Big Easy Bike Tours.** Guided tours start at $49 for a three-hour excursion. ⊠ *Faubourg Marigny* ☎ *504/377–0973* ⊕ *www.bigeasybiketours.com.*

▮ BOAT TRAVEL

BY FERRY

The ferry ride across the river to Algiers is an experience in itself, offering great views of the river and the New Orleans skyline as well as the heady feeling of being on one of the largest and most powerful rivers in the world. Pedestrians enter near the Spanish Plaza and the Riverwalk shopping area and board the Canal Street Ferry from above. Bicycles board from below on the left of the terminal; cars are no longer allowed on the ferry. The trip takes about 5 minutes; ferries leave on the hour and half-hour from the east bank (New Orleans) and on the quarter-hour and three-quarter-hour

from the west bank (Algiers)—they run from 7:15 am to 8 pm on weekdays, 10:45 am to 8:15 pm on Saturdays, and 10:45 am to 5:45 pm on Sundays. Be sure to check return times with the attendants if you are crossing in the evening—it's no fun to be stranded on the other side. There are wheelchair-accessible restrooms on the ferry.

Information Canal Street Ferry ⊠ *Bottom of Canal St., at Convention Center Blvd.* ☎ *504/376–8180* ⊕ *www.friendsoftheferry.org* ⛴ *Free.*

CRUISES

Large cruise lines like Carnival, Norwegian, and Royal Caribbean International depart from New Orleans.

For more information, visit the Port of New Orleans website at ⊕ *www.portno. com* or call ☎ *504/522–2551.*

Cruise Lines American Cruise Lines ☎ *800/460–4518* ⊕ *www. americancruiselines.com.* **Blount Small Ship Adventures** ☎ *866/556–7450* ⊕ *www. blountsmallshipadventures.com.* **Great American Steamboat Company** ☎ *888/749–5280* ⊕ *www.americanqueensteamboatcompany. com.* **Travel Dynamics International** ☎ *800/257–5767* ⊕ *www. traveldynamicsinternational.com.*

▮ BUS AND STREETCAR TRAVEL

GETTING AROUND BY BUS AND STREETCAR

Within New Orleans the Regional Transit Authority (RTA) operates a public bus and streetcar (not "trolley") transportation system with interconnecting lines throughout the city. The buses are generally clean and on time and run on a regular schedule from about 6 am to 6 pm. Smoking, eating, and drinking are not permitted on RTA vehicles. Buses are wheelchair accessible, as are the Canal Street, Riverfront and Loyola Avenue streetcar lines; the Saint Charles line streetcars are not.

ROUTES

The riverfront streetcar covers a 2-mile route along the Mississippi River, connecting major sights from the end of the French Quarter (Esplanade Avenue) to the New Orleans Convention Center (Julia Street). Nine stops en route include the French Market, Jackson Brewery, the Aquarium of the Americas, Canal Place, the World Trade Center, the Riverwalk, Woldenberg Park, and the Hilton Hotel. This streetcar operates every 20 minutes during peak hours and every 40 minutes in the morning and evening, daily, from 7 am until 10:30 pm.

The historic streetcars of St. Charles Avenue run from St. Charles Avenue at Common Street to the Riverbend at Carrollton Avenue roughly every 10 minutes for most of the day. This line continues on along Carrollton Avenue and stops at Claiborne Avenue in Mid-City. Streetcar service on St. Charles Avenue runs 24 hours a day, though wait times can be as long as 30 minutes between 11:30 pm and 3 am. Because the tracks are undergoing preventative maintenance, service may be interrupted along part of the route. In these instances, shuttle service is provided; check the RTA's website for up-to-date information.

A third streetcar line runs along Canal Street from the river near Harrah's Casino to either City Park or the Cemeteries. Going from Harrah's Casino to the Cemeteries, it passes every 16 minutes. As it gets closer to City Park, it passes every 30 minutes. The Canal Street line operates from 5 am to about 3 am, with longer waits after midnight.

The newest streetcar line, which opened in early 2013, goes along Loyola Avenue and covers the CBD and French Quarter. It departs from the Union Passenger Terminal every 15 minutes between 6 am and 11:30 pm on weekdays, heads to the French Market Station and makes stops at Canal Street and Harrah's Casino. A $135 million expansion, set to run past the CBD and the French Quarter and then eastward into Tremé, the Faubourg Marigny, and Bywater, is in the works.

COSTS

Bus and streetcar fare is $1.25 exact change plus 25¢ for transfers. Unlimited passes, valid on both buses and streetcars, cost $3 for one day, $9 for three days, and $55 for 31 days. The daily passes are available from streetcar and bus operators; three-day and 31-day passes are available at many local hotels and at most Walgreens.

Bus and Streetcar Information
RTA ☎ 504/248–3900 ⊕ www.norta.com.

TICKET/PASS	PRICE
Single Fare	$1.25
One-day Jazzy Pass	$3
Three-day Jazzy Pass	$9
31-day Jazzy Pass	$55

▌CAR TRAVEL

CAR RENTALS

If you plan to stick to the highly touristed areas of New Orleans, you may want to keep it simple and use taxis, streetcars, and the airport shuttle. However, if you plan to travel beyond the French Quarter and the Garden District, renting a car is a good idea.

If you do decide to rent a car, rates in New Orleans begin at around $40 per day ($250 per week) for an economy car with air-conditioning, automatic transmission, and unlimited mileage. Prices do not include local tax on car rentals, which is 13.75%, or other surcharges, which can add another 10%–15% to your cost. All the major agencies, including Alamo, Avis, Budget, Hertz, and National Car Rental, have outlets in New Orleans.

FROM NEW ORLEANS TO	ROUTE	DISTANCE
Atchafalaya Basin	I-10	124 miles
Avery Island	I-10, U.S. 90	136 miles
Baton Rouge	I-10	80 miles
Breaux Bridge	I-10, U.S. 31	130 miles
Lafayette	I-10	136 miles
Oak Alley	U.S. 44	60 miles
Opelousas	I-10, U.S. 190	136 miles
San Francisco Plantation	U.S. 44	35 miles
St. Francisville	I-10, U.S. 61	105 miles

GASOLINE

Gas stations are not plentiful within the city of New Orleans. The downtown area is particularly short on stations. Head for Rampart Street if you need gas while in the downtown area. If you're in Uptown, there are stations along Carrollton Avenue.

PARKING

Meter maids and tow trucks are plentiful in the French Quarter. Avoid spaces at unmarked corners: less than 15 feet between your car and the corner will result in a ticket. Watch for temporary "no parking" signs, which pop up along parade routes and for film shoots. The Central Parking website can help you find lots and garages around town.

Garages Central Parking ⊕ www.neworleans.centralparking.com.

ROAD CONDITIONS

Surface roads in New Orleans are generally bumpy, and potholes are common, thanks to the city's swampy, shifting terrain and extensive live-oak roots. Along St. Charles Avenue use caution when crossing over the neutral ground (median); drivers must yield to streetcars and pedestrians along this route. Afternoon rush hour affects New Orleans daily, and backups on Interstate 10 can start as early as 3 pm. Ongoing construction on Interstate 10 may cause delays.

▌ TAXI TRAVEL

Cabs are metered at $3.50 minimum for up to two passengers, plus $1 for each additional passenger over two people, and $2 per mile. If you're trying to hail a cab in New Orleans, try Decatur Street, Canal Street, or outside major hotels in the Quarter or the CBD. Otherwise, call.

During Mardi Gras it can be extremely difficult to get a cab; plan an alternate way to get home (or enjoy the party until public transportation starts up again in the morning).

Taxi Companies American Taxi ☎ 504/299–0386. **United Cabs** ☎ 504/522–9771 ⊕ www.unitedcabs.com. **Veterans** ☎ 504/367–6767. **White Fleet-Rollins Cab Co.** ☎ 504/822–3800. **Yellow-Checker Cab** ☎ 504/525–3311.

▌ TRAIN TRAVEL

Three major Amtrak lines travel to and from New Orleans Union Passenger Terminal. The Crescent, operating daily, runs to and from New York and Washington, D.C., via Atlanta. Also daily, the City of New Orleans runs to and from Chicago, via Memphis. Running three times weekly, the Sunset Limited runs to and from Los Angeles, via Tucson and Houston.

Information Amtrak ☎ 800/872-7245 ⊕ www.amtrak.com. **Union Passenger Terminal** ✉ 1001 Loyola Ave. ☎ 504/299-1880.

TRAIN ROUTE	SERVES	APPROX. COST
City of New Orleans	Chicago	$130
Crescent	New York	$180
Sunset Limited	Los Angeles	$290

ESSENTIALS

▌ CHILDREN IN NEW ORLEANS

The "Family Affairs" column, published once a month in the *Times-Picayune*'s Friday arts and entertainment insert, *Lagniappe,* lists upcoming events for families and kids. The Louisiana Children's Museum, the Audubon Zoo, and the Insectarium often have activities that are both educational and fun.

Be sure to plan on visiting the French Quarter, but avoid Bourbon Street. Things are out in the open, whether you plan to see them or not. In the evening, Bourbon Street quickly becomes overloaded with large, noisy, and drunk crowds.

If you're renting a car, don't forget to arrange for a car seat when you reserve.

Local Information New Orleans Convention & Visitors Bureau ⊠ *2020 St. Charles Ave., Garden District* ☎ *800/672–6124, 504/566–5011* ⊕ *www.neworleanscvb.com.*

▌ DAY TOURS AND GUIDES

Given the variety of perspectives available in the city of New Orleans, a package tour can be a good option, especially for first-time visitors. Highlights will likely include the French Quarter and Riverwalk, with daytime visits to spots like Audubon Zoo, the Garden District, and possibly a plantation or swamp tour.

BUS TOURS

Several local tour companies give two-to four-hour city bus tours that include the French Quarter, the Garden District, Uptown, and the lakefront. Prices range from $30 to $70 per person. Both **Gray Line** and **New Orleans Tours** offer a longer tour that combines a 2-hour city tour by bus with a 2-hour steamboat ride on the Mississippi River.

New Orleans Tours leads city, swamp, and plantation tours and combination city–paddle wheeler outings. **Tours by**

Isabelle (the oldest tour company in New Orleans, operating since 1979) runs city, swamp, plantation, and combination swamp-and-plantation tours.

For visitors interested in seeing the scope of the impact of the 2005 storm and keeping the local economy in motion, **Gray Line** and **Tours by Isabelle** both offer tours of Hurricane Katrina damage and recovery. For the more personal experience, choose **Tours by Isabelle**.

PLANTATION TOURS

Full-day plantation tours by bus from New Orleans, which include guided tours through three antebellum plantation houses along the Mississippi River, are offered by **Gray Line** and **New Orleans Tours.**

Tours by Isabelle includes a stop for lunch in its full-day plantation package that traces the history of the Cajun people. The cost of lunch isn't included. Also available is the Grand Tour: a full-day minibus tour that includes a visit to one plantation, lunch in a Cajun restaurant, and a 2-hour boat tour in the swamps via either a speedy airboat or a peaceful bayou pontoon boat with a Cajun trapper and raconteur.

RIVERBOAT CRUISES

The New Orleans Steamboat Company offers narrated riverboat cruises and evening jazz cruises up and down the Mississippi on the steamboat *Natchez,* an authentic paddle wheeler. Ticket sales and departures for the *Natchez* are at the Toulouse Street Wharf behind Jackson Brewery.

New Orleans Paddlewheels has a Mississippi River cruise aboard the *Creole Queen*. Highlighting the port and French Quarter, this cruise leaves twice daily from the Riverwalk. There is also an evening jazz dinner cruise from 8 to 10 (boarding at 7 pm, which is also when the band starts playing and the cash bar opens); tickets are available for the dinner (a Creole buffet) and cruise, or just the cruise and live music. The company also offers a cruise to

Chalmette Battlefield, the site of the Battle of New Orleans, which provides an opportunity to learn about the 1815 battle and tour the battlefield, the Malus-Beauregard House, and the Chalmette Monument. The ticket office is at the Poydras Street Wharf near the Riverwalk.

SPECIAL-INTEREST TOURS

Macon Riddle's Let's Go Antiquing offers personalized shopping itineraries of the city's antiques stores, galleries, or boutiques based on your interests and preferences (not all tours are about antiques). The number for appointments is her residence; don't be afraid to leave a message.

The New Orleans School of Cooking, in the heart of the French Quarter, offers classes on Cajun and Creole cuisine. Visit the website for details about class schedules and rates.

SWAMP TOURS

Exploring an exotic Louisiana swamp and traveling into Cajun country is a highlight for many visitors. Dozens of swamp-tour companies are available. You can check at your hotel or the visitor center for a complete listing. *Many do not provide transportation from downtown hotels, but those listed below do.* Full-day tours often include visiting a plantation house.

WALKING TOURS

Free 1-hour walking tours along the Mississippi River levee, with a discussion of the interaction between the river and the city, are given daily at 9:30 am by rangers of the Jean Lafitte National Historical Park and Preserve. Tickets are available at the Jean Lafitte Parks French Quarter Visitor Center starting at 9 am on the morning of the tour. Check the National Park Service website for details. Tickets are free, but tours are limited to 25 people. Two-hour general history tours, beginning at the 1850 House on Jackson Square, are given Tuesday through Sunday at 10 and 1:30 by Friends of the Cabildo.

Several specialized walking tours conducted by knowledgeable guides on specific aspects of the French Quarter and the Garden District are also available; Tours by Isabelle and Historic New Orleans are reputable companies.

The cemeteries of New Orleans fascinate many people because of their unique aboveground tombs. Save Our Cemeteries conducts guided walking tours of St. Louis No. 1 as well as Lafayette No. 1. Reservations are generally required.

Voodoo- and spiritual-themed tours are popular in New Orleans, and several companies, including Haunted History Tours, Historic New Orleans Walking Tours, and New Orleans Spirit Tours all have spooky options to choose from.

Contact Information Friends of the Cabildo ☎ 504/523-3939 ⊕ www.friendsofthecabildo. org. **Gray Line** ☎ 800/233-2628, 504/569-1401 ⊕ www.graylineneworleans.com. **Haunted History Tours** ☎ 888/644-6787, 504/861-2727 ⊕ www.hauntedhistorytours. com. **Historic New Orleans Walking Tours** ☎ 504/947-2120 ⊕ www.tourneworleans. com. **Honey Island Swamp Tours** ☎ 985/641-1769 ⊕ www.honeyislandswamp. com. **Jean Lafitte National Historical Park and Preserve: French Quarter Visitors Center** ⊠ 419 Decatur St., French Quarter ☎ 504/589-3882 ⊕ www.nps.gov/jela/french-quarter-site.htm ⊘ Daily 9-5. **Jean Lafitte Swamp and Airboat Tours** ☎ 800/445-4109, 504/689-4186 ⊕ www.jeanlafitteswamptour.com. **Let's Go Antiquing** ☎ 504/899-3027 ⊕ www.neworleansantiquing. com. **New Orleans Paddle Wheels** ☎ 800/445-4109, 504/529-4567 ⊕ www.creolequeen.com. **New Orleans School of Cooking** ☎ 800/237-4841, 504/525-2665 ⊕ www.neworleansschoolofcooking. com. **New Orleans Steamboat Company** ☎ 800/365-2628, 504/586-8777 ⊕ www.steamboatnatchez.com. **New Orleans Tours** ☎ 504/592-1991 ⊕ www.notours.com. **New Orleans Spirit Tours** ☎ 504/314-0806 ⊕ www.neworleanstours.net. **Save Our Cemeteries** ☎ 504/525-3377 ⊕ www.saveourcemeteries.org. **Tours by Isabelle** ☎ 877/665-8687, 504/398-0365 ⊕ www.toursbyisabelle.com.

GAY AND LESBIAN TRAVEL

New Orleans has a large gay and lesbian population spread throughout the metropolitan area. The most gay-friendly neighborhood is the French Quarter, followed by the Faubourg Marigny, just outside the Quarter. Most bars for gay men are within these neighborhoods; lesbians may have to head to bars on designated Girls' Nights, such as the one held Thursdays at the Country Club, in Bywater.

Throughout the year there are a number of gay festivals. The biggest is Southern Decadence, held Labor Day weekend. The city also has gay-friendly guesthouses and bed-and-breakfasts, particularly along Esplanade Avenue.

Faubourg Marigny Art and Books is the last independent gay-focused bookstore in New Orleans, and it's a good resource for LGBT information around town.

Ambush, a local newspaper that's published twice monthly, provides lists of current events in addition to news and reviews. You can find this publication at many gay bars and at Faubourg Marigny Art and Books.

Local Sources Faubourg Marigny Art and Books ✉ 600 Frenchmen St., Faubourg Marigny ☎ 504/947–3700 ⊕ www.fabonfrenchmen.com.

HEALTH

The intense heat and humidity of New Orleans in the height of summer can be a concern for anyone unused to a semi-tropical climate. Pace yourself to avoid problems, particularly dehydration. Pollen levels can be extremely high, especially in April and May. Know your own limits and select indoor activities in the middle of the day; you'll find the locals doing the same thing.

MONEY

Prices throughout this guide are given for adults. Substantially reduced fees are almost always available for children, students, and senior citizens.

ATMs can easily be found on Decatur, Royal, and Chartres streets, close to Canal, at most gift shops, and in most bars in the French Quarter. These machines generally have high fees, but there are some that advertise fees as low as 99¢. As anywhere, use common sense when withdrawing cash and be aware of your surroundings. If getting cash at night, try to use machines in more populated areas.

ITEM	AVERAGE COST
Cup of Coffee	$2
Glass of Wine	$7–$10
Glass of Beer	$3–$6
Po'boy	$6–$10
One-Mile Taxi Ride	$3.50 plus $2 per mile
Museum Admission	$6–$22

PACKING

New Orleans is casual during the day and casual to slightly dressy at night. A few restaurants in the French Quarter require men to wear a jacket and tie at dinner. Take comfy walking shoes.

In winter you'll want a coat or warm jacket, especially for evenings, which can be downright cold. In summer pack for hot, sticky weather, but be prepared for air-conditioning bordering on glacial, and bring an umbrella in case of sudden thunderstorms. Leave the plastic raincoats behind (they're extremely uncomfortable in the high humidity). In addition, pack a sun hat and sunscreen lotion, even for strolls in the city, because the sun can be fierce.

Insect repellent will come in handy if you plan to be outdoors on a swamp cruise or in the city dining alfresco; mosquitoes come out in full force after sunset in warm weather.

▌ SAFETY

New Orleans has long drawn unwelcome attention for its high crime rate. Tourists are seldom the target of major crimes but can, like other citizens, be the target of pickpockets and purse-snatchers. The New Orleans Police Department regularly patrols the French Quarter. Still, common sense is invaluable.

Know where you're going or ask the concierge at your hotel about the best route. In the French Quarter, particularly if you're on foot, stay on streets that are heavily populated. In other areas of the city it is often advisable to drive or take a taxi. High-end neighborhoods and derelict properties back up to one another throughout New Orleans, making aimless strolling a bad idea outside the Quarter. Try to stick to the recommended walks and areas in this book, and be aware of your surroundings.

Call a taxi late at night or when the distance is too great to walk; this is even more important if you've been drinking.

▌ TAXES

A local sales tax of 9% applies to all goods and services purchased in Orleans Parish, including food. Taxes outside Orleans Parish vary and are slightly lower. Due to a state revitalization program, art sold in designated "cultural districts" is exempt from state or local sales tax. Most businesses whose wares are tax-free have signs pointing this out, but be sure to ask if it's unclear.

Louisiana is the only state that grants a sales-tax rebate to foreign shoppers who are in the country for no more than 90 days. Look for shops, restaurants, and hotels that display the distinctive tax-free sign, and ask for a voucher for the 9% sales tax tacked on to the price of many products and services. Present the vouchers with your plane ticket and passport at the tax rebate office at the Louis Armstrong New Orleans International Airport, near the American Airlines ticket counter, and you can receive up to $500 in cash back. If the amount redeemable is more than $500, a check for the difference will be mailed to your home address. Call the airport refund office for complete information.

Contact Airport Refund Office ☎ *504/467-0723* ⊕ *www.louisianataxfree.com.*

▌ TIPPING

A standard restaurant tip is 15%; if you truly enjoyed your meal and had no complaints, then perhaps 20% is a better amount. If you use the services of the concierge, a tip of $5 to $10 is appropriate, with an additional gratuity for special services or favors. Always keep a few dollar bills on hand—they'll come in handy for tipping bellhops, doormen, and valet parking attendants, and for rewarding the many fine street musicians who entertain day and night. As always, use your discretion when tipping.

▌ VISITOR INFORMATION

For general information and brochures, contact the city and state tourism bureaus *below.* The New Orleans Convention & Visitors Bureau's website is a comprehensive source for trip planning, hotel and tour booking, and shopping in the city; you can also download brochures, coupons, walking tours, and event schedules, as well as find links to other helpful websites. The Louisiana Office of Tourism offers the same with a focus on the entire state.

Contacts Louisiana Office of Tourism
☎ *800/994-8626* ⊕ *www.louisianatravel.com.*
New Orleans Convention & Visitors Bureau
☎ *800/672-6124, 504/566-5011*
⊕ *www.neworleanscvb.com.*

ONLINE RESOURCES

The Louisiana Department of Culture, Recreation and Tourism's website gives a general overview of tourism in Louisiana, especially recovery efforts after Hurricanes Katrina and Rita.

New Orleans Online provides basic trip planning and travel tools. The city's official site has updates on local issues and government affairs, as well as a list of licensed bed-and-breakfasts and historic homes for short-term stays and an interesting "City Stories" section that profiles residents of note. It includes links to the *Times-Picayune* newspaper, with news stories, nightlife, and more.

For those visitors interested in contributing to the ongoing recovery of the neighborhood and city, the Louisiana Serve Commission's website (⊕ *www. volunteerlouisiana.gov*) has a section about opportunities to volunteer while on vacation called "Voluntourism" that can link you up with numerous opportunities.

The website of the *Gambit* weekly newspaper does a good job of representing varying perspectives on life in the city and has a comprehensive events calendar.

The French Quarter site gives great links to event, accommodations, and parking information, as well as an interactive French Quarter map. And for that something extra, *Experience New Orleans* has links to a blog, podcast, and fun video tours, in addition to the standard tourist sites.

For general information about events, hotels, and restaurants, check the official New Orleans travel site. For Louisiana music coverage (plus other entertainment news), *OffBeat* magazine's website is a good bet, as is the radio station WWOZ, which streams online and maintains a music calendar. Everything you need to know about the New Orleans Jazz & Heritage Festival can be found at its website. A site devoted entirely to Mardi Gras includes histories, parade schedules, and other specific Mardi Gras information.

For arts happenings around town, the Arts Council of New Orleans website has a calendar of art, music, dance, film, theater, literature, and culinary events in the city. The site also includes an artist directory and other resources.

All About Louisiana The Louisiana Department of Culture, Recreation and Tourism ⊕ *www.crt.state.la.us.*

All About New Orleans City of New Orleans ⊕ *www.nola.gov.* **Experience New Orleans** ⊕ *www.experienceneworleans.com.* **Frenchquarter.com** ⊕ *www.frenchquarter. com.* **Neworleans.com** ⊕ *www.neworleans. com.* **New Orleans Online** ⊕ *www.neworleansonline.com.*

Music, Festivals, and Events
Arts New Orleans ⊕ *www.artsneworleans. org.* **Mardi Gras New Orleans** ⊕ *www. mardigrasneworleans.com.* **New Orleans Jazz & Heritage Festival** ☎ 504/558–6100 ⊕ *www.nojazzfest.com.* **OffBeat Magazine** ☎ 504/944–4300 ⊕ *www.offbeat.com.* **WWOZ** ☎ 504/568–1239 ⊕ *www.wwoz.org.*

Periodicals The Times-Picayune ☎ 800/925–0000 ⊕ *www.nola.com.* **Gambit** ☎ 504/486–5900 ⊕ *www. bestofneworleans.com.*

INDEX

PHOTO CREDITS

NOTES

NOTES

NOTES

NOTES

NOTES

NOTES

NOTES

NOTES

NOTES

NOTES

NOTES

NOTES

NOTES

ABOUT OUR WRITERS

Nathalie Jordi lived in Miami, London, County Cork, and New York City before finding her true home in the Faubourg Marigny area of New Orleans five years ago. She has written for, among other publications, the *LA Times, Bon Appetit, Food & Wine, Travel & Leisure, Conde Nast Traveler,* and the *New York Times.*

Alexis Korman is a freelance food, wine, and travel writer who traded the Big Apple for the Big Easy in 2012. She serves as food editor for *Wine Enthusiast Magazine,* writes for Fodor's, Premier Traveler, and the Daily Meal, and is co-founder of an artisanal kombucha project in New Orleans called Big Easy 'Bucha.

New Orleans native Susan Granger has been chronicling the food, fashion, and culture of the Crescent City for 15 years as a writer for the *Times-Picayune* newspaper and its website, NOLA.com. She lives within walking distance of Magazine Street, which puts some of the city's best boutiques just steps from her door.

Cameron Todd has been in love with New Orleans since she first visited the city 15 years ago. Now a Mid City resident, she's pursuing an MFA in fiction writing at the University of New Orleans, while continuing her mission to visit every bar in New Orleans—for research purposes, of course.

Words Made Flesh

Volume II

Biblical Reflections
For Year B

Fr. Thomas Rosica, CSB

Canadian Conference of Catholic Bishops
Ottawa

Library and Archives Canada Cataloguing in Publication

Rosica, Thomas
    Words made flesh / Thomas Rosica.

Contents: Vol. 2. Scripture reflections for Year B.
ISBN 978-0-88997-607-8 (v. 2).--ISBN 978-0-88997-662-7 (set)

    1. Church year meditations. 2. Bible. N.T. Gospels--Homiletical use.
3. Catholic Church--Prayers and devotions.
I. Catholic Church. Canadian Conference of Catholic Bishops II. Title.

BX2170.C55R67 2012   242'.3   C2011-908327-2